654

THE ART AND SCIENCE
OF VICTORIAN HISTORY

THE ART AND SCIENCE OF VICTORIAN HISTORY

by Rosemary Jann

OHIO STATE UNIVERSITY PRESS : COLUMBUS

Copyright © 1985 by the Ohio State University Press
All Rights Reserved.

Library of Congress Cataloging-in-Publication Data

Jann, Rosemary, 1949-
   The art and science of Victorian history.
   Bibliography: p.
   Includes index.
   1. Historians—Great Britain. 2. Historiography—
Great Britain—History—19th century. 3. Great Britain—
Historiography. I. Title. II. Title: Victorian History.
DA3.A1J36   1985   907'.2041   85-13651
ISBN 0-8142-0390-6

FOR MY PARENTS

CONTENTS

	Introduction	xi
I.	Thomas Arnold: History as Practical Evangel	1
II.	Thomas Carlyle: History as Secular Prophecy	33
III.	Thomas Babington Macaulay: History as Whig Via Media	66
IV.	James Anthony Froude: History as Protestant Apologia	105
V.	John Richard Green: History as National Biography	141
VI.	Edward Augustus Freeman: History as Past Politics	170
	Conclusion: Desired Presents and Re-ordered Pasts	207
	Epilogue: Amateur Ideals and Professional Identities	215
	Notes	235
	Index	263

ACKNOWLEDGMENTS

I am grateful to the many colleagues whose support and suggestions have contributed to this study. Lawrence Evans and Christopher Herbert helped shape early drafts with their thoughtful and probing criticisms. Particular thanks are due Bill Heyck: as a friend, a guide, and an example, he has left his mark on my work in more ways than I have been able to acknowledge. I am also deeply indebted to Barry Qualls. With characteristic generosity he offered thorough readings of the final drafts; this essay would have been much the poorer without his insights, and the task of revision much more difficult without his encouragement. Others who provided useful comments about various parts of the manuscript include Laura Kendrick, Janet Larson, Steven Putzel, John Osborne, David Roos, and members of the Rutgers Social History Group, in particular Andrew Abbott. I appreciate the help and hospitality of Dr. D. A. Rees, Archivist of Jesus College, Oxford, who made available to me letters from Green and Freeman in the College collection. The Associated Colleges of the Midwest, the Newberry Library, and the Rutgers Research Council provided release time and financial support for my research, for which I am grateful. Final thanks go to Laura Kendrick, Susan Crane, and Elissa Greenwald, who helped me prepare drafts of the manuscript, and to Donald Dunlap and Steven Putzel, who provided word-processing assistance above and beyond the call of duty.

INTRODUCTION

Poetry, Divinity, Politics, Physics, have each their adherents and adversaries; each little guild supporting a defensive and offensive war for its own specific domain; while the domain of History is as a Free Emporium, where all these beligerents peaceably meet and furnish themselves; and Sentimentalist and Utilitarian, Sceptic and Theologian, with one voice advise us: Examine History, for it is "Philosophy teaching by Experience." —Thomas Carlyle, "On History," 1830

The historical was indeed the common coin of the nineteenth century, the currency of its most characteristic art, the security for its most significant intellectual transactions. Defenders of absolutes, rational or religious, learned to use history as an asset and not a liability; uneasy relativists found some compensation in its didactic value. Rival ideologies competed for its sanctions. Poets and scientists found in it their inspiration. The Victorians plundered the past for the raw stuff of imagination and shaped what they found to their own political, social, and aesthetic ends. The explanatory power of the biological, the developmental, and the narrative made the historical

Introduction

method the preeminent paradigm of their age. It asserted its authority over science and social science; it became the "philosophical" way of understanding national as well as personal identity. The Victorians found that learning to harness "the Time Spirit of the Nineteenth Century" was the best way to escape being driven by it.[1]

Formal works of history illuminate most fully the strategies essential to the nineteenth century's conquest of time. They are documents central to both the philosophical and the literary dimensions of the Victorian mind. They stand at the intersection of its two ways of knowing, the rational and the imaginative. They perfectly reflect that conflation of the scientific, the historical, and the philosophical characteristic of Victorian thought, and that didactic use of the imagined real that was central to its art. This study uses representative examples to explore the strategies at work in Victorian historical writing and the needs served by such strategies. My purpose is not to reconstruct a "Whig history" of the profession, although the transition from the man of letters to the professional historian is part of my story. I am primarily concerned with examining the ways certain nineteenth-century historians negotiated intellectual and moral dilemmas specific to their age. I wish to trace in their historical writings the shape of the Victorian mind, not the priorities of the future.

I characterize the writing of history as an activity that exploited the didactic strategies of both science and literature (as the Victorians understood them) to affirm order and value in human society. Like so many Victorian thinkers, the historian attempted to bring the methodological authority of the physical sciences to the study of man's past. Though acknowledging the limitations of his evidence, he considered himself to be "scientific" or "philosophical" because he analyzed historical data in a systematic and inductive way and because he derived from his facts patterns and laws capable of guiding the present and anticipating the future. Such laws were urgently needed given the force with which the rapid current of change was undermining traditional assumptions and authorities. The Victorians' narrative histories served the same purposes as the rest of their serious literature: to identify what Henry Sidgwick called some "higher unity of system" that could provide for both continuity and change.[2] These histories reflected what to George Eliot was the "conservative-reforming" impulse of the period: that attempt to reconcile progress with permanence, to formulate values and institutions that could be both dynamic and stable. Not the least important

Introduction

factor in this attempt was the historian's demonstration that the "scientific laws" of history vindicated, rather than threatened, his assumptions about social and spiritual order.

This demonstration required the historian to reject the materialist and determinist biases inherent in a Utilitarian or Positivist empiricism. He wished to be "scientific" without sacrificing his belief in the primacy of free will and moral law—the belief that alone made man fully human. The imaginative dimension of the Victorian history played an essential role in protecting and substantiating this belief. On one level, of course, quite practical concerns motivated the compelling narratives, vivid portraiture, and self-consciously fictive techniques that were the stylistic trademark of the "literary" history: the historian wished to attract as large as possible an audience to profit from his message. But his aesthetic strategies also testified to the complex functioning of imagination as a way of knowing and understanding the past. In order for historical evidence to have "philosophical" credibility, the historian had to resuscitate the living reality from the dead facts. Believing that the essential truths of man's past were spiritual rather than material, he needed imagination in order to recover them. Having privileged morality, will, and emotion in historical explanation, he turned naturally to a narrative mode with the affective richness to do them justice. The creative side of his endeavor was also essential to the didactic. To fashion a coherent narrative that "explained" the past was in effect to guarantee its meaningfulness; the assertion of narrative order was an assertion of moral order as well. The style that characterized "literary" history was inseparable from the value judgments and didactic intentions embodied in it.

Like many Victorian writers, the historian abjured the willful falsity of the invented and claimed instead the higher authority of events that had "really" occurred. But in practice he exploited the tactics of both romance and realism. Rendering the historical foreground as a pageant of heroism affirmed the potential for human greatness and the meaningfulness of moral choice; it released the reader from the limits of the ordinary but not from the pressure of duty and emulation. The commonplace asserted different but no less important claims. The historian's concern with his heroes' humanizing foibles and their public personae, his attention to the life of the people and the life of the court revealed the conviction he shared with Victorian realism: that the quotidian too was the stuff of vital realities, that the

Introduction

most mundane phenomena often disclosed the highest truths. He shared the novelists' didactic strategies as well. Assent to the truths of history was finally as much an act of extended sympathy as of rational accord.

The historian's target was not what George Eliot called the ready-made sympathy elicited by generalizations and statistics. Like the artist, the historian aimed to provide instead the "raw material of moral sentiment,"[3] to convert readers into participants by providing them with a past so detailed and credible that they lived rather than merely observed it. Narrative and ethical order also merged on the highest level, as the historian emplotted over this carefully authenticated reality the triumphant archetypes of romance: the successive stages of Arnoldian progress that incorporated cyclical time in Christian time, the trial and triumph of Froude's Protestantism, the Whig history's "familiar optimistic shape of loss and restitution,"[4] Carlyle's apocalyptic vindication of the True. Qualifications abounded and emphases differed in these patterns—in Carlyle, for instance, the victory of righteousness seems more a threat than a solace—but their consoling power and their authority were intended to be the same.

Ultimately, both the "aesthetics of sympathy" and the need to demonstrate meaningful system blurred the distinction between the created and the discovered.[5] *Wissenschaftliche* order merged with the secularized teleology of romance to render the scientist's objectivity simply a pose. The historian's undertaking was essentially one of affirmation rather than induction. Historical "reality" became more sociologically complex, but it was still molded by desired truths. For these very reasons, the Victorian history tells us more about the ways the Victorians wished to shape their own experience than about the shape of the past itself.

I have chosen six practitioners of the art and science of Victorian history to form the basis of this study: Thomas Arnold (1795-1842), Thomas Carlyle (1795-1881), Thomas Babington Macaulay (1800-1859), James Anthony Froude (1818-1894), John Richard Green (1837-1883), and Edward Augustus Freeman (1823-1892). This selection reflects their importance relative to their own age. The popularity and prominence of their major works and the significance of the imaginative dimension to their didactic purposes weighed heavily in my choice. Most important was the self-consciousness of their relationship to their audience. They shared a sense of vocation. Each chose the historian's role to deliver himself of a vision of the past that

Introduction

he hoped would do for society what it had done for him: order and make sense of the present. I passed over writers like Sharon Turner or Henry Hallam, whose concern with the past was more thoroughly antiquarian than imaginative, as well as historians who, because of their Utilitarian or Positivist biases, ultimately contributed more to the emergent social sciences than to narrative history *per se*. The professional priorities of later Victorians like William Stubbs and S. R. Gardiner were influential enough to accord them separate treatment in the epilogue.

The six represent a range of approaches. Thomas Arnold is the most eminent historian of what Duncan Forbes called the Liberal-Anglican School.[6] At the beginning of the period he provided the classic statement of the morality and unity of western history. Inspired by German romanticism more than Broad Church Christianity, Carlyle attempted to achieve the same ends as Arnold with a secularized supernaturalism. Macaulay is the foremost of the Whig historians, and Green serves as the major social historian of that same tradition. Like Freeman and Froude, Green found that he had to redefine and defend his identity as historian when the rival professional model began increasingly to assert its claims in the closing decades of the century. Froude's supporters considered this disciple of Carlyle's to be the chief defender of the "literary" history against the encroachment of positivistic science; his detractors found him the most blatant example of dilettantism. Froude's nemesis, E. A. Freeman, is a transitional figure: one of the most vocal spokesmen for the new professionalism, as a practicing historian he was in many ways as deeply traditional as any of the six.

To provide a comparative framework for examining the cultural function of the historian, each chapter asks similar questions about theory and practice. What factors defined the historian's interest in and conception of history? How did he understand and how did he balance the need to be philosophical and "scientific" with the need to re-create the past as art? What assumptions controlled the patterns or laws he found in the past, and what peculiarly Victorian needs did his explanatory model serve? In particular, how did he balance the respective claims of the great individual, the social group or class, and the spirit of the age in his explanation of change and causality? What conception of progress did he offer? What value judgments about relevant historical experience did the selectivity and treatment of his research imply? How did he shape historical narrative to engage the

Introduction

imagination as well as the reason of his readers? My examination of specific historical interpretations focuses not so much on the opinions themselves as on the ways in which characteristic biases originate and influence historical analysis in other areas. My consideration of methodology is not intended to be exhaustive, but to furnish valid bases of comparison among the six. Each chapter pays increasing heed to the emerging confrontation between popular and professional historiography. Although professionalization challenged fundamental assumptions about the cultural functions of history and the historian, I will argue in the epilogue that this challenge ended in a compromise rather than a split: that in England, the continuing vitality of the values served by "literary" history shaped professionalism in unique ways.

To establish a common context for the individual analyses that follow, some attention to the major intellectual traditions that converge in the art and science of Victorian historiography is in order. The methods and assumptions of Enlightenment, romantic, and "scientific" historiography play significant if varied roles in the work of each writer. Although the Renaissance had introduced an appreciation of time and process into the static medieval world view and raised the standard of historical research, essentially uncritical attitudes towards texts persisted. The use of history as a polemical weapon during the religious and political controversies of the seventeenth century had so discredited it that by the early eighteenth century many held history in contempt as little more than "popular tale-telling, aimless antiquarianism, or political propaganda."[7] Johnson's and Addison's scorn for the slight abilities and superficial results of contemporary historians was characteristic; Hume undertook his *History* in the belief that "style, judgment, impartiality, care—everything is wanting to our historians."[8]

In one sense, then, the *philosophes*' task was to establish the legitimacy and importance of historical knowledge, and this they largely accomplished, notwithstanding exaggerated nineteenth-century claims about their "antihistorical" bias. Their empiricist orientation emphasized the importance of documentary support, while their fight against all forms of superstition set new standards in the critical scrutiny of source materials. As William Robertson defined it, "to relate real occurrences, and to explain their real causes and effects, is the historian's peculiar and only province"; he has "no title to claim

Introduction

assent, unless he produces evidence in proof of his assertions."[9] Robertson amassed an unprecedented amount of material in his attempt to compose the "authentic" history of Scotland. In the same way, Gibbon felt compelled as much by "a sense of duty" as by his "curiosity" to draw from the "fountain-head" of original sources wherever possible in the *Decline and Fall*.[10] This resort to the "fountain-head" represented a deliberate rejection of evidence based on faith, tradition, or conjecture, and thus formed part of a larger attempt to assess the reliability of sources in a more critical spirit.

The Enlightenment historians significantly advanced history's explanatory power as well by subordinating facts to system. The eighteenth century had inherited a long tradition of contempt for mere erudition. For Hume as for others, the problem with the "dark industry" of the antiquarian was that his indiscriminate heaping-up of facts ignored or obscured the meaningful pattern of history. "The part of an historian is as honourable as that of a mere chronicler or compiler of gazettes is contemptible," said Gibbon.[11] The historian had also to be a philosopher; he had to discern amidst the chaos of data the shaping principles of human action and to display them in such a way as to teach and guide his audience: "History," Gibbon wrote, "is for the philosophic spirit what gambling was for the Marquis de Dangeau. He saw a system, relationships, and order there, where others saw only the caprices of fortune."[12] It was the historian's duty to illustrate the links between events, to determine those general causes which form the springs (*Ressorts*) of action in history: only then was he writing *en philosophe*. Enlightenment thinkers in effect applied the same intellectual tools to both nature and history: their purpose in investigating both was to replace transcendental with empirical causes. Man might have no access to metaphysical truths, but he could, by examining the phenomena of experience critically, determine the relationships between facts and express these in terms of rules or laws. History could become part of what Hume called "a science of man" to the extent that it involved a systematic effort to derive general explanations for human conduct from empirical observation.[13] From his repository of concrete and verifiable evidence about human experience, the historian could formulate "general theorems" that enabled him "to comprehend, in a few propositions, a great number of inferences and conclusions."[14] Such theorems in turn greatly simplified his decisions about what constituted "relevant" data.

Introduction

The process of shaping and selection necessary to demonstrate the system in history was as much artistic as philosophical. Hume argued, "The unity of action . . . which is to be found in biography or history, differs from that of epic poetry, not in kind, but in degree."[15] Yet the *philosophe* was a man of letters in the highest sense not merely because his stylistic treatment pleased, but because it instructed: artistic selection and control were means to an end. Gibbon drew much the same distinction between Livy and Tacitus as Bolingbroke did between Herodotus and Thucydides: the former was merely an "agreeable story-teller"; the latter illustrated a "chain of events and fill[ed] our heart with the wisest lessons."[16] Narrative order reinforced ethical order. Vivid representation also served didactic ends. History was, after all, "philosophy teaching by *examples*"; the effectiveness of its "wise lessons" depended upon "a just and perfect delineation of all that may be praised, of all that may be excused, and of all that must be censured."[17]

Notwithstanding these attempts to make historical study more critical and more "philosophical," the Enlightenment's largely unexamined assumptions about progress and human nature diluted its objectivity and its appreciation of historical relationships. Obsessed by the rise and fall of "civilization," the *philosophes* judged men and events by their relationship to eighteenth-century definitions of rationality and progress. "Barbarous ages," if treated at all, were so handled that their "deformity" might teach the present "to cherish, with the greater anxiety, that science and civility which has so close a connexion with virtue and humanity."[18] No fact was important for its own sake. The abridgment necessary to demonstrate history's order and lessons justified the historian in excluding as irrelevant all that he lacked sympathy with: the primitive, the irrational, the uncouth.

His assumptions about human nature narrowed his focus in more significant ways. The Enlightenment historian was not interested in studying men and women so much as in trying to abstract "man in general" from the evidence of human history.[19] His task was to disengage from the folly and fanaticism of the past the "constant and universal principles" of man's "true" nature. In effect the Enlightenment tried to include human nature in the presumed uniformity of the natural world, for the lessons of philosophical history could be practically applied only in a realm where men were considered everywhere and at all times the same. This is precisely what Hume assumed:

Introduction

> Would you know the sentiments, inclinations, and course of life of the Greeks and Romans? Study well the temper and actions of the French and English: You cannot be much mistaken in transferring to the former *most* of the observations, which you have made with regard to the latter. Mankind are so much the same, in all times and places, that history informs us of nothing new or strange on this particular. Its chief use is only to discover the constant and universal principles of human nature, by showing men in all varieties of circumstances and situations, and furnishing us with materials, from which we may form our observations, and become acquainted with the regular springs of human action and behaviour. These records of wars, intrigues, factions, and revolutions, are so many collections of experiments, by which the politician or moral philosopher fixes the principles of his science; in the same manner as the physician or the natural philosopher becomes acquainted with the nature of plants, minerals, and other external objects, by the experiments, which he forms concerning them.[20]

The *philosophes*' treatment of human nature had inherent limitations. They conceived men as complexes of psychological traits rather than as complex individuals. Hume could present contradictory aspects of historical figures, but he made little attempt to synthesize them into a personality. He de-emphasized or dismissed as inconsistent traits that did not fit and rejected as incredible motives he could not sympathize with. His *History of England* may be read as a more concrete elaboration of those abstract principles laid out in the *Treatise on Human Nature*.[21] Gibbon's "human nature" was limited in similar ways. He too ascribed "the different characters that mark the civilized nations of the globe . . . to the use, and the abuse, of reason,"[22] and relied heavily on the vices and virtues of the Romans to explain the rise and decline of empire. The "springs" of national character led to the same sort of "ruling passions," writ large, that dominated individuals.

Despite the Enlightenment's scientific pretensions, *a priori* assumptions clearly limited its laws and stunted its empiricism. Romantic historiography was still indebted to its pioneering efforts, however. Historicism's emphasis on sympathy built upon the eighteenth century's commitment to observation. The connectedness of philosophical history was at least a first step toward nineteenth-century organicism. The *philosophes*' ideal of progress, however unhistorically conceived, did allow the possibility of development through time that would be exploited (to different ends) by following generations. The work of Montesquieu, Voltaire, and Hume ac-

Introduction

knowledged the importance of social, cultural, and intellectual factors in historical explanation. Gibbon advanced farthest toward a recognition of the complexity of forces—rational and irrational, material and immaterial—contributing to national consciousness, and he was best able to conceive a more flexible and relativisitic causality. Finally, the Enlightenment established conclusively the authority of the historian as man of letters, a literary artist of powerful intellect and broad humanistic culture, and asserted the legitimacy and importance of "philosophical" history: comprehensive, synthetic, and didactic.

The watershed for the shift in historiographical models was the French Revolution. It epitomized the Enlightenment's attempt to free itself from the dead hand of the past by trying to destroy it, to build a new society on reason rather than on tradition. At the same time, the Revolution's results illuminated some of the blind spots of the Enlightenment mind. As the source of historical change, the Revolution replaced the reasoning individual with a mass movement, driven by unpredictable and often irrational impulses. It showed the authority of abstract reason to be as inadequate as that of a naive fundamentalism in explaining human behavior. These changes prepared the way for a crucial feature of romantic historiography: the historicism that shifted attention from the general to the specific, from the mechanical to the organic, and from the judgmental to the sympathetic. As Friedrich Meinecke explained it, "The essence of historism is the substitution of a process of *individualising* observation for a *generalizing* view of human forces in history."[23] Revolting against the concept of life and mind governed by a single static law, the romantic reasserted the value of the concrete, the individual, and the suprarational. Against the abstract rationality of the Enlightenment, Coleridge claimed, "Reason never acts by itself, but must clothe itself in the substance of individual understanding and specific inclination, in order to become a reality and an object of consciousness and experience."[24] To writers like Johnson who counseled the poet not to number the streaks of the tulip but rather to exhibit "such prominent and striking features, as recall the original to every mind," Blake flatly replied that "to Generalize is to be an Idiot. To Particularize is the Alone Distinction of Merit."[25] Rather than selectively ransacking past ages for confirmation of a uniform human nature and valuing them only as they resembled the present, the historicist held all ages "immediate to God," in Ranke's words.

Introduction

The new historian endowed nations and peoples with the diversity, uniqueness, and complexity of personalities, viewing societies not as arbitrary aggregates of individuals but as "quasi-biological entities which defied analysis by the exact quantitative methods of chemistry and physics."[26] Like the organism's, the nation's component parts existed in dynamic interdependence, so that individual men, values, and institutions could be understood only as products of an entire complex of conditions. Events were not the result of rational decisions governed by general laws of human nature, but cross-sections of a wider and continuous field of forces. Mechanical laws of cause and effect could not account for the underlying identity of the organism despite its movement through time. The nation's dynamic individuality required an evolutionary concept of change to reconcile permanence and development. The physical growth of the plant, the intellectual and spiritual growth of the individual, provided the romantic historian with models for the histories of peoples and institutions. In the same way, Thomas Arnold conceived a nation's history as its "biography," and Carlyle charted "cycles and seasons" for the mind of mankind.

Accepting the developmental nature of change prevented the romantic historian from seeing his own values as ultimate, or from regarding past beliefs merely as errors. To apply an arbitrary standard to the past was to distort it: his task rather was to open himself unjudgmentally to the unsystematic variety of historical forms in a given age, seeking not resemblances with the present, but the era's own self-justifying identity. He restored to the past much that had been beneath the "Dignity of History" in the eighteenth century, or that, like custom and myth, had been largely inaccessible to its rationalistic analyses. The romantic derived national consciousness from a much wider range of data—geographical, social, and cultural, as well as political—and considered the testimony of the masses as important as that of monarchs and ministers.

More importantly, romantic thought legitimized the role of imagination in the historical enterprise. Dissection into abstract categories perverted the nature of a biological entity: the romantic past had to be "felt, or intuited, or understood, by a species of direct acquaintance."[27] To gain access to it, the historian had to follow Herder's advice: "First sympathize with the nation . . . go into the era, into the geography, into the entire history, feel [*einfühlen*] yourself into it."[28] Before he could understand the significance of facts he had to

Introduction

"resuscitate" them: he had to re-create the past in all its specificity before it would divulge its unique unifying principles. Clearly, the mechanical reason and superficial fancy of Hume and Hartley were inadequate to such a task. It took a faculty like Coleridge's constitutive secondary imagination to discern the unity underlying past events. Only when knowing the truth became an essentially creative process could perception be imaginative without becoming imaginary, based on the senses without being limited to their evidence. And only then could history as an act of imaginative projection and identification claim to expose a truth about the past that had been inaccessible to both fictionalizing chroniclers and rationalistic *philosophes*.

The romantics tried to reclaim science as well as imagination from the *philosophes*. Enlightenment science, essentially mechanical, aimed to rank data on a single scale of value, to subsume individuality in uniformity. The understanding of romantic science was relational and organic; it illuminated individuality by investigating the organism's development in time. For the historicist, as Peter Gay explains it, the idea that man possessed not a fixed nature but an individual history made the historian "the master scientist. The historian is the student of change; the central reality of the world is change—who more important, then, in the scheme of things, than the historian? Again, while other scientists seek universal laws, the historian strives to understand individuals on their own terms, and since individuality is the central reality of men, who more important for the study of man than the historian?"[29] In an even more significant sense, the very constitutive power that made the imagination of the romantic historian "poetic" made it "scientific" as well. Susan F. Cannon demonstrates the distinction made by Wordsworth and echoed by Victorians between "sciences of classification" that gave only "worthless, superficial knowledge" and those "true sciences" that revealed "wider and wider interrelationships" leading "to an understanding of the system of the world and therefore . . . eventually to God."[30] The same ability to perceive relationships was associated with what Philip Harwood, in his 1842 analysis of "The Modern Art and Science of History," called "the historic, scientific imagination": that faculty that knew how to "recreate worlds out of the loose, chaotic elements furnished by chroniclers and bards." The modern historian became "scientific" not by classifying phenomena but by "combining the scattered and fragmentary parts into wholeness and unity, and giving a plan to the mighty maze" of past life.[31]

Introduction

The links between the scientific and the poetic, the empirical and the romantic, bear stressing, for they had important ramifications in nineteenth-century historiography. The romantic historian's desire to sympathize with the object, to realize it in all its individuality, was not just compatible with but essential to his "scientific" apprehension of it. Understanding "the *symbolism* of facts," as Harwood put it,[32] might have involved a more conscious creativity than the *philosophe* acknowledged, but it still began with the historian endeavoring to look steadily at his subject and ended with the identification of history's ordering principles. The romantic historian's search for laws and patterns led directly to the imposition of what Hayden White calls a particular emplotment and argument on the historical field.[33] But this made him not less inductive or scientific than his Enlightenment predecessors—simply different in his conception of what constituted valid unities and interrelationships. His desired order required a different kind of narrative. Historians might argue throughout the century about which "plot" was correct, but their duty to demonstrate some kind of order would remain central to their claim to be "scientific."

Neither was a romantic emplotment by definition incompatible with the call for a more rigorous evaluation of source materials, the other major principle upon which "scientific" history rested. The older model of organized, systematized knowledge embodied in *Wissenschaft* could provide the basis for order in history. It was the increasing prestige of the physical sciences that prompted the historian to seek analogous ways of isolating, testing, and evaluating his data. Although as the century wore on, such "scientific" methodology was more and more often linked to assumptions and emplotments inimical to romantic history, quite the opposite was true at the outset. The work of Barthold Niebuhr and Leopold van Ranke, both professors at the University of Berlin, provided the romantic historian with an example of how he could obtain greater objectivity and rigor in the classification and analysis of documents without forfeiting his wider and more sympathetic approach to the past. At Berlin from 1810 to 1859, Niebuhr introduced stricter methods for evaluating the authenticity of source materials. Like the romantic historian, however, he valued classes over individuals and customs over law-givers in explanations of the historical process. He first gave serious attention to the hitherto neglected ballads of Rome as a valid source for its early history and broadened the base of historical research to include a much

Introduction

wider range of data. His ability to make critical methods of textual analysis serve the ends of imagination would exercise particular influence on Thomas Arnold's treatment of myth in the *History of Rome.*

Ranke likewise had allegiances to both romantic and "scientific" historiography. In the spirit of Niebuhr, he made the evaluation of evidence more "scientific" by insisting on strictly contemporary sources and then by analyzing them in light of the author's temperament, allegiances, his probable access to correct knowledge, and the extent of his agreement with other sources. Ranke's intention, as announced in the famous preface to his earliest work, was to move the historian from value judgments to analysis: "To history has been assigned the office of judging the past, of instructing the present for the benefit of future ages. To such high offices this work does not aspire: It wants only to show what actually happened [*wie es eigentlich gewesen*]."[34] This emphasis on the facts of history was motivated as much by Ranke's rejection of the romanticized histories of Scott as by his repudiation of the value judgments of the Enlightenment. After comparing one of Scott's characterizations in *Quentin Durward* with that of Commines, he wrote, "I found by comparison that the truth was more interesting and beautiful than the romance. I turned away from it and resolved to avoid all invention and imagination in my works and to stick to facts."[35]

But if history *"wie es eigentlich gewesen"* rejected the biases of both Enlightenment rationalism and historical romance, Ranke was far from endorsing a positivistic empiricism. Particularly outside Germany, exaggerated claims for the objectivity of his methods obscured his affinities with romantic history.[36] He asserted the authority of the empirical and the objective to aggrandize the "more interesting and beautiful" truth he sought, but this truth was to be known through a distinctly romantic sympathizing with individualized facts. It was precisely because the past was to be re-created in all its specificity that only the most concrete, the most factual data could provide the materials for the historian. Ranke's claim that "every epoch is immediate to God," his fascination with historical personalities, his idealist assumptions, as well as his use of ballad materials and folk traditions, further ally his sympathies with those of the romantics. Central to Ranke's historiography were foregone conclusions about the preeminence of national identity that prevented his investigations from be-

Introduction

ing any more genuinely inductive than the romance and rationalism he rejected. Ranke's adoption of a more rigorous treatment of sources did not prevent the meaning of history from being as much created as discovered. "Scientific" history increased the range and reliability of historical data, but the plots it constructed out of those data provided not so much a greater, but simply a different, truth than that of romantic history.

As the century went on, the growing eminence of the factual made the subjectivity latent in "scientific" history harder to perceive and more heretical to assert. When historians began to professionalize, they often based their claims to expertise on their scientific research methods, seemingly analogous to those that insured the authority and prestige of the physical scientist. What Ranke meant as a modest disclaimer was converted into a boast that the historian actually could achieve a "scientific" exactitude in showing things as they "really" had been. The almost exclusive concentration of the Rankean school on political and diplomatic documents added to fears that historical study had to satisfy a narrowly positivistic kind of factuality in order to be scientific. The rise of Positivism, the true heir to Enlightenment rationalism, further encouraged this belief. Because positivistic science, which claimed to reduce human behavior to laws as simple and monolithic as those that ruled the natural world, rested on similar claims to complete objectivity about the data of history, scientific historiography and the scientism of Comte often became conflated in the popular mind. In the second half of the century, attacks on a "science of history" often meant attacks on the Positivist's determinism. Methodological issues were further confused by criticisms of "literary" history that made superficial scholarship the necessary counterpart of a vivid narrative. As a result "scientific" history remained implicated in the materialism of much nineteenth-century science, "literary" history in the license of much imaginative literature, despite widespread underlying agreement on the importance of both critical research methods and effective style in historical writing.

Of more significance than methodology *per se* in distinguishing the professional's "scientific" position from that of the "literary" historian was his conscious shift in priorities. The professional's highest responsibility was not to instruct or entertain the general public but to advance knowledge in the field. In order to preserve the scientist's disinterested commitment to facts, many scholars felt they had at least

Introduction

publicly to reject the popular historian's search for moral lessons and the popular audience's presumption to judge their work—in effect, to reject the duty and the authority of the Victorian sage.

The historians I consider exemplify varying blends of Enlightenment, romantic, and "scientific" assumptions about history. In England historical writing remained the domain of the man of letters for the better part of the century. At both Oxford and Cambridge, chairs of modern history went traditionally to literary men; Charles Kingsley won the Regius Professorship at Cambridge as late as 1869. It was an age in which a civil servant like George Grote or a lawyer like H. T. Buckle could achieve an international reputation for historical research, an age when best sellers by Macaulay or Green could rival the popularity of contemporary fiction.[37] It was the last age in which the historian could expect to command the attention of a large and relatively homogeneous audience of educated general readers and to rest his authority on his ability to teach and uplift rather than on his advance of historical knowledge.

Each of these six historians built his public role on a private, essentially romantic, attachment to the past. Each recognized the importance of imagination to historical reconstruction. Most openly endorsed the romantic view that in order to understand the past event, the historian had to relive it through an act of sympathetic projection, and that to convince readers of its importance, he had to resuscitate it through an act of literary creation. "Literary" history was philosophical in the highest sense because it claimed a poetic insight into the "symbolism of facts." It revealed spiritual truths inaccessible to mere reason and compelled the moral sense to acknowledge their reality. These historians had also learned from the romantics a widened appreciation of what constituted relevant historical data. Their very "realism" depended upon closer attention to history's sociological and physical environment. Although in actual practice most achieved only limited success in integrating geographical, social, and cultural data into the political account, all recognized the importance of such materials to a full understanding of historical change. They were particularly sensitive to the insights that myth, legend, and popular literature offered into the mind of the past.

At the same time, all understood and accepted the new standard of thoroughness and critical analysis demanded of the historian who would establish his facts on a scientific basis. Each wished to aggran-

Introduction

dize the authority of his interpretation by basing it on an inductive investigation of the past. Whether acknowledged or not, however, the accuracy of facts was not an end in itself, but a means of increasing the credibility of the laws and patterns each saw in history. Most did little or no research in primary sources; those who did, like Macaulay and Froude, compromised their claims to accuracy and completeness by the ways in which they used such data. Ultimately, none possessed the conviction, important to both historicism and "scientific" objectivity, that facts were important for their own sake. Each judged facts by the extent to which they vindicated *a priori* assumptions about order and meaning in history. Each sought proof of the operation of laws necessary to make sense of the present.

These laws differed in crucial ways from those of the Enlightenment historians, of course. Macaulay was alone in tacitly accepting the eighteenth century's belief in man controlled by associationist laws of pain and pleasure and measured against a uniform rationality, and even he believed that he was reacting against just such "abstract" theories. The others set out consciously to refute this behavioral model as it resurfaced in Utilitarianism and Positivism and to reassert the greater power of morality and free will in human history. Where the *philosophes* had based progress on the triumph of reason and posited a single scale of civilization by which to measure all cultures at all times, the Victorians conceived progress as essentially moral and were capable of a more relativistic appreciation of values and customs. Their organic conceptions of development permitted them to treat ideas, institutions, and customs not as man-made artifacts but as products of historical growth whose relationship to their own time deserved understanding and respect.

Nonetheless, all based their judgments on implicitly unhistorical standards. Arnold and Carlyle superimposed their own vision of moral order on the past in order to demonstrate that history vindicated God's laws. Froude employed a double standard of credibility in order to fit the Tudors to a similar proof. The Whig historians rehabilitated the "dark" ages scorned by the Enlightenment and invoked natural growth and practical accommodation to sanction progress in uniquely English institutions. But in defining this growth by nineteenth-century priorities and evaluating past events in terms of their contributions to the present's triumphant political balance, the Whigs proved as myopic as the *philosophes*. Finally, the "literary" historian's responsibility to shape, to judge, and to justify was in-

Introduction

compatible with the kind of detachment and restraint mandated by professional history. His primary responsibility was not to his facts but to his duties as teacher; relativism and objectivity became equally culpable if they prevented clear judgments of right and wrong. His object was not history for its own sake, but for the sake of a wider society in growing need of guidance and reassurance. When emerging professionals began to shift their allegiance from the needs of the general audience to the demands of their peers, they repudiated—or seemed to—a vital cultural function. To measure the dimensions of that function is the goal of the chapters that follow.

I

THOMAS ARNOLD
HISTORY AS PRACTICAL EVANGEL

Thomas Arnold served many nineteeth-century historians as he did former students: he was an abiding presence, a stern guide, a demanding example. In various ways he furnished a prototype for the historiographic traditions that followed. Keenly aware of the increased importance of both scholarship and artistry to historical writing, he set out to emulate Niebuhr in his critical evaluation of source materials as well as in his imaginative resuscitation of the past. He suffused both processes with a moral earnestness characteristically Victorian and thereby turned historical writing into a didactic tool vitally important for his time. Of even greater significance for the characteristic intellectual dilemmas of the period was his concern to reconcile the truths of reason with the truths of belief. His developmental model of historical change accommodated the relative and the absolute, the constantly evolving with the permanently fixed, and thus provided his contemporaries with a means of diffusing the destructive potential of scientific thought for the bases of belief. Suitably defined, scientific understanding became an aid, not an obstacle, to Christian duty, and the "natural" sanctioned the political and moral change Arnold desired for his own society. Arnold's historian could challenge Utilitarians with an analysis of progress that was "philosophical" without being materialist or mechanical. If the firmness of Arnold's faith in these reconciliations throws him into poignant relief against the sceptical generation that followed, his conviction that Christian ethics could be a practical force in shaping society retained its inspiration even when cut loose from dogmatic orthodoxy. This conviction informs his conception of history as well as makes his work especially important to interpreting the forms and purposes of Victorian historical writing.

Arnold's intellectual development was shaped by his willingness to wrestle with the "multitudinousness" that threatened to overwhelm his son. Thomas Arnold's greater confidence in the ultimate harmony of the created world gave him the energy for his struggle, but it made the task of integrating the moral, the intellectual, and the emotional no less demanding of active effort. His characteristic combination of Christian earnestness and scholarly rigor first emerged when his studies for ordination led him to "distressing doubts" about the "proof and interpretation of the textual authority" supporting several of the Thirty-Nine Articles.[1] He undoubtedly took John Keble's advice to "pray earnestly for help and light from above and turn himself more strongly than ever to the practical duties of a holy life" (LC, 16), but his reservations remained, and he took Priest's Orders in 1828 only upon being allowed to explain his objections to the presiding Bishop. In Arnold's discomfort over Subscription, we first hear the undertone of a continuing anxiety that historical criticism might threaten belief. He faced the challenge of the Higher Criticism most directly in his sermons on scriptural interpretation, but we should also consider his histories as further attempts to confront and to reconcile conflicts between doctrinal truth and historical understanding.

The work of Arnold's middle years was diverse but motivated by consistent intellectual concerns. He produced his first work on Roman history, a series of articles collected as the *History of the Later Roman Commonwealth*, in the mid-twenties. During the same period, he also taught himself German in order to read Niebuhr and other Germans and began ten years work on his edition of Thucydides. We can find early evidence of his theory of historical development at Rugby, where he adjusted his treatment of different forms to their relative levels of intellectual and moral maturity. The famous educator actually gained more notoriety as a controversialist in the late twenties and early thirties. Arnold's reaction to the widespread social distress of these years characteristically fused moral and intel-

Thomas Arnold

lectual impulses. He considered it part of a Christian's duty to promote the welfare of the poor, but advocated systematic research into all pertinent aspects of lower class existence as the most effective means of alleviating their suffering.[2] Believing that physical well-being had to build on a moral foundation, he freely mixed religious homilies with economic and political critiques in his short-lived *Englishman's Register*, aimed at effecting "Christian Reform." A similar mixture of motives informed his skirmishes with the Tractarians. He found their increased emphasis on sacraments and clergy decidedly at odds with his desire for comprehension of dissenters and the merger of church and state, and he attacked their rejection of progress as "unhistorical." By choosing to live in the past, Oxford effectively abdicated moral and intellectual leadership, leaving the people it should guide to their own presentist and utilitarian biases. Typically, Arnold found it hard to distinguish between *"intellectual error"* and *"moral wickedness"* in the Tractarian position, and the intemperate tone of articles like his "The Oxford Malignants" played a significant role in depriving him of two prospective bishoprics in the thirties.[3]

Arnold's complex conception of intellectual responsibility quite naturally informed his historical writings. He began his *History of Rome* at Rugby and published the first volume in 1838. The second followed in 1841, and the third, nearly complete at his death, was hardly needed to cement his reputation as a historian. That had been recognized in 1841, when he was appointed to the Regius Professorship of Modern History at Oxford. His *Introductory Lectures on Modern History* proclaimed a new breadth and relevance for historical study and, by implication, a new stature for the historian—a stature confirmed by crowds unprecedented in the history of the Chair. A. P. Stanley's agenda for future lectures suggests that Arnold would have continued to use his position to integrate his historical, religious, and social concerns: to act on his

> long cherished intention of bringing the "Politics" of his favorite Aristotle to bear on the problems of modern times and countries,—his anxiety to call public attention to the social evils of the lower classes in England, which he would have tried to analyze and expose in the process of their formation and growth,—his interest in tracing the general laws of social and political science, and . . . his longing desire . . . of unfolding all the various elements, physical and intellectual, social and national, by which the moral character of the Christian world has been affected. (LC, 590-91)

History as Practical Evangel

In his eminently practical way, Arnold would have made the lectures into his own "Tracts for the Times," had he not died suddenly in June of 1842.

We can appreciate the centrality and peculiar intensity of historical study for Arnold only after grasping the extent to which a scientific and a moral understanding of the world were to him equivalent. "The pursuit of knowledge for its own sake, and for the mere indulgence of our intellectual appetite," he considered no more worthy than "an excessive desire for food for its own sake, for the gratification of our bodily appetite" (MW, 148). But ultimately he viewed "all science, whether natural or moral, as a matter of duty rather than of simple knowledge" (MW, 411). Like other members of what Susan F. Cannon has called the "Cambridge Network" of scientists and Broad Churchmen,[4] Arnold refused to confine the pursuit of knowledge within narrow theological bounds, for he was convinced that the search for truth in whatever field could not threaten the fundamental bases of faith and, when rightly valued, could indeed be a positive support to them. Neither the substance nor the methods of scientific investigation were subversive of Arnold's goals. Using the term *science* in the sense of *Wissenschaft*, Arnold could conceive of only one possible sphere of "Truth" and thus could see no reason why the truths of natural and moral knowledge should ever contradict one another. Of course man's highest happiness was moral, so that knowledge of the physical world could not in itself be adequate to its fulfillment. But a man who was one of Buckland's "most earnest and intelligent" students, and who maintained a life-long interest in geology, could hardly be considered hostile to scientific study. "The discovery of truth" in all fields he considered "more or less our duty . . . for the benefits of others . . . or for the improvement of our own powers of mind, that so we may act our part in life more efficiently" (MW, 412).

More importantly, he adopted as being best suited to this "discovery of truth," and thus best suited to the fulfillment of our "duty," procedures similar to those of the natural sciences: the critical evaluation of evidence, and the inductive method of observation, generalization, and verification. He was convinced that only "by the study of facts, whether relating to nature or to man, and not by any pretended cultivation of the mind by poetry, oratory, and moral or critical dissertations," would "the understandings of mankind . . . be most improved, and their views of things rendered most accurate."[5] Facts alone led to a "philosophical" understanding of the principles that structured the moral and the physical worlds. The mind could "exert the very fulness of its power" (MW, 404) only when it was engaged in understanding "the laws or causes by which . . . phenomena are regulated" (MW, 410), and these must be determined by the scientific method. The duty to achieve such "philosophical" understanding was ultimately moral: mastering those laws would allow mankind to "form [Nature] or reform her for our own purposes," and teach us "after our most imperfect measure to learn to work like" the God who authored them (MW, 408). In this way a scientific understanding of the world became an asset rather than a liability in the Christianizing of daily life, and the scientific verification of truth an inherently moral undertaking.[6] One's duty as a Christian was better to understand, so as more fully to conform to, the laws by which God regulated the moral and physical world. Arnold's relentless search for the laws that could reveal the truth—whether it be in scriptural, historical, or scientific study—was thus inseparable from his mission as a Christian and infused with a similar earnestness.

Once shown to be the preeminent moral science, history could play a key role in this educational process. Arnold believed that only the study of biblical prophecy had a better claim to direct man's attention to general principles of good and evil in the world: "Whatever there is of greatness in the final cause of all human thought and action, God's glory and man's perfection, that is the measure of the greatness of history."[7] Indeed, Arnold ended his short-lived appointment as Examiner in the Arts at the University of London because it did not require that the professors of such "moral subjects" as history be Christian (LC, 428). Since he considered it the historian's highest duty to "encourage the love of all things noble and just, and wise and holy" (LC, 406), he felt called upon to disparage current, more limited conceptions of this calling. He deplored the classical tradition that considered historical writing no more than a source of literary fame to the author or a "means of giving pleasure" to an audience.[8] He sternly condemned the poetic license of modern work for leading at best to frivolity, at worst to falsification: "We may hope that the folly is now gone by of studiously painting the manners, institutions and events of ancient times in colours most strongly contrasting with everything which we know from our own experience. The pictures thus produced were striking and beautiful indeed, but nothing practical could be learnt from them, since they displayed a world as unreal as the fantastic creations of romance."⁹

Like Carlyle and many another early Victorian critic of "romantic" literature, Arnold felt the artist shirked his duty if he entertained at the expense of truth. But Arnold had reason to fear that even legitimate historical writing could be subverted to escapist ends, becoming another form of that "intellectual indulgence" he equally condemned. Stanley's conjecture that writing the *History of Rome* afforded Arnold "a refuge from the excitement and confusion of the present," a retreat from "the painful and conflicting thoughts roused by his writings on political and theological subjects" (LC, 268), hints at potential struggles with the temptations of escape. Elsewhere Arnold openly expressed worries that the life of the scholar might deflect his energies from the duties of the Christian reformer. "How earnestly one desires to present to one's mind a *peopled landscape* of Gaul, or Germany, or Britain, before Rome encountered them" he wrote to Chevalier Bunsen; "And yet, these indulgences of our intellectual faculties match strangely with the fever of our times, and the pressure for life and death which is going on all around us" (LC, 311).

Arnold thus had both a personal and a public stake in proving history's practicality. By demonstrating that historical study was scientific and not merely antiquarian, he could make it proof against escapism or self-indulgence. And so as he advised his Oxford audience, "We must remember also not so to transport ourselves into the fourteenth century as to forget that we belong really to the nineteenth; that here, and not there, lie our duties; that the harvest, gathered in the fields of the past, is to be brought home for the use of the present" (L, 313-14). Not the details themselves, "which are generally worthless," but the "great changes, both physical and moral" (LC, 310-11) which they could be shown to document, had practical importance for guiding the present. "Antiquarianism is no teacher of wisdom" because the antiquarian lacked "that comprehensive view which becomes the true historian." Although many of Arnold's assumptions about historical reality were quite romantic, this "comprehensive view" entailed the same things for him as it had for the men of the Enlightenment: the ability to discern beneath the apparent randomness of history general patterns that "may really assist in shaping and preparing the course of the future" (L, 84). Far from advocating an historicist immersion in the spirit of past ages, Arnold felt the historian had a duty to judge the past by the priorities of the present. He especially criticized historians like de Barante who, after "having shown himself most capable of analyzing history philosophically" in earlier works, had chosen in his study of the dukes of Burgundy "to forfeit the benefits of his own wisdom" and describe "the fourteenth and fifteenth centuries no otherwise than might have been done by their own simple chroniclers" (L, 314).

Arnold consciously modeled the historical researcher on the scientist: both tried to separate "what is accidental and particular from what is essential and universal."[10] He had no doubt that proper inductive methods would yield "truths of historical science" (L, 63) when applied to the facts of the past. Because historical periods were not viewed "in combination with one another," he argued, "perception of the general law" was obscured by "circumstances which interfere with its regular operation" and the "scientific character" of historical study was not acknowledged (L, 306). Reveal these laws by induction and comparative analysis, however, and human history became not just "a mere aggregation of particular actions or characters, like the anecdotes of natural history but . . . besides this the witness to general moral and political truths, and capable when rightly used, of bringing to our notice fresh truths which we might not have gained by *a priori* reasoning only" (L, 307).

In practice Arnold's investigation rested upon *a priori* moral universals that subverted induction to the same extent as had the *philosophe*'s rationalistic ones. He proclaimed himself

> firmly persuaded . . . that setting out with those views of man which we find in the Scriptures, and with those plain moral notions which the Scriptures do not so much teach as suppose to exist in us, and sanction; the laws of history, in other words, the laws of political science, using "political" in the most exalted sense of the term . . . may be deduced, or . . . confirmed from it with perfect certainty, with a certainty equal to that of the most undoubted truths of morals. (L, 305)

Arnold projected onto history the moral order he assumed in all human affairs. For a mind so heavily regimented by general principles, an objective measure of the individual datum was virtually impossible. Stanley describes his "unwillingness . . . to act in any individual case, without some general law to which he might refer," suggesting that "at times it would almost seem as if he invented universal rules with the express object of meeting particular cases" (LC, 80). Contemporary political and ecclesiastical controversies merged in his mind with "the prototypes of the various forms of error and wickedness" denounced in the Bible, and "living individuals . . . and existing principles, became lost to his view in the long line of images, past and future, in which they formed only one link" (LC, 150). In such a mind, historical induction inevitably confirmed patterns established by "undoubted truths."

Too much depended upon the existence of these truths to allow the historian to accept the scientist's objectivity along with his authority. Arnold was keenly aware of the damage that could be done to the bases of belief if historical events were allowed to be random in their occurrence or relative in their significance, or worse yet, if historical and scientific criticism could be shown to compromise revealed truth. If historical study could not demonstrate the functioning of moral law, "we should be driven to the extremity of scepticism; truth would appear indeed to be a thing utterly unreal or utterly unattainable" (L, 306). This placed great responsibility on the historian. Nothing was more culpable than a relativism that deprived laws of their sanction, nothing so insidious for a Christian society. Even impartiality—if it meant to write "as if there were no truth attainable in the matter, but all was mere opinion" (LC, 577)—became morally remiss. Once convinced that political and moral truths existed, the historian could not "but wish them to be seen and embraced by others."[11] Thus it was far from "partiality to say that the support of a bad cause is itself evil, the support of a good cause is itself good" (L, 301-2). As Duncan Forbes explains it, the impartiality of the Liberal Anglican historians did not mean having no standpoint, but rather having the best one—the Christian one.[12]

Imposing such a viewpoint allowed Arnold to side-step the challenge that history's sheer variety posed to universal and permanent truths. He objected to Strauss's scriptural interpretation not because it was too sceptical but because it was not scientific enough.[13] According to Arnold's disciple Bonamee Price, Arnold showed in his sermons that the most advanced insights of historical and scientific criticism could be used to place "the supernatural inspiration of the sacred writers on an imperishable historical basis . . . proof against any attack which the most refined modern learning could direct against it" (LC, 168). Arnold was able to turn the Higher Criticism against itself because the "scientific" principle revealed by his "*a priori* inquiry" into scripture was that its "lower," "historical" sense was of a different order from the higher, universal, spiritual meaning of

Thomas Arnold

each text.[14] He could apply the "general rules of interpretation" to the historical side of the Bible without fear because he knew the validity of its "higher" meaning could not be undermined by its imperfect realization in history. Arnold was able, in Price's words, to reconcile "the progress of knowledge with Christianity" by limiting the sphere in which critical methods had validity, rather than by attempting to prove biblical accounts literally correct.

Arnold overcame scepticism in the secular realm by similarly ruling invalid all challenges to the bases of his belief. The "laws" of political science possessed in his mind the same certainty as did the tenets of Christian conduct because they were in essence the same thing: "The truths of political science belong as much, I think, to an historian, as those of theology to a Professor of Divinity" (LC, 577). As Stanley reminds us, "The Greek science, πολιτιμὴ, of which the English word 'politics,' or even political science, is so inadequate a translation" meant for Arnold "society in its connexion with the highest welfare of man" (LC, 170). Moral perfection was the end of both civic and individual development and was guided by the same laws. Once assume these laws—and he confessed perplexity that any could doubt them—and the lessons of history neatly followed. Since Arnold was sure that only the presence of some "disturbing causes which may be clearly pointed out" could prevent such laws from promoting the good of nations, he could conclude that to oppose them was simply "to uphold what is bad" (L, 306-7).

For Arnold the "unity of history" derived in part from the continuing validity of these laws. Believing that the "general rules" of "political wisdom" had remained the same for all western society made the classics contemporary and the study of ancient history not "an idle inquiry about remote ages and forgotten institutions, but a living picture of things present, fitted not so much for the curiosity of the scholar, as for the instruction of the statesman and citizen" (LC, 148-49). But Arnold's unity meant more than uniformity. He based history's practicality on an interpretive tool more powerful than the manifestation of universal laws, always and everywhere the same. In an appendix to his translation of Thucydides, Arnold enunciated a theory of development that gave the additional "scientific" sanction of organic similarity to historical comparisons. Inspired by Vico, this master law of history held that "states, like individuals, go through certain changes in a certain order. . . . But they differ from individuals in this, that though the order of the periods is regular, their duration is not so; and their features are more liable to be mistaken, as they can only be distinguished by their characteristic phenomena."[15] This law provided the demonstrable regularity in human history necessary to a philosophical understanding of it, while still respecting the uniqueness of the developmental process in individual states. Only nations at the same stage of development could be validly compared. To impose upon history the "artificial divisions" established by political events was to be arbitrary and unscientific: "History is to be studied as a whole, and according to its philosophical divisions, not such as are merely geographical and chronological."[16] Every society had an ancient and a modern history, so that "ancient history" was misnamed, because it really constituted the "modern history of the civilization of Greece and Rome." Empirical comparison of similarities between past and present would make clear that "in our moral and political views, in those matters which most determine human character," there existed a "perfect resemblance" between moderns and ancients (MW, 349). As a result the ancient world provided data directly relevant to the historian's theorizing about modern society—data possessing "all the value of a mass of new and pertinent facts, illustrative of the great science of the nature of civilized man" (MW, 350).

This "science" was governed not by the static categories of man in general, but by the stages through which a biological organism matured. It could account for change without sacrificing identity and recognize relative degrees of development without foregoing valid generalizations about the developmental process as a whole, or about the organism as an entity. The significance of this qualified relativism is demonstrated by the ways it conditioned Arnold's theorizing in other areas. At Rugby the lower standard of morality he tolerated among younger boys paralleled that historically tolerated during "the boyhood of the human race" (LC, 68). Their limited development justified flogging, though reason and responsibility were the appropriate means of enhancing the sixth form's greater moral maturity. The "principle of accommodation" Arnold used to interpret scripture similarly adjusted rules to circumstances. By claiming that "God's revelations to man . . . were adapted to his state at the several periods when they were successively made,"[17] he could argue that injunctions given to one age were only binding upon another to the extent that their circumstances were similar. This provided an escape from the intellectual discrepancies created by literal interpretation of scripture, and more importantly, established grounds for the permanent relevance of Christian doctrine. For Arnold as for Carlyle, appreciating relative stages of development ended by shoring up rather than undermining what each defined as permanent principles.

Like Carlyle too, Arnold justified his diagnosis of present problems with an appeal to the past—an appeal that merged the authorities of the historical, the natural, and the divine. The organic metaphor lent urgency to the reform movements of the early nineteenth century because it stressed the inevitability of change and the dangers inherent in attempting to subvert the natural maturation of the state. In Arnold's case, however, the state "naturally" progressed toward greater freedom and complexity. The tendency of society was to "become more and more liberal" as the source of authority shifted from birth, to wealth, to numbers.[18] Progress toward wider participation represented the growth of moral as well as political maturity. The transition from aristocracy to plutocracy was analogous to the transition from childhood to manhood:[19] accepting the responsibility of self-government encouraged "that practical vigour of mind" which, when properly cultivated, was "the greatest earthly blessing of which mankind are susceptible" (LRC, 2:257-58). Since "all the world is by the very law of its creation in eternal progress" (LC, 224), attempting to resist the expansion of self-government would be like trying to defy the order of nature and, by implication, the moral order of God's plan for human development.

Arnold's conviction that this kind of political progress was organically necessary helps explain those attitudes toward revolution and aristocracy that so alarmed the Tories in the twenties and thirties. As he explained to Chevalier Bunsen, he took the revolutionary turmoil of the thirties as a "sign infallible" of the irreversible breakup of the old order. Trying to hinder it could only "derange the process of the new birth which must succeed it" (LC, 281). Government by aristocracy was to Arnold "the greatest source of evil throughout the world" (LC, 447), because, by attempting to preserve the status quo, they had themselves provoked violent disruptions of the social order: "Considering the people as children, they have restrained the child, but they have not educated him; considering them even as lunatics, they have confined the lunatic, but have often so irritated him with their discipline as to make his paroxysms more violent and more incurable" (L, 276). In distinction to Carlyle and other early Victorian conservatives, Arnold stressed that the aristocracy's responsibility was to "train up" the lower orders "to the independence of manhood," to elevate and enlighten their inferiors, preparing them for popular rule.[20]

But those who branded Arnold a dangerous radical missed the inherently conservative assumptions behind such views. As his reading of Roman history repeatedly makes clear, he condoned expanded popular power only when "the natural progress of things" (i.e., the spread of wealth and education) made the people "ripe for it" (R, 1:340-41). Giving them too much power too soon would be as "unnatural"—as subversive of God's providence—as refusing to change at all (R, 1:491). Like Macaulay and other Whigs, Arnold championed reform as the best means of preserving the underlying continuity of national institutions. "Every new institution should be but a fuller development of, or addition to, what already exists," he wrote. "If things have come to such a pass in a country, that all its past history and associations are cast away as merely bad, Reform in such a country is impossible" (LC, 503). To reject tradition and ignore history as did the Chartists was to be a "slave," not a citizen (MW, 494). Believing that a nation could no more deny its past than could a person the formative events and associations of his own life, Arnold cultivated an attitude toward progress that encouraged further growth while respecting national heritage; in this way the English could achieve "Democracy without Jacobinism" (LC, 679 n.).

Human or natural models of change increased Arnold's leverage on an undesirable status quo but also posed the problem of decay. To allow the history of western culture to be cyclical without being circular, he needed to argue that improvement had been incremental even though development repeated the same pattern in every society. To image all history as a static repetition of identical cycles would have negated the moral progress implicit in Christianity. Like other Liberal Anglican historians, Arnold believed that modern history exhibited "a fuller development of the human race, a richer combination of its most remarkable elements" (L, 26), because it incorporated and improved upon the moral excellence attained by previous cultures. Unlike Carlyle and Froude, he felt that overvaluing the past was more dangerous than undervaluing it; glorifying former times tended to hinder progress by "depriv[ing] us of the advantages of our own superior experience" (LC, 195). To idolize either classical antiquity or the middle ages was to permit the possibility that humanity had degenerated over time—a conclusion thoroughly incompatible with Arnold's belief that history was the arena for the gradual perfecting of the human race.[21] He allowed that material progress might be equivocal in its nature, but not moral progress:

> . . . while the advance of civilization destroys much that is noble, and throws over the mass of human society an atmosphere somewhat dull and hard; yet it is only by its peculiar trials, no less than by its positive advantages, that the utmost virtue of human nature can be matured. And those who vainly lament that progress of earthly things, which, whether good or evil, is certainly inevitable, may be consoled by the thought that its sure tendency is to confirm and purify the virtue of the good.[22]

Holding center stage in this historical arena was the nation rather than the individual. History was foremost "the biography of a political society or commonwealth" (L, 5). The institutions of the advanced state were necessary to cultivate the moral maturity Arnold desired in its subjects. The nation expressed the common life and common purpose of its members; it focused their efforts to accomplish its divinely appointed work. The struggles of even the greatest heroes were of interest not for their private triumphs but for their advance of the state; the Hector who subordinated himself to his country's good was more noble than the selfish and self-sufficient Achilles (R, 3:386-87). Even nations diminished in importance when viewed through the wider lens of western culture. The individual struggles of the Romans and Teutons were significant not in themselves but for their advance of civilization. These peoples had been chosen by Providence to play leading roles in the spiritual biography of western man.

As inheritors of this legacy, the Victorians bore a grave responsibility. The possibility of regression always qualified the inevitability of progress for Arnold. "Nations, like individuals," he wrote, "have their time of trial; and if this be wasted or misused, their future course is inevitably evil" (R, 1:252). Indeed, in the history of Rome itself loomed the specter of possible defeat: "The great improvements of our own days may at some future period be again cut short" (LRC, 2:386). His confidence in the continuity of progress was qualified by the eschatological anxiety that "modern history appears to be not only *a* step in advance of ancient history, but *the* last step; it appears to bear marks of the fulness of time, as if there would be no future history beyond it" (L, 28). Because he saw "no new continents peopled by youthful races, the destined restorers of our worn-out generations" (L, 30), he ruled out the possibility of a "third period of human history" beyond classical and modern. It was the apocalyptic culmination to his pattern of progress that gave historical writing its urgent practicality. If "our existing nations are the last reserve of the world," he wrote, "its fate may be said to be in their hands—God's work on earth will be left undone it they do not do it. But our future course must be hesitating or mistaken, if we do not know what course has brought us to the point where we are at present" (L, 31). On man's success in discerning, understanding, and applying the laws of history rested the fate not just of England, but of God's favored people on earth. And the historical scientist, by virtue of his command of these laws, guided the spiritual as well as the political destiny of the world. He was not just a scholar, but a sage.

II

We can clearly trace the ramifications of Arnold's theories about history in his analysis of sources, his artistic reconstruction of the past, and his judgments on men, events, and nations. For Arnold as for Carlyle, the danger of scepticism intensified the responsibility of research. As he warned in his eighth lecture, "If historical testimony be really worth nothing, it touches us in one of the very divinest parts of our nature, the power of connecting ourselves with the past. For this we do and can do only through knowledge which we must call historical." If no veracity could be expected from historical statements, if no facts could be established from the physical evidence of past civilizations, "our life would be at once restricted to the span of our own memory; nay, I might almost say to the span of our own actual consciousness. For if no other man's report of the past is to be credited, I know not how we can defend the very reports of our own memories" (L, 282-83). Identity itself rested on the truths of memory. Like Wordsworth's child and man, England too could claim a unified self: her political life was "made up wholesomely of past and present, so that the centuries of English History are truly 'bound each to each by natural piety' " (LC, 680). Critical analysis of source materials must not be allowed to produce radical scepticism about historical truths, lest the basis for life-giving continuity—the integrity of the individual organism over time—be destroyed. That is one reason why Arnold so admired Niebuhr's analytical skills. The master possessed an "instinctive power of discerning truth" where others saw only myth: he "has rescued from the dominion of scepticism much which less profound inquirers had before too hastily given up to it" (R,

1:218) and thus affirmed the historical validity of Rome's "childhood."

Evaluating the credibility of historical data took on a characteristic high seriousness for Arnold. It was not enough for the historian to be impartial or free from dishonesty: he must have "an earnest craving after truth, and utter impatience not of falsehood merely but of error" (L, 293). Significantly, as in scriptural interpretation, Arnold considered the "scientific" treatment of source materials not only a means to truth, but the best guarantee of reaching it. In his "Introductory Dissertation on the Credibility of Early Roman History," he compared the evaluation of historical data to that of "natural philosophy": what would be unthinkable in the sciences—the confounding of all evidence, regardless of its reliability, with fact—must also be avoided in the study of history "if we wish to establish the great doctrines of history on the same sure base with those of natural philosophy."[23] Arnold's "cross-examination" of historical witnesses is clearly inspired by Niebuhr's methods for evaluating textual reliability. He tried constantly to be aware of the prejudices, affiliations, and temperaments that color the testimony of his sources. He pointed out, for instance, that Livy and Dionysius had relied upon the annals of great Roman families, and that "each successive version of these, as men's notions of their early history became more and more romantic, would omit whatever seemed inconsistent with the supposed purity and nobleness of the times of their forefathers" (R, 1:239-40). Elsewhere in the *History of Rome* he was careful to separate disinterested observation from prejudice in accounts rendered by participants, and he remained alert to the ways that friendship between historians and their subjects could restrain criticism and exaggerate praise (e.g., R, 3:382-83).

Although Arnold was keenly aware that the modern historian could no longer gain a "reputation for learning" (R, 1:476) merely by repeating the accounts of the ancients, his own work was far from original. His primary materials were those available to any educated man of the time: the standard accounts and the more modern attempts to reconcile them, chief among them Niebuhr's. Arnold followed Niebuhr very closely in volumes 1 and 2 of the *History of Rome*, although he insisted that his work was more than "a mere compilation," insofar as his "own reading and comparison of the ancient authorities" was the foundation of every paragraph (R, 2:v). Of particular significance for Arnold's romantic sense of national identity, he followed Niebuhr in restoring the myths of early Rome to its history. Like the German and British romantics before him, Arnold believed that the best means of discovering the essence of "racial" identity lay in the literature it had produced. He was aware that given "that wider view of the connection of races and languages, which we have learnt of late to entertain," historians could no longer "cast . . . aside as mere fables" the "mythic reports" of a nation's origins (R, 1:481). Besides valuing myths for the "germ of truth" that might be recovered from them, Arnold was also committed to a theory of history that stressed the organic integrity of all manifestations of national life at any given stage of its development. The epigraph from Mackintosh that opens the *History of Rome* acknowledges the value Arnold placed on the emotional "facts" of national identity: "The old songs of every people, which bear the impress of their character, and of which the beauties whether few or many must be genuine, because they arise only from feeling, have always been valued by men of masculine and comprehensive taste."

Even in researching later periods Arnold considered popular literature of unique historical importance. His lectures particularly recommended a period's second- and third-rate literature to the student. In a peculiarly Carlylean image, Arnold compared this literary "rubbish" to "mere moss" which "becomes in the lapse of ages, after being buried in its peat bed, of some value as fuel; it is capable of yielding both light and heat" (L, 75). He found the "colloquial peculiarities" of contemporary histories and the "particularity" of an age's legal style also worthy of attention because they helped resuscitate the past; in reading them the audience could feel "we are in some sort hearing" the voices of contemporary speakers (L, 67). The end of research was ultimately to galvanize these remains into some semblance of the once living whole. Literature was merely the most accessible form of the wealth of sociocultural data needed to reveal "not what existing accounts may have recorded of a people or a race, but what the people or race really was, and did; we wish to conceive a full and lively image of them, of their language, their institutions, their arts, their morals; to understand what they were in themselves, and how they have affected the fate of the world" (R, 1:476-77).

Arnold's attention to the geographical evidence also deserves note, as it would be shared by Carlyle, Freeman, and especially Green. Buckland had first kindled Arnold's scientific curiosities; their continued vigor manifested itself in plans for a major work "on the connection between the revolutions of nature and those of mankind" that would demonstrate that "nature, no less than human society, contains tokens that it had a beginning, and will as surely have its end" (R, 1:498). Geography also had a romantic appeal for one who shared Wordsworth's quasi-religious attachment to the Lake District around his own Fox How. In his Oxford lectures, Arnold recommended the study of geography not just as a pedagogically useful starting point for political history, but also because it contained "so much . . . of the most picturesque and poetical character; so much of beauty, of magnificence, and of interest, physical and moral" (L, 123-24). Just as the life of a nation could to him become as distinct "as that of an individual," so too the terrain of a country could take on an anthropomorphical individuality. "Let me once understand the real geography of a country," he claimed, "its organic structure . . . the form of its skeleton, that is, of its hills; the magnitude and course of its veins and arteries, that is, of its streams and rivers: let me conceive of it as a whole made up of connected parts; and then the position of man's dwellings . . . becomes at once easily remembered, and lively and intelligible besides" (L, 125-26). In geographical evidence an understanding of organic relationships was quite literally the key to meaning; reverence for the poetic feelings nature awakened was the best guarantee of "scientific" accuracy in reconstructing its past. Arnold criticized Polybius because the "tameness" of his accounts of alpine passes crossed by Hannibal revealed that "not one spark of feeling" had been awakened in him by the sublime; the "unpoetical character" of his mind made his descriptions so "unscientific" as to be unrecognizable.[24] Landscape provided history's most palpable terrain. It took the eye of imagination to glimpse its true contours, a collaboration of poetry and science to fix its extent. It was not just a backdrop, but a vital part of historical understanding.

Arnold's conception of his artistic tasks was informed by a similar complexity of moral and creative vision. The writing of history posed more than a literary problem: an inadequate narrative failed to make sense of the past. So long as it lacked coherent shape, the historical account could not demonstrate the unfolding of God's will in the universe. Like a paleontologist trying to make the argument from design, the historian was left with only scattered bones; what gave them identity and unity, "the face, figure, and mind of the living man are lost to us beyond recall" (R, 2:82). He had to impose order lest vision become nightmare. His task was to "supply, and arrange into an intelligible whole, the disjointed and seemingly unmeaning images, which our fragments of information offer, as perplexing and incongruous as the chaos of a dream" (R, 3:460-61). Arnold admired Niebuhr's artistic abilities as much as his scholarship, for his integrative genius allowed him to retrieve "from much, that to former writers seemed a hopeless chaos, . . . a living picture of events and institutions, as rich in its colouring, as perfect in its composition, as it is faithful to the truth of nature" (R, 1:219).

Arnold's early conversion to Wordsworthian romanticism had helped convince him that only art could render this coherent truth adequately. His college friend J. T. Coleridge had first introduced Arnold to the *Lyrical Ballads.* In Coleridge's eyes becoming a "zealous disciple" of Wordsworth was of peculiar advantage to Arnold, whose practical bent too often inhibited his "feeling for the lofty and imaginative" (LC, 12). Doubtless Wordworth's ideas also played a role in convincing Arnold that *"Poetical feelings* are merely . . . all the highest and purest feelings of our nature. . . . The very essence of poetry is, that it exhalts and ennobles us, and puts us into a higher state of mind than that which we are commonly living in" (MW, 252-53). It was natural that as an historian he should draw upon these feelings in himself and appeal to them in his audience. When Arnold confessed to his brother-in-law in 1841 that he had begun to regard his own *History of Rome* "more and more with something of an artist's feeling as to the composition and arrangement of it" (LC, 549), he implied a spiritual and imaginative intensity different in kind from the ancients' concern with mere style. Haunted even in sleep by images of famous events, he tried to maintain this identification and sympathy in the creative process as well. J. C. Hare conjectures that Arnold's manuscript lacked footnotes because "after having impregnated his mind with the liveliest conception he could gain of the events he was about to record . . . he was unwilling to interrupt the flow of the narrative by pausing to examine the details of the documents" (R, 3:iv). Where he lacked personal experience of the kind of events portrayed, he trusted in "his general knowledge of human nature, his love of great and good actions, his sympathy with virtue, his abhorrence of vice" to "assist him in making himself as it were a witness of what he attempts to describe" (R, 2:vii-viii). Upon the authenticity of this witnessing rested the credibility of the historian's message; his highest credentials were moral, not scholarly.

Arnold also had quite pragmatic reasons for his artistic choices. It was impossible "to communicate any interest to history," he feared, "if it must only record events and not paint actions" (R, 2:562). History had great potential as a didactic weapon; a lively narrative filled with "painted" scenes and portraits was the best means of reaching a wide audience. Consistently, the needs of the general reader took precedence over those of the fellow scholar in shaping Arnold's histories. He wished to make his translations "as good as any which they are publishing in Germany" but was also anxious that their scholarly apparatus not seem superfluous to a "man of plain sense" (LC, 63-64). He undertook his own history of Rome because he feared that Niebuhr's "discoveries and remarkable wisdom" would not become "generally popular in England" unless rendered in a form "more adapted to our common taste" (R, 1:vii). "Common taste" favored a higher proportion of story-telling narrative to scholarly "dissertations." Arnold excused the excessive length of volume 2 by claiming that further abridgment would deprive it of the interest and particularity that most effectively impressed the memory. Although generally scrupulous about the reliability of historical data, so that at one point he relegated conjectures to an appendix because they were not definite enough "to claim the name of history" (R, 2:307), elsewhere he allowed audience expectations to override his reservations. He relied on the traditional chronology for the consuls and tribunes of Rome because it was fixed in readers' memories in a way Niebuhr's more accurate version was not. In Rome's earliest history he was content to flesh out "an outline of undoubted truth" with specifics that were at least "clear from manifest error" and that still preserved "some of its most remarkable details, which may be true, and are at any rate far too famous to be omitted" (R, 1:531-32). Although vigilant against the distortions of fantasy, Arnold remained sensitive to its emotional power. He consciously chose to include events that "are so striking in their incidents, as to acquire the interest of a romance, and thus retain their hold on the imaginations and moral feelings of all ages and countries" (R, 3:259-60). Memory and imagination were the keys to living history; the "romance" that nurtured both must not therefore be sacrificed completely to the "spirit of inquiry and of fact" (R, 1:99).

Arnold's treatment of the legends of early Rome offers the most interesting examples of his attempts to preserve this "romantic" quality. Like Macaulay in the *Lays of Ancient Rome*, Arnold sought to capture the voice as well as the message of the ancient world. Too sophisticated a style would be anachronistic; one too prosaic would destroy the poetry. No man could tell "such stories in a civilized age in his own proper person, with that sincerity of belief, nay even with that gravity which is requisite to give them their proper charm" (LC, 432). Just as Wordsworth attempted to approximate the "language really used by men" in his poems of rural life, so too Arnold presented the early legends of Rome in what he called "an antiquated and simple language"; in fact, he told J. T. Coleridge that Wordsworth had seen and approved of this treatment (LC, 432). Arnold considered it irreverent to follow too closely the most obvious model, the Bible, but its stylistic impress still lingers. In the legend of Aeneas that opens the *History of Rome*, Arnold combines touches of archaic diction and syntax with balanced cadences to reinforce the mythic details of the story:

> When the fatal horse was going to be brought within the walls of Troy, and when Laocoon had been devoured by the two serpents sent by the gods to punish him because he had tried to save his country against the will of fate, then Aeneas and his father Anchises, with their wives, and many who followed their fortune, fled from the coming of the evil day. But they remembered to carry their gods with them, who were to receive their worship in a happier land. They were guided in their flight from the city, by the god Hermes, and he built for them a ship to carry them over the sea. When they put to sea, the star of Venus, the mother of Aeneas, stood over their heads, and it shone by day as well as by night, till they came to the shores of the land of the west. But when they landed, the star vanished and was seen no more; and by this sign Aeneas knew that he was come to that country wherein fate had appointed him to dwell. (R, 1:1-2)

Even in the later history of Rome, Arnold found himself falling "insensibly" into the same measured pace and antiquated inversions when confronted by stories historically true in substance but filled with "romantic" details, like that of the Gauls' attack on the Capitol (R, 1:545). Arnold hoped this treatment would charm, but he also intended it to serve more practical ends: it made clear to "the most careless reader" that the legends were distinct from "real history" (R, 1:x, 20). Arnold follows these early legends with analyses, often based on a comparison of variants, designed to determine how much of the ancient tales could be accepted as true. Still, he distinguished between fictions calculated to minister to national or individual vanity, and those which were "imaginative but honest . . . not professing to impart exact knowledge, but to delight, to quicken, and to

Thomas Arnold

raise the perception of what is beautiful and noble" (R, 1:393). If the former deserved oblivion, it would be "irreverence" to neglect the latter, serving as they did some of the highest aims of historical writing.

Reverence and identification were the keynotes of Arnold's reconstruction of people and events as well. Nowhere were they more important than in his handling of characterization. Although Arnold never indulged in hero-worship for its own sake, he too believed that respect for true superiority lay at the base of the modern social order and could hardly retain its credibility in the present if it could not be made understandable and admirable in the past. The myths of ancient Rome served this end by providing some of the commemoration that was traditionally "due to the memory of illustrious names" (LRC, 1:26). But "real history" demanded recognizable individuals; these transformed the "landscape" into "an historical picture." A more powerful means of inspiring understanding and admiration was the historian's ability to "multiply in some sort the number of those with whom we are personally and individually in sympathy." Enabling the reader "to recognise amidst the dimness of remote and uncongenial ages, the features of friends and of brethren" laid on him a claim to belief and assent forged from a common humanity (L, 74). Arnold lamented that the utter lack of "materials for painting portraits" made his account not only inferior to Niebuhr's, but contrast sadly with "those inimitable living pictures with which Carlyle's History of the French Revolution abounds" (LC, 448). He strove to compensate for this lack in a number of ways.

Dialogue provided one means of increasing the reality of characterization. Arnold felt it "quite essential" to present the legends dramatically, "making the actors express their thoughts in the first person, instead of saying what they thought or felt as narrative" (LC, 432). Such was the style of the Bible and Herodotus, works from commensurate stages of cultural development. For later periods, too, he occasionally fashions direct quotations from the classical sources (e.g., R, 3:69), notwithstanding his conviction that such speech-making had too easily degenerated into mere rhetorical affectation in many of the ancients. Having criticized Livy for drawing "the Romans of every period in the costume of his own times,"[25] he invents speeches only when they would authenticate "the peculiar views of [a] party or time"—for instance, Servius Maluginensis' opposition to the Licinian laws (R, 2:48ff.). And yet, while taking care to antiquate the language appropriately so as to preserve the flavor of the period ("and if ye had ever found me to be your enemy, it had been ill done in you to have tried me yet again this seventh time"), Arnold cannot help finding in Maluginensis' situation a somewhat anachronistic vindication of the uses of Christian revelation. He similarly superimposes the perceptions of one culture upon another when he advises his audience to read Chatham's speech against the Franco-American coalition in order to duplicate the drama of Appius Claudius's arguments aginst peace with Pyrrhus (R, 2:497). Both cases suggest the extent to which Arnold's appreciation for particularity remained controlled by private typologies.

Of course, allusions or comparisons to more modern events also allowed Arnold to tap the strong enthusiasms and vivid memories of his audience and to use them to charge characters with more immediate significance. Arnold exploits both the awe and the patriotism of the English by comparing Hannibal's sixteen-year struggle against Rome to Napoleon's against England; the personal magnetism of the warrior is balanced against the moral necessity of his defeat in both cases (R, 3:63). He encourages his readers to view with greater sympathy the apparent mixture of faith and scepticism in Scipio's behavior by suggesting his resemblance to Cromwell. Such comparisons easily shade into projections of desired similarities, however. Arnold decides that given Scipio's "nobleness of soul," he must have felt the contemporary reverence for the invisible and the divine (R, 3:384-85). What appears to be hypocrisy Arnold explains as the result of conflict in one longing to believe, yet repelled by the "palpable falsehood" of Paganism. What seem to us to be time-bound assumptions are of course to Arnold permanent truths that render charges of anachronism irrelevant.

Arnold's insistent faith in heroism controls his attempts to illuminate the minds and characters of great men, so that these figures become not so much fully realized individuals as fulfillments of his own ideals. In Scipio's case he sides with Livy because his "truer feeling . . . taught him that a hero cannot be a hypocrite." For Arnold, the stature of both Hannibal and Scipio endowed them with a manifest personal "ascendancy" that he assumes must have overpowered the minds and allegiances of lesser men. In the absence of conclusive data, he finds no bars to the best construction of equivocal behavior, as when he assumes that Hannibal's fervent patriotism was what enlisted his support of action that wore the appearance of savage cruelty (R, 3:133). This devotion to his country's honor becomes the keynote of Arnold's reconstruction of Hannibal's state of mind. He follows the classical sources in portraying Hannibal as haunted night and day by "his strong sense of being the devoted instrument of his country's gods to destroy their enemies" (R, 3:70). His own inventions reinforce this characterization as they expand the reader's capacity for sympathy and imagination. Here, for instance, he encourages us to think with Hannibal riding beneath the walls of Rome:

> If anything of disappointment depressed his mind at that instant; if he felt that Rome's strength was not broken, nor the spirit of her people quelled, that his own fortune was wavering, and that his last effort had been made, and made in vain; yet thinking where he was, and of the shame and loss which his presence was causing to his enemies, he must have wished that his father could have lived to see that day, and must have thanked the gods of his country that they had enabled him so fully to perform his vow. (R, 3:246)

The reader's satisfactions are complex. Not only is he for the moment privy to the great man's thoughts; confident of the superior strength of the unified state and the ultimate piety of the hero's intentions, he can also give himself over to the vicarious pleasures of both vengeful victory and poignant defeat.

The individuality of Arnold's characters, especially his heroes, is finally subsumed by the ethical imperatives they serve. On the broader stage of western history, Rome's ends outweighed Hannibal's in importance and necessarily qualified Arnold's final estimation of his defeat. Arnold acknowledges the ability of great individuals like Hannibal to embody the history and "the living spirit" of an entire nation. He pays homage to others whose own hands had shaped the course of time—to Philip of Macedon, for instance, or to Dionysius of Syracuse, "who outtopped by his personal renown the greatness of the events in which he was an actor" (R, 1:438). But his belief that the state was "the ultimate power in human life" had to put into perspective even the greatest heroes. Ultimately, great men could act permanently only by forming great nations: "brave and able as Dionysius was, active, and temperate, and energetic," he failed because "he left behind him no beneficial institutions; he degraded rather than improved the character of his countrymen" (R, 1:475). Hannibal's selfless devotion to the good of his nation made him a Hector to Scipio's Achilles, but was inadequate to compensate for Carthage's inherent cultural deficiencies. Perhaps Arnold is warning himself as much as his audience against "our tendency . . . to admire individual greatness far more than national." Rome's triumph, he insists, demonstrated "the wisdom of God's providence. . . . It was clearly for the good of mankind, that Hannibal should be conquered: his triumph would have stopped the progress of the world." He urges those who regretted Hannibal's defeat to consider how isolated Carthage was, and how ill-fitted to "bind together barbarians of every race and language into an organized empire, and prepare them for becoming, when that empire was dissolved, the free members of the commonwealth of Christian Europe" (R, 3:64-65). Admiration for individual preeminence was finally less important than—and perhaps distracted from—reverence for the providential, which operated on the level of the nation.

Here was a more challenging dramatic problem: Arnold's didactic purposes required that the identity of the state be realized with as much intensity as that of its great individuals. He follows the romantic historian's lead in seeking "national personality" in phenomena such as race, language, religion, and institutions. In the *History* he provides periodic if necessarily sketchy inventories of various aspects of Roman culture—their art and literature, their religious festivals, their public works, and the sources of their wealth—in order to establish the character of the people at important junctures (R, 1:ch. vi; 2:446 ff.). He also follows his contemporaries in assuming that certain political traits were innate to certain "races." The love of institutions and order, the reverence for law, and the subordination of individual to social good characterized both the Greeks and the Romans, needing only the addition of Teutonic morality and domestic virtue to produce a racial mixture uniquely suited to promote Arnold's ideal Christian democracy. Arnold uses laws to reveal "the deliberate mind" of a society. This was particularly true of property laws, since in his moralized political order the possession of property "calls forth and exercises . . . forethought, love of order, justice, beneficence, and wisdom in the use of power," thereby determining the social maturity of a given civilization (L, 19). Arnold tries, for instance, to incorporate his investigations of various land tenures into a "sort of Domesday Book of Italy after the Roman Conquest" (LC, 514) that would, like England's, reveal social as well as economic relationships.

Although he believed that a state's political history at times obscured its "infinitely more important" social condition, in most places in the *History of Rome* he had in large part to rely on the former to gauge the latter. In its first half, his sympathy and interest

Thomas Arnold

focus on the struggle of the commons to gain legitimate power, his criticisms on the obstructions created by burgher and aristocrat to such "natural" progress (R, 1:229; 2:19-20; 2:271-72). In volume 3, however, his sympathies begin to shift, in part because the aristocracy had shown itself willing to share power gradually, but more importantly, because he found in them a needed embodiment of the "spirit, and wisdom, and power of Rome" (R, 3:64), of a collective heroism to counterbalance Pyrrhus and Hannibal. Believing that "against a whole nation of able and active men the greatest individual genius of a single enemy must ever strive in vain" (R, 2:463-64), Arnold needed to make the aristocracy demonstrate the same purity of motive he expected from great heroes. The "unyielding magnaminity" (R, 3:64) with which the Roman aristocracy devoted themselves to the defense of the commonwealth against Hannibal—their fidelity under duress (R, 3:158), their willingness to endure personal sacrifice (R, 3:191), their generosity to the commons and the colonies in the face of a greater danger without (R, 3:169)—all support Arnold's claim that they deserved their ascendancy (R, 3:342). Roll calls of great Roman families were the easiest way to individualize this group. Elsewhere Arnold tries to render the nation imaginatively palpable by re-creating the collective experience of citizens, just as he had tried to reconstruct the thoughts of great men. A series of particulars sketches in the Romans' fears at learning of Hannibal's approach (R, 3:244), for instance, or their jubilation after Hasdrubal's defeat at Metaurus (R, 3:377-79). Without data to support such particularity, however, he more often has to treat the nation metaphorically: Rome was the rock standing unshaken in the torrents of war, the special agent of divine providence, against which even the greatest powers were fated to struggle in vain (R, 3:146, 244).

Arnold's attempts to objectify his conception of national life finally carry less narrative weight or interest than his more conventional efforts at military history. Even if the ancient annals had not justified this emphasis, Arnold's belief that military heroics excited "our deep sympathies" would have. Battles had to be either useful or uplifting to justify inclusion: campaigns deserved full coverage only when they contained valuable military lessons or were so striking as to command "the imaginations and moral feelings of all ages and countries." Unlike the "feeble bickerings" of the decaying Greek states, the "varied and eventful story" of Hannibal's Italian campaigns laid such a claim on soldier and general reader alike; so too did the Sicilian wars, preserving as they did "the immortal names of Syracuse and Archimedes" (R, 3:260). Arnold was convinced that the truth about combat could be discovered neither by those who placed all the good on one side, nor by those "unbeliever[s] in all heroism," who brought "every thing down to the level of a common mediocrity; to whose notions, soldiers care for nothing but pay or plunder, and war is an expensive folly, with no fruit but an empty glory" (L, 301). He takes care in his own accounts to weigh the various merits of conflicting sources, reminding his audience, for instance, of the reasons each side would have for misrepresenting the circumstances of the original Pyrrhic victory at Asculum (R, 2:509) and allotting praise and blame to both sides where due. Guided by his own faith in heroism, however, he willingly credits Livy's claims that when Nero revealed his secret plan to destroy Hasdrubal's reinforcements, his troops "felt the glory of their mission, and shared the spirit of their leader"—that, spurred on by the "universal enthusiasm" of the people, "the soldiers would scarcely receive what was offered to them: they would not halt; they ate standing in their ranks; night and day they hastened onwards, scarcely allowing themselves a brief interval of rest" (R, 3:369). And yet, notwithstanding the traditions preserved and the reverence inspired by military history, Arnold never forgets that other virtues outweigh the soldier's: he criticizes Nero's injustice and inhumanity toward the vanquished as much as he does Hasdrubal's decision to face certain death with his troops rather than escape to serve his country once again (R, 3:375-76).

The moral power of military history depended upon the historian's ability to make it vivid and comprehensible to a general audience. Arnold draws upon a variety of devices to personalize and make immediate his battle scenes. The Napoleonic wars were still fresh in memory and charged with emotion; hence, Sentinum becomes the Austerlitz of the second Samnite War (R, 2:346), and Hannibal's deliverance of Capua is likened to Napoleon's of Dresden (R, 3:231). To convey a clear and concise idea of military tactics, Arnold presents them in layman's terms and often from the point of view of participants. It is more than a mere rhetorical flourish, he claims, to compare the destruction of the Carthagenian fleet at Syracuse to the "destruction of the giants by the thunder of Jove" (R, 1:466)—such was the comparison actually suggested to eyewitnesses "amidst the excitement and enthusiasm of the actual spectacle." The queer but deadly instruments that helped deliver the city a second time come to life through the eyes of the astounded Romans. Those who were not shot at through loopholes by invisible enemies saw long poles "like the arms of a giant" dropping stones on their heads and grappling hooks reaching down to upset their ships. So daunted by these "strange and irresistible devices" did they become that, "if they saw so much as a rope or a stick hanging or projecting from the wall, they would turn about and run away, crying 'that Archimedes was going to set one of his engines at work against them' " (R, 3:286-87). The audience is clearly meant to share in the enemy's amusement at such spectacles and to see the human side of warfare.

Closeups on individuals afford another means of humanizing the scale of battles and of personalizing even the most legendary experiences. In Hannibal's crossing the Alps, our interest focuses as much on the personal drama as on the military feat. We join Hannibal at the summit where, according to Polybius, he tried to rally his despairing troops:

> He called them together; he pointed out the valley beneath, to which the descent seemed the work of a moment: "That valley," he said, "is Italy; it leads us to the country of our friends the Gauls; and yonder is our way to Rome." His eyes were eagerly fixed on that point of the horizon; and as he gazed, the distance between seemed to vanish, till he could almost fancy that he was crossing the Tiber, and assailing the capitol. (R, 3:89-90)

The infectious self-confidence that arouses his troops at Cannae in the face of daunting odds again impresses us with the power of Hannibal's personality and the extent of his daring and ambition. The narrative that follows this closeup is typical: Arnold counterpoints the main lines of the traditional account with a limited amount of analysis and picturesque detail. He opens with the obligatory review of the troops, but also captures small details of weather that help one to visualize the scene: the dusty wind that blew into Roman faces, the rising sun that "flashed obliquely on their brazen helmets . . . and lit up the waving forest of their red and black plumes" (R, 3:139). He attempts some explanation of the Romans' strategic mistakes and furnishes comparisons to help his readers grasp the scene: the Roman army advanced like the English column at Fontenoy, the final carnage found parallel only in the Greeks' butchery of the Persians at Platea. For the most part, everyone acts in character in this set piece: the stones of the Balearian slingers fall "like hail" on the Roman line, the Numidians pursue the enemy with unwearied speed and unspar-

History as Practical Evangel

ing ferocity, the Romans struggle on "against all hope by mere indomitable courage" (R, 3:140-42).

Arnold's battle pieces remain largely conventional: they preserve "details too famous to be omitted" and do not significantly modify the standard accounts. However, what Hare called Arnold's "singular geographical eye" supplied observations that were genuinely original. Arnold was among the first to adopt an attitude that soon became customary: that the historian had a duty to visit sites in person, to confirm the accuracy of his descriptions but also to sympathize with and understand events more fully. His use of detail gathered in such trips also anticipated techniques used by later historians to draw the reader into the scene. He frequently included "personal recollections" from his Roman travels in the *History* because he thought they would "give an air of reality to the narrative greater than it ever could have from maps" (LC, 549). His references to the geography of present day Ascoli, for instance, help explain the success of Pyrrhus's elephants against ancient Asculum (R, 2:505). Having seen "those strange masses of rock which rise here and there with steep cliffy sides" out of the Rhone makes it easier for him to understand how a detachment of Hannibal's troops were able to cross it and cut off the Gauls (R, 3:76). Elsewhere, he recalls the modern day scene only to stress past differences. The famous harbor of modern Carthegena was in ancient times a lagoon so shallow that at low tide Scipio's troops could cross it on foot, giving credence to their general's claims that Neptune himself had intervened on their behalf. Although the country around the Metaurus River was in Arnold's day an "open, joyous, and habitable region," Hasdrubal was trapped while retreating through it because "the dark masses of uncleared wood still no doubt in many parts covered the face of the higher plain," and the river below, "not to be judged of by its present scanty and loitering stream, ran like a river of a half cleared country, with a deep and strong body of waters," thus preventing his passage (R, 3:372). Arnold's frustration over the vagueness of Polybius's account was compounded by his fear that "accustomed as we are . . . in the present century, to regard the crossing of the Alps as an easy summer excursion, we can even less than our fathers conceive the difficulties of Hannibal's march, and the enormous sacrifices by which it was accomplished," confronted as he was by glaciers instead of the blue lakes and "the bright hues of the thousand flowers, which now delight the summer traveller on the Col of the Little St. Bernard!" (R, 3:480-81). Geographical evidence afforded a measure of eye-witness credibility to the historian, of eye-witness participation to the reader. Placing the reader in the scene gave historical imagination a habitation. Overlaying the familiar present with a stranger, wilder past then made sharper the need for a conscious act of projection preliminary to sympathy and understanding, a conscious surrender of modern assumptions and scepticism preliminary to accurate vision.

Arnold's keen interest in geography helped make his accounts of military campaigns among the most graphic and immediate in the *History*, at least in part because visiting sites afforded a kind of firsthand insight that his fragmentary and contradictory sources would always deny him. In the final analysis, however, the *History of Rome* was innovative in neither its artistry nor its scholarship. Despite his belief in the importance of the social and personal dimensions of the past, the *History* remained predominantly a political history, for Arnold lacked the visionary powers to illuminate the lacunae in his sources. As both Stanley and Hare acknowledged, his strength lay in "combining what was already known, rather than in decyphering what was unknown" (LC, 160; R, 3:viii). He admired "the richness of [Niebuhr's] learning and the felicity of his conjecture" all the more because he could not share them, could not duplicate the "personal characters and . . . distinct events" that the German divined so confidently. On the other hand, despite his keen sense of his own dramatic failures in this regard, the dimensions of his history are true to his own predilections. The nation, as represented by its internal political development, was more important than "personal characters"; the central fact of Roman history was its fulfillment of providence by military defeat of Hannibal. The Roman annals needed a critical and chastening appraisal, but only so that their tale of national triumph could be accepted with a more "scientific" certitude, and their life of the state be read in moral terms.

Arnold's faith in the order and benevolence of God's world, in the living reality of those supreme truths which study of that world could only vindicate, unified his life and thought to a degree that many in later periods could only envy. This faith remains a major source of his appeal and importance for contemporaries. It gave him the confidence to meet head-on the forces that threatened disunity in his society. When demographic as well as ideological forces were driving a wedge between Church and State, he tried to reunite them by redefining their roles, making religion practical and government moral.

History as Practical Evangel

Realizing the danger of allowing scientific and historical modes of analysis to be sufficient to an understanding of the world, he co-opted both and enlisted them in the service of belief. Seeing that in a modern age faith would weaken unless it could be made both intellectually and spiritually acceptable, he devised an interpretive model that could acknowledge the validity of new critical methods without abandoning to them the fundamental bases of belief. Dedicated to progress but well aware of the limitations of a strictly Utilitarian conception of it, he substituted the higher usefulness of historical lessons for the calculus of pain and pleasure. Sensing how deep was the channel of conservatism in English life, but appreciating the strength of the current of change working against it, he offered an organic model of development that would accommodate both, making reform the highest respect for one's forefathers, as well as the fulfillment of one's duties to the present.

Arnold's skill in reconciling potentially subversive impulses becomes clear when his approach to history is put in perspective. In his understanding of national identity, in his broadened conception of the range of data needed to document that identity, in his respect for myth, legend, and other forms of imaginative literature as source materials, and in his concern for resuscitating the life of the past rather than merely recording events, he was deeply influenced by romantic historiography. His organic model of change and progress also owes much to romantic thought, as does his reverence for the past as something that touches us "in the divinest part of our nature." But his deepest temperamental biases were more in harmony with the systematizing "philosophical" spirit of the Enlightenment. He too tended to view all history as a repository of facts that could be shown to document general laws once inductive methods were applied. He also believed that such laws could then be used deductively to judge specific cases, and to offer practical guidance for the present. Although he could appreciate the specificity and uniqueness of certain kinds of historical data, his intellectual bent was pervasively generalizing and essentially anti-historicist: data were useful only when they had been categorized according to universal types. Imaginative sympathy with past events could move him deeply but never convert him, for he went to the past as one of the faithful seeking confirmation, not as a doubter seeking proof. Resuscitation of the past was the result, not the cause, of conviction; it allowed him to experience and to represent more fully those particular cases that confirmed what he needed to believe were eternal laws. Knowing that he lacked evidence for the kind of fully realized, fully dramatized narrative he advocated, he still chose Roman history; Rome's ability to illustrate laws of development strategically important for his own day quite outweighed its sketchiness in unique "biographical" detail.

But if his methods were similar to those of eighteenth-century historians, his ends were different in ways that fundamentally transformed his means. In his hands a philosophical, scientific view of history confirmed the validity of those very moral truths that the Enlightenment historian had intended to explode. The regularity that Arnold's scientific laws confirmed lay not in the static duplication of the same standards for all ages but in the recognition of relative standards for different stages of growth. The order of these stages gave a scientific regularity to the historical process, a regularity that made comparison and generalization about similar stages and the overall pattern of history possible, without necessitating that specific phenomena in given stages be uniform from culture to culture. Arnold's "science of man" was fully compatible with Christian belief; for him, the authority of the natural order and the authority of the moral order were one and divine, so that the pursuit of truth could only end in the better understanding of God's will.

Arnold's attitude toward historical study was highly influential for his contemporaries because it answered so many of their needs. Here was a scholar who embraced the methods of German erudition and introduced a new scientific rigor into historical study, thus promising to put history's truths on an objective basis. Here too was an artist whose narratives were both imaginatively satisfying and braced with a healthy dose of didactic uplift. But most importantly, here was a great religious teacher who reassured his age that history, rightly understood and properly applied, could be shown to confirm society's fundamental ethical beliefs and give eloquent testimony to a divinely ordained order. He could convince the public that the historian had a vital and noble role to play as sage and teacher, one who could derive the laws of history and show how these could be used to guide society through what often seemed like a troubled future. Arnold's concrete contributions to historical scholarship in England were not so important as this tone of high moral seriousness and practicality that he lent to it. It would be heard again and again in the Inaugural lectures of Regius Professors of Modern History, which after his tenure tended to be manifestos of the historian's assumptions about the morality

History as Practical Evangel

and practicality of historical study.[26] Although he didn't live long enough to give his theories full embodiment, he provided a statement of purpose and direction that would not be seriously challenged until much later in the century.

What Arnold found in history, he had himself brought to it. The deepest foundations of his faith admitted no challenges, and so inevitably all endeavors—intellectual, artistic, scientific, political, pedagogical—wound up confirming faith. Followers who set out to examine the bases of belief with the same intellectual rigor but without the foregone conclusion that they were true found them all too susceptible to erosion by scientific and historical modes of criticism, and were left without an adequate means of coping with the relativism that resulted. Arnold's supreme confidence in the certainty of belief was the gift of an earlier age, but his attempts to make Christian ethics a major force in secular life retained its appeal even when the rare unity of the intellectual and the spiritual that Arnold achieved had broken down. History, as the best proof of a divine order for believers and the best alternative to one for those who doubted, would play a major role in this process of secularization in the years that followed.

II

THOMAS CARLYLE
HISTORY AS SECULAR PROPHECY

Thomas Carlyle confronted his century in an uneasy relationship: as a prophet he spoke directly to the Victorian spiritual dilemma, but his preachings grew increasingly incompatible with the actual direction of change in his day. Despite their resistance to many of his views, the Victorians heard in Carlyle one of the most eloquent testimonies to their will to believe. He voiced their own desire for a source of permanent value capable of sustaining human community on earth and their longings for transcendence beyond it—sustaining these against the slow erosion of the orthodoxy and authority that had formerly ordered their world. His historical writings provide the core of this testimony, because history—that is, Carlyle's mystically conceived history—became this source of value. Even as they denounced the status quo, his major works (*The French Revolution*, 1837; *Past and Present*, 1843; *Cromwell's Letters and Speeches*, 1845; and *Frederick the Great*, 1858-1865) affirmed sustaining bonds between old and new. And for all their idiosyncrasies, his histories both formed and reflected influential historiographical traditions.

Their political and religious differences make Carlyle's and Arnold's agreements about historical study more significant. Carlyle too yearned to forge a consciousness in which the religious, the intellectual, and the practical were one. Like Arnold's, his resounding conviction that history was the revelation of God's will moving in the

History as Secular Prophecy

world of man increased his sense of urgency about turning history from escapist to practical ends. This belief also created high expectations for the historian, whose job it was to rescue from oblivion proof of the supernaturalism of daily life. Central to human history was man's attempt to create order out of chaos; likewise, the historian's chief task was to create meaning out of the randomness of the historical record. Lacking the orthodoxy of Arnold's religious belief, however, Carlyle also lacked his confidence in the ultimate unity of all truths. His search for order entailed greater risks and his prophecies concealed deeper anxieties.

Arnold's confidence in this unity allowed him to adapt the systematizing instincts of the Enlightenment to romantic and Christian ends. Carlyle's romanticism—the most radical of any Victorian historian's—was fundamentally antisystematic. His transcendentalism made no compromise with material fact. He also stood in the most profound opposition to the developing tradition of "scientific" historiography in his day. It would not be fair to say that his unparalleled success at forging a sympathetic communion between reader and past was achieved at the expense of accuracy; his scholarship was far more scrupulous than he is often given credit for. But his historical understanding was essentially metaphorical and symbolic, making it not so much incompatible as incommensurate with the goals and methods of more traditional historiography. His scholarship served the ends of a visionary, not a scientific truth. The laws he acknowledged were of a different order than those conceived by the philosophical historian of the past or the "political scientist" of the future. Their purpose, however, was the same: to affirm that some deeper regularity patterned the disparate phenomena of human life.

Carlyle's early lapse from orthodoxy left him far more vulnerable than Arnold to the tyranny of fact and reason. His "fusion of poetry, history, and religion" represented an attempt to salvage the tenor of belief from its discredited vehicles and to break the hold of a merely mechanistic rationality.[1] "Natural Supernaturalism" provided a secularized way of retaining intact Calvinist notions of God and individual duty. The conception of history that he adapted from the German romantics provided a secular scripture, an alternative testimony to God's presence in the world. History also provided a means to reconcile the poetic to the factual. Like Arnold, Carlyle realized that empiricism could be satisfactorily answered not by substituting a higher fictional reality but by obliterating the distinction between the poetic and the real. He redefined history to do just this. Although he began by believing that poetry most suitably embodied the ideal in human life, the biographical gradually edged out the fictional in significance as his developing transcendentalism drew his attention from the invented to the actual.[2] He came to prefer "*any* fact, relating especially to man,"[3] for being able to reveal truth in a way works of mere poetic "sensibility" could not. He demoted fiction to no more than man's attempt to substitute his paltry history for God's. The "smallest historical *fact*" was superior to the "grandest *fictitious event*" because it "did actually occur; was, in very truth, an element in the system of the All, whereof I too form part."[4] History was a "perpetual Evangel,"[5] the record of mankind's "whole spiritual life" (E, 2:84). "Genuine poetry" became "the right interpretation of Reality and History" (E, 3:79). Like Arnold, Carlyle transformed history into a genre that could exploit the creative talents of the artist while disarming Victorian suspicions against frivolous or misleading fictions; his history was real and visionary at the same time.

Carlyle also wished to make the historian the master scientist as well as the master poet. In an 1831 notebook entry, he revealed his hopes that history might provide a truly "scientific" and "philosophical" way of grasping the "whole" of divine reality formerly accessible only to poetry:

> I see some vague outline of what a *Whole* is; also how an individual Delineation may be "informed with the Infinite"; may appear hanging in the universe of Time and Space (partly): in which case is it a Poem and a Whole? Therefore, are the true Heroic Poems of these times to be written with the *ink of Science*? Were a correct philosophic Biography of Man (meaning by philosophic *all* that the name can include) the only method of celebrating him? The true History (had we any such) the true Epic Poem?—I partly begin to surmise so.[6]

Carlyle needed a "science" far more transcendental than Arnold's to find the infinite in the finite, however. He meant for the "historical scientific fact" to oppose not just fictions, but the "formulas" used by the mechanistic sciences of the early nineteenth century to "dispense with God" and to scale down the mystery of creation to easily quantified limits.[7] The implications of such formulas had proved too threatening to allow him to share Arnold's confidence that the regularity of law guaranteed the meaningfulness of facts. Carlyle had fallen back from orthodoxy onto the premise that facts at least were created by God and inviolable. Lest man's systematizing admit the

History as Secular Prophecy

possibility of rival realities, he had to deny "formulas" the power to do more than "label," "compound," and "separate" data. Finally, only a science that promised an unmediated contact with facts could preserve their integrity for him. Far from entailing the scientist's detachment, this contact presupposed a commitment to seeing the "infinite" spiritual reality behind the phenomena of this world.

The *philosophes* offered Carlyle the historiographical counterpart to this false science. Finding intolerable the conclusions offered by their "death's-head Philosophies 'teaching by example,' "[8] he denounced their method of writing history. History was not philosophy teaching by examples but "an address (literally out of Heaven, for did not God order it all?) to our *whole* inner man." The first step toward realizing its miraculous nature "is that we *see* the things transacted, and picture them out wholly as if they stood before our eyes;—and this, alas, of all considerations, is the one that 'dignity of History' least thinks of."[9] The *philosophes* had not only refused to "look fixedly at the *Thing*" itself—they had substituted a "wretched politico-metaphysical Abstraction" for it (E, 3:326). No wonder that for them the past was not a soul-sustaining reality but a "godless Impossibility" (PP, 239).

Carlyle redefined history so that its meaningfulness depended upon coherences beyond the reach of formula, on patterns invisible to the merely empirical eye. It took the talents of a poet-seer to reconstitute the organic relationships that united the parts into a harmonious whole. Dryasdust, "being himself galvanic merely," could produce only "Chaos," "Dungheaps," "Shot-rubbish," and "dust Whirlwinds"—pointless compendia of inert data. He was but an antiquarian, an artisan—one of those men "who labor mechanically in a department, without eye for the Whole" (E, 2:90). Carlyle's ideal historian, on the other hand, was a "Psalmist," an "Iliadist," "the highest Shakespeare producible."[10] He was an artist whose "rhythmic nature"—his ear for the deeper harmonies and internal correspondences—allowed him to "inform and ennoble the humblest department with an Idea of the Whole, and habitually know that only in the Whole is the Partial to be truly discerned" (E, 2:90). False science could only dissect and atomize; it could not discern the interrelating of parts through which history, like poetry, like nature itself, became meaningful and vital. Society was an organism, not a machine; the wholeness of its history was that of a reticulation, not of a calculus. Each of us was a thread woven by the "Loom of Time" into a "magic web" of historical phenomena, held fixed in a pattern on a "warp of mystic darkness" (E, 3:181), knitted into the "Enormous Tissue of Existence never yet broken."[11] We owed our sense of belonging—indeed, our very identities—to the relationships that thus enmeshed us. This network also maintained the continuity of ideas and beliefs so that some could "continually gravitate back to us" and, in a new form, "enrich and nourish us again" (FG, 1:16). Truths that had stood the test of time emerged in the "beatified bodily form" of tradition. Man remained "socially" and "spiritually alive" because he was able to breathe the "life-element" of these accumulated truths (HS, 316). Not all parts of the past possessed this vital power. The true "Art of History, the grand difference between a Dryasdust and a sacred Poet," lay in the ablity "to distinguish well what does still reach to the surface, and is alive and frondent for us."[12]

The historian's privileged vision gave him great power over the "eyeless" manipulators of fact. He could free the fact from dead abstractions and restore it to the living process that gave it meaning. He could rejuvenate "the Thing itself" where others built only painted waxworks (E, 3:326). He could discern which beliefs were permanently vital and could translate the "mystic heaven-written Sanscrit" into a "Bible of World-History" (E, 3:251). But with great power went even greater risks for one who thus bore the responsibility for history's meaningfulness. Carlyle might proclaim as loudly as Arnold that the permanent verities endured and manifested themselves to any who had (spiritual) eyes to see, but he was much more anxious that the facts might elude him. His peevish attacks on the Dryasdusts who reduced history to an "infinite grey void" sprang from his own alarm at finding the past melting into "sheer formlessness" and "unintelligible maundering" (OC, 1:10) as he groped for meaning. Those individual events that he could prove to have been real served as no more than the kindling of a "wooden lucifer" in the "void night"—only a moment of illumination for the spiritual eye to see into the heart of the mystery.

For Carlyle as for Arnold, human identity was sustained by its connectedness to a palpable past; "man was still man" only so long as he could identify a continuous and vital history with which to refute the Everlasting No. If it were impossible to prove that heroes had once existed, it would be "as if we had done no brave thing at all in this Earth;—as if not Men but Nightmares had written of our History!" (OC, 1:6). If the historian could not make the past "melodious"—

resonant with a deep organic unity—"it must be forgotten, as good as annihilated; and we rove like aimless exiles that *have* no ancestors, whose world began only yesterday."[13] Without historical proof of filiation, Carlyle would have left a spiritual orphan; without concrete verification of the infinite truth, he would have lost his grip on those spiritual moorings he had so carefully constructed to replace defunct orthodoxy, and drifted once more into that confused whirlpool of values in which so many Victorian minds would flounder.

Like many of his contemporaries, Carlyle found a willed belief better than none at all. For all his exaltation of the authority of fact, he was no more truly scientific or historicist than Arnold. Too much depended on the outcome of investigation to allow him to risk his poetic vision to empirical proof. George Levine aptly calls his turn to history and to the "primacy of 'fact' " after *Sartor* "probably not so much an expression of willingness to trust experience as an escape from the need to trust it."[14] Carlyle saw only those facts that confirmed the lessons he needed to make sense of his own world. René Wellek argues persuasively that "Carlyle was never able to keep consistently to the historical point of view . . . he always introduced a set of ethical standards which are not derived from history itself and which prevent him from judging the individuality of a man or time by its own inherent criteria."[15] Despite his political differences with the Whigs, Carlyle agreed with them that "there is no use of writing of things past, unless they can be made in fact things present."[16] His polemical purposes similarly undermined sympathy and obscured the historical context of the event. Like the Whigs he deduced the "facts" of the past from the moral and political order he wished to impose upon the Victorian present.

Carlyle's conception of change offered a powerful reinforcement to the patterns he saw in history and to the reordering he desired for the present. In change as in unity, his model was an organic one. This allowed for the inevitable transformation of social structures and for the persistent vitality of essential truths. The analogy between human history and nature began as a speculation in an early notebook ("Has the mind its cycles and seasons like Nature, varying from the fermentation of *werden* to the clearness of *seyn*; and this again and again; so that the history of man is like the history of the world he lives in?"[17]) and achieved certainty in *The French Revolution*, where civilization is an organism progressing through cycles of growth, decay, and rebirth. Earlier essays had elaborated on the nature of these cycles. Ages

Thomas Carlyle

of scepticism alternated with those of faith, didacticism with poetry, stability with revolution. In his "Early German Literature," Carlyle also drew explicit comparisons (not unlike Macaulay's) between the "history of the universal mind" and that of the individual: youth was a time of "poetic recognition" that must inevitably give way to "scientific examination" (E, 2:283).

He dealt more literally than Arnold with the threat of decay built into this cyclical model. Arnold and the Whigs stressed the continuity of progress, the improvement that survived collapse. Although Carlyle's belief in a purposeful universe unfolding according to a divine, if inscrutable, will also implied that cycles spiraled upward, his system was more a series of renewals than a continuum. Destruction was not only inevitable but salutary. Only through decay could "a prurient element, rich with nutritive influences," be formed to nourish new life.[18] Only after conflagration could the Phoenix rise from its ashes, and only when the "deserted edifices" were torn down could people go forward down the "thoroughfare" of human progress.

Where other historians used organic cycles to lend a scientific regularity to history, Carlyle's theories of change were finally "consciously unscientific and even anti-scientific."[19] For Arnold, the fact that all nations went through the same stages of development made possible the derivation of standard principles governing their growth: lessons from one stage of development could be applied with equal justice to corresponding stages in the lives of other organisms. Carlyle's cycles proceeded according to no law except that of the inevitability of change itself. The fact of periodic change was clear, but his periods were far less uniform than Arnold's, and he was far more likely to stress their uniqueness. Still less did Carlyle share any real sympathy with the positivists' attempts to reduce history to laws capable of predicting the future, despite parallels between St. Simonian theories and his own.[20] Carlyle's insistence on the fundamentally irrational and uncontrollable nature of historical change was his means of refuting just such "mechanical" philosophies. History's unpredictable energy defied simplistic "cause and effect speculators" who attempted to read "the inscrutable Book of Nature as if it were a Merchant's Ledger" (E, 2:91). In that "web" of history, causation was conceived not as a " 'chain' or line, but rather as a tissue, or superficies of innumerable lines, extending in breadth as well as in length, and with a complexity, which will foil and utterly bewilder the most assiduous computation" (E, 1:399).

History as Secular Prophecy

The unpredictability built into Carlyle's system finally made continuity problematic, and progress even more so. Arnold and the Whigs used the organic metaphor to emphasize conservative, orderly progress. They tried to make the very process of innovating traditional, arguing that accommodating the new when times were ripe was the best means of preserving continuity. For Carlyle change was fundamentally catastrophic rather than gradualist, having more in common with the conversion experience than with uniformitarianism. Carlyle's idea of history was not a linear progression, not an accommodation of old to new, but a constant reassertion of the permanently and transcendently true. This required renewal, not preservation, and could not be achieved without a complete destruction and purgation of the old. There could be no compromise with what was already dying; only apocalypse could cleanse the old world of its corruption.

This vision could reassure Victorians that although change might be violent, catastrophic, and unpredictable, it ended by resurrecting those ideas and beliefs most essential to human life. The destruction of old forms they saw around them need not mean simply loss, but loss preparatory to greater gain. More important, however, were the uses of Carlyle's theory of change as a weapon against a recalcitrant society. Insisting on the unpredictability of change disqualified the "computators" of the mechanistic world view and moved historical analysis to moral ground, accessible only to believers. The only real "law" governing change was that God's decrees could not long be transgressed without retribution, and that only what conformed to eternal truth would survive. History's one lesson was to cleave to the good and abhor evil. The historian used his privileged vision to choose his own manifestations of this law. The theory of cyclical destruction gave Carlyle a *deus ex machina* to rid society of those institutions he could not tolerate, a means of imposing poetic justice where the rationalist saw only random process or mechanical cause and effect. This model plausibly interpreted the French Revolution's destruction of the *ancien régime*, but fell increasingly short of the new reality that followed. Fundamentally out of sympathy with the advance of democracy in a way Arnold (or the Whig) was not, Carlyle looked in vain in his own day for proof of progress toward the truth that his theories insisted upon. He locked himself into a more and more rigid resistance to advances that contradicted his desired order.

Thomas Carlyle

By the time he wrote *Frederick the Great*, that rigidity had already started to constrict his confidence about history itself.

Carlyle's organicism finally justified only a faith in process, not a certainty of its end. He left progress explicitly open-ended. He had early on adopted Schiller's dictum that truth *"immer wird, nie est,"* that truth is never an achieved absolute, but rather an infinitely changing, infinitely progressing entity. This left the human soul free to "develop itself into all sorts of opinions, doctrines, which go on nearer and nearer to the truth." But it also left the process permanently unresolved: "All theories approximate more or less to the great Theory, which remains itself always unknown."[21] Only on the largest scale and in the most general terms did progress occur, and even then, since complete knowledge was God's alone, this process never reached a specific fulfillment in time. Denied the assurance of arrival, Carlyle clung instead to the importance of movement. In "Signs of the Times" he took ferment as a sign of vitality and of advance:

> However it may be with individual nations, . . . the happiness and greatness of mankind at large have been continually progressive. Doubtless this age also is advancing. Its very unrest, its ceaseless activity, its discontent contains matter of promise. . . . This is as it should be; for not in turning back, not in resisting, but only in resolutely struggling forward, does our life consist. (E, 2:80)

As that promise of advance was not fulfilled, "work" became for Carlyle an end in itself: the continual struggle of the soul never sure of its election—sure only of the damnation that awaited the idle or despairing, the death that succeeded "passive inertness" in the organism.

Some critics have also considered Carlyle's heroes *dei ex machina* that allowed him to ignore the role of groups and institutions in historical change. In truth, he acknowledged the contributions of all three, although he weighted them differently. Given his conviction that true history lay in the engagement of the individual with the infinite, it was inevitable that the biographical interest would dominate. As he explained in "Biography," the life of any human being possessed a "scientific interest" insofar as it instructed others how to cope with the "Problem of Existence." As the struggle of "human Freewill against material Necessity" called "the Sympathy of mortal hearts into action," it also became "the sole Poetry possible" (E, 3:44-45). A vivid likeness of human life was not in itself enough to make biography poetic, however. Although he complimented Scott for demonstrating that "the bygone ages of the world were actually filled by living men, not by protocols, state-papers, controversies and abstractions of men," Carlyle considered the Waverley novels lacking in any interest deeper than that aroused by "contrasts of Costume" (E, 4:76-77). He was still harsher on Robertson's *History of Scotland* for providing only a "little Scandalous Chronicle" of Mary Stuart, "a Beauty," and Henry Darnley, "A Booby who had fine legs" (E, 3:82), when the historian should have been chronicling the effects of the Reformation. The biograpical was not an end in itself, but a means of illuminating the individual's engagement in the cosmic struggle between good and evil.

The power of heroic free-will against necessity is complicated by the fact that Carlyle depicted change, especially revolutionary change, as operating on a scale far greater than that of any individual and believed that "the strongest man can but retard the current partially and for a short hour" (E, 3:122). Although he claimed that "not by material, but by moral power, are men and their actions governed" (E, 1:400), in "Diderot" he gave both sides their due:

> It is a great truth, one side of a great truth, that the Man makes the Circumstances, and spiritually as well as economically is the artificer of his own fortune. But there is another side of the same truth, that the man's circumstances are the element he is appointed to live and work in; that he by necessity takes his complexion, vesture, embodiment, from these, and is in all practical manifestations modified by them almost without limit; so that in another no less genuine sense, it can be said Circumstances make the Man. (E, 3:229)

In this essay he concluded that men had to be judged by the conditions of their own time, although these never absolved them from the supreme duty of recognizing and furthering the right. Nonetheless, Carlyle's heroes were preeminently suited to serve these ends because of their ability to see through circumstances to the essentials at their core. They were "original men" who could "converse with this universe at first-hand" (HS, 345). Like Frederick, they swept aside sham; like Johnson, they believed where others only supposed; like Cromwell, they discerned the "inarticulate divineness" of present and future "beyond the letter and the rubric" (OC, 2:169). For these reasons they were in the best position to "determine, not what others do, but what it is right to do" (E, 3:89). They were "modellers, patterns," "revealers" of God's purposes, whose role it was to "articulate" for lesser men the best way "to conform themselves to the Eternal Laws" of the universe (HS, 1-2).[22] They played the key role in social change and stability. Carlyle's histories show that only the action of an individual hero—like Napoleon, or Abbot Samson, or Frederick—could recompose social chaos into new order. Heroes were responsible for institutionalizing the "law of habit that makes roads everywhere through the pathless in this universe" (HS, 177); they were the chief objects of *"imitation,* that all-important peculiar gift of man, whereby Mankind is not only held socially together in the present time, but connected in like union with the past and the future" (E, 2:394). They were custodians of the Traditions that gave meaning to human life; in worshipping heroes man celebrated his own need for, and understanding of, a divinely appointed order.

Notwithstanding the preponderant importance of heroes in human history, Carlyle did not entirely neglect lesser men, as is shown by his proposal that "the Court, the Senate and the Battlefield" recede in favor of "the Temple, the Workshop and Social Hearth" (E, 3:83). He found the conventional stuff of history—"empty invoice-lists of Pitched Battles and Changes of Ministry"—as barren as "Philosophy teaching by Experience" and sought instead to restore "the innumerable peopled luminous *Days"* in all their fullness (E, 3:325; PP 49-50). The corollary of his belief that "history is the essence of innumerable Biographies" was that "Social Life is the aggregate of all the individual men's lives who constitute society":

> The inventions and traditions, and daily habits that regulate and support our existence, are the work not of Dracos and Hampdens, but of Phoenician mariners, of Italian masons and Saxon metallurgists, of philosophers, alchymists, prophets, and all the long-forgotten train of artists and artisans; who from the first have been jointly teaching us how to think and how to act, how to rule over spiritual and over physical Nature.   (E, 2:86-87)

These men were at least as relevant an object of the historian's attention as the Dracos and Hampdens themselves. In principle this recognition of the life of the "common man" suggests the democratizing influence of the romantic historians and their efforts to write the "biography" of whole nations and peoples. In actual practice Carlyle's conception of historical development limited his attention to lesser men as much as did his individualizing brand of hero-worship. The real value of mariners and masons lay in their very obscurity: their work contributed to the silent growth of a healthy social organism. When minor figures do find a place in his writings, they function as "emblems" of historical phenomena beyond their control. They are effects, not causes, of cosmic change.

The same point might be made about Carlyle's handling of institutional, political, and sociological forces. He might have agreed with Arnold that the way people were governed gauged the moral health of their society, but he lacked all interest in the political machinery by which this governing was accomplished. He scornfully dismissed "Redbook Lists, and Court Calendars, and Parliamentary Registers" as but "eddies" in the "Life-Current" (E, 3:81). Laws and constitutions were not the "life of man" but merely the house in which it was led. His attitude in *The French Revolution* is typical: the Constituent Assembly could devise no more than "a theory of irregular verbs," for any constitution that "images" the conviction of real men (FR, 1:215) was sanctioned by a cosmic Necessity, and could never be produced by parliamentary debate. He gives little attention to the constitutional issues involved in *Cromwell* and skims over Frederick's peacetime accomplishments to return to his battles (FG, 5:198). On the other hand, he did acknowledge the specific class issues operating in the French Revolution. The Girondes had in his eyes tried to exploit the Sansculottes in their attempts to bring about a republic of "Respectabilities and Decencies," in which the "Moneybag of Mammon" would replace the "Feudal Fleur-de-lys" (FR, 3:115). Naturally their pitiful attempt to mount a government based on sham was incapable of controlling the organic force of the mob, who represented a genuine and necessary outburst of nature, the embodiment of anarchy capable of destroying the old order but not of building a new. Carlyle's symbolic treatment of class finally precluded any more literal probing of the issues involved, however. He saw a hierarchical class structure as a biological imperative of the social organism and dealt with social groups only in terms of the role he prescribed for each. The "Twenty-five Millions," "the Sanscullotism," are never more than personified abstractions, their needs not differentiated beyond the primal imperatives for food and leadership.

For Carlyle society denoted not so much a set of institutions as the structure of belief embodied in institutional forms. His approach was designed explicitly to refute those who had mistaken the materials of purely "local" history—politics, battles, laws, etc.—for the spiritual realities appropriate to "universal" history. In reacting against the conventional approach, however, Carlyle tended to lose sight of the actual weave of institutions, politics, economic and legal systems in his haste to get beyond them to the forces of which they were merely the vesture. G. M. Trevelyan defended him by claiming that he accurately understood and portrayed the effects of these factors on the people involved,[23] but this does not compensate for neglecting their structure.

The strengths and weaknesses of Carlyle's theorizing spring from the fact that it is essentially metahistorical. He wished to use the authority of history to go beyond history. He focussed on the cosmic realities behind historical appearances and enjoined his readers to look through facts to higher truths that redeemed the failures of the phenomenal world. The alternative to traditional faith he thus offered had the same vulnerability as the old one. Assent was finally a matter of belief, not of proof. By treating phenomena as merely appearances, he ruled out verification by fact alone. He simply refused to fight on the same ground as those who read the "facts" differently. The emotional power of his vision was enough to draw many across with him in a leap of faith. Yet if his willed belief delivered many from "Descendentalism," it abandoned to the limits of rationalism still more who could not make that leap, since he left no middle ground between his vision and blindness.

II

To obtain the assent that transcended reason, Carlyle needed to create a past so experientially real that it compelled the reader's presence in his vision. His desire to capture both the spiritual essence and the fact that embodied it, to reconstruct the very "life of man," posed new challenges to the researcher. The historian had both to see and to divine; he had to be the scientist as well as the artist to make history disclose its meaning: " 'Stern Accuracy in inquiry, bold Imagination in expounding and filling-up; these,' says friend Sauerteig, 'are the two pinions on which History soars' " (E, 3:259-60). We must ask then how "stern" were Carlyle's own standards. On the face of them, his research methods seem as unconventional as his narrative techniques. He claimed that after trying various approaches, involving everything from note books and bundles to paper bags filled with slips of paper, he resolved to avoid taking notes at all by simply marking relevant passages in his sources. As he explained in an 1845 letter:

> On the whole [I] try to keep the whole matter simmering in the *living* mind and memory rather than laid up in paper bundles or otherwise laid up in the inert way. For this certainly turns out to be a truth: Only

what you at last *have living* in your own memory and heart is worth putting down to be printed; this alone has much chance to get into the living heart and memory of other men.[24]

If "The Guises" can be taken as typical of a work in progress, this process meant that the construction of the main narrative line took precedence over the validation of exact names, dates, and quotations. Parenthetical notes mark the places where these are to be inserted, if indeed they could ever be found. Despite this somewhat fragmentary approach, Carlyle was keenly aware of the importance of solid factual data, prizing even insignificant primary sources that could make the event "luminous" far more than he did the "sifting and straightening out of . . . old cobwebs" in more comprehensive secondary accounts.[25] He also acknowledged high standards of thoroughness and accuracy. In writing *The French Revolution*, he took full advantage of the source materials just coming into print and probably used twice as many books as he cited.[26] When he found that he had included an incorrect account of the French warship "Vengeur," whose crew supposedly refused to surrender and went down shouting "Vive la République!", he published a full account of his investigation of the error in *Fraser's Magazine* (E, 4:208-25). Elsewhere he showed himself capable of a Rankeian cross-examination of sources, and offered to lay his interpretations open to comparison with the primary sources (FG, 2:235).

But it must finally be said that his earnestness to find the truth was simply not strong enough to counterbalance his ambivalence about the scholarly side of historiography. When he compared the historian to Orpheus returning to the underworld, he was doing more than striking a pose: he really did feel that "he that would investigate the Past must be prepared for encountering things unpleasant, things dreary, nay, ghastly [for] the Past is the dwelling of the Dead" (HS, 314). His constant lamentation over the difficulty of his task and his vituperative outbursts against earlier historians sprang from his anxiety to prove his view of the past correct. The more elusive his epic portrayal became, the more he blamed the Dryasdusts for not having the vision to provide the materials he needed. Also, the more likely he was to resort to "abridgment" and "immense omission" in an effort to suppress "large tracts" of "mere pedantisms, diplomatic cobwebberies, . . . and inhuman matter" (FG, 3:309). Arguing that if " 'wise memory' is ever to prevail, there is need of much 'wise oblivion' first" (OC, 1:41) too often meant that what did not fire his imagi-

Thomas Carlyle

nation, like the details of political, legal, or ecclesiastical squabbles, or what threatened to diminish the epic stature of his heroes, was simply dismissed or sloughed over with a few elliptical metaphors. It also meant that the authenticity of what fit with his own conception of a movement or hero was not tested so rigorously as that which was unfavorable. Arnold made this point about the "Vengeur" case, claiming that Carlyle should have been more wary, knowing the unreliability of his source.[27] Wellek sees a similar gullibility in the matter of the Squire papers, a set of letters and documents allegedly written by Cromwell, of which "copies" were sent to Carlyle by an extremely eccentric retired sea captain.[28]

Cromwell's *Letters and Speeches* offers other examples of the way Carlyle's preconceptions could compromise scholarly standards. After publishing what purported to be a complete edition, he was deluged with various new materials, some privately held, but others that he had overlooked in published sources. Carlyle asserted that as a rule "the new Contributions to any Edition have been slight" (OC, 1:vii), notwithstanding his addition of more than thirty new letters in the Appendix alone. Even had he integrated these into the text, it is apparent that Carlyle would have refused to sacrifice the synthetic form he had already given his "Cromwelliad." A biographer, he proclaimed, should worry less about whether later interpolations might improve his book "as a practical Representation of Cromwell's Existence" than about whether it would be "swollen out of shape by superfluous details, defaced with dilettante antiquarianisms, nugatory tag-rags" (OC, 1:viii). The priorities of hero-worship and artistic harmony clearly outweighed those of scholarship. Carlyle's concern for eliminating any trace of pedantry that might hinder the general reader explains in part some editorial changes in what he called "the authentic utterances of the man Oliver himself." In order to make the materials easier to read and understand, he alleviated the "encumbrance" of Cromwell's spelling and tried to help "bring out the struggling sense" (OC, 1:79) by adding words (in brackets) here and there. But despite Carlyle's lofty claim that he considered it his supreme duty "to avoid altering, in any respect, not only the sense, but the smallest feature in the physiognomy, of the Original" (OC, 1:79), Reginald Palgrave ably demonstrated that he was neither thorough nor entirely forthright about his scholarship. Judging him according to the standards of the new "scientific" historiography in 1887, Palgrave faulted him for inaccurate transcriptions, misrepresentation of his sources, and failure to consult the manuscript version of some speeches or to compare modern versions with ones of higher authority. Damning by any standard is Palgrave's evidence that Carlyle added misleading interpolations and punctuation, that he omitted words, phrases, and even whole sentences, and that he suppressed several passages unfavorable to his heroic view of the Protector.[29]

It is not enough to excuse such failings by saying that Carlyle's purposes were more poetic than historical; he himself would have rejected the implications of this distinction. Criticism is warranted precisely because he portrayed himself as a heroic truth-seeker, wrestling with cosmic forces that threatened to doom men to oblivion. But then again, if he was little different in these respects from the partisan historians of his own and earlier ages, the truly innovative aspects of his approach to research should not be ignored. In his attempts to hear the voice and feel the pulse of the past, he embraced the same wider conception of evidence as Arnold and Macaulay. He too advised the beginning historian to "*read* himself *into* the century he studies" (E, 4:237), no mean feat considering that for him "all Books, . . . were they but Song-books or treatises on Mathematics, are in the long-run historical documents" (E, 3:167). Even the sheet music of the *Ça-ira* could contribute its spark to the rekindling of past consciousness. Carlyle also valued portraits and memoirs for their insight into the human side of history. He relished the gossipy accounts of a Boswell, a Jocelin de Brakelond, or a Princess Wilhemina because they viewed the world with the real "human *eyes*" that history books did not possess (FG, 1:378). Although he deplored the subjectivity of such sources, their glimpses into historical reality fitted his own episodic, anecdotal style too congenially for him to be highly discriminating in their use.

Like Arnold he prized geographical evidence as much as imaginative. Geography was one of the "two windows of history" because for him too familiarity with the physical setting of an event allowed him to possess it imaginatively.[30] Driven by the demands of his pictorial imagination, he sent Mill to look at the sites important to "The Diamond Necklace," and his brother to report back on Versailles and on the Place de Grève, where the Tree of Liberty had stood. Maps of Paris, groundplans of the Bastille, technical accounts of the embankment of the fens in Cromwell's day, all allowed him to locate himself, both figuratively and literally, in past experience. The same craving for empathy encouraged several "pilgrimages" to "Cromwell-

Thomas Carlyle

land," where he emotionally relived the experience of his hero in Ely Cathedral, in his farmyard, and at Dunbar field on the anniversary of Cromwell's triumph there.[31] Carlyle considered the topography of battle sites particularly essential to studies of wartime: Richard Brooks has amply documented the extent of his 1858 tour of German battlefields and the process whereby its results were worked into the narrative of *Frederick the Great*.[32] No fact, provided that it could illuminate some corner of a past reality, was beneath the "Dignity of History" for Carlyle.

The brilliant eccentricity of Carlyle's style may obscure the objectives he held in common with fellow historians: resuscitation, identification, sympathy, and conversion—in that order. Fearing that "till *we* become Believers and Puritans in our way, no result will be arrived at" in the attempt to reform society,[33] he aimed to convince his quack- and cant-ridden contemporaries that the belief and moral purpose they lacked had been realities in the past, and to provide them with the opportunity to "connect" themselves imaginatively with those same feelings once again (OC, 1:1). Carlyle's peculiar obsession with the symbolic immanent in the actual did make him the most stylistically innovative of the six historians. He became convinced early that the historian needed to invent a new "language," one "melodious," "musical," and "poetic" enough to turn fragments into wholes, documents into experiences. He needed a spectrum of frankly fictive techniques to create a narrative that destroyed the intervening lapse of time, immersed the reader in the event, and allowed him to enter directly into the spiritual dimension of historical reality.

The French Revolution introduced a range of effects to achieve these ends. Its very allusiveness—to Merovingian Kings, to Boston Harbors black with tea, to Feasts of Morals mounted by Philosophe-Sentimentalism—draws readers into the narrative by implying their preexisting intimacy with a more densely populated historical realm. Carlyle forgoes a discursive analysis of issues and antecedents in favor of impressionistic evocations of mood and conjurations of symbols. The oracular tone of his digressive sermons and incantations encourages the sense that his narrative operates above the level of prosaic and limited reality. The nominalization and pluralizing of names and beliefs—the "Courtierisms, Conquering Heroisms, Most Christian Grand Monarque-isms, Well-beloved Pompadourisms" that obscured the inevitable arrival of revolution, for instance— signal the reader that individual men and events are being translated

History as Secular Prophecy

into those abstract truths and spiritual realities that coursed beneath the appearances of life. The frequent use of the present tense reinforces the immediacy and dynamism of events and draws in the audience as living witnesses.

The obstacles to restoring a contemporary understanding of events preoccupied Carlyle. As his hypothetical researcher "Smelfungus" explained it, past events were like living plants that eventually decayed into layers of peat: the higher generations pressed upon the lower, "squeezing them ever thinner" (HS, 64) and obscuring the original contours of significance. One hoped that this process would leave standing some "high peaks," some major events, that could give their name to the entire region. More often great actions proved "historically barren," while the smallest took root in the moral soil and grew to cover "whole quarters of the world."[34] To complicate the historian's task still further, in retrospect he often failed to distinguish between "the real historical Transaction" and the "more or less plausible scheme and theory of the Transaction" that tried to "account" for it in the present.

In order to rediscover the meaning of the event for himself, the historian had in effect to abandon any attempt at artificial historical perspective, any theory about the event. His goal was to attain vision from an internal perspective by achieving complete sympathy and identification with past actions. Hedva Ben-Israel calls the process of creating true history for Carlyle "as subconscious as the process of creating poetry was in Wordsworth's theory. To promote a genuine reaction, a historian makes sure that the picture that gives the stimulus is authentic. Once the right reaction has been brought about, it is this which directs the recreation of reality."[35] Historical art, Carlyle explained to Sterling, thus began with a "thorough *intelligence* of the fact to be painted. . . . This once *blazing* within one . . . one has to take the whole dexterity of adaptation one is master of" and "contrive to exhibit it one way or other."[36] To allow the reader a correct appreciation of historical relationships required "the best insight, seeking light from all possible sources, shifting its point of vision withersoever vision or glimpse of vision can be had" (FR, 1:214). In his "exhibition" of the event, the historian needed in particular to overcome the fact that "narrative is *linear*, Action is *solid*" (E, 2:89). The continuity of linear narrative, with no more than mechanical cause and effect explanations at its disposal, could not be

Thomas Carlyle

true to the chaotic interplay of historical forces or the multidimensionality of historical experience.

Carlyle tried to compensate for the distorting linearity of narrative by consciously manipulating perspectives. In what C. F. Harrold called his "synoptic view," he was constantly juxtaposing the present condition of an object or event with its past and future condition.[37] H. M. Leicester analyzes this same process by dividing Carlyle's modes of presentation into "prospective" and "retrospective" points of view.[38] In the first the historian's *ex post facto* knowledge about the event was suppressed, so that the experience of it was limited to the immediate and excluded knowledge of the event's outcome or of alternative possibilities. The retrospective view superimposed the missing dimensions of the event—the causes, results, and future significances that only time could reveal. The advantage of the "prospective" view lay in its ability to duplicate the immediacy of an experience unfolding on the spot, making the reader a witness and, in some cases, a participant.

For instance, in recounting the royal family's attempted escape to Varennes in *The French Revolution*, Carlyle positions himself with the reader as a contemporary observer with no privileged knowledge or hindsight to elucidate the scene. Present tense verbs subvert the linearity of narrative by evoking a perpetual present. "We observe" Count Fersen often using his Ticket of Entry without realizing what it means (FR, 2:158). On the night of 20 June 1791, we watch anonymous figures enter the glass coach in the Rue de L'Echelle: hooded dames with children, "a thickset Individual, in round hat and peruque," who springs a shoe buckle and stoops to reclasp it, a "Lady shaded in a broad gypsy-hat" who touches her *badine* to the spoke of Lafayette's carriage. Even when the Lady is revealed as the Queen, the indeterminacy of the event is prolonged by questions that leave open its outcome: "But is Fersen on the right road?" "If we reach Bouillé? If we do not reach him?" In the process the point of view also shifts so that the reader shares the feelings of the royal party. Carlyle often forged this kind of identification for the narrator, increasing the immediacy of the action and the authenticity of his voice by merging himself with participants. Thus he is alternately a seventeenth-century courtier ("I myself . . . have often assisted at Ben's Masques . . . and endeavoured to make acquaintance with a fair friend or two" HS, 75), a gossipy neighbor of Cromwell ("Doctor Simcock has told friends of mine that he suffered under terrible hypochondria, and had fancies about the Town-Cross" HS, 203), or a foot soldier on the rainy eve of the battle of Dunbar ("We English have some tents; the Scots have none" OC, 2:205). This abandonment of the omniscient voice forced the reader to sacrifice pat explanations that tried to "account" for the event and instead to try to experience it for himself.

The "retrospective" view, on the other hand, revealed that every occurrence was part of a broader network of significance, full of immanent meaning. As Leicester points out, the procession of the States General in volume 1 of *The French Revolution* was not just the description of a concrete event: it introduces all those figures who will emerge as important in the ensuing narrative. By the end of the chapter, "the brief moment of the procession has been filled up with references, images and significances that were not actually available at the time of occurrence, but that body forth the hidden meanings which even then, Carlyle would maintain, were present."[39] Elsewhere Carlyle employs slightly different techniques to implicate seemingly minor facts in larger patterns of meaning and to reveal the interweavings of history's web, invisible to the eye fixed only on one nexus. He often depended upon a panoramic sweep of vision that came to rest, prophetically, on those objects that were or that would become most pregnant with significance. A geological explanation of the Bog of Lindsey opened up to include a survey of all the famous men who had dwelt there, starting with King Cnut and funneling down to Cromwell (HS, 58-60). The account of Cromwell's early biography (OC, 1: chap. 4) includes not just incidents in Oliver's life, but milestones in the religious controversy that shaped his later career: the Hampden Court Conference, the Gunpowder Plot, the collapse of the Spanish Match. Carlyle also notes the coincidence of Shakespeare's death— ending the first "World-great Thing" of English History—with the beginning of the second "World-great Thing," the "Armed Appeal of Puritanism," in the form of Oliver's admission to Cambridge. Such a lamination of events makes clear that history possesses not a linear causality but a layered solidity of meanings, in which each moment expands outward in all directions to influence others.

Carlyle's other answer to the limitations of linear narrative was to make his method purposefully fragmentary. Substituting for the conventional continuity of major events a series of close-ups on the most suggestive occurrences achieved several ends. Like the manipulation of points of view, it too defied conventional causality and the

Thomas Carlyle

flattening perspective induced by *ex post facto* theories about events. More importantly, his preference for the "minor" details afforded a way of demonstrating the fecundity of even the smallest germ of historical reality and of exalting the luminous God-made fact. As he pointed out in *Past and Present*, the very "intermittence" of Jocelin's record duplicated the mingled inscrutability and certainty of Nature itself (PP, 46). This quality guaranteed the superiority of his account to fictions that invented what they could not authenticate and to annals that buried the significant fact in a deluge of shot-rubbish. The prosaic detail was particularly useful in helping the reader "domesticate himself" in scenes foreign to his own sceptical age; "Dryasdust Torpedoism" could never convince him that the seventeenth century had been "an actual flesh-and-blood fact" with "colour in its cheeks" and a belief worth dying for in its heart (OC, 1:79-80). In the escape to Varennes, Louis's shoe buckle and Marie's *badine* function in a similar way: their very insignificance convinces the reader of the authenticity of the scene. Carlyle most often relied upon the telling detail to epitomize a whole range of sociocultural phenomena. For instance, *The Marriage of Figaro, Paul et Virginie,* and *The Chevalier de Faublas* offers the final indictment of the advanced decay of French morality (FR, 1:59-60); the new style of Empire dandyism in dress and dance signifies the "reclothing" of French culture after the Terror (FR, 3:292-93).

On a larger scale, this fragmentary method often approximates the approach Carlyle praised in Schiller's *History of the Revolt of the United Netherlands*: "The work is not stretched out into a continuous narrative; but gathered up into masses, which are successively exhibited to view, the minor facts being grouped around some leading one, to which, as to the central object, our attention is chiefly directed. This method of combining the details of events, of proceeding as it were, *per saltum*, from eminence to eminence, and thence surveying the surrounding scene, is undoubtedly the most philosophical of any."[40] "Philosophical," that is, in that it allowed the historian to show the contours of "Universal History" while still exploiting the particularized factuality of events. The volume subtitles of *The French Revolution*, for instance, locate its "eminences": the Bastille, the Constitution, and the Guillotine. Likewise, each book takes its name from the major event, locale, or body highlighted within: "The Feast of Pikes," "Varennes," "Parliament First." Volume 3 offers the most forthright examples of what Carlyle also referred to as his "compendious, grandiose-massive way" of summing up events.[41] There his avowed intention was to "splash down what I know in large masses of colours, that it may look like a smoke-and-flame conflagration in the distance."[42] Throughout these elliptical passages, repeated epithets, phrases, labels, and personifications act as leitmotifs to remind the reader of emerging themes and to create a degree of cohesion in an otherwise fragmentary account. On one level the fragmentary method works to convince the reader that the relationship between historical facts is that of metaphor, not of cause; actions are not the "effects" of one another, but are rather linked by their common significations of a larger implied historical whole, inaccessible by direct observation.

On another level the fragmentary method forces the reader to confront the very process of understanding history, particularly in *Frederick the Great*. There Carlyle also passes over large areas, providing only "glimpses"—selected incidents presented "as if caught-up by some sudden photograph apparatus" (FG, 3:41)—that allowed the reader to "conceive" the "actuality of this business" for himself. Elsewhere his attempts to force the reader into imaginative participation become even more insistent: he rapidly sketches in the outline of the action, then invites the reader to complete it with his own details (FG, 3:134-35). In the process the reader begins to share in the historian's endeavor to interpret and reconstruct the past. As the massive work proceeds, the growing heaps of undigested data and the broader gaps in narrative continuity put more and more responsibility on the reader. In this sense John Clive has described *Frederick the Great* as a *bildungsgeschichte*, in which the reader as protagonist gains self-knowledge and insight by sharing the same experiences the historian underwent in his search for truth. To Morse Peckham, however, the eventual breakdown of narrative coherence in later volumes reveals Carlyle's gradual loss of faith in the possibility of penetrating sham to read the world as a symbol of the divine.[44] Thus a narrative method that began as a search for more profound explanations of historical truth ended in Carlyle's tacit admission that all historical explanation was at best illusory.

Notwithstanding their ultimate subversion of narrative integrity, Carlyle's methods were highly effective in realizing specific people and events. His treatment of character makes good use of the telling detail. Indeed, minor characters themselves function as such details, synecdoche for larger phenomena. The angry old women in *Past and*

Thomas Carlyle

Present, their property confiscated in lieu of reaping silver, brandish their distaffs not just against the *Cellararius*, but against all the misrule of Hugo's tenure (PP, 64). Jenny Geddes takes aim at all decayed sacramentalism when she pitches her stool at the Anglican priest (OC, 1:96). The vividly specific types who labor to complete the Field of Mars for the Feast of Pikes make palpable the way "Patriotism" inspired and leveled an entire society. Carlyle presents a mosaic in which "long-frocked tonsured Monks, with short-skirted Water-carriers, with swallow-tailed well-frizzled *Incroyables* of a Patriot turn" labor side by side, where "snowy linen and delicate pantaloon" alternate with the "soiled check-shirt and bushel-breeches." "Does one distrust his brothers?" answers "a certain person" of wealth when warned against leaving his watches unguarded; at once anonymous and specific, he exposes the beautiful but flimsy "noble-sentiment" that only hastens collapse in a society incapable of weaving sentiment into duty (FR, 2:57-59). The "antiquarian" clothing of Cromwell's cousins is used to somewhat different effect. Their "fringed trouser-breeches" and "starched ruff," vividly real again for the moment of the historian's notice, only underline the disintegrating power of time, which has rendered their "soul's furniture" as quaintly antiquated as their "spanish boots and lappet caps" (OC, 1:102).

The figurative significance of such characters and details finally works against the very literalness of their portrayal. All their luminous uniqueness is a means to an end. Like metaphors, their importance lies not in the image itself but in the relationships it reveals. In this context H. M. Leicester has argued that "there are really two sets of characters going under a single set of names" in Carlyle's histories: "the actual men, whose real nature is lost in the past and therefore unknowable; and Carlyle's *leitmotifs*, which act out the parts allotted to them" in the drama of Universal history.[45] Characters embody not individual personalities but historical purposes: the historian's "compressive imagination" concentrates the entire Reign of Terror in Marat, the spiritual bankruptcy of all France in the Arch-Quack Cagliostro. In the process John Holloway has said, "Their individuality is volatized and disintegrated by the abstractions of which they are the vehicles."[46] Carlyle breathes life into minor characters so that they can give their testimony to the reality of attitudes, beliefs, phenomena, but after their task has been accomplished, he as easily exchanges them for other "emblems" that serve his purpose just as well.

Major characters are realized more fully as individuals, although

History as Secular Prophecy

their individuality is finally subordinated in similar ways to figurative ends. Like others of his contemporaries, Carlyle believed that sympathy with the public man rested on a humanity shared with the private one within. Here the commonplace detail played an important role in helping the audience to recognize in even the most legendary beings kindred worthy of sympathy and compassion, while at the same time offering its own tacit commentary on the significance of human actions. Queen Sophie Charlotte's smuggled pinch of snuff at Friedrich Wilhelm's coronation is not only in character with the familiar, down-to-earth woman Carlyle earlier "reads" in her portrait; that "symbolic pinch of snuff" also represents a quiet protest against cant and ostentation, a grasp of realities that her son inherits (FG, 1:53). Carlyle passes over the fifty-seven questions asked at Louis's trial in favor of the bit of bread he begs of Chaumette after withdrawing from the Salle de Convention: "The King eats of the Crust . . . asks now, What he shall do with the crumb? Chaumette's clerk takes it from him; flings it out into the street. Louis says, It is pity to fling out bread, in a time of dearth." The muted pathos of this exchange invites our sympathy for the "poor innocent mortal" who "so quietly . . . waits the drawing of the lot," but Carlyle expects us also to sense the irony in this solicitude for mere crumbs, come too late to a monarch unseated by Twenty-five Hungry Millions (FR, 3:93-94).

Carlyle took most literally the romantic injunction to resuscitate the past. He advised readers to "repress . . . that too insatiable scientific curiosity" about the details of history so that their *"aesthetic feeling"* could free their imaginations (E, 3:360), and relied himself on techniques frankly dramatic and at times fictional to restore characters to a fully credible humanity. Dialogue fashioned from source documents is a standard device in his histories; his choice of Cromwell's letters and speeches confirms his regard for authentic speech. His desire to make his dramatizations serve his own didactic and artistic ends increasingly blurs the boundaries of his evidence. In *Frederick the Great* he will sometimes fashion exposition into his own version of quoted dialogue, claiming, "that or something equivalent, indisputably was" (FG, 4:118), or will cite as actually spoken what he allows might be only "a mere French epigram, . . . put down for fact" (FG, 6:273). Sometimes he even renders the commentary of his source historians in a colloquial voice, as when he makes Henry Lloyd (*History of the Late War*) reply to hopes of an easy French victory, "No general will permit himself to be taken in flank with his eyes open; and the King of Prussia is the unlikeliest you could try it with!" (FG, 6:273). In addition to personalizing his narrative, Carlyle thus makes Lloyd reinforce precisely the characterization he is creating; like Arnold, he uses invention to flesh out the full dimensions of heroism.

His artistic license extends farther yet in the battle of Hohenfriedberg. There he translates Frederick's actual words into distinctly Carlylean turns of phrase ("You see the ranks beginning to shake, and jumble towards indistinctness"), phrases that project onto Frederick the historian's own contempt for the French (FG, 5:125). The sources barely mention Frederick's irritation at Adjutant Gaudi's discomposure as the enemy approaches. From them Carlyle extrapolates a pungently specific vignette that epitomizes the plain-speaking Frederick of his imagination:

> "Well, and if he do? No flurry needed Captain!" answered Friedrich,— (*not* in these precise words; but rebuking Gaudi, with a look not of laughter wholly, and with a certain question, as to the state of Gaudi's stomachic part, which is still known in traditional circles, but is not mentionable here). (FG, 6:273-74)

Such fictive techniques make palpable Carlyle's claim that the eye of the imagination often saw more deeply into the essence of the man than the eye of the pedant, for all his data. Sometimes he also took literally his comment that the historian must become a Shakespeare, resorting to frankly histrionic devices in order to recapture the drama inherent in historic encounters. Rather than follow verbatim the account of an audience with Frederick "reported by the faithful pen" of the English Ambassador, Robinson, Carlyle "compresses" it in order to make the King's character "vividly significant." Moreover, he stages the reenactment as a one-act play, starring the young Frederick who easily punctures the hot-air balloons of diplomacy with the inflexible steel of Realpolitik. The frame combines the appeal of spectacle (complete with *dramatis personae*, costumes, stage directions, and lines) with parenthetical insights that illuminate the real feelings and thoughts of each participant (FG, 4:231 ff.). No State Paper could allow the reader to experience the past as a dramatic transaction, to see it from the inside out. Carlyle similarly restores the dynamic dimension to history in his "extensions" of Cromwell's speeches. He scatters stage directions in brackets throughout the text, here indicat-

History as Secular Prophecy

ing the audience's response—"hear! hear!" "a grim smile on some faces"—there the mode of delivery—"Oliver's voice somewhat rising"—even stopping occasionally to correct the misapprehensions that "Groans from Dryasdust" indicate (OC, 3:46-59). These devices pull three-dimensional characters from the linear narrative, set into motion the drama frozen by time into *tableaux*. And yet we must to a large extent agree with Emerson: "We have men in your story and not names merely; always men, though I may doubt sometimes whether I have the historic men."[47] Carlyle defied the limitations of time and memory by creating a credible humanity to plead for belief and assent, but their testimony supports his vision of the past, not necessarily their own.

We find the same concerns and devices in Carlyle's treatment of action, particularly in his battle scenes. Although he might profess to esteem "the Social Hearth" over "the Battlefield," military history loomed large, particularly in *Cromwell* and *Frederick*. In fact it served Carlyle's purposes just as well if not better than domestic history. Like Arnold, Carlyle did not find warfare indiscriminately interesting. Battles deserved to be remembered when they proved to have been the "travail-throes of great or considerable changes" (FG, 4:144). It was not necessary to furnish the strategist with materials for study, however; just enough detail "to assist the reader's fancy in conceiving it a little" for himself (FG, 5:120) would do. Rich in action, emotion, and heroism, battle scenes provided direct opportunities to forge an imaginative link between the reader and his ancestors, and thus to reconnect him with the values they found worth fighting for. Carlyle consciously appeals to the layman's eye and the brother's heart. Battles emerge from the dusty pages of the tacticians with a human face and compelling verisimilitude.

The main intention of his version of the storming of the Bastille, for instance (FR, 1:186-95), is to duplicate the experiential reality of the scene rather than to provide an exact account of military maneuvers: the fact that the cannon of the *Gardes Françaises* played the key tactical role in taking the Bastille is obscured in the jumble and rush of events. Throughout the account, Carlyle maintains a tension between the imaginative and the moral by shifting back and forth between the vividly immediate and the ultimately symbolic impact of events—the prospective and the retrospective views. Present tense verbs, speech set in dialogue, syntax as choppy as the action itself, draw the reader into the action until he and the historian merge with

Thomas Carlyle

the participants: "We fall, shot; and make no impression!" Against a chaotic background, Carlyle's focus skips from individual to individual, closing in just long enough to grasp their personal response to these events or to prefigure their role in later ones. Concurrently, the voice of Carlyle the moralist is pealing out its judgment: "Wo to thee, DeLaunay, in such an hour, if thou canst not, taking some one firm decision, *rule* circumstances." Typically, events seem to accomplish themselves: "straw is burnt," "blood flows," and, at the crucial moment, "sinks the drawbridge . . . rushes-in the living deluge: the Bastille is fallen!" Each individual action is propelled by the same relentless inevitability possessed by the Revolution as a whole, because this "Fire-Mahlstrom" is the instrument of divine judgment on a corrupt France.

In the battle scenes of *Cromwell* and *Frederick*, Carlyle goes out of his way to restore human interest and draw the reader into the action. By translating source documents into direct address and slipping into present tense verbs and first person pronouns, he converts the reader from spectator into participant. He is more successful than Arnold in exploiting his firsthand knowledge of battle sites: by shifting from his modern day impressions to the field's appearance on the day of a famous battle he achieved what Emerson called a "stereoscopic" time-effect, drawing the reader from present into past. In *Cromwell* Carlyle often drops the formal and omniscient voice and lets one or two eye-witness narratives suffice for the battle account (OC, 1:175-77). Their insight into authentic human emotion is more important to him than their military accuracy or completeness. Elsewhere, Carlyle simply hands over full responsibility to the reader, advising him to imagine a battle for himself as "the most enormous hurlyburly, of fire and smoke, and steel-flashings and death-tumult, ever seen in those regions" (OC, 1:187). Carlyle's account of Dunbar battle (OC, 2:197-209) furnishes a useful illustration of these techniques in action. He begins with present day Dunbar, then invites the spectator to look landward to "a barren heath of Hills." In front of them we find Oliver's tents, pitched on a "very uneven tract of ground; now in our time all yellow with wheat and barley . . . but at that date only partially tilled . . . [and] terribly beaten by showery winds that day, so that your tent will hardly stand." In the space between "our times" and "your tent," Carlyle has already merged the Victorian with the Roundhead. He dwells on one relatively insignificant event: Lesley's capture of a one-armed Puritan musketeer on the day before the bat-

History as Secular Prophecy

tle. He quotes the man's defiant answers to Lesley because Carlyle sees in this "most dogged handfast man" a symbol of Puritan tenacity. Carlyle then closes in on the battlefield itself, conjuring his readers to "look even with unmilitary eyes at the ground as it now is" until some "small glimmerings of distinct features," "some spectrum of the Fact," become visible, and they can see that "the footprint of a Hero, not yet quite indistinguishable, is here!" The reader's participation is further reinforced as Carlyle surveys the battle lines on the rainy eve of Dunbar—"We English have some tents; the Scots have none"—and as he continues to refer to Cromwell's troops as "we" for the rest of the account. The fighting itself he conveys in one rapid-fire paragraph that sacrifices exact detail to achieve a sense of confused movement and emotion. The action shifts in short present tense sentences from one side to the other, from men's thoughts to their actions, until we "break them, beat them, drive them all adrift" and the Scottish army is "shivered to utter ruin."

Like characterization, battle scenes in *Frederick* exercise even greater dramatic license to achieve drama and identification. Brooks demonstrates how Carlyle combed his travel notebooks and his sources for picturesque, anecdotal details to personalize and highlight individuals in the major battle scenes in this work. Straining for a plausible reality, he actually invented emotions, actions, and likely dialogue to flesh out the human shapes dessicated by his military sources. For instance, by furnishing thought, action, and speech he helps us to "fancy" Niepperg's reaction when Frederick's attack surprises him at dinner: "Quick, your Plan of Battle, then? Witherward; How; What? answer or perish! Niepperg was infinitely struck; dropt knife and fork: 'Send for Römer, General of the Horse!' " (FG, 4:121). Later in the same account of Mollwitz, he invents dialogue to suggest the frustration of Römer's troops—"Are we to stand here like milestones, then, and be all shot without a stroke struck?" (FG, 4:124)—and to imply the comradery among the men whom Winterfield encourages with, "Steady, *meine Kinder*; fix bayonets, handle ramrods!" (FG, 4:127-28). Admitting that "no human pen can describe" nor intellect discern how the Prussians triumphed at Sterbohol, he substitutes instead a brief vignette that imagines Field Marshall Schwerin turning back his retreating troops with a *"Heran, meine Kinder,"* the cry they take up "with hot tears" as he falls: *"Heran,* On!" until "they manage to do the work at Sterbohol" (FG, 6:134-35). The mousetrap image in the battle of Hohenfriedberg and the "Theseus and the Mi-

Thomas Carlyle

notaur over again" at Zorndorf are other inventions like the "Heran" that organize and focus an event for the reader. Carlyle's narratives proclaim that the emotional reality of an event is more important than its literal occurrences; they attempt to make his reader understand the past by experiencing it with contemporaries. At their best his techniques create a comprehension beyond the merely historical, but they are controlled by and finally limited to a past he invented to make sense of the present. The more his confidence in his own vision faltered, the more insistently he imposed his fictions on an uncooperative or fragmentary reality. As a result we wind up agreeing with contemporary reviewers, who found the work "a curious psychological study, more interesting and valuable perhaps in a History of Thomas Carlyle than a History of Frederick the Great."[48]

The idiosyncrasies of Carlyle's style always made his reputation as an historian controversial. He never succeeded in convincing his contemporaries that the created and the historical were one and the same. In fact his works played an important role in defining the split between "scientific" and "literary" history from its beginnings. The *Saturday Review* began to distinguish between the two as early as 1858, when J. F. Stephen used *The French Revolution* to exemplify "the especial advantages and disadvantages of the literary temperament" in the historian. Pointing out the ways imaginative excess could falsify history, Stephen expressed a fear common among defenders of "scientific" history: that the more powerful the historian's literary ability, the greater the potential for misleading readers.[49] Robert Vaughan had similarly criticized *Cromwell* for sacrificing "proof" to "vivacity."[50] *Frederick* of course deviated farther and farther from what reviewers expected in a history, distorting perspective and obscuring the leading facts of the epoch in an effort to entertain.[51] Because they considered it a particular abuse of his genius to glorify might as right, reviewers claimed *Frederick* as proof that the "literary" historian was as dangerous a moral teacher as he was unreliable a scholar.[52] By the 1880s, when the battle lines between "men of science" and "men of style" had been clearly drawn, Carlyle was almost uniformly condemned by defenders of professionalism as "a literary historian pure and simple."[53] Oscar Browning's analysis of Carlyle's factual errors in the flight to Varennes exemplified the attack of the academic historian on the artistic license of his "literary" rivals.[54] Looking back in 1886 on *The French Revolution*, Frederic Harrison noted the change in critical climate: "A generation ago the

History as Secular Prophecy

influence of it was great; it is now seen to be a poem, with the vision, the movement, the exaggeration of poetry, but without the one indispensable quality for history, solid historical science and true social philosophy."[55] With the general public, however, Carlyle's influence remained great. In the closing decades of the century, he was held up as a paradigm for the strengths as well as weakness of "literary" history.

Taking Carlyle's measure as an historian is no simple matter. Like Arnold he combined elements of various historiographic traditions. His theory of history was romantic in its organic concept of change, in its focus on the process of spiritual revolution, and in its recognition of the contributions of the life of the common man to the life of nations. He also borrowed techniques and attitudes characteristic of the romantic poet. The prophetic role he assigned to the historian, the merging of historian and event that preceded the act of imaginative reconstruction, and his attempt at forging a new language that could portray the spiritual dimension of events, all link him to romanticism. But in practice his sternly moralistic purposes prevented him from escaping the judgmental tendencies of preceding historians, and thus restricted the process of empathetic identification so fundamental to romantic historicism. The overriding purpose of his histories was to impress upon his readers the lesson learned in the history of the Jews: all men must keep God's commandments or become the instruments of His wrath. His Calvinistic biases were constantly imposing on events and characters a set of ethical standards not derived from history itself.

If Carlyle's elevation of human history to the level of cosmic drama gave his work a timelessness that other historians may not be able to claim, it also entailed serious drawbacks. Because his interest in events was essentially metaphorical or allegorical, he rarely gave them the close analysis that they demanded. He largely ignored his own collectivistic and developmental theories about the way history operated. Unlike Arnold he tended to reduce any epoch to a kind of psychomachia in which institutions, law, economics, politics, or class were only effects, not causes, of change. While asserting that custom, convention, and tradition played a vital role in human activity and thought, Carlyle seldom went beyond a symbolic explanation of their interrelationship. With characters as with institutions, his sins were usually those of omission. The allegorical function he attributed to individuals always limited the depth of their characterization. When faced with evidence incongruous to his own formulation of a character's importance, he did not misrepresent so much as he simply ignored. Undeniably he possessed a rare ability for bringing historical characters back to life, but they walked as the ghosts of his own prejudices and not as self-validating personalities.

Out of his very weaknesses, however, come some strengths. If he was insufficiently critical of those men who represented the forces of good, he escaped the cynicism of utilitarian theories that reduced all motivation to the level of pleasure or pain. If he allowed a metaphorical view of an event or character to preclude rigorous analysis, at least in the case of *Cromwell* and *The French Revolution* he provided a much-needed corrective to prevailing prejudices. If he depended too heavily on moral absolutes as standards of judgment, they did save him from what were later recognized as the dangers of excessive historical relativism: a refusal to judge, a blind trust or equally blind fatalism concerning the course of history. If his techniques drew more heavily on the subjectivity of the poet rather than on the professionalism of the scholar, they allowed for a dimension in historical writing rare in later days of overspecialization. Carlyle, in James Russell Lowell's phrase, saw "history, as it were, by flashes of lightning";[56] the luminous clarity and insight of his best passages more than atone for the intervening obscurity.

We should also keep in mind that Carlyle's conception of history, whatever its limits, suited the needs and interests of the Victorians. Without making them feel they were escaping from their duty in the present, he offered them reconnection with the "vigorous whole-life" of "rough strong times, wherein those maladies of ours had not yet arisen" (E, 4:56). His view of change acknowledged the mutability of material things that was so constant a reality to them while offering reassurance that the "organic filaments" of spiritual continuity still survived destruction of the familiar. He devoted his major works to the most thorough changes in modern Europe, seeking ways to interpret the changes of his own day. These works acted as both a warning to his own age to follow God's laws and a reassurance that in the long run Good would triumph. His transcendental conception of time and history satisfied Victorian hunger for moral uplift while allowing his readers to forget the specific theological dilemmas of their own age. The theory of hero-worship, however repugnant its objects, offered a heartening denial of the diminution of individual stature in a randomly determined universe and a means of obtaining secular saints

History as Secular Prophecy

for a generation now forced to live by "Admiration, Hope, and Love." Natural Supernaturalism held out the promise of spiritual transcendence without requiring a repudiation of the facts of this world, thus suggesting a means of unifying the scientific, the religious, and the imaginative, faculties that seemed to many to operate at cross purposes.

That Carlyle's teachings could not retain their orginal credibility tells us as much about the times as the man. In one respect he—unlike Arnold—simply outlived that generation for which the contradictory pulls of science and religion could be balanced without fragmentation of belief. He had made a leap of faith to conquer scepticism, but in the latter half of the century that leap simply fell short of the realities of the age. As the century wore on, the scientific conception of change and progress silently refuted claims that history was governed by divine purpose and direction. The progress of religious scepticism made Natural Supernaturalism all the more attractive as an inspiring, if vague, alternative, but one that either failed to provide practical objects for worship, or that expressed itself in a worship of force repellent to the Victorian moral sense. The changing social fabric most decisively distanced Carlyle from his times. The sage seemed an atavism in an age of professionalism and specialization, the hero-worshipper an anomaly in an age of democracy and mass culture. Carlyle's refusal to acknowledge democracy's strength in the modern world was his most unhistorical blindspot. With the repudiation of his social teachings implicit in the political drift of the latter nineteenth century, what had begun in him as an appreciation for individual excellence and wise guidance hardened into a blind absolutism and worship of force that repelled readers otherwise quite receptive to the moral quality of his message.

That Carlyle could be so wrong-headed about the actual course of change in his own day only underlines the fact that his strengths and weaknesses were those of the visionary. He was a powerful critic of his own society, but an inadequate reformer, because in the long run he wanted not to confront time and change so much as to overleap them into a world of eternal verities. He had a keen insight into the spiritual malaise of his age and a profound understanding of man's spiritual needs. However else they may have failed, his histories succeeded admirably in nourishing these. One reviewer noted that in failing to realize his own version of utopia, Carlyle had also failed in his wish to make *"himself . . . the hero of this modern age."*[57] One suspects,

Thomas Carlyle

however, that it was precisely his example—as one voice struggling with incomparable eloquence to express man's continuing need to reaffirm the possibilities for faith, order, excellence, and transcendence—that assured his heroic value even for an age that outgrew his teachings.

III

THOMAS BABINGTON MACAULAY
HISTORY AS WHIG VIA MEDIA

That the two most acclaimed historical artists of their era, Thomas Babington Macaulay and Thomas Carlyle, could be so emphatically different provides an important commentary on the Victorian frame of mind. If Thomas Carlyle was the prophet most opposed to his age, Thomas Macaulay was, in Leslie Stephen's words, the very Prince of Philistines.[1] If Carlyle epitomized the Victorians' yearning for a natural supernaturalism, Macaulay epitomized their pragmatism and dogmatic common sense. Where Carlyle illuminated the mystery of the past with romantic imagination, Macaulay flooded its shadows with enlightened rationality. While Carlyle enacted his age's painful transcendence of the Everlasting No, Macaulay sidestepped its most painful moral and intellectual dilemmas. No wonder Carlyle found Macaulay "unhappily without divine idea," and Macaulay considered him a "charlatan."[2] Yet Macaulay's tendency to yoke rather than to reconcile the dichotomies of his age makes him the more powerful a spokesman for the Victorian middle classes whose historical tastes he consciously shaped. His startling literary success argues that his vision of history satisfied powerful and widely felt needs even for those who fully acknowledged his limitations.

Macaulay no less than Arnold and Carlyle tried to reconcile the demands of reason and imagination in a form of history both scientifically sound and artistically compelling. He too sought in the past a

Thomas Babington Macaulay

stable center for a diversifying society. But his version of the "Whig view of history" sought not so much to locate a source of moral value in history as to substitute a political order for that moral one. He institutionalized an interpretation and infused it with a patriotic self-satisfaction that cut across party lines. By showing how English institutions reconciled tradition and innovation, Macaulay provided a secularized source of meaning and stability. Shaped by a yearning for order no less powerful than Carlyle's, his view of history proved more useful because it co-opted rather than tried to subvert democracy. He used the past to endow Victorian success with ethical value and, in so doing, provided a focus for national pride and identity. His overwhelming popularity resulted as much from his reassuring view of progress and permanence as from the brilliant style that reinforced it, a style making as few demands on understanding as his explanation of history did on faith. The shallowness of his response to the intellectual crises of his time should not detract from his importance as a barometer of Victorian taste and thought. He reveals the trouble spots of nineteenth-century consciousness no less because he tried to sidestep where he could not transcend. The theoretical incongruities beneath the monotonous lucidity of his style yield important insights into the transitional state of Victorian historiography.

John Clive and others have helped clarify how Macaulay's early years contributed to the "making of the historian."[3] He shook off much more easily than did Arnold and Carlyle the effects of his stern religious upbringing in the Clapham sect. His father's typically evangelical disapproval did little to decrease Macaulay's lifelong passion for novels and other imaginative literature. As early as his Cambridge days, his continuing respect for evangelical codes of conduct was no longer matched by a similar doctrinal orthodoxy. With orthodoxy he discarded any reliance on a moral truth transcending time and place—the kind of reliance that focused Carlyle's and Arnold's historical consciousness. His own focus was always more political than religious. His Whig view defined itself against the backdrop of the Napoleonic wars abroad and the continuing potential for revolution at home. As pressure for reform mounted in the twenties, he like Arnold became convinced of the inevitability of change and looked to history to justify the accommodations it required. The early essays and his fragmentary *History of France* articulated ideas that coalesced in his parliamentary speeches in support of the first Reform Bill.[4] The extension of the franchise became part of a tradition of change that preserved by progressing and ordered by expanding the privileges necessary to maintain balance. These views would become the pattern for all his further thought on history and the state.

The characteristic bent of his literary temperament formed early as well. Cambridge debating encouraged the versatility of imagination and rhetorical acuity that would become as crucial to the historian as to the M. P. His work on the Indian legal code further sharpened his facility for marshalling historical examples to support general principles. The *Lays of Ancient Rome* (1842), whose publication Arnold encouraged, proved even more dramatically than the *Essays* Macaulay's skill in reconstructing the mind of the past. That same skill combined with his highly gratifying view of the English past to make the first two volumes of the *History* best sellers in 1849 and to secure the triumphant success of the third and fourth volumes in 1855. Although when he died in 1859 the *History* covered barely one fourth of his original prospectus, it was no less suitable a monument to his rhetorical genius and to his complacent vision of Victorian success.

Macaulay's use of history mediated specific conflicts in a mind marked by pronounced contrasts. At first glance his intense imaginative devotion to the past matches oddly with his bumptious enthusiasm for progress. His sternly empirical rationalism seems scarcely compatible with his romantic love of time-traveling, of imagining himself "in Greece, in Rome, in the midst of the French Revolution" or in conversation with famous historical figures.[5] In fact, the peculiarly quantitative nature of his imaginative capacities allowed him to indulge his fancy while still satisfying the demands of reason. As he explained to his sister Margaret, it was his very love of "castle-building" that encouraged the accuracy with which he retained facts: "Precision in dates, the day or hour in which a man was born or died, becomes absolutely necessary. A slight fact, a sentence, a word, are of importance in my romance" (LM, 1:171). Although Macaulay valued the conscious fantasies of "romance" too much to be a mere rationalist, he used imaginative detail in a thoroughly practical and quantitative way to increase the reality of what he knew was only an illusion.

If anything, his particular exercise of imagination ended by more effectively divorcing fact from fantasy. As Margaret Macaulay pointed out, she and Tom were imaginative without being "romantic"; their reveries allowed them to escape into a fantasy world but "would never make us do a foolish thing, or indulge very extravagant expectations, in which we should not be borne out by what we see passing in the world around us."[6] History was in this respect a perfect outlet. It provided a fully-formed imaginative world while remaining true to the laws of experience; it indulged the fancy while remaining firmly rooted in fact. Macaulay's handling of the *Lays* reinforces this distinction. The mythic part of ancient history appealed to him because it possessed that "peculiar character, more easily understood than defined, which distinguishes the creations of the imagination from the realities of the world in which we live."[7] The boundaries between the real and the unreal were so clearly marked that there was no chance of confusing them; one could escape completely into the latter without jeopardizing one's status in the former. Arnold, too, had expected the "poetic" quality of the myths to distinguish them from "real history," but for him the poetic also gave access to a spiritual insight closed to Macaulay.

Macaulay's distance from Carlyle is even greater. Carlyle valued facts over fiction because facts were a means of transcending the limits of mortal experience and gaining access to a higher truth; Macaulay valued facts because they more clearly defined those limits. Where both felt *a priori* deduction to be an inadequate means of accounting for reality, Carlyle opposed "formulas" because they intervened between man and divine reality, while Macaulay in effect replaced faith in any such reality with faith in facts alone.[8] Where Carlyle attempted to interpret events by seizing on the revelatory details and illuminating their spiritual significance, Macaulay argued by piling up examples of similar circumstances and generalizing from them. Jane Millgate calls his process of reasoning "illustrative and analogical rather than analytic."[9] It determined truth not through a cognitive leap to a higher reality but by the sheer weight of similar cases.

Even had Macaulay's characteristic intellectual biases not drawn him to history, his more complex emotional needs would have, as George Levine and others have shown.[10] He took up the *History* after his return from India and the loss of his two favorite sisters, Hannah to marriage, Margaret to death. He was frustrated by the opposition his legal reforms had aroused and disenchanted with public office. The "desertion" of the sisters upon whom he had concentrated his strong affections intensified his desire to retreat from active life. In a telling letter to Margaret, he confessed that his disappointment over Hannah's engagement had intensified his "passion for holding converse with the greatest minds of all ages and nations, my power of forgetting what surrounds me, and of living with the past, the future, the distant, and the unreal."[11] The writing of history became far more than an avocation: it became a way of establishing an ideal world that guaranteed him protection from the emotional risks and losses of real life: a controlled world of reason and experience, a source of emotional sustenance and intellectual stability more dependable than anything his own life afforded. In this sense Macaulay represents another variation on that Victorian pattern of outer confidence and inner doubt. His reiterated conviction that the present was superior to the past did not prevent history from offering a static retreat from the disequilibrium that change and progress necessarily caused.

His desire to balance the claims of reason and imagination and of change and permanence shapes his theorizing. Although he did not possess a coherent philosophy of history, certain ideas first articulated in the 1828 essays "History" and "Hallam's Constitutional History" provide a working definition: history should combine reason and imagination, it should use particular examples to identify general principles of human conduct, and it should document not just public events, but the "silent revolutions" in thought and taste of which those events were only the outward signs. "History, at least in its state of ideal perfection, is a compound of poetry and philosophy," wrote Macaulay in the Hallam essay: "It impresses general truths on the mind by a vivid representation of particular characters and incidents" (W, 5:162). Unfortunately, in his own day poetry and philosophy were treated as "hostile elements": historical fiction invested the past with flesh and blood, but the historical essayist had "to extract the philosophy of history, . . . to trace the connexion of causes and effects, and to draw from the occurrences of former times general lessons of moral and political wisdom" (W, 5:162). Macaulay's ideal historian would combine the sculptor's eye for external reality possessed by Sir Walter Scott with the anatomist's eye for structure and causality possessed by Hallam; ideal history would join the coloring of a "painted landscape" with the "exact information as to the bearings of the various points" supplied by a map (W, 5:163). Only thus could history provide instruction "of a vivid and practical character" that would be not merely "traced" on the mind, but "branded into it" (W, 5:160). Macaulay's ideal history was to perform a task that in "Milton" (1825) he had considered impossible in a modern age: to unite "the incompatible advantages of reality and deception, the clear discernment of truth and the exquisite enjoyment of fiction" (W, 5:7).

Thomas Babington Macaulay

In other words it was to accomplish what Macaulay himself did in his highly factual fantasy world.

Macaulay's insistence on the mutual exclusivity of reason and imagination proceeded as much from his belief that "as civilisation advances, poetry almost necessarily declines" (W, 5:4) as from his attempt to be imaginative without being "romantic." The very factors that made history more "scientific" decreased its imaginative vigor. For Macaulay as for Arnold, history became "philosophical" insofar as it identified those principles of conduct that comprised "the science of government." Like other "experimental sciences" that arrived at generalizations through induction, historical interpretation was generally in a "state of progression" (W, 5:145). Because the modern historian had a wider inventory of experience on which to base his reasoning, he surpassed the ancient in the ability to distinguish "what is local from what is universal; what is transitory from what is eternal; to discriminate between exceptions and rules; to trace the operation of disturbing causes; to separate those general principles which are always true and everywhere applicable from the accidental circumstances with which . . . they are blended" (W, 5:151). However, this march of mind robbed history of its "picturesque" qualities; the generalizations necessary to advance knowledge blunted the particularity necessary to "brand" them into the imagination. Macaulay wished to restore this imaginative vividness to history while remaining faithful to its "scientific" purposes. As Levine has argued, he sought in history what many Victorian writers sought in realistic fiction: "a genre which allowed critical intelligence and a greater fidelity to the possibilities of real experience to combine with what remained of modern man's enfeebled imaginative powers."[12]

To achieve this reconciliation, Macaulay, like Carlyle, reversed the relationship of creativity in fiction and history, although with significantly different effect. He did not share the realist novelist's belief that fiction could—and should—test and explore reality. He considered fiction "essentially imitative. Its merit consists in its resemblance to a model with which we are already familiar." Fiction was in effect deductive, history inductive: "In fiction, the principles are given, to find the facts: in history, the facts are given, to find the principles." As a result behavior that ran contrary to expectations was "shocking and incongruous" in novels, but "delightful as history, because it contradicts our previous notion of human nature, and of the connections of causes and effects." "What is called the romantic part of history is in fact the least romantic" (W, 5:131), for it could serve to enlarge and correct one's expectations about human nature. History could thus satisfy the demands of both the imagination and the reason: it allowed one to indulge one's propensity for the exotic, the improbable, the fantastic, while retaining its didactic function.

In actual practice Macaulay succeeded in reconciling imagination and reason in history only by severely limiting both. For him the transforming creativity of the romantic artist was not just unnecessary to the historian, but positively inappropriate. It was rather a "lower kind of imagination" that the historian required: "The object of [his] imitation is not within him; it is furnished from without. It is not a vision of beauty and grandeur discernible only by the eye of his own mind, but a real model which he did not make, and which he cannot alter" (W, 6:83). Since Macaulay's reality did not possess the spiritual dimensions of Arnold's and Carlyle's, reconstructing it was a matter of imitating the seen, not intuiting the unseen. Carlyle would of course have dismissed the results of Macaulay's historical inductions as lying "formulas." For him and for Arnold, the aim of shaping detail into narrative was to break the tyranny of appearances. They relied on the eye of the spirit to illuminate the pattern beyond the facts. For Macaulay narration created an accurate illusion of an unquestioned reality. It selected and arranged such parts of the truth as most nearly "produce the effect of the whole" (W, 6:83). This process depended wholly upon the eye of the senses; Macaulay's conception of the true gave him no cause to seek further testimony.

Macaulay's conception of science was as mechanical as his conception of imagination, and it depreciated fact in a way equally contrary to the romantic temperament. At first glance his hostility to deductive reasoning and his enthusiasm for concrete detail might seem to undermine the character types and behavioral "laws" that obstructed a historicist appreciation of individuality. In practice treating historical facts as merely the "materials for the construction of a science" (W, 6:259) prevented Macaulay from valuing or completely comprehending any fact or event for its own sake. Despite his keen eye for telling detail, he still believed that "facts are the mere dross of history. It is from the abstract truth which interpenetrates them . . . that the mass derives its whole value" (W, 5:131). To him no past event was intrinsically significant; it was valuable "only as it leads us to form just calculations with respect to the future" (W, 5:155) or reveals "a

Thomas Babington Macaulay

general truth" about human nature (W, 6:260). This of course is significantly different from Ranke's belief that all ages were immediate to God, or even Carlyle's dedication to ideas that still bore spiritual fruit in the present. For Macaulay, the legacy of history was a set of generalizations by which likely outcomes could be calculated; for Carlyle, a set of spiritual absolutes that no man or nation could transgress with impunity.

Macaulay's reductively pragmatic approach to historical laws effectively ruled out any absolute, political or moral. Notwithstanding his early attacks on the Utilitarians for their dependence on "abstract" theory, he shared their goals—to provide the greatest good for the greatest number—and he favored whatever political strategies would bring this about. He might use scientific analogies to describe the "laws" of political science or talk about the "philosophy of history" (W, 5:543),[13] but his own laws designated neither universal relationships nor a philosophical basis for government. They were, at most, thoroughly pragmatic rules of thumb. The declaration that "a good government, like a good coat, is that which fits the body for which it is designed" (W, 7:687) summed up the extent of Macaulay's "philosophy." All other values yielded to utility. Constitutions were evaluated not by ideals served or traditions preserved, but by how well they suited the needs and interests—and thus increased the happiness —of those subject to them. A "wise man" valued liberty itself not as something "eternally and intrinsically good" but rather for the "blessings" of political stability and progress that resulted from it (W, 7:686). Even party allegiances paled before such worldly wisdom. Joseph Hamburger demonstrates that as both politician and historian Macaulay was less a Whig than a trimmer.[14] He favored not a consistent party line, but rather those forces that stabilized opposing political interests in order to achieve the balance necessary for prosperity and progress. The illogic of political positions was irrelevant so long as they achieved their ends (see, e.g., W, 2:367). Macaulay was in a sense more ruthlessly utilitarian than the Utilitarians themselves.

The gap between Macaulay's conception of the "laws of political science" and Arnold's was of course even more profound. Arnold assumed that the political order mirrored the ethical order and that its laws confirmed the "undoubted truths" of morality. For Macaulay, "all questions in morals and politics are questions of comparison and degree" (W, 5:152). The landscape of political action was not a path marked by absolutes, but rather a shadowy "frontier where virtue and vice fade into each other" (W, 2:189). In this territory the exigencies of political expedience shaped "laws," not timeless standards of right and wrong. His belief that "no man ought to be severely censured for not being beyond his age in virtue" (W, 6:18) might point toward a relativism not characteristically Victorian, but it also revealed a profound disillusionment with the possibility that any permanent ideals transcended ordinary experience the way Arnold's Christianity or Carlyle's Natural Supernaturalism did. Macaulay was largely spared from imposing alien standards of conduct on other ages because he acknowledged the value of no ideal standard.

Although in their dominant sense, "laws" merely described logical expectations about behavior, there was one law that possessed a prescriptive authority amounting to divine decree: the overall progress of human civilization. Macaulay in places treated society's advance as simply the logical outcome of the development of experimental science and of the individual's drive to better his position. But elsewhere he added the sanction of God and Nature as well. He took the "natural tendency of the human intellect to truth" and of "society to improvement" as evidence of those "general laws which it has pleased [God] to establish in the physical and in the moral world" (W, 5:365). It was no more logical to expect to stem progress than to "change the courses of the seasons and of the tides" (W, 8:73). The necessary and predictable advance of civilization in this sense attained a status Macaulay accorded to no other phenomenon in his world of transient values. And, John Clive points out, Macaulay had sound reasons for these conclusions. Looking around him he saw a world that *was* demonstrably better—in morals, in social consciousness, in religious zeal—than the age that preceded it, largely as a result of reforming impulses like those that inspired the Clapham sect. Evidence of material progress would thus merely have "reinforced the lesson taught by the confident Evangelicalism of Macaulay's youth" and gained for itself a quasi-religious authority. The man who found the Crystal Palace a sight "beyond the dreams of the Arabian romances" (LM, 2:226) did not merely welcome the material advances of the industrial revolution, but found in them "the source of something akin to what the Romantic poets were finding in nature."[15] This significantly shifted the emotional fulcrum for Macaulay's assessment of history. For Carlyle the persistence of tradition sanctified the present. Macaulay, on the other hand, reverenced tradition because of the present successes it had made possible.

Thomas Babington Macaulay

The full implications of this reorientation were to an extent masked by Macaulay's rhetoric. His argument for progress gained strength from organic analogies similar to Arnold's and Carlyle's. Comparing the development of nations to that of individuals in "Milton" allowed him to argue for a cultural as well as an individual maturation toward logic and abstract reasoning. In the *History* this analogy insured continuity in national identity: "the groundwork of [national] character" had remained "the same through many generations, in the sense in which the groundwork of the character of an individual may be said to be the same when he is a rude and thoughtless schoolboy and when he is a refined and accomplished man" (W, 1:330-31). More importantly, this developmental model allowed Macaulay to argue that nations, like individuals, needed forms of government adapted to their relative stage of maturity: "The very means by which the human mind is, in one stage of its progress, supported and propelled, may, in another stage, be mere hindrances" (W, 1:37). Like Arnold he supported reform because the "law of growth" governing societies decreed that as the people's strength and experience increased, government could "no longer confine them within the swaddling bands . . . of their infancy" (W, 8:75). They must be accorded political power commensurate with their increased intellectual and economic strength in order to bring "the legal order of society into something like harmony with the natural order" (W, 8:84).

Like the natural order, the pattern of history was also governed by cycles. For Macaulay this meant that societies advanced through a series of actions and reactions in politics and public opinion. It also meant that for no nation was development without limit. The fact of decay gave cause for optimism, because the death of social organisms contributed to new birth. Here the metaphors are distinctly Carlylean: "The corruption of death" after Charlemagne's fall ultimately "ferment[ed] into new forms of life" (W, 6:389); the Reformation and French Revolution had acted like volcanoes whose fiery deluges ended by fertilizing the soil they devastated (W, 5:595). But there was cause for melancholy as well. For all his commitment to the march of mind, Macaulay did not see England forever in its vanguard. Arnold looked in vain for new races to carry on the next stage of development; Macaulay could envision a time "when some traveler from New Zealand shall, in the midst of a vast solitude, take his stand on a broken arch of London Bridge to sketch the ruins of St. Paul's" (W, 6:455). More often, however, he took the shorter view, assuring his audience that despite the "recoil which regularly follows every advance," the great tide of progress was steadily coming in on English shores (W, 6:97).

The rhetoric of organic change is deceptive, for beneath it lay assumptions that significantly distanced Macaulay's position from Arnold's and Carlyle's. His enthusiasm for the present was only one distinguishing factor. His model of progress was actually closer to that of the Utilitarians and the Scottish conjectural historians. The notion of developmental stages he derived from the latter allowed him to dismiss as primitive whatever challenged his norm for civilization.[16] By measuring all societies on one and the same scale he ruled out Arnold's appreciation of how different nations could translate a common pattern of development into terms appropriate to themselves. Praising the ancients at the moderns' expense irritated him because by virtue of their very modernity his contemporaries occupied a higher rung on the ladder of progress. There was, after all, no "well authenticated instance of a people which has decidedly retrograded in civilisation and prosperity" without the agency of external calamity (W, 5:366). More importantly, his measure of "civilization" ruled out the moral growth that Carlyle and Arnold considered essential to the social organism. Improvement in the physical realm meant the increase of material prosperity and population; in the intellectual realm, it meant the dispersion of superstition and the march of mind toward scientific rationalism. By moral improvement Macaulay meant little more than the change in manners from rude to refined, barbarous to humane. Once he contrasts the modern gentry's polish and accomplishments with the "unrefined sensuality" of their swilling, swearing counterparts in 1685, it does not occur to him to look for further proof of moral advance (W, 1:250). Not only did he ignore spiritual progress in the sense Arnold intended—he saw it as impossible: "A Christian of the fifth century with a Bible is neither better nor worse situated than a Christian in the nineteenth century with a Bible" (W, 6:457-58).

Macaulay epitomized that "faith in machinery" that Matthew Arnold would later single out as the "besetting danger" of Victorian society. His concept of cycles reinforced not the organic integrity of all social organisms but a mechanical cause and effect. Situations are not so much evolved as provoked by opposite extremes. The license of the Restoration was caused by the prudery of Puritanism, the violence of revolutions corresponded to the degree of misgovernment that brought them about. That is why the balancing hand of the trimmer was so necessary. The whole logic of trimming was averse to the kinds of catastrophic destruction of the old that Carlyle deemed necessary to purify society. For Macaulay the goal was to effect change through a series of accommodations between old and new, action and reaction. For the sake of social stability he was quite willing to tolerate much of the corruption that Carlyle was eager to purge. Compromise, not conversion, was always his desideratum.

Macaulay's attitude toward the individual distanced him farthest from Arnold and Carlyle. To the "cool and philosophical" observer like Macaulay, the human nature that drove all men amounted to little more than enlightened self-interest responding quite predictably to pain and pleasure. Believing that "man . . . is always the same," he also assumed that marked differences between two generations could be explained solely by the differences in "their respective circumstances" (W, 5:217). The mainspring of historical change was for him neither ideals nor heroes, but an externalized "spirit of the age." Macaulay declared unequivocally that the age formed the man, not the man the age. Just as no man should be expected to rise above the morality of his time, neither could he escape its prevailing mental climate. The progress of society in all its forms—political, economic, cultural, and intellectual—operated with a momentum and an inevitability of its own. Changes destined to occur would do so independently of specific men, great or small. He declared that

> without Copernicus we should have been Copernicans,—that without Columbus America would have been discovered,—that without Locke we should have possessed a just theory of the origin of human ideas. Society indeed has its great men and its little men, as the earth has its mountains and its valleys. But the inequalities of intellect, like the inequalities of the surface of our globe, bear so small a proportion to the mass, that, in calculating its great revolutions, they may safely be neglected. (W, 5:85)

There was little room for Carlylean hero-worship in such a fundamentally deterministic view of change, or even for the recognition of original genius. Even in the arts the laws of progress "operate with little less certainty than those which regulate the periodical returns of heat and cold, of fertility and barrenness." The "electric impulse of change" reduced Shakespeare to a shock wave of the Reformation, Wordsworth to a spark of the French Revolution. There was no Carlylean transmutation in this galvanic current, no reciprocity in the social organism. No man could resist "the influence which the vast mass, in which he is but an atom, must exercise on him" (W, 6:353). Those who appeared to lead society "are, in fact, only whirled along before it; those who attempt to resist it, are beaten down and crushed beneath it" (W, 8:73).

Macaulay's complacency with the modern, his celebration of both progress and continuity, and his faith in the "laws" of history all come together in the "Whig view of history" he epitomized. As Herbert Butterfield demonstrated,[17] the Whig view denotes an attitude toward the past as much as a particular political affiliation: the tendency to judge events by the degree to which they led toward the condition of the present. The major drawbacks to this view lay in its tendency to fashion precedents where there were only superficial resemblances and to attribute causality where only sequence existed. Macaulay was aware of how this bias could operate, particularly in England where the appeal to precedent had always played so large a role in political debate. And yet so clear to him were questions of correct and incorrect political action, of improvement and regression, that he could not see when he was himself guilty of judging the past by the present. Like Arnold he did not think that making allowance for the past state of political science and morality precluded "looking at ancient transactions by the light of modern knowledge." It was in fact "among the first duties of a historian to point out the faults of the eminent men of former generations" (W, 6:94). His comments on Halifax in the *History* make clear his most significant criterion for judgment. What distinguished Halifax from other contemporary statesmen was that "through a long public life, and through frequent and violent revolutions of public feeling, he almost invariably took that view of the great questions of his time which history has finally adopted" (W, 4:127). Macaulay might try to re-create in loving detail the circumstances that produced the thoughts and feelings of his ancestors, but finally only those men whose judgments were vindicated by later developments earned the historian's full esteem and sympathy. His praise for James Mill's histories reveals the goals of his own as well:

> We know of no writer who takes so much pleasure in the truly useful, noble, and philosophical employment of tracing the progress of sound opinions from their embryo state to their full maturity. He eagerly culls from old despatches and minutes every expression in which he can dis-

cern the imperfect germ of any truth which has since been fully developed. He never fails to bestow praise on those who, though far from coming up to his standard of perfection, yet rose in a small degree above the common level of their contemporaries. It is thus that the annals of past times ought to be written. It is thus, especially, that the annals of our own country ought to be written. (W, 6:95)

J. W. Burrow illuminates the tensions in traditional Whiggism that Macaulay tried to reconcile.[18] Nineteenth-century Whigs needed to steer between the conservative's "antiquarian" insistence on precedent and the radical's repudiation of it, to balance a reverence for tradition against the practical need to adapt political institutions to changing social and economic reality. Macaulay largely adopted the "Whig compromise," which looked for precedent not in an "ancient constitution" but in the thirteenth-century parliament and which held that the Glorious Revolution reaffirmed norms more ancient than the aberrant Stuart despotism. Lest Tories block further change by viewing 1688 as a new and final precedent, it was also important to make further progress traditional as well. "In the very act of innovating," England had "constantly appealed to ancient prescription," Macaulay argued (W, 5:634); this helped make her revolutions defensive, her reforms preservative. The argument for continuity was still crucial, but this continuity demanded accommodation to social and economic progress as the polity matured. By claiming that "the present constitution of our country is, to the constitution under which she flourished five hundred years ago, what the tree is to the sapling, what the man is to the boy" (W, 1:20), Macaulay could make the trimming and compromise he advocated essential to the "natural" development of the political organism.

Macaulay's interpretation had a peculiar appeal in the early years of the century, marked by the agitation for reform and the fear of revolution. John Clive points out that in the years preceding the first Reform Bill, political positions were often so overlapping and amorphous that history became "an enkindling agent, supplying touchstones and confrontations lacking in the contemporary situation."[19] For Macaulay England's seventeenth-century vindication of both popular representation and ancient tradition provided a paradigm for the change he wished to see in the present. By lifting the civil wars to the level of a "great conflict between . . . liberty and despotism, reason and prejudice," in which "the destinies of the human race were staked on the same cast with the freedom of the English people" (W, 5:23), Macaulay gained additional rhetorical leverage on his audience. He could then capitalize on patriotic pride by stressing the parallels between the nineteenth and the seventeenth centuries:

> It will soon again be necessary to reform that we may preserve, to save the fundamental principles of the Constitution by alterations in the subordinate parts. It will then be possible, as it was possible two hundred years ago, to protect vested rights, to secure every useful institution, every institution endeared by antiquity and noble associations, and, at the same time, to introduce into the system improvements harmonizing with the original plan. It remains to be seen whether two hundred years have made us wiser. (W, 5:237)

In this way what might have been a subversion of ancient authority was transformed into the fulfillment of a noble tradition. What might have represented a threat to stability and prosperity manifested the type of political behavior that, by insuring domestic stability, had been responsible for the march of mind and material progress in the last two hundred years. Macaulay brought the argument full circle after 1832 by claiming that the English had been able to effect a reform amounting to a revolution "by the force of reason, and under the forms of law" because their "moderation and humanity" were themselves "the fruits of a hundred and fifty years of liberty" (W, 5:624-25).

Macaulay's version of the Whig view also allayed fears that England might be pulled into the tides of revolution sweeping the continent in the first half of the century. The threat of revolution, should accommodation through reform fail, was an important argument for change. Macaulay held up the organic continuity of English institutions as proof that England would not go the way of France. This continuity made England quite different "from those polities which have, during the last eighty years, been methodically constructed, digested into articles, and ratified by constituent assemblies" (W, 3:465)—and which, he need not have added, endured bloody revolutions to put those constitutions into force. The strength of the English lay in the fact that they "have seldom looked abroad for models; they have seldom troubled themselves with Utopian theories; they have not been anxious to prove that liberty is the natural right of men; they have been content to regard it as the lawful birthright of Englishmen" (W, 5:634). In short they had been able to depend on history rather than abstract theory to sanction government, and had been able to accommodate change without completely breaking with the past. Completing chapter 10 of the *History* in November 1848, when "all around us the world is convulsed by the agonies of great nations," Macaulay drove his point home: "Now, if ever," he wrote, "we ought to be able to appreciate the whole importance of the stand which was made by our forefathers against the House of Stuart." England remained a center of calm because the English had "never lost what others are wildly and blindly seeking to regain. It is because we had a preserving revolution in the seventeenth century that we have not had a destroying revolution in the nineteenth" (W, 2:397-98).

The Whig tradition, Burrow notes, allowed the English "to cherish the past while denying it binding force."[20] In Macaulay's hands this tradition became a powerful device for mediating between the need for permanence and the inevitability of change in the Victorian period. Macaulay took major credit not only for popularizing this view of government, but for endowing it with a quasi-religious intensity all Englishmen could share. What he could not find in human relationships or public life—a source of permanent value that could still accommodate change—he found in his interpretation of history.

II

If Macaulay bore the impress of Enlightenment thought far more deeply than did Arnold or Carlyle, the ways he redefined the scope and nature of historical writing showed that romantic influences also marked his work. He wanted the historian to reclaim those details appropriated by the novelist in order to illustrate the history of the people as well as the history of government: "to call up our ancestors before us with all their peculiarities of language, manners, and garb, to show us over their houses, to seat us at their tables, to rummage their old fashioned wardrobes, to explain the uses of their ponderous furniture" (W, 5:162). He expressed the same interest in sociological detail that animated Carlyle and the same contempt for the "dignity of history" because it had led earlier historians, "for fear of alluding to the vulgar concerns of private life . . . [to] take no notice of the circumstances which deeply affect the happiness of nations" (L, 2:56). The circumstances that most influenced this happiness, "the changes of manners and morals, the transitions of communities from poverty to wealth, from knowledge to ignorance, from ferocity to humanity," Macaulay defined as "noiseless revolutions" whose "progress is rarely indicated by what historians are pleased to call important events" (W, 5:156). That he intended to rectify such errors in his own *History* he makes clear in its opening pages:

> It will be my endeavour to relate the history of the people as well as the history of the government, to trace the progress of useful and ornamental arts, to describe the rise of religious sects and the changes of literary taste, to portray the manners of successive generations, and not to pass by with neglect even the revolutions which have taken place in dress, furniture, repasts, and public amusements. I shall cheerfully bear the reproach of having descended below the dignity of history, if I can succeed in placing before the English of the nineteenth century a true picture of the life of their ancestors. (W, 1:2-3)

The famous third chapter of the *History* offers the clearest example of how he achieved this end. The survey of everything from agriculture to urban growth, literature to economics, entertains readers with curious detail but also resuscitates for them an otherwise alien past. Interwoven throughout the rest of the work one also finds commentary on everything from the rise of newspaper printing to the ingenious stockjobbing swindles induced by the glut of middle-class wealth (W, 3:612-13; 4:171). Most often his source was the literature—popular more so than belletristic—of the period. In the discussion of stockjobbing, Macaulay refers to the parodies of such swindlers in Shadwell's plays; in another instance, Tom Brown's *Descriptions of a Country Life* (1692), he documents the hardship of the middle classes by noting that "in this year, wine ceased to be put on many hospitable tables where [Brown] had been accustomed to see it, and that its place was supplied by punch" (W, 3:592). Macaulay was scarcely exaggerating when he replied to critics that only someone who had also "soaked his mind with the transitory literature of the day" was capable of judging the accuracy of his portrayals in chapter 3 (LM, 2:162n.).

In addition to supplying and corroborating specific details, literary sources were used by Macaulay as they were by Carlyle and Arnold, to document the values and beliefs of an age or nation. He defended even the most licentious Restoration comedy for "the light it throws on the history, polity, and manners of nations" (W, 6:491). In the spirit of Carlyle's celebration of Boswell, Macaulay pronounced a set of love letters to be worth their weight in state papers for illustrating the mind of the time (W, 6:261). He too advocated a process of "reading oneself into" a period and often spent hours in the British Museum, turning over seventeenth-century pamphlets, tracts, and newspapers; in doing so, he wrote, "The mind is transported back a century and a half, and gets familiar with the ways of thinking, and with the habits, of a past generation" (LM, 2:196).

A random scan of his footnotes suggests further the breadth and diversity of his research: architectural and geographical detail, notes of visits to historical locations, lists of sources collated into one account, extrapolations from population and industrial statistics, notes from foreign sources, ballads, old maps, manuscripts recently published by antiquarian societies, all can be found there and in the text itself. He also pored over manuscripts in the Archives of the House of Lords with a zest only a fellow parliamentarian could share, and underlined their authenticity with references to parchments "embrowned with the dust of a hundred and sixty years" and cancellations and emendations on the original (W, 2:468; 3:626). This journal entry made shortly after the publication of volumes 1 and 2 suggests the amount of research he considered necessary before sitting down to write:

> I have now made up my mind to change my plan about my History. I will first set myself to know the whole subject:—to get, by reading and travelling, a full acquaintance with William's reign. I reckon that it will take me eighteen months to do this. I must visit Holland, Belgium, Scotland, Ireland, France. The Dutch archives and French archives must be ransacked. I will see whether anything is to be got from other diplomatic collections. I must see Londonderry, the Boyne, Aghrim, Limerick, Kinsale, Namur again, Landen, Steinkirk. I must turn over hundreds, thousands, of pamphlets. Lambeth, the Bodleian and the other Oxford Libraries, the Devonshire Papers, the British Museum, must be explored, and notes made: and then I shall go to work.   (LM, 2:157-58)

As did Carlyle he considered field research essential to take in the atmosphere of historical places like Turnham Green (site of the assassination attempt in Chapter 21) and to collect concrete detail that could be found nowhere else (LM, 2:234-35). Trevelyan claimed that "the notes made during his fortnight's tour through the scenes of the Irish war are equal in bulk to a first-class article in the Edinburgh or Quarterly Reviews" (LM, 2:159). On-the-spot research also provided an opportunity to investigate fortifications, to sketch ground plans of city streets, and to interview any "inhabitant who was acquainted with any tradition worth the hearing" (LM, 2:159).

History as Whig Via Media

Macaulay's shrewd and sceptical temperament proved a keen weapon in determining the credibility of his sources, although that shrewdness also proved susceptible to partisan misuse. He was adept at singling out the reliable parts of a given account—St. Germain's *Life of James the Second*, for instance—by distinguishing between sections based on personal memoir and the self-interested revisions of James's son or the later work of an "ignorant compiler" (W, 2:313 n.). In other cases he uses discrepancies in the different accounts of an incident to argue against the credibility of certain sources (e.g., W, 2:413 n.). Although most contemporary critics acknowledged his vast learning, some challenged him on specific points. James Spedding charged with some accuracy that Macaulay willfully ignored published refutations and corrections of his *History*, or at best corrected only errors of detail while leaving substantially inaccurate interpretations standing.[21] More damaging charges were made by John Paget, who showed that Macaulay often overgeneralized from literary sources, applying casual or obviously biased comments to an entire country or group and selectively ignoring contradictory evidence, even in the same source. Paget was the chief defender of Marlborough, one of Macaulay's blackest villains, and he refuted Macaulay's defamation with copious evidence. He also made clear how Macaulay's biases make the same faults—conjugal infidelity, for instance—venial in the good William, detestable in the evil James. Identical virtues were respected in one and condemned in the other, and sources discarded as unreliable when they refuted Macaulay's prejudices were willingly appropriated when they concurred.[22]

In the hands of his most thorough critic, Sir Charles Firth, Macaulay came off reasonably well in accuracy and breadth of documentation, especially considering the limitations of the data available in his time. In his *Commentary on Macaulay's History of England* (1938), Firth gave Macaulay credit for having rested his narrative on a greater mass of evidence than could be claimed by any of his predecessors. He admitted, however, that compared with Ranke's, Macaulay's treatment of his sources was relatively superficial: Macaulay stood completely outside "one of the great achievements of the nineteenth century," the "development of a more scientific method of treating historical evidence." Firth echoed Paget's criticism that Macaulay was less critical with those sources that corroborated him than with those who questioned his interpretations.[23] Macaulay was always too much the rhetorician to be a sober judge. His analysis of data, while possessing the outward trappings of thoroughness, left his fundamental prejudices untouched.

Although it was most often the brilliance of the rhetorician and not the insight of the poet that Macaulay brought to the creative part of the historian's task, he approached his artistic responsibilities with quite as much gravity as Carlyle. He repeatedly stressed the ephemerality of his review essays as works of art, but he sat down to write the *History* with "the year 2,000, even the year 3,000, often in [his] mind" and believed he "sacrificed nothing to temporary fashions of thought and style."[24] At the same time, he frankly sought wide popular success, as his famous claim indicates: "I shall not be satisfied unless I produce something which shall for a few days supersede the last fashionable novel on the tables of young ladies" (LM, 2:52). His desire to reach a wide audience was grounded in intentions no less serious than those of Arnold and Carlyle. Macaulay considered novelistic techniques, in particular the illustration of general conditions with "appropriate images," essential to "branding" practical instruction on the mind. He desired popular success not as an end in itself, but as the sign that he had reached a significant portion of the new and rapidly growing reading public of the mid-nineteenth century. Too few of those "who read for amusement" could be attracted by the gravity of a Mill or the obscurity of a Niebuhr.[25] Macaulay intended to interest and to please those readers "whom ordinary histories repel" (LM, 2:210).

His purposes in gaining the ear of this public were manifold. Macaulay chose his subjects with the express purpose of filling in gaps in his countrymen's knowledge of the success story of their own empire. He likewise hoped the *History* would illuminate a portion of their past that was "even to educated people almost a terra incognita" in the 1840s (LM, 2:52). Apart from the better understanding of human nature or specific arguments for political precedent to be gained from the *History*, Macaulay felt that England deserved an account of her heritage consistent with her modern stature. As we have seen, for him the imaginative value of the past gained force from the imaginative power of the present. Who else could have gone to the Great Exhibition and "felt a glow of eloquence, or something like it" that inspired "some touches which will greatly improve my [account of] Steinkirk" in the *History* (LM, 2:166)? Believing, as did Arnold and Carlyle, that "a people which takes no pride in the noble achievements of remote ancestors will never achieve anything worthy to be remembered with pride by remote descendants" (W, 2:585), Macaulay set out to justify that pride in a way all his contemporaries could appreciate.

His unique style owes much to this concern to make his writing widely accessible. Trevelyan attributed its great clarity to "an honest wish to increase the enjoyment, and smooth the difficulties, of those who did him the honour to buy his books" (LM, 2:169). Indeed, the biography is filled with references to making transitions without distracting the reader, to arranging ideas so as most effectively to illuminate complex relationships, to fashioning passages that "read as if they had been spoken off, and may seem to flow as easily as table talk" (LM, 2:182, 211, 213). According to his nephew, "He thought little of recasting a chapter in order to obtain a more lucid arrangement, and nothing whatever of reconstructing a paragraph for the sake of one happy stroke or apt illustration" (LM, 2:165). However, this preoccupation with ease and effect had its drawbacks: too often ideas were tailored to fit the demands of style, rather than vice versa. His was a prose that asserted rather than persuaded, that tried to convince with the sheer weight of accumulated effects—highly patterned word pairs and repetitions, periodic phrasing, biblical and poetic cadences, assonance, alliteration—rather than the careful working out of a complex argument.[26] His recurrent patterns of allusion, point, and antithesis provided an influential model for "high popularisation" later in the century, but its very adaptability to the prose of "opinion, information" and "political persuasion" blunted his style's effectiveness in dealing with any subject requiring subtler and more evenhanded consideration.[27] Macaulay's stylistic trademark, the balanced antithesis ("It is because we had freedom in the midst of servitude that we have order in the midst of anarchy" W, 2:398), inevitably encouraged pat formulas rather than fine distinctions. His much vaunted clarity was the appropriate counterpart of his "unquestioned faith in the obviousness of truth" and of his impatience with all that was not accessible to reason, logic, and common sense.[28]

The larger narrative structure of his major work is shaped by a similar concern for entertaining and instructing and by similar limitations in perspective and insight. For all its "propulsive" drive forward, there is a peculiarly static quality to the *History*.[29] Macaulay effectively renounces the tension of suspense in the majestic opening paragraphs: we read on, safe in the knowledge that this historical romance will have the archetypal happy ending. Once he has established the essential pattern of obstacles overcome, contraries reconciled, crimes punished and virtues rewarded, it remains for us simply to sit back and enjoy the way he can dramatize and particularize the story. Macaulay clearly wanted to control this narrative as completely as he did his private historical "romances," and he knew that for all its excesses, melodrama had safer limits than genuine drama. Suggesting alternative outcomes to specific events as he periodically does only heightens "the reader's sense of the fatality of events which have actually occurred," in William Madden's words; we have the sense of watching characters "enact their appointed destinies" rather than exercising free will.[30] The dynamic of the narrative is controlled by the same pull of opposites that renders his phrasal antitheses so brittle. J. W. Burrow maps the *History* as "the agony of the constitution followed by deliverance and partial renewal."[31] The same general pattern is duplicated in intermediate cycles of factiousness and reconciliation that advance the action. The outcome is perhaps no less inevitable than in Carlyle's histories; for both men *the* archetypal need in human history was for order to master disorder. But where Carlyle knew the daemonic had to take its course, Macaulay constantly tried to control it. He polarizes the dynamic of experience where Carlyle celebrates its multiformity. With Macaulay we feel the limits, not the potentiality, of the possible. Conflict and tension may arise, but Macaulay manages them in a predictable way: opposing extremes are reconciled in compromise, basic laws of political science and human nature are vindicated, justice—be it divine or secular—is satisfied. The overall arrangement of the *History* indulges the imagination, while never leaving any doubt that the "laws of reason and experience" will be confirmed.

Macaulay's management of detail also reflects his characteristic intellectual biases. His passion for concrete examples (the exact facts and dates that were crucial to his historical "romances") sharpened his eye for telling detail and made his use of it in the *History* particularly effective. Never content with a generalization, he always strove to gather together a representative sampling of concrete examples to make it explicit. He drives home the "barbarism" of the northern shires in 1685 with the ferocious bloodhounds, the fortified farmhouses, the stones and boiling water ready to meet the plunderer (W, 1:223-24), and makes palpable the economic chaos caused by James's issuance of base money in "a mortgage for a thousand pounds . . . cleared off by a bag of counters made out of old kettles" (W, 2:566). Detail could also imply moral judgments. Macaulay accomplishes two ends by bringing before us the fine paintings, Japanese cabinets, and Parisian tapestries that filled the apartments of the Duchess of Portsmouth. He makes vividly particular Charles's extravagant indulgence of his favorite, while tacitly commenting on the vanity of human wishes when she collapses in grief over his death "in the midst of this splendour" (W, 1:337).

This elaboration of detail was clearly in keeping with Macaulay's dislike of abstractions and his tendency to define by examples rather than by analysis. It also widened the appeal and accessibility of the past by demonstrating the impact of major events on a quotidian reality recognizable to every reader. Macaulay's motivation, however, is less George Eliot's commitment to "the faithful representing of commonplace things" than the desire to reinforce his own claim that the welfare of the state was based on the well-being of individuals. To allow his readers to "enter into the feelings" of British exultation when the French fleet was routed at La Hogue, Macaulay attributes them not just to national pride, but to a sense of relief that he renders tangible: "The island was safe. The pleasant pastures, cornfields and commons of Hampshire and Surrey would not be the seat of war. The houses and gardens, the kitchens and dairies, the cellars and plate chests, the wives and daughters of our gentry and clergy would not be at the mercy of the Irish Rapparees . . . or of French dragoons" (W, 3:552). In a similar vein, to show how little misgovernment affected the common people, he summons up a crowd of tactile, sensuous images: "Whether Whigs or Tories, Protestants or Jesuits were uppermost, the grazier drove his beasts to market: the grocer weighed out his currants: . . . the harvest home was celebrated as joyously as ever in the hamlets: the cream overflowed the pails of Cheshire: the apple juice foamed in the presses of Herefordshire" (W, 4:189). The examples are so appealing that it is easy to overlook the materialistic assumptions that inspire them: that economic well-being and physical security are the measure of all things.

Analogous biases characterize his treatment of place, notwithstanding Macaulay's fascination with historical sites. He manipulates detail not just to re-create scenes, but to exact judgment. His sketch of Covent Garden in the seventeenth century gains impact from well-placed specifics, but also from the proximity of high to low: "Fruit women screamed, carters fought, cabbage stalks and rotten apples accumulated in heaps at the thresholds of the Countess of Berkshire and of the Bishop of Durham." The disorder that was in itself a sign of social backwardness is summed up in the haranguing mountebanks and dancing bears who congregated each night within yards of Winchester House (W, 1:280). Usually comparisons between past and present are much more explicit. Macaulay's attempts to reinforce the differentness of the past almost always end by congratulating the materially better present:

> We should greatly err if we imagined that the road by which [James II] entered that city bore any resemblance to the stately approach which strikes the traveller of the nineteenth century with admiration. At present Cork . . . holds no mean place among the ports of the empire. The shipping is more than half what the shipping of London was at the time of the Revolution. The customs exceed the whole revenue which the whole kingdom of Ireland, in the most peaceful and prosperous times, yielded to the Stuarts. The town is adorned by broad and well built streets. . . . In 1689, the city extended over about one tenth part of the space it now covers . . . a desolate marsh . . . covered the areas now occupied by stately buildings. . . . There was only a single street in which two wheeled carriages could pass each other. (W, 2:531-32)

The "gigmanity" Carlyle scorned becomes Macaulay's measure of success: the Manchester without a single coach in 1688 supported twenty coachmakers in 1841; the Leeds of seven thousand souls now numbered its people one hundred fifty thousand (W, 1:267). The "facts" speak for themselves. Macaulay's "stereoscopic" vision propelled readers toward the present rather than engaging them more fully in the past. When Carlyle looks around Samson's Bury St. Edmonds, he sees water not yet polluted by the dyer's chemistry, land not yet possessed by the Steam Demon. He mourns Time as both a bearer and a devourer. Macaulay faces resolutely forward. He senses the factories, the gins, the market emporium not yet there as a loss, a disorienting absence (W, 1:266-67).

Macaulay lacked any romantic sensitivity to landscape that might have provided other dimensions to place. He could wax eloquent about the pastoral idyll of modern Killiecrankie, where fine summer days find the "angler casting his fly on the foam of the river . . . or some party of pleasure banqueting on the turf in the fretwork of shade and sunshine." His object, however, is only to heighten the barbarity of the ravine in William's day, when the river suggested to "our ancestors thoughts of murderous ambuscades, and of bodies stripped, gashed, and abandoned to the birds of prey" (W, 3:82-83). He dryly comments that modern ecstasies over the Highlands' sublimity were made possible only by civilization's advance: "A traveler must be freed from all apprehension of being murdered or starved before he can be charmed by the bold outlines and rich tints of the hills" (W, 3:42). But his limitations go beyond this. Even in his cityscapes we are allowed to indulge in quaint and picturesque detail only so that we feel the presentness of the modern day more fully. Macaulay lacked what Burrow calls "a kind of imaginative archaeology, a sense of man's shaping and penetration of the landscape through many generations."[32] This sense allowed Carlyle to see the past as both containing and nourishing the present. Macaulay did not deny the heritage of the past, but he did impoverish its complexity. In all other realms but the political, the uncouth oddity of former societies was indulged only because it was outgrown, and in that sense, denied. Macaulay condescended where Carlyle revered; to him the facts argued not for the continuing reality of habit but for its outdatedness.

The same kind of condescension diminishes his success in re-creating the mind of the past. Macaulay defends popular literature and lore as worthy evidence notwithstanding the "large mixture of fable" found in such materials. Whether true or false, such tales "were heard by our ancestors with eagerness and faith," and thus furnished important insights into the mind of the past (W, 1:300). Too often, however, psychological insight gives way to celebrations of the march of mind. To Macaulay the rumors that circulated at Charles's death furnish

> a measure of the intelligence and virtue of the generation which eagerly devoured them. That no rumour of the same kind has ever, in the present age, found credit among us, even when lives on which great interests depended have been terminated by unforeseen attacks of disease, is to be attributed partly to the progress of medical and chemical science, but partly also, it may be hoped, to the progress which the nation has made in good sense, justice, and humanity. (W, 1:345)

Macaulay is always too busy propagandizing to sympathize. As George Levine points out, he includes the superstitions of the vulgar because they indulged the reader's taste for the exotic, the fantastic, the fictional, while not transgressing the dictates of reason maintained by the "mature" mind.[33] He could exploit their affective potential as evidence of a more primitive form of consciousness without losing the modern perspective.

He uses representative social types in similar ways. Purporting to demonstrate that no natural inferiority existed between Celt and

Thomas Babington Macaulay

Saxon, Macaulay exploits the apparent inferiority and simultaneously celebrates the virtues of modern civilization. He first titillates his audience with all the lurid detail of Highland savagery—huts swarming with vermin, men smeared with tar, meals of grain and dried blood. But he redeems himself from mere sensationalism by pointing out that "an enlightened and dispassionate observer" would even then have predicted that the civilizing influence of Protestantism, English, and a good police force would make the clans the Saxons' equal (W, 3:46-48). The uncouth country squire of chapter 3 is a similar exaggeration intended to congratulate contemporaries on one hundred and fifty years of social progress.

Macaulay's condescension to the uncouth and the irrational, combined with his mechanistic conception of human nature and his subordination of the man to his age, limit severely his powers of characterization. Just as major events unfold in a preestablished pattern, individual actions conform to an essentially static conception of character. Jane Millgate identifies this approach with that of the seventeenth-century genre of Character. The individual is perceived as a "whole rather than as something developing in time; qualities and actions are treated of in essence rather than in sequence; works and opinions are invoked as illustrations in the service of a static judgment and not as the motive power by which a dramatic presentation is moved forward."[34] Since major changes in consciousness or government come about of their own accord, Macaulay's characters need only typify the spirit of the age. For this purpose individual complexities merely get in the way: stereotypes throw the real forces of change into higher relief. Hence, those portraits that round out the sociological contours of his narrative are marked by the distortion of caricature rather than the faithfulness of miniatures. Even his major characters are too externalized: we know William's "bitter and cynical smile" (W, 2:222), and the meager, wrinkled face that betrayed Danby's ambition (W, 2:194), but the internal man eludes us. No wonder Carlyle found Macaulay's characters "a series of empty *clockcases*."[35]

Macaulay's characterizations are flattened by the paradoxical linking of opposing qualities. This was more than a stylistic tic, although obviously his balanced antitheses made such contrasts irresistible: "The Puritan was made up of two different men, the one all self-abasement, penitence, gratitude, passion, the other proud, calm, inflexible, sagacious. He prostrated himself in the dust before his Maker: but he set his foot on the neck of his king" (W, 5:38-39). He might deplore the two equally distorted views of the Highlander, one a "coarse caricature" by scornful Cavaliers, the other a "masterpiece of flattery" by romanticizing moderns (W, 3:52). But his own portraits thrived on the same kind of contrasts. The Highlanders combined sordid barbarity with admirable valor. The country gentleman "spoke with the accent of a carter," but "was ready to risk his life rather than see a stain cast on the honour of his house" (W, 1:252). Even major characters are inconsistent rather than complex. His James I is "two men, a witty well-read scholar, who wrote, disputed, and harangued, and a nervous, drivelling idiot, who acted" (W, 6:167).

Macaulay has no real patience with, or insight into, psychological complexity. Leslie Stephen was among the first to note his resulting tendency to reduce individuals to "bundles of contradictions" rather than trying (as Carlyle would have) to find some underlying organic unity that would integrate disparate personality traits.[36] He has no appreciation for a devotion to ideals that could unify character or transcend self-interest. He shares none of Arnold's trust in the purifying power of heroism, none of Carlyle's belief in the ways faith transforms the man. The spiritual ideals that draw Carlyle to the seventeenth century are to Macaulay merely fanaticism: a manifestation of mental imbalance dangerous to the state.

The realist novelist, the Eliot or the Trollope, might similarly deflate the pretensions and posturing of romantic heroism by exposing the all-too-human foibles of their protagonists. But their purpose is to deepen our sympathy by confronting us with evidence of a shared fallibility. Macaulay wishes us to assume the superiority of that "cool and philosophical observer" who frankly acknowledges the absurd inconsistencies of human nature. He had found himself all too vulnerable to betrayed ideals and contradictions between emotion and reason. His way of controlling these is to adopt an attitude of complete cynicism. He criticizes the tendency of earlier historians to make individuals overly consistent personifications of good or bad because he claims that no such purity of motive or character could survive the assault of circumstance or betrayal by one's passions. After all, had not everyone seen "a hero in the gout, a democrat in the church, a pedant in love, or a philosopher in liquor" (W, 7:685)? He professes only scorn for those who would think otherwise: "as if history were not made up of the bad actions of extraordinary men . . . as if nine-tenths of the calamities which have befallen the human race had any other origin than the union of high intelligence with low desires" (W, 6:175). It is because Macaulay knows that "the line of demarcation between good and bad men is so faintly marked as often to elude the most careful investigation," and not because he appreciates the ambiguities of human personality, that he sees character as black *and* white, but without shades of grey (W, 7:685). To expect consistency from individuals is as unreasonable as to expect prediction from "abstract" theory: the laws of experience prove that in personality as in political action, all is just rough give-and-take between extremes.

His theory of *Zeitgeist* and his far-reaching cynicism make it difficult to talk of heroes in his work. William and James dominate the *History*, but as embodiments of political vice and virtue moving toward inevitable rewards and punishments, not as men. In keeping with the Whig view, those men who supported the triumphant cause were by definition heroic in the broader scope of history. The *Essays* suggest that "the great body of the middle class" would have become in a sense the collective hero of the *History*. They shared leadership in the march of progress that summed up his vision of English history: "The higher and middling orders are the natural representatives of the human race. Their interest may be opposed in some things to that of their poorer contemporaries, but it is identical with that of the innumerable generations which are to follow" (W, 5:265). Cromwell succeeded not because of his Puritan zeal, but because "no sovereign ever carried to the throne so large a portion of the best qualities of the middling orders" as he did (W, 5:214). Chief among these qualities is the instinct for order and self-control so important to Macaulay personally. Burrow characterizes Macaulay's Hastings and Clive as other middle-class conquerors whose manly energies mold an effeminate, decadent east into empire. The bourgeois respectability of Macaulay's own day depended upon the same concern for manliness and order; such respectability connoted not manners alone, but opposition to the revolutionary "state of nature" that for Burrow represents Macaulay's deepest fears for society: the unleashing of lawless ambition, the riot of fanatical delusions, "the negligence or hatred of all boundaries to will, passion and appetite." The "middling orders" continued to offer the clearest examples of the traits Macaulay had historically associated with the Whig balance between absolutism and radicalism: rational control of feeling, openness, accountability, decorum, propriety.[37] Seen in this light, the *Essays* and the *History* become attempts to provide the Victorian middle classes with a history of their own rise to power over the preceding two centuries—the process by which they shed the backward ways of the seventeenth century and aligned themselves with values and behavior that insured the triumphs of constitutional and social order in the present.

The very desire for control and clarity that stunted Macaulay's rendering of character made him a highly effective narrator. He rivaled the latest novel by borrowing many of its techniques. If his narrative "I" is less obtrusive than Eliot's or Trollope's, its coercing presence is felt throughout. It summarizes Macaulay's didactic intentions at the outset and allies the reader with it in the "we" whose proper reactions—pride, shame, awe—it is constantly prescribing. Macaulay carefully controlled the pace of dramatization, narrative, and transition for maximum effect. He alternates chapters of exposition with those of action and intensifies the sense of endings by closing chapters and volumes with climactic events: the fall of the Hydes, the flight of James, the proclamation of William and Mary. By his own admission he embellished his account with "grand purple patches" (LM, 2:204) that catered to his audience's taste for high drama and memorable tableaux. Like Carlyle, he emphasized peaks in the action—Charles on his deathbed ("And do not let poor Nelly starve"), Jeffries on the Bloody Circuit ("Show me a Presbyterian, and I'll show thee a lying knave")—by rendering his sources in direct address.[38]

Although Macaulay lacked Carlyle's profound capacity for empathy, he found ample opportunities for identification, particularly in political debate. From a wide range of debates and documents concerning James's deposition, he constructs speeches that he puts into the mouths of the statesmen of the day: "If, these politicians said, we once admit that the throne is vacant, we admit that it is elective" (W, 2:375). As he proceeds tags like "so the politicians said" recede into the background and Macaulay seems to place himself among the "we" he paraphrases (see also W, 2:310). Shifts into the present tense and first person work in similar ways to pull the reader into the train of events leading up to the Popish plot:

> The reigning King seemed far more inclined to show favour to [the Catholics] than to the Presbyterians. . . . The Catholics had begun to talk a bolder language than formerly. . . . At this juncture, it is rumoured that a Popish plot is discovered. A distinguished Catholic is arrested on suspicion. It appears that he has destroyed almost all his papers. A few letters, however, have escaped the flames. (W, 6:107)

Thomas Babington Macaulay

And yet, where Carlyle's use of the present tense helps to dissolve the artifice of linear narrative, Macaulay's always reminds us of the showman behind the scenes. Those paraphrased speeches are too contrivedly Macaulayean in their balance and tension. He may rightly claim to restore the voice of "a whole literature which is mouldering in old libraries" when he reconstructs Tory or Whig positions, but the tonal ironies are distinctly his own: "The sycophants, who were legally punishable, enjoyed impunity. The King, who was not legally punishable, was punished with merciless severity" (W, 2:405-7). Macaulay's art is finally an ingenious ventriloquism, not Carlyle's transforming magic.

Still, as a showman, his histrionic talents were considerable. As we would expect from one who tended naturally to frame even his own experiences as historical set pieces,[39] he remains keenly attuned to the literary potential of events that, like the trial of the Bishops, retained "all the interest of a drama" even when "coolly perused after the lapse of more than a century and a half" (W, 2:171). He carefully orchestrates this event to join high drama with human interest, historical immediacy with historical perspective. After assembling the cast of characters—the prosecution and defense teams—he reconstructs the legal maneuvering with a barrister's eye. Arguments over technicalities are ticked off and dispensed with one by one, with the pivotal exchanges rendered in dialogue. All seems in order. The bishops are on the point of being acquitted when the importunity of one of their own counsel delays the proceedings just long enough to bring the Lord President with damning evidence against them. Macaulay quotes from contemporary letters to authenticate the "intense anxiety" that prevails that night as the jury deliberates. Although voices "high in altercation" are heard within the jury room, "nothing certain was known" until, in the "breathless stillness" of the courtroom the next morning, the verdict of "Not Guilty" is delivered (W, 2:177).

The action ranges from the most personal to the most symbolic. We have human interest. One of the jurymen, the King's brewer, comes alive again in his bitter complaints: "If I say Not Guilty, I shall brew no more for the King; and if I say Guilty, I shall brew no more for anybody else" (W, 2:171). We learn that Thomas Austin's stout resistance ("I will stay till I am no bigger than a tobacco pipe" W, 2:177) personally faced down the last hold-out for a guilty verdict. We have melodrama. As his people and his troops celebrate his defeat, James, the villain of the piece, slinks away with an ominous, "So much the worse for them" (W, 2:179). We have epic scale. By tracing the crowd's reactions to the verdict, Macaulay enlarges the stage on which the drama is acted and underscores its status as a national event. He follows the shouts of triumph as they echo from the benches and galleries, to the great hall, to the throng outside, to the boats covering the Thames, until it seems that all London reacts with one voice. We get sensational detail in the guise of historical curiosity. Surveying the "spectacles" that drew the "common people" that night provides him a characteristic way of informing and entertaining at the same time. While tacitly deploring the "grotesque rites" involved in burning effigies of the Pope, Macaulay takes this opportunity to refresh his readers on the more colorful aspects of this "once familiar pageant" (W, 2:181). And we get a moral. The account ends as do most of his set pieces, with an elongation of historical perspective. This event stands alone in English history as the one time when love of Church and love of Freedom were in harmony. Macaulay is thus able to close with another variation on that favored pattern of reconciled opposites, as Tories and Whigs, Dissenters and Churchmen, join symbolically in the "vast phalanx" against the government.

Although wars of ideas interest him more than wars of arms, Macaulay as fully exploits the dramatic interest of his battle pieces. He increases their immediacy with conventional techniques—quoted battle cries, details of weather, references to terrain he has himself visited. He paces and orders action for maximum effect, duplicating the mounting tension at crucial junctures in terse, declarative sentences, or rapidly shifting from one part of the fighting to another. Military life includes elements of pure spectacle he finds irresistible. Under the pretext of the recording sights "well fitted to gratify the vulgar appetite for the marvelous" in William's entry into Exeter, he converts the procession into a brilliant mummery. Clearly he expected the exotic Africans in turbans and feathers and the Swedish horsemen in black armor and fur to dazzle his own audience as much as they did the simple throng at Exeter (W, 2:258). The story of the old woman who dodges through the drawn swords and curvetting horses to touch the hand of the deliverer is another concession to the anecdotal, although it also affords him an opportunity to drive home the historical significance of the moment: perhaps, he speculates, she is a zealous Puritan who had waited twenty-eight years for this deliverance, or perhaps she had lost a son to Sedgemoor or the Bloody Circuit. Here as elsewhere the roll call of famous warriors in William's train provides an opportunity to commemorate their other famous exploits. The immediacy of such scenes is thus enriched with the deeper resonance of a noble tradition.

Like other historians of his era, Macaulay surveyed warfare with a civilian's eye. Technical maneuvers recede in favor of details that enliven and humanize the scene. What we remember about Steinkirk is less the fighting than the carefully disordered neckerchiefs that took their name from it—a reference to the "glittering . . . lace and embroidery hastily thrown on and half fastened" by the French princes roused from "their couches or their revels" to head their army (W, 3:581). A man's tactics are less important than his mettle; each account includes closeups on selected heroes and cowards (e.g., W, 3:295-96). William is always at his best in battle: "Danger acted on him like wine, opened his heart, loosened his tongue, and took away all appearance of constraint from his manner" (W, 3:296). He inspires the Eniskilleners with touching gratitude at the Boyne. The light of memory softens his features still further at Landen: "Many years later grey-headed old pensioners who crept about the arcades and alleys of Chelsea Hospital used to relate how he charged at the head of Galway's horse, how he dismounted four times to put heart into the infantry, how he rallied one corps which seemed to be shrinking: 'That is not the way to fight, gentlemen. You must stand up close to them. Thus, gentlemen, thus' " (W, 4:23). These eye witness accounts convey William's personality and suggest the human element in military experience far more convincingly than a technical account could have.

Macaulay pulls out all the stops to bring the first half of the *History* to a rousing close with the siege of Londonderry. He first intensifies the desperation of the besieged inhabitants with grisly detail. As famine spreads, dogs "battened on the blood of the slain" become luxuries and rats are eagerly hunted and greedily devoured (W, 2:579-80). Although even in their extremity the general cry remains "no surrender," there are not wanting voices that murmur, "First the horses and the hides; and then the prisoners; and then each other."[40] Having brought the people to the verge of atrocity, Macaulay steps back to reveal relief finally at hand. English ships attack the boom that blockades the river. The action seesaws back and forth in spare, paralleled exchanges:

> The huge barricade cracked and gave way: but the shock was such that the Mountjoy rebounded, and stuck in the mud. A yell of triumph rose from the banks: The Irish rushed to their boats, and were preparing to board: but the Dartmouth poured on them a well directed broadside which threw them into disorder. . . . The Mountjoy began to move, and soon passed safe through the broken stakes and floating spars. But her brave master was no more. (W, 2:582)

The use of detail here makes the people's relief no less palpable than their desperation. To replace the dogs and rats come "great cheeses, casks of beef . . . kegs of butter . . . ankers of brandy." "It is easy" for the historian "to imagine with what tears grace was said" by men who the preceding night had dined on tallow and salted hides (W, 2:582).

Such human drama prevails throughout. Its "peculiar interest" lies not in the military maneuvers, which would have "moved the great warriors of the Continent to laughter," but to the fact that it was a contest "not between engineers, but between nations; and the victory remained with the nation which, though inferior in numbers, was superior in civilisation, in capacity for selfgovernment, and in stubbornness of resolution" (W, 2:583). The reality of this account gains amplitude from Macaulay's visits to the site. We can easily imagine him reliving the siege as he roamed Londonderry in search of landmarks that anchored his personal "romance" at the time and certified the authenticity of the scene in the *History*. He has talked to people who tasted the fruit of the pear tree by which Lunday escaped (W, 2:547); he knows that gardeners still find skulls and thighbones beneath the flowers in what was once the besiegers' burial ground (W, 2:555).[41] At the end of the piece, we walk the walls and streets of the city with him, reverencing the relics found there and calling to mind the annual commemoration of the siege. Although deploring the racial animosities such ceremonies keep alive, Macaulay considers this respect for the past fundamental to national greatness. The *History* itself, of course, is dedicated to the same consecration of memory.

Macaulay's brilliant management of detail and action is rightly acclaimed. In the final analysis, however, there is something oddly distancing about his style, for all the vivid life in the panorama, for all the force of the argument. Macaulay's richly quantitative imagination ends by constricting rather than by expanding the multidimensionality of the past. For Carlyle detail symbolizes the whole. For Macaulay detail sums it up. The weight of detail is always pressing toward judgments that too much imaginative sympathy might subvert. Macaulay's desire to control experience works against the surrender that such sympathy demands; his commitment to empiricism impoverishes other dimensions of reality. The surface of the action is so highly polished that the reader must remain an observer. As theater it is incomparable, as argument overbearing. Yet even Macaulay's contemporaries left it without that deeper emotional assent that genuine imaginative participation brings.[42]

The rise and fall of Macaulay's stock as an historian is no less representative of Victorian tastes than the man himself. Opinion was always divided about the vices and virtues of his style. Early reviewers like Thackeray, Bagehot, and William Greg agreed in admiring Macaulay's brand of "intellectual entertainment," his ability to combine "conscientious and minute research" with a style as "irresistible as the most absorbing novel."[43] The perils of that style were nonetheless clear: it oversimplified issues and turned analysis into polemic. Archibald Alison and Margaret Oliphant were particularly apprehensive about the way "the power of the rhetorician" overpowered the "reflection of the sage" in his pages.[44]

At the same time, there was striking agreement with the essence of Macaulay's interpretation of British history. James Moncrieff claimed the *History* as a "great national work" that had for the first time illustrated the true nature of the Constitution. David Brewster wished that an abridged version might be prepared as "the safest expositor of our civil and religious liberties" for the schools. Despite Mrs. Oliphant's qualms about Macaulay's exaggerations, she too rejoiced that "a story so brilliant, lifelike, and vivid, a chronicle so dignified and able, should mirror forth to the public of England the beginning of the modern era of national history—the groundwork and foundation of the liberties and blessings of our own time." Even John Croker, long Macaulay's political and literary adversary, declined to dispute the *History*'s account of "the progress of the constitution." His very dismissal of this interpretation as commonplace shows how widely shared was the Whig view.[45] The chorus of praise for Macaulay's celebration of English history predictably reached a crescendo at his death in 1859. One expects to find the *Edinburgh* reviewers applauding his expansion of Whig principles until "they embraced the noblest destinies of man." It is more surprising, particularly considering the *Saturday*'s stern standards for historical writing, to find J. F. Stephen in qualified agreement. Whatever the limitations in Whig principles of continuity and precedent, Stephen wrote, "It is an unquestionable truth that their assertion has been closely allied, not only with a course of national greatness and prosperity unequalled in human history, but also with a spirit of reverence and affection for the past which in other countries has hardly ever been separated from a love for despotism and bigotry."[46]

By 1876 when the *Life and Letters* was reviewed, attitudes toward historical writing were changing, and a second generation of Victorians was ready to condemn as Philistine what their fathers had praised as art. Macaulay's very representativeness proved his limitations. Froude identified "the key to his extraordinary popularity" as the fact that "what his own age said and felt, whether it was wise or foolish, Macaulay said and felt." John Morley and Leslie Stephen dealt the most telling blows. For Morley it was "Macaulay's substantially commonplace" ideas that made him so "universally popular" with the new generation of middle class readers: "His Essays were as good as a library: they made an incomparable manual and vade-mecum for a busy uneducated man, who has curiosity and enlightenment enough to wish to know a little about the great lives and great thoughts, the shining words and many-coloured complexities of action, that have marked the journey of man through the ages." Macaulay succeeded by his unparalleled skill in offering "incense" to the popular idols of patriotism and freedom; his "unanalytical turn of mind kept him free of any temptation to think of love of country as a prejudice, or a passion for freedom as an illusion." Stephen broadened these criticisms by linking Macaulay's "contempt of the higher intellectual interests" to the pervasive Whiggism and Philistinism of the middle classes. He found in Macaulay no genuine "experiential philosophy," only common sense and a "crude empiricism." Nevertheless, like Morley, Stephen could not deny that the successes of his age were due largely to those "deep-seated tendencies of the national character" that Macaulay epitomized. He might deplore the narrowness of Macaulay's patriotism, but he admitted that "it implies faith in the really good qualities, the manliness, the spirit of justice, and the strong moral sense of his countrymen." Macaulay's "manliness," that Victorian code word for rectitude, common sense, blunt straightforwardness, and transparent honesty, found admirers among many of Macaulay's critics in an age increasingly given over to aestheticism, doubt, and compromise.[47]

With increasing frequency Macaulay was also held up as a prime example of those offenses to which "literary" historians were particularly prone. Morley found his "habitual recourse to strenuous superlatives . . . fundamentally unscientific and untrue." Oliphant chided audiences taken in by his style: "To see Macaulay followed by Froude should have been a sharp lesson to such lovers of the picturesque." Cotter Morison blamed Macaulay's indifference to "the most important reform in historical studies ever made," the application of "a critical method to the study of the past," on the fact that he "cared for little beside his own success as an historical artist." Like Morison, Stephen felt that Macaulay's "unscientific" approach obscured the true "causes and nature of great social movements."[48]

But Macaulay found defenders, too. Far from finding impartiality necessary, the *Eclectic* reviewer considered it the historian's duty to judge characters and events from a clear position—"the more liberal and expansive indeed the better." In view of her earlier criticism, it is noteworthy that by 1892 Mrs. Oliphant was recommending Macaulay as a healthy antidote for the latest casualty of professionalized history, the "lecture-dried student, whose interest in history only tends to the answering of questions at an examination, or . . . to endowing posterity with a set of cut and dried annals."[49] Several critics had begun to defend the differences between Macaulay's kind of popular history, which brought "the matured results of scholars to the man in the street in a form that he can remember and enjoy," and that scientific scholarship which was by definition more restrained in style and more restricted in appeal.[50] Others renewed claims that his services to British patriotism more than compensated for his scholarly failings.[51] As late as the 1920s, the *History* was still being recommended as "one of the best instruments we possess for beginning the education of future citizens."[52] Macaulay was finally so representative as to become a national institution despite his limitations.

But those limitations remain. Despite the breadth of his experiences in the world—far wider than those of Carlyle and Arnold—Macaulay never overcame the limits of his singularly "inexperiencing nature," as Bagehot called it.[53] He was essentially the same man at 59 that he had been at 20; if the circumstances of his own life had not penetrated his biases, there was little reason to expect the circumstances of the past to do so. His imaginative impartiality was not matched by a similar impartiality of sympathy. He could depict the past in vivid detail but was incapable of reaching beyond its surface realities. For him human nature was too uniform, self-interest too much stronger than principles, to allow any reality beneath the surface. The style was indeed the man: it was capable of great clarity and force, but little subtlety or insight. It conveyed vigor without passion, light without heat. His ability to produce clear contours from masses of evidence, to assert narrative control over vast quantities of information, amounted to a kind of genius, but was achieved at the cost of an oversimplification which to many minds denied the highest purposes of historical writing.

Herein lie his greatest differences from Carlyle. Gladstone noted that despite their radical political and philosophical differences they were both honest if highly partisan, more powerful in expression than in thought. But there was nothing in Macaulay to correspond to the spiritual dimension Carlyle created in history.[54] To be sure, some contemporaries angered by Carlyle's denigration of the present or bewildered by his "riot of the imagination" valued Macaulay for being pedestrian.[55] But Stephen knew that to gain "clearness and definition Macaulay has dropped the element of mystery" in human life. He could make the past come alive, but he lacked the ability "to emancipate us from the tyranny of the present . . . to raise us to a point at which we feel that we too are almost as dreamlike as the men of old time."[56] Even in an increasingly secularized age, there remained a longing for some kind of transcendence that Macaulay's historical writings could not fulfill.

And yet, despite Macaulay's emotional and imaginative limitations, it is incorrect to say that his mind issued "straight from the eighteenth century, completely untouched by the Romantic movement."[57] It is true that his dominant traits were Augustan. His cynical and mechanistic view of human nature, his materialistic and rationalistic conception of progress, his complacency with the present, precluded the empathy that could grasp the spirit as well as the substance of the past, or could appreciate its passions as well as its appearances. His "science" stressed classification and prediction, not discovery and induction. His foregone conclusions about the inevitability of progress and the dominance of self-interest and inconsistency in human nature were as tyrannical as any of the "abstract theories" for which he had so much scorn. They precluded an objective view of the past, they blunted an appreciation of the fact for its own sake, just as much as Arnold's and Carlyle's quite different moral assumptions. Still, Macaulay was undeniably touched by the romantic spirit of his age. His avid interest in evidence of popular culture, his desire to

Thomas Babington Macaulay

broaden the sociological dimensions of history, his fascination for time traveling, his vivid particularity in re-creating the past, his ability to make his readers spectators, if not participants, in historical moments, all register the influence of romantic historiography on his work. If romantic thought had relatively little impact on his metaphysical assumptions, it still opened up to his readers a new and immensely influential relationship with the past.

I would argue that his amalgamation of eighteenth- and nineteenth-century historiography was more representative of the transitional state of many Victorian minds than was Carlyle's transcendental union of the two. Macaulay offered his contemporaries all the romantic strangeness of the past while reassuring them that they still lived in a world accessible to reason and common sense. Just as his own work as an historian provided a psychic retreat from the risks and disorder of real life, so too his historical writings offered his readers an emotionally satisfying portrait of their past without challenging their beliefs or disturbing their prejudices. The Whig view of continuity reconciled progress with permanence and reassured his contemporaries that, far from sacrificing tradition to progress, their present achievements represented the vindication of the most vital principles of their national identity. By substituting the ideals of political and intellectual liberty for more conventional religious or chivalric ones,[58] he provided a secularized source of value that retained its usefulness even as traditional orthodoxies began to crumble. If he did not attain the vision of the Victorian sage, neither did he incur its dangers. Discipleship to Macaulay never meant risking the security of belief for a leap of faith one might not be able to complete. Although his conventionality might be a limitation in the eyes of posterity, it constituted his chief value for many contemporaries. If he led his readers into new territory, it was not a wilderness of vaporous or exploded ideals, but a past as familiar as the present, because he reconstructed it in the same image. From its dim reaches emerged the familiar contours of national character and political structure so dear to the present. His genealogy of bourgeois liberalism gave the Victorian middle classes a stabilizing sense of identity while lending all the authority of history to continued development in the future.

Macaulay was the greatest of the nineteenth-century popularizers. He was instrumental in fostering the taste for history in a rapidly widening audience and in shaping their expectations about its purposes. Demonstrating the humanizing force of patriotism, he gave the historian as man of letters new stature in the public eye and made historical writing part of the national literature. His historical narratives retain their brilliance as works of art even while many of their assumptions mark them as artifacts of a world view already breaking down at his death. They epitomize the realistic romances dear to the Victorian historical imagination and illuminate its longing for both order and progress.

IV

JAMES ANTHONY FROUDE
HISTORY AS PROTESTANT APOLOGIA

Hilaire Belloc hinted at the paradoxical nature of Froude's life when he described him as "kneaded right into his own time and his own people . . . in tune with, even when he directly opposed, the class from which he sprang, the mass of well-to-do Protestant Englishmen of Queen Victoria's reign."[1] The sources of opposition were plentiful. From the scandalized outcry that met *The Nemesis of Faith* to the indignation that succeeded the *Life of Carlyle*, the chain of controversies forming that life stretched unbroken. And yet the links were forged from issues typically Victorian. Froude's rejection of the Gospel of Newman for the Gospel of Carlyle was a paradigm of the 1840s; that same gospel made his consequent hostility to Liberalism in all its forms conventionally unorthodox in the fifties and sixties. His unabashed support for white Anglo-Saxon supremacy aggravated the sorest points of racial and cultural relativism in the seventies and eighties. As an historian too he was at the center of the ideological storms of his day. By rehabilitating the Tudors, his *History of England* challenged aspects of the Whig view with an alternative explanation of modern success. As if that were not controversial enough, the popular appeal of his brilliant style and the suspect nature of his scholarship turned Froude into a test case in the definition of professional authority.

There is a tension of paradox in Froude's writing and thinking

History as Protestant Apologia

about history that shows the stress of intellectual dilemmas widely shared. In history he confronted the conflict between knowledge and wisdom, the need to prove versus the need to believe. He was a dogmatic doubter, both a chastiser and a celebrator of English ways. Although he rebuffed the challenge of opposing beliefs, both theological and scientific, by denouncing all interpretation as fictional, such scepticism actually freed him to argue more forcefully for his own providential fictions. He combined a Macaulayean belief in the overwhelming power of *Zeitgeist* with a Carlylean worship of heroes; a whiggish justification of past policy by present successes with a Tory conception of the ideal social order. In his historical interpretations, hard-headed English pragmatism fulfilled transcendental ideals. Although he argued eloquently for sympathy with the past, judgment repeatedly subverted sympathy. The vision he projected back in time answered highly personal needs, but it also shaped the Victorians' public identity in important ways.

The impress of Froude's early years on his historical writing was deep and direct beyond comparison with his five contemporaries. After his mother's early death, his stern father and his adored brother Hurrell exercised a predominant influence over his emotional and intellectual life.[2] His father's disappointment and his own humiliation were keen when he failed to follow Hurrell's brilliant academic example. He was brought home from three "wasted" years at Westminster and left to his own desultory studies in his father's library. There, while his brother was emerging as a leader of the early Oxford movement, James Froude was first encountering modern historians like Gibbon and Sharon Turner. His understanding of both the English past and English Protestantism jarred oddly with the historical reversals implicit in Hurrell's Tractarian doctrines.

Froude finally entered Oriel College in 1836, under the shadow of his brother's recent death. The priesthood had always been supposed his ultimate destination, and he took deacon's orders in 1845, convinced that his belief in the general truth of the Gospel outweighed his growing confusion about its proofs. In his early years at Oxford, Froude attempted to resist the "strange fascination" of John Henry Newman by remaining purposefully aloof from the circle in which Newman tried to include him. Nevertheless, he clearly felt the attraction of the Tractarian position in those turbulent forties that called all institutions into doubt. He feared that he might have succumbed to the movement that was "sweeping with it the most brilliant of the

James Anthony Froude

rising generation" had it not been for the countervailing influence of Carlyle and Emerson. Their writings taught him that the basis for religion must be found in "the present reality of our actual life and experience," rather than in ingenious arguments for the historical continuity of the Church (B, 72).

Ironically enough, Newman reinforced these conclusions by enlisting Froude's help on "The Legend of St. Neot" for his *Lives of the English Saints*. Rather than strengthening Froude's faith, this "excursion among the Will-o'-the-wisps of the spiritual morasses" convinced him of the futility of trying to satisfy the intellect with historical proofs for Christian belief.[3] Instead of following Newman into Romanism to end his continuing "confusion and perplexity" about religion, Froude decided that he had mistaken his profession and began to think how he might escape the legal strictures that bound him to it. He was planning to resign his fellowship at Exeter quietly and take a teaching post in Tasmania when his *Nemesis of Faith* unleashed a storm of controversy in 1849. The story of a young clergyman who resigns his orders and converts to Roman Catholicism laid bare Froude's continuing spiritual dilemmas; it also made the authorities question his fitness as a teacher and revoke their offer of a position.

Thus was Froude cut adrift in 1849, in his own eyes a martyr to intellectual freedom, but a pariah at Oxford and once again a disappointment to his family: a prime example of the intellectual and emotional casualties of the 1840s. In light of the catastrophe of his clerical career, his choice of historian as an alternative vocation takes on particular significance; in view of his complicated relationship to the Oxford movement, so does the subject matter of his major work. Having retreated to North Wales with his wife in 1850, he soon settled down to work on a book-length treatment of Elizabeth's reign. The vocation of historian clearly represented a safe footing in the doctrinal quagmire that had proved so ruinous for him. In beginning the *History*, Froude wrote, "I had done with speculation over the insoluble problems. I was feeling ground under my feet, and was actively engaged on what promised to be a profession with which I could support myself" (B, 172). An 1853 letter to Charles Kingsley further demonstrates his hope of building out of the factual material of history a bulwark against the dangerous currents of conflicting theory. After scornfully dismissing the theological wrangling that led to F. D. Maurice's expulsion from King's College, he defends his own decision to stick to his project, for "at any rate [in writing history] one has substantial stuff between one's fingers to be moulding at, and not those slime and sea ladders to the moon 'opinion.' "[4]

Like Carlyle caught in the crossfire of conflicting ideologies, Froude sought in history a refuge from scepticism; like him too, he concentrated on periods that could refute the most threatening of those theories. Writing the *History of England from the Fall of Wolsey to the Defeat of the Spanish Armada* served emotional needs far more important than the merely economic ones that had led him to take it up. Burrow notes its national recapitulation of Froude's autobiographical pattern: the pilgrim's progress from false to true faith.[5] The *History* allowed Froude once and for all to exorcise the dangerously attractive spirits of Newman and Hurrell by repudiating the Tractarian view of the Reformation. At the same time it served as an atonement to his father, who was convinced by its success not just that Froude's view of Henry was correct, but that good might finally come of his son after all (B, 200). Froude also regarded the work as a formal recantation of his heterodoxy at Oxford. Hoping to be considered for the vacant Regius Professorship of Modern History in 1858, he offered his attempts to "clear the English Reformation and the fathers of the Anglican Church from the stains which have been allowed to gather on them" as proof that "if I ever return to Oxford it will be with the object of defending the Church of England from all enemies within and without" (B, 273). In the *History*'s final pages, written in 1870, Froude still pursued the enemy of Roman superstition—a superstition even more dangerous in the present insofar as it threatened to betray society to the "godless secularity" of modern science by divorcing Christianity from intellect.[6] Clearly in writing this history, he found not just an alternative career, but in many respects an alternative creed, one far more useful than the doctrinal orthodoxy he had forsaken.

Despite its controversial interpretations of the Tudors, the *History*, which appeared in two-volume installments from 1856 to 1870, firmly established Froude's claims as a major historian. His second major work, *The English in Ireland in the Eighteenth Century*, appeared from 1872-74 and stirred up a furor on both sides of the Irish Sea for its dogmatic insistence that "might makes right" when dealing with an "inferior race" like the Celts. Froude's biographical studies of Becket, Julius Caesar, and John Bunyan also appeared in the seventies and increased his reputation as a popularizer. All this popu-

James Anthony Froude

lar success made him the target of professional criticism. His scholarship had been subject to attack throughout the sixties; the Becket study only intensified the assaults of his most strident critic, E. A. Freeman, who consistently attempted to make an example of Froude's alleged dilettantism. This did not prevent Froude from succeeding Freeman as Regius Professor upon the latter's death in 1892. Having recently published a follow-up volume to the *History, The Divorce of Catherine of Aragon*, he produced three more works based on his Oxford lectures during his two short years as Regius Professor: *The Life and Letters of Erasmus, English Seamen in the Sixteenth Century*, and *The Council of Trent*. Although Froude made some effort to induct students into the mysteries of manuscript research, his work in the Regius Chair was informed by the same beliefs in the preeminently moral and imaginative nature of history that he had enunciated forty years earlier.

Notwithstanding the relief with which Froude retreated from theology to history, his relationship to historical facts was from the first problematic. His early speculations made him sound like the most sceptical historian of his age. He responded to the dogmatism of both orthodox faith and positivistic science with a "theory of history" that declared all such theories merely projections of what one wished to believe about what one could not know. Lured into a spiritual wilderness by Tractarian claims to provide "objective" validation for the "subjective" truths of religion (SS, 4:227), Froude reacted by denying objective truth to all formulas, religious, political, and philosophical. Like Carlyle he argued that theories "vitiate[d] the observation of fact," that formulas struck "half the life" out of truth.[7] But where Carlyle had tried to transcend the division between the truths of knowledge and the truths of belief, Froude felt he could only disarm the challenge of history to faith by making these two types of truth mutually exclusive. Carlyle had claimed poetic history as the truly real; Froude turned all historical knowledge into fiction.

Writing "A Legend of St. Neot" molded his thinking about both religious and historical knowledge. In its introduction he admitted that hagiography represented not historical fact but edifying myth, a product of the biographer's imagination. Rather than distinguishing religious from secular history on these grounds, however, he went on to hold that the difference between this biography and our own was merely one of degree. "We all write Legends," and all history is "more or less fictitious,"[8] insofar as we relate facts not as they really happened, but as they appear to us. Memory can not retain facts in isolation, so it rearranges them "in a more conceptional order" according to its preexisting prejudices. Just as increasing years modify our interpretations of personal history, so too each age absorbs and fuses and remodels historical facts to suit its own altered perspective. History, he wrote elsewhere, is like "a child's box of letters" (SS, 1:1); we can rearrange its facts to spell whatever message we wish.

Like George Eliot's similar admission that she presented not the facts in themselves, but men and things as mirrored on her mind, Froude's proclamation that "all history is mythic" actually ended by throwing greater weight on the testimony of the myth-maker.[9] As if like Eliot in a "witness-box,"[10] the historian was sworn to represent accurately his personal vision. This witnessing depended not on sight but on insight, not on facts but on belief. Far from concluding that legends like Neot's were meaningless because "untrue," Froude argued that their meaningfulness depended on their spiritual message, not on their verifiability. The soundest empirical facts were valueless if their story taught us nothing about moral truth. All interpretation might be based on assumptions, but not all assumptions were for Froude equally valid.

Froude manipulated his sceptical attitude toward historical facts so as to protect assumptions crucial to his own values. He might warn, for instance, that "the most earnest efforts of intellectual sympathy" could but half solve the enigma of history (H, 4:14), or that "no effort of the imagination . . . will ever enable us to place ourselves exactly in the position of any man."[11] Such pessimistic claims were simply maneuvers to deflect a pseudoempiricism that excluded morality from its assumptions about "human nature." Arguing that all historical theories were subjective and all facts malleable not only undercut an untenable fundamentalism, but served equally well to deny the "destructive" conclusions of positivistic science, whose claims had been forcefully established by H. T. Buckle's *History of Civilization in England* (1857-61). In "The Science of History" (1864), Froude denied Buckle's assertion that historical study could imitate science by arguing that its facts could be neither exhaustively nor accurately determined, let alone repeated experimentally. He had graver objections to Buckle's pretensions to predict future behavior, since such predictions could rest only on the Utilitarian assumption that human action was controlled by a "law" of self-interest. So long as one believed, as did Froude, that moral choice could override material necessity, that man was neither consistently selfish nor consistently noble, there was no adequate science of him: "You will make nothing of him except from the old-fashioned moral—or, if you please, imaginative—point of view" (SS, 1:16).

Although Froude in a sense by-passed facts, he arrived at the same position as did Carlyle—that point at which the moral and the imaginative became one in willed belief, where spiritual truths were transmuted into "the great poem of human history" ("Inaugural," 143). He risked nothing by admitting that this poem's interpretation depended entirely upon one's assumptions about life's ultimate value, because he never doubted the superior truth of his own assumptions. For the believer, one romance formula preempted all other myths. There was no danger of real relativism for a man convinced that "one lesson, and only one, history may be said to repeat with distinctness; that the world is built somehow on moral foundations; that, in the long run, it is well with the good; . . . it is ill with the wicked" (SS, 1:14). He might describe the past as one endless flux of creeds, opinions, and manners, but he never doubted that "the moral law is written on the tablets of eternity" (SS, 1:18). Just as much as did Carlyle and Arnold, he believed that the student's duty was to determine "the rule under which we are governed by the Almighty Lord of the world . . . to what forms of faith or action is the grace of God most emphatically rewarded."[12] The answer to such questions would allow the student to see through the controversies that had so long perplexed human history to the one truth in their midst.

At times he wrote as if this ideal truth were scarcely attainable in the fallen world of human time. Man would never write "faithful and literal history . . . until perfect knowledge and perfect faith in God shall enable him to see and endure every fact in its reality; until perfect love shall kindle in him under its touch the one just emotion which is in harmony with the eternal order of all things" (SS, 1:369). But in the meantime, the most important facts of human existence were still proof against the onslaught of so-called "scientific" approaches to history and were uncompromised by ephemeral ceremonies and dogmas. Like Carlyle, Froude defined the "fundamental axiom of all real life" in conveniently nondoctrinal terms: holiness, purity, and "obedience to the everlasting laws of duty" (H, 2:44) best served God. Here were goals one needed no controversial theology to reach and that no scientific proofs could suspend.

Froude's distinction between the higher truths of imagination, creativity, and faith and the lower ones of reason, philosophy, and intellect led him naturally to a poetry rather than a science of history. For all his scepticism, he could not simply dismiss facts. Even while acknowledging the influence of interpretation on data he still admitted that history "depends on exact knowledge, on the same minute, impartial, discriminating observation and analysis of particulars which is equally the basis of science" (SS, 2:462). He tried to resolve the contradictions in his position by making the historian's ability to perceive such particulars depend on a "high faith" capable of uniting Intellect (which, working alone, was merely destructive) with the "creative faculties— . . . Love, Idea, Imagination" (SS, 1:369). He claimed to avoid the distortion of formula by focusing on "facts" of emotion and action—facts whose integrity could be preserved only by the conditions of art: "If Poetry must not theorise, much less should the historian theorise, whose obligations to be true to fact are even greater than the poet's. If drama is grandest when the action is least explicable by laws, because then it best resembles life, then history will be grandest also under the same conditions" (SS, 1:23). He found the most perfect history in Shakespeare's plays, where actors, circumstances, and motives existed as dramatic facts unmediated by interpretation. It is no coincidence that Shakespeare wrote during that epoch whose political and spiritual health it was Froude's purpose to illuminate. He explicitly linked what he considered a healthy society to an accurate poetic vision. Shakespeare's "directness of insight" and "breadth of sympathy" would again be possible only when "the common sense of the wisest and best" had replaced the theorizing of factions and when all "speculative formulas" had surrendered to "the few but all-important truths of our moral condition" (SS, 2:487). This, of course, is effectively to prejudge which traits insight and sympathy will confirm as factual and to assign his own assumptions the status of axioms, not theories.

Conceiving history as a stage on which "good and evil fight out their everlasting battle" (SS, 1:16-17) suited Froude's hero-worshipping purposes in a number of ways. "To myself the object of history is to discover and make visible illustrious characters, and pay them ungrudging honour," he affirmed in his Inaugural Lecture as Regius Professor: "The history of mankind, says Carlyle, is the history of its great men. To find out these, clear the dirt from them and place them on their proper pedestals, is the function of the historian. He cannot have a nobler one" ("Inaugural," 162). To science the individual was nothing, the species all. Only the conditions of art allowed the individual his full weight and dimensions. Only poetry was adequate to re-create the greatest natures (SS, 1:337). By conjuring up "real human creatures who would bleed if we pricked them,"[13] the historian appealed directly to the identification and sympathy necessary for moral education. By restoring heroes to their full proportions he enlarged the ethical capacities of every reader:

> The address of history is less to the understanding than to the higher emotions. We learn in it to sympathise with what is great and good; we learn to hate what is base. In the anomalies of fortune we feel the mystery of our mortal existence, and in the companionship of the illustrious natures who have shaped the fortunes of the world, we escape from the littlenesses which cling to the round of common life, and our minds are tuned in a higher and nobler key. (SS, 1:24)

Although Froude was as unequivocal as Carlyle about the importance of great individuals to history, he allowed more weight to the spirit of the age, which established the conditions by which the hero's achievements were to be judged. Indeed, at times he rivals Macaulay in the weight he assigns to historical circumstances. He claims that even the great individual genius of a Shakespeare or a Raphael "is never more than the highest degree of an excellence which prevails widely round it, and forms the environment in which it grows" (H, 1:74). Convinced that the Reformation "could never have been brought about constitutionally according to modern methods" (B, 202), Froude portrayed it from the beginning as the work of the two powerful sovereigns, Henry and Elizabeth. But he defined Henry as a "practically effective" leader precisely because he was advanced "only slightly beyond his contemporaries." In such leaders "the motive force which bears him forward is not in himself, but in the great tidal wave of human progress. He is the guide of a great movement, not the creator of it, and he represents in his own person the highest average wisdom, combined necessarily in some measure with the mistakes and prejudices of the period to which he belongs" (H, 3:71). There is little opportunity here for the penetrating and molding intellect of the Carlylean hero. Those leaders who could read the signs of the times at best rode the crest of the "tidal wave," those who could not were left in its wake.

If some of Froude's metaphors sound Macaulayean, they serve a significantly different model of change. We find in both men the usual organic analogies. For Macaulay, however, the individual was merely a passive receptor of the current of progress; for Froude he was the instrument of Providence. Macaulay might use the authority of the natural for rhetorical leverage, but his "nature" served rationalistic ends and argued for an underlying uniformity in human experience. History was cyclical because without the trimmer's balancing hand mankind was constantly oscillating between extremes. Like Carlyle's, Froude's model of change allowed him to stress the uniqueness of ages unfolding according to a divine, if mysterious, plan. Froude's particular historical arguments depended upon the spontaneity, irrationality, and irreversibility of organic process. He too recognized cyclical alternation in history: times of increasing knowledge alternated with periods of consolidation and "moral cultivation" (H, 1:11-12). But unlike Macaulay's, his cycles insured diversity, not uniformity. Cyclical change refuted the rationalist's appeal to a law of averages because it left no two generations exactly alike.

Froude relied on the Carlylean cycle of institutional growth, decay, and rebirth to justify the Reformation. He too viewed institutions as but the outward forms of eternal truths, forms that remained vital only so long as they credibly represented man's relationship to heaven. While still green and young, the Catholic Church had nourished its people. When it reached the end of its life cycle, as all institutions must, its language became dead, its symbols hollow, its "living robe of life . . . a winding-sheet of corruption" (H, 2:45). Not just Henry, but nature herself, decreed its demise. All honorable men, once they realized that their religion no longer corresponded to truth, turned away from its dead forms and fell back upon "the naked elemental life" (H, 2:46). The very spontaneity with which discontent sprang up among Teutonic people everywhere proved that Protestantism was rooted in an appreciation of vital and invincible truths. Luther's spark only ignited an explosion that, like the French Revolution, fulfilled a higher imperative, consuming away the rotten fruit and clearing the ground for new growth (H, 2:39). This vindication of elemental truths was beyond conscious human control: "The genius of change . . . car[ed] little for human opposition . . . the truth stole into men's minds they knew not how" (H, 4:441).

Froude's argument for organic necessity actually worked less to diminish the role of the individual than to celebrate (as did the Whig view) those who had supported the "right" cause. Its most important use was to rationalize desired political and social behavior. The Tudors had correctly read the "signs of the times"; the organic as well as

James Anthony Froude

the divine sanctioned their ends and so justified their means. In the *English in Ireland*, the natural "law" that might makes right justified the repression of an inferior people. Since the world was so constituted that man must be ruled by strength, "nature also has allotted superiority of strength to superiority of intellect and character."[14] Ireland's inability to win her freedom militarily was proof that she lacked the maturity to justify self-rule. *Julius Caesar* summed up Froude's tract for the times. Statesmen could not prevent the inevitable decay of outworn institutions, he argued, but could check the progress of the evil by recognizing the symptoms in time. According to his own diagnosis, Victoria's England shared the ills of Caesar's Rome: birth had been superseded by wealth, religion by cant, patriotism by party. Popular government had given control of the state to those who could not even control themselves. The lesson was clear: the "forces . . . which control the forms in which human things adjust themselves" would once again make an end of free institutions unless duty and justice replaced pleasure and material expediency as the basis of government.[15] Froude's "forces" in effect exchanged the materialist necessity of Utilitarianism and Positivism for a moral necessity which, while no less binding, insisted on the importance of self-sacrifice and individual responsibility.

Froude, like Carlyle, used organic change selectively; cycles justified the preservation of an approved status quo and sanctioned the destruction of undesirable institutions. But his conception of change lacked the apocalyptic violence of Carlyle's. It was more evolutionary than revolutionary. Even movements so clearly propelled by truth as the Reformation coalesced slowly, moved forward hesitantly, and preserved fragments of old and new in glaring contradiction (H, 1:161). Froude's need to justify the Reformation was intensely personal and complex. The influence of this justification on his model of historical change necessarily introduced strain and ambiguity into his argumentation about progress and decline. It was not enough for Froude to vindicate the Reformation by proclaiming that it discarded falsehood for truth. He wanted the extra sanction that subsequent social and intellectual progress gave to the Reformers' choices. Although he admitted that he found the true interest of the past not in the growth of "material and mechanical civilisation" but in the drama of human emotion (SS, 1:17), he used sociocultural evidence no less polemically than Macaulay or Carlyle to reinforce his judgments. Fleshing out the ethnic and economic proportions of the Reformation in England provided him with further means of demonstrating its historical importance and inevitability.

Endorsing Victorian conceptions of race, for instance, he presents the new religion as being taken up instinctively by the Teutonic mind, with its "craving for a higher life" (H, 2:39). The Reformation plays a crucial role in the intellectual and material progress that constitute Froude's own version of the march of mind. Because their minds were freed from the old religious superstitions, England's merchants were more receptive to the astronomical innovations revolutionizing sea travel and consequently were able to lay the base for her maritime prosperity and colonial empire. The influx of highly skilled Protestant emigrants fleeing the persecution in Holland and Flanders further strengthened the economy. As a result the English flourished, but because of the "Spaniard's choice" of Catholicism, "his intellect shrivelled in his brain, and the sinews shrank in his self-bandaged limbs"—a fate typical of Celts (H, 8:436). Looking with satisfaction at England's power and influence in the nineteenth century, Froude concluded that the Reformation had been "the root and source of the expansive force which has spread the Anglo-Saxon race over the globe, and imprinted the English genius and character on the constitution of mankind."[16]

Although this view of progress lent a brisk argumentative momentum to parts of the *History*, it deepened inherent contradictions in Froude's position. This march of mind was implicitly out of step with the silent, organic, un- (if not anti-) intellectual growth Carlyle associated with true faith. Making Protestantism the religion of "men of active and original vigour of understanding," while resigning Catholicism to the uneducated, the "imaginative," and the traditional (H, 7:10), undercut distinctions Froude himself maintained elsewhere between the theoretical sophistry of the false faith and the unreflective simplicity of the true. We might attribute these contradictions to Froude's rhetorical opportunism, his willingness to switch from wily Jesuits to superstitious dupes as needed to make his point. Such opportunism does explain many contradictions in his argument. But the very dynamic of that argument is controlled by more profound conflicts that cannot be resolved so easily.

Not the least of the paradoxes of Froude's *History* is the deeper undertow of nostalgia for a lost world that pulled against this triumphant wave of progress. Although Burrow reminds us that Froude's

James Anthony Froude

enthusiasm for Anglo-Saxon empire glorified a national and not a commercial triumph,[17] it still conflicted with his equally intense enthusiasm for the feudal. The forward thrust of Froude's Protestant ideal carried him inevitably toward a deeply antipathetic present. It was part of his strategy to make explicit the differences between this present and the past. His most comprehensive examination of economic and social evidence occurs in chapter 1, "The Social Condition of England in the Sixteenth Century." An obvious parallel to Macaulay's chapter 3, this discussion seeks not to celebrate the extent of modern advance but to assess its limitations. Froude's version of Carlyle's medieval idyll is intended to reconfirm the spiritual choices made by men and masters in the sixteenth century. But Froude had to strike some damaging emotional compromises in order to aggrandize both the wisdom and virtue of the old society and the progress that left this world in its wake.

Froude portrays sixteenth-century England as a society in which the rules of political economy were neglected in order "to bring the production and distribution of wealth under the moral rule of right and wrong" (H, 1:91); a world before labor was looked upon as a market commodity, in which men were held together "by oaths, free acknowledgments, and reciprocal obligations" rather than by the "harsher connecting links of mutual self-interest" (H, 1:26). In his eyes a law that raised the cost of cloth by limiting weavers to two looms was motivated not by a desire to restrict trade but to retain the people "in the condition not of 'hands' but of men" (H, 1:63). The guild system existed not to monopolize commerce but to enforce honest dealing in honest goods (H, 1:56). Overlooking their use in controlling scarce labor after the Plague, Froude disposed of the stringent vagrancy laws as legislation that simply "harmonized with the iron temper of the age, and . . . answered well for the government of a fierce and powerful people, in whose hearts lay an intense hatred of rascality, and among whom no one need have lapsed into evil courses except by deliberate preference for them" (H, 1:90). Even when confronted with the palpable discrimination of the forest laws, he professed to believe that "they served only to enhance the excitement [of poaching] by danger" and cited the Robin Hood ballads as evidence of the "warm genial spirit" with which such petty class warfare was conducted (H, 1:72). All in all, in Tudor society "the people were ruled as they preferred to be ruled" by an aristocracy who demonstrated their fitness as leaders by their self-sacrifice in defense of their country (H, 1:45) and by their submission to the "moral authority" of legislation like the sumptuary laws (H, 1:25).

The essential health of this body politic naturally insured the healthiness of the spiritual choices it made. Demonstrating that the majority of the populace under Henry were "prosperous, well-fed, loyal and contented" at once refuted Whig arguments about Tudor tyranny and forced specific parables on a present dominated by atomistic democracy, buccaneering capitalism, and political economy. But Froude's is an idyll already dissolving as he contemplates it. He detects the snake of greed and self-interest already stealing into the feudal paradise as the commercial middle classes gain in power under the Tudors. Although he pointedly notes that forced military training was an effective deterrent to "self-seeking tendencies in the mercantile classes" (H, 1:71), he must concede that mammonism soon destroyed the feudal constitution.

Macaulay and Green were able to maintain the forward thrust of the Whig view by allying Protestantism to the expansion of middle class power. They could celebrate the development of modern intellect, industry, manners, and politics as analogous manifestations of one unified current of progress. For Froude the course of history was divided against itself. The energy of the new religion propels him forward, the decay of the social system drags him back. The progress that he had needed to label inevitable for the sixteenth century left him longing for the harmony of the past and explaining away the disharmonies of the present. Carlyle was saved from escapism by his ability to universalize his heroes and project them into the present. Froude's heroes were too thoroughly controlled by the spirit of their age. His own struggles with faith and doubt had left him overawed by the mutability of ideals. A willed transcendence was for him more a hope than a possibility. Despite his discipleship, he could never comfortably adopt Carlyle's decisive voice. History itself had taught him that it was impossible to predict the future: "We should draw no horoscopes . . . we should expect little, for what we expect will not come to pass" (SS, 1:18). Arguing that change worked in mysterious ways was for him more a defense against the unknowable than a defiant assertion of faith. His calls for reform hold out only warning of punishment, not a vision of a reformed world. He tried to evade modern political and economic realities by abandoning progress itself as mythic and seeking refuge in the permanently true. Duty, self-sacrifice, and self-control were verities sufficiently nonsectarian to offer a key to all mythologies, but they left too many troubling details still in need of interpretation. Much of what struck Froude's contemporaries as paradoxical in his writings resulted from his unwillingness to trust either facts or ideals completely. Even the most universal truths at times needed a pragmatic rationale; even the most practical means required the extra sanction of providential ends. Building myths out of an all too fallible reality required constant, often unacknowledged, compromise.

II

For Arnold and Carlyle, identity itself rested upon the historian's ability to retrieve the truth about the past. Froude, on the other hand, had conceded that even "our knowledge of one another is mythic . . . for in every act of perception we contribute something of our own" ("Inaugural," 153). Far from following this conclusion into solipsism, however, Froude arrived at what was at least superficially a considerably more "scientific" conception of contemporary documentation and a notably more historicist point of view. Precisely because he considered it impossible to reach an objective understanding of the past, he argued that readers must either accept the impressions of events formed by contemporaries competent to judge them or "give up history in despair."[18] Far from scorning "parchment Chartularies" as did Carlyle, Froude looked to them for the real life of the past. He advocated studying the statute books of the sixteenth century because in them one found "the deliberate expression of [our ancestors'] collective thought, on the high questions of faith, and life, and law, and duty"—a glimpse of the "inner side" of human experience, of the secret passions and motives that alone made intelligible the "outward" history of wars and politics ("Teaching History," 73). The language itself exhaled an atmosphere in which "the forms of departed things rise up and take shape before you" ("Inaugural," 159). Nor was it only the imaginative value of primary sources that Froude prized. His Carlylean defense of fact against formula led him to defend the pedagogical importance of texts in terms strikingly similar to those Freeman used while debating the first reforms at Oxford. Froude scorned the "universal knowledge" purveyed by London University, and he argued that unless teaching in the new school of Modern History at Oxford were to fall to the level of Gower Street or the popular press, the close reading of manuscript sources for limited periods must replace the cramming of epitomes and historical compendia "philosophised into unity" by the theories of modern speculators ("Teaching History," 57).

Moreover, Froude practiced what he preached far more thoroughly than did Freeman. He made exhaustive studies of manuscripts at the newly opened archives in Simancas, Spain, as well as consulting documents in the archives of Paris, Brussels, and Vienna, at Hatfield House, the British Museum, and the Rolls House. In order, he claimed, to enable his readers to form their own opinions, he swelled the *History* with copious extracts from original documents and manuscript sources in which "the principal actors unfold their character and motives in their own language."[19] Convinced that history would be "but a dumb show of phantoms" without some investigation of the daily life beneath the official events, he also amplified his research with a range of sociocultural evidence. His first chapter employs statistical projections of population to gauge the country's material growth (H, 1:13), inventories of country homes and banquet menus to suggest genteel life styles (H, 1:47-52 n.), and comparisons of wages and prices with modern buying power to determine the relative standard of living enjoyed by workers (H, 1:28-35). Like other historians working under romantic influences, he also paid particular attention to evidence of the popular mind—the literary, the legendary, the irrational.

In actual practice it was neither historicist sympathy nor "scientific" objectivity that Froude was after in his devotion to contemporary evidence, but support for a particular kind of polemic. Objectivity was no part of his historian's responsibility. He freely admitted that he considered "moderate views . . . but the husk of history; the real grain is beaten out before they can be manufactured." A student left adrift in noncommital studies was likely to become hopelessly confused or, worse yet, fall into "a somewhat trenchant scepticism as to the credibility of any history whatsoever" ("Teaching History," 59). This end Froude feared as much as did Arnold and Carlyle. Impartiality was not only foreign to human nature but also, where great questions were at issue, was "but another name for an unworthy indifference" ("Teaching History," 78). Looking back at the *History* in *The Divorce of Catherine of Aragon*, Froude claimed no such impartiality: "I believe the Reformation to have been the greatest incident in English history. . . . I am unwilling to believe more evil than I can help of my countrymen who accomplished so beneficent a work,

James Anthony Froude

and in a book written with such convictions the mythical element cannot be wholly wanting."[20]

As we have already seen, it was not all theorizing about the past that Froude objected to, but theorizing that disagreed with his own "myths" about history and human nature. Carlyle had feared that the sceptical, utilitarian mentality of the 1840s would render incomprehensible a period of genuine faith like the seventeenth century; Froude professed similar anxieties about the Reformation. He identified the salient trait of modern historians as a talent for depreciation, for reducing the stature of great men to fit the limited moral and intellectual understanding of the general reader.[21] He doubtless had in mind Macaulay's contemptuous dismissal of Cranmer when he singled him out as being especially guilty of taking "mean and low views of men, and of human nature" (B, 544). Modern political economists similarly considered human nature incapable of the self-sacrifice and moral character Froude assumed in the Tudor aristocracy. The prevailing fashion of interpreting the past, he complained, was to seek the causes of great movements in the whims and caprices of mean minds and thus to reduce merry old England to "the nursery of everything most pitiful, most base, and most contemptible" ("Teaching History," 71). Froude claimed that by using contemporary documents, he could rescue the reputation of Reformation leaders from the cynicism of modern "philosophers" as well as from the calumnies of Catholic fanatics.

Froude's own sympathies prove to be as selective as those he criticizes. For instance, he accepts the evidence of the popular mind only when it corroborates his point of view. He cites popular ballads to establish the outcry of a "high-minded people" against ecclesiastical corruption (H, 1:190) or quotes street ballads to create a sense of widespread indignation over what he has presented as the cold-blooded murders of Darnley and Murray (H, 9:83; 9:590 n.). He might be more respectful than Macaulay of religious belief, but only if it revered a living truth and not a dying sham. Catholicism is usually the religion of the weak-minded in his pages. Reports of signs and portents illustrate the "fevered imaginations" of Catholic fanatics at the return of Mary Tudor (H, 5:308) or at the death of Edward (H, 6:15). The craving after prophecies in the 1530s is not just symptomatic of intellectual revolution, but the logical result of a religion built on superstition; it is particularly to Henry's credit that he remained proof against such madness (H, 2:192). Froude examines at length the Nun of

History as Protestant Apologia

Kent's jeremiad against the divorce, only to dismiss her as a young woman of bad health and irritable nerves, whose success exemplified merely the charlatanism of the Church and the perennial insatiability of human credulity (H, 1:295). His prejudgments stunt empathy almost as thoroughly as did Macaulay's.

What appeared to be an effort at historicist reconstruction in the *History* usually became a not-so-subtle form of special pleading. Froude chose to take state papers at face value because their self-serving pronouncements affirmed his own assumptions about the righteousness of the Reformation. The Statute book presented events as originating not in the venality or caprice of self-interested individuals, but as "rising out of the national will, and expressing the national judgment" ("Teaching History," 66)—in other words, as a spontaneous flowering of the spirit of the age. It was hardly any wonder that Froude found that "the story of the Reformation as read by the light of the statute book is more intelligible and consistent than any other version of it, doing less violence to known principles of human nature, and bringing the conduct of the principal actors within the compass of reason and probability" (H, 3:355 n.). Indeed, it would have violated his conception of "human nature" to assume that "statesmen engaged in so magnificent an enterprise" as the Reformation "would make themselves accomplices in enormous crimes, the complacent instruments of a licentious and capricious tyranny."[22] He fell back on false dilemmas to establish guilt or innocence: if Anne Boleyn were not guilty then one would have to assume that English noblemen and gentlemen had degraded themselves in inventing the heinous charges against her; if Mary Stuart had not masterminded Darnley's murder, then Elizabeth and her advisors must be condemned for imprisoning her.

The latter conclusions were simply inadmissable for one who had in effect already determined on his own "Whig view" of Reformation history. The legislation of Henry VIII was to Froude no less than "the Magna Charta of the modern world." It allowed England to accomplish peacefully what had been achieved in Europe only by long and bloody wars. The Reformation in England represented for Froude what the Glorious Revolution had for Macaulay: in both "the stake played for was the liberty of mankind."[23] Once concede that the choices of the sixteenth century had been vindicated by the nineteenth and writing history became a simple matter of selectively reconstructing events so that they anticipated future success. This method conveniently conflated past motives with present results, allowing Froude to press for agreement on the grounds that "if the present law of England be right, the party in favour of the divorce was right" (H, 1:118 n.).

To be sure, Froude's reassessment of the period served some useful functions. By stressing the political significance of Henry's various marriages, he toned down the portrait of the capricious Bluebeard and revealed a monarch driven at least as much by policy as by personal inclination. More often, however, his historicist arguments were undermined by double standards. For instance, he conceded that Catholics and Protestants were alike guilty of persecution, and that given the spirit of the age, it was unreasonable to expect either to have acted differently (H, 10:251). Catholics, however, he blamed for lacking the humanity that could have overridden the political logic of their position (H, 1:165); Protestant persecution, on the other hand, was but "the natural resource of a vigorous government placed in circumstances of extreme peril." Had Elizabeth's ministers "been embarassed with modern scruples" about "outrooting . . . truth" through torture, her government would have come to a swift end (H, 10:293-94).

Froude was caught in a dilemma: he wanted to mount a Macaulayean argument for pragmatism while retaining for his favorite causes a Carlylean purity of purpose. He called awkwardly on Providence to justify executions that Macaulay could have accepted as mere expediency. Froude chooses to see an "even hand of justice" at work repaying Catholics for the persecution of heretics (H, 2:328) and excuses even "needless cruelty" as "an instance of the wide justice of Providence, which punishes wrong by wrong, and visits on single men the offences of thousands" (H, 3:270). Providence exacted Catherine Howard's execution as well, in a rather selective retaliation against those who had disfigured its high ends by mixing them with "worldly intrigues" (H, 4:139). Although growing ever wearier with the machinations of Reformation politics, Froude chose to believe that "the good remained, the corrupt perished"—that the higher morality of the ends justified and ultimately overrode the questionable morality of the means. In short, his apparent historicism and relativism were argumentative ploys. He drew upon the contemporary justification of events because it provided a self-validating view of the transactions in question. He did not so much judge the past on

History as Protestant Apologia

its own terms as choose the rationalization most consistent with his own beliefs. Viewing the English Reformation through the long perspective of three hundred years of Protestant success, he confused his enthusiasm for its effects with a just assessment of its causes.

Froude set out consciously to revise history. Taking fiction and drama as his models, he aimed quite as frankly as Macaulay at popular success, for he realized the power of art as an instrument of conversion. In keeping with his pronouncement that history was "only a stage on which the drama of humanity is acted out" ("Inaugural," 162), he framed much of the action as theater: the divorce is a "great drama" unfolding act by act, Cromwell the protagonist in a lesser "tragedy" (H, 2:443; 3:474). In line with his argument that the truest art was based on unmediated facts and taught best when it taught least, much of his "characterization" consists of long quotations (or paraphrases presented as direct quotations) from the letters, speeches, and papers of public figures and from contemporary views of colleagues. Anne Boleyn's ravings in her cell, he points out, are "as touching as Ophelia's" but claim a higher authority: they are not just a poet's invention, but the actual words of a suffering fellow mortal (H, 2:467). At times Froude goes beyond mere quotation, condensing documentary evidence into dramatized dialogues. Thus we see the Emperor Charles "wincing" and "muttering" at Paget's plain speech; we attend court as Henry accuses the heretic Lambert in person; and we witness Mary Stuart's confrontation with John Knox (H, 4:377; 3:314-15; 7:377). Like Carlyle, Froude prized even incidental evidence if it could offer an authentic insight. He records a stray letter from an English gentleman because it kindles "a small spark of English life" during the visitation of the monasteries (H, 2:418), and includes the story of Dalaber's persecution which, in its "minute simplicity, brings us face to face with that old world, where men like ourselves lived, and worked, and suffered, three centuries ago" (H, 2:54). For Froude as for George Eliot, the testimony of eye witnesses "like ourselves" pleaded for the sympathy and understanding based on recognition of a shared humanity. Froude accorded these dramatic truths of emotion and experience an authority he denied to other kinds of historical interpretations.

Froude's other means of restoring credibility and human interest to history lay in his novelistic talent for clothing abstractions in a fabric of concrete particulars. He rivaled Macaulay in his ability to individ-

James Anthony Froude

ualize the experience of the past and to suggest the way change permeated the daily reality of an entire society of people "like ourselves":

> Every parish pulpit rang with the divorce, or with the perils of the Catholic faith; at every village ale-house, the talk was of St. Peter's keys, the sacrament, or of the pope's supremacy, or of the points in which a priest differed from a layman. Ostlers quarreled over such questions as they groomed their masters' horses; old women mourned across the village shopboards of the evil days which were come or coming. (H, 1:291-92)

Froude's was less Carlyle's eye for symbol than Macaulay's eye for the startling antitheses that revealed social cleavage. The disorder produced by great intellectual change springs vividly to life in the "peasant theologians" who come to blows as they dispute the mysteries of justification over their ale, or in the lawyer who lifts a small dog in derision as a priest lifts the host (H, 3:341, 343). Froude employs similar economy of detail to establish the full ignominy of superstition's overthrow in an Oxford where "the divinity schools were planted with cabbages" and "laundresses dried clothes in the School of Arts" (H, 5:255).

The situation Froude portrays, when extremes of Protestant and Catholic fanaticism threaten to rend the social fabric, fits a peculiarly Macaulayean pattern. However, Froude's interest is less in exploiting sensational polarities than in transmuting them into something more closely resembling that "galvanic mass" of forces Carlyle saw moving chaotically toward revolution. In the early stages of reform, Froude tells us, "each separate human being . . . was whirled along the rapids which formed the passage into a new era" (H, 3:219). To capture the confusion of change in progress he passes before our eyes a series of fleeting images like the "pictures in a magic slide"— representative events that convey us with a present-tense immediacy into both sides of the conflict. First we view a friar mendicant condemning heresy in a local village. "The friar disappears. A neighbour of the new opinions . . . takes his place, and then begins an argument" denouncing him (H, 3:219-20). "The slide again moves" and "we are in a village church" where a groom from the court scornfully challenges the sainthood of Becket, depicted there "in a window gorgeously painted." "We are next at Worcester, at the Lady Chapel, on the eve of the Assumption," where a citizen publicly mourns the desecration of the Virgin's statue (H, 3:222). By the time this slide show ends, the contradictions of England's movement forward, "rocking and reeling" into the new age, have been effectively captured in Froude's kaleidoscopic vision. We have been made to sympathize with both the loss and victory entailed in this "under-current of the war of opinions, where the forces were generated which gave to the time its life and meaning" (H, 3:219).

For all his special pleading, there is a degree of impartiality and wonder in Froude's re-creation of the past that Macaulay could not claim. It is not just that he was willing (like Carlyle) to invite the reader to "call his imagination to his aid, and endeavour, if he can, to see the same object in many shapes and many colours, to sympathize successively with those to whom the Reformation was a terror, and with those to whom it was the dearest hope" (H, 3:61). Froude's own imaginative eye was keen to the nuance and detail that authenticated empathy. Despite his distaste for Catholicism, he pities its mutilation in terms that make us share the pain: "It was no light thing to the village peasant to see the royal arms staring above the empty socket of the crucifix to which he had prayed" (H, 5:64). He helps us feel the baldness of loss in chapels after the statues had crashed from their niches by imagining the sunlight that "stared in . . . on the whitened aisles" and the commandments written on whitewashed walls "where the quaint frescoes had told the story of the gospel to the eyes of generation after generation" (H, 5:47). He finds heroic virtues, "courage and self-sacrifice" beautiful in enemy and friend alike; martyrdom, so long as it was "nobly borne," is worth our witnessing whether in those who "bought England's freedom with their blood" or those who were tinged with the sunset glory of an old faith (H, 2:338-39).

Yet nostalgic sentiment is finally no match for prejudice.[24] Despite Froude's encouragement that we judge and feel for ourselves the positions of both sides, his partisanship controls our sympathy, and his judgments limit our experience of the past. Froude held to the righteousness of his cause with a Carlylean tenacity and indignation. Truth vindicates itself with a relentless inevitability that truncates empathy. Change is a tide whose flow cannot be turned, a seed forcing relentlessly through the soil, a clock inexorably counting down to the hour of reckoning:

> Slowly the hand had crawled along the dial-plate; slowly as if the event would never come: and wrong was heaped on wrong; and oppression cried, and it seemed as if no ear had heard its voice; till the measure of

James Anthony Froude

the circle was at length fulfilled; the finger touched the hour, and as the strokes of the great hammer rang out above the nation, in an instant the mighty fabric of iniquity was shivered into ruins. (H, 1:193)

He never permits the imaginative interest of history's pageantry to carry us away from the judgment exacted by God. Witnesses to Thomas More's execution, we are allowed to find uplifting the cheerful faith with which he meets his death. But More's own eloquence is swiftly drowned out by the voices of Protestant martyrs "crying underneath the altar" for vengeance from "the throne of the Most High" (H, 2:377). The cosmic righteousness of retribution for Catholic wrongs necessarily trivializes our sympathy for More the man.

The coronation of Anne Boleyn reveals a similar antagonism between sympathy and judgment. There is something distinctively Carlylean in this set piece that grafts the immediate onto the symbolic and turns brilliant spectacle into a sermon on the vanity of human wishes. Froude spares no effort in bringing back to life "the blazing trail of splendour" that once filed down London streets, now so "black and smoke-grimed," but then "radiant with masses of colour, gold, and crimson, and violet" (H, 1:424-25). The rich costumes, the glittering jewels, the fountains running with wine, the monuments and tributes, all coalesce in an extravagant pageant at whose center we find "fortune's plaything of the hour, the Queen of England—queen at last— . . . breathing the perfumed incense of greatness which she had risked her fair name, her delicacy, her honour, her self-respect, to win" (H, 1:425). Froude poses Anne as both symbol and victim of the social earthquake convulsing her society: a "poor silly soul" tempted into moral chaos by the fatal gift of greatness. We are inclined at least to pity, if not to sympathize with her, when Froude clouds the sunshine of her triumph with a foreshadowing of that day three years hence when she would leave the Tower "a poor wandering ghost, on a sad tragic errand, from which she will never more return" (H, 1:426). In the long run, however, Froude knows we cannot sympathize with both Henry and Anne, and at the moment of her coronation he exacts at her expense the indignation for Catherine's treatment that he would not allow us to direct against the King. When Anne was anointed Queen, he asks,

> Did any vision flit across her of a sad mourning figure which once had stood where she was standing, now desolate, neglected, sinking into the darkening twilight of a life cut short by sorrow? Who can tell? At such a time, that figure would have weighed heavily upon a noble mind. . . .

History as Protestant Apologia

> But Anne Boleyn was not noble and was not wise,—too probably she felt nothing but the delicious, all-absorbing, all-intoxicating present. ent. (H, 1:429)

He tries to manipulate our pity into disgust at the callous vanity of the other woman in this maudlin melodrama, and to prepare us for the adultress' further outrages against womanly feeling. In the process, however, his Carlylean grip on transcendent truths slips and the heavy-handedness of the special pleader takes over. Froude's censoriousness makes his sympathy for her seem condescending and insincere.

This need to judge and justify constantly intervenes between us and Froude's characters. He might aspire to create an "overmastering human interest" in history that "transcends explanation,"[25] but in practice he does not trust human interest alone. In analyzing Henry's marriages, for instance, he maneuvers the reader through a maze of double standards. While commending Henry for letting political expedience override sentiment in divorcing Catherine, he blames Pope Clement for letting "worldly prudence"—in the person of Emperor Charles—enter into his deliberations on the divorce. He applauds Henry's decision to force the dispute to an issue by marrying Anne Boleyn and yet condemns her for acquiescing to such an equivocal position. He argues that the personal feelings of Catherine and Mary should not be allowed to obstruct a national good, but summons up considerable pity for Henry's personal dislikes and domestic unhappiness in order to justify his divorces.

Froude in effect wants to make a Carlylean hero out of Henry—a hero who acts rather than talks, who defends order against chaos, who instinctively separates sham from truth. Although he blames the "barren disputings" in which Henry entangles himself on his early theological training, Froude is clearly embarrassed that it took the King so long to trust to his "instincts as an English statesman" and affirm the simple truth in his heart rather than entering into a "legal labyrinth" to justify the divorce (H, 1:268-70). Froude is obviously relieved when Henry is forced to defy the Pope openly. In contrast to the distracted Clement who snivels and fawns, falls back on "Italianate cunning" when flattery will not serve, he can pose Henry as a Frederick the Great, a general in a state of war, with no time to mince words in his swift commands for swift obedience (H, 2:235-36). In the end Froude argues that Henry's "honest inconsistency," the trait of "men of practical ability in times of change," was in fact the key to his ultimate success. It allowed him to bring the nation through "the hardest crisis in its history" without revolution and to lay the foundations of modern England (H, 4:490, 492). Guided by common sense rather than theory and exonerated by time, Henry is, as Burrow suggests, a distinctively whiggish hero—notwithstanding Froude's efforts to endow him with Carlylean grasp on transcendent truths.[26]

Froude needed villainy as much as heroism to maintain the tension in his "mythic" view of the Reformation. If Henry is the incarnation of the silent truths of Protestantism, Mary Stuart is the epitome of Roman Catholic duplicity. Froude is wary of the sentimental and sensational appeal she traditionally had for English readers. By exaggerating rather than blunting the drama of her life he makes its obvious theatricality proof of all the falsehood for which she stands. She is from the beginning never more than a wily hypocrite and consummate actress, a genius that thrived only in the "uncertain twilight of conspiracy" (H, 8:83). Her religion would have been enough to condemn her in his eyes, but he will not allow her sincerity even in that. Elizabeth's equal in intellectual gifts, Mary lacked her ability to feel "like a man an unselfish interest in a great cause" (H, 7:368). She cared only for the gratification of her own selfish passions, and "sacrificed her own noble nature on the foul altar of sensuality and lust" (H, 9:44). To be sure, she gains a certain stature in her very villainy. Froude accords her grudging admiration for her physical courage and singlemindedness, both of which contrast markedly with Elizabeth's ambivalence and vacillation. Scenes in which she figures most prominently—the murders of Rizzio and Darnley, for instance—are among the most lively in the second half of the *History*. But Froude allows us to appreciate them only because we know they are virtuoso performances by a woman who sins with full knowledge of her guilt. When facts are missing, invention makes his cause. He encourages us to sympathize with Darnley's growing fears by suggesting that Mary's plan to remove him to the isolated Craigmillar "had an ominous sound. The words were kind, but there was perhaps some odd glitter of the eyes not wholly satisfactory" (H, 8:365). He makes her assumed complicity in Darnley's murder even more appalling by imagining that she went to bed, "to sleep, doubtless—sleep with the soft tranquility of an innocent child," after leaving Darnley to his fate (H, 8:370).

Froude controls our point of view to the end. It is not enough that we merely witness Mary's execution: its "human interest" derives

History as Protestant Apologia

from our "knowing" that it was all a charade. In Froude's eyes there is no doubt of this: "It would be affectation to credit her with a genuine feeling of religion." Mary's insistence that she died as a martyr to her faith rather than as a conspirator against Elizabeth's life was but a last desperate gesture at a revenge that might outlive her (H, 12:352). Her very effrontery earns her his back-handed compliment: her fortitude in the face of death was all the more noteworthy because it could not spring from devotion to a higher cause (H, 12:353). The "elaborate care" with which she prepared to encounter her end provides evidence of how skillfully she stage-managed her last performance. She exchanges the plain grey dress for a sumptuous black satin hung with crucifixes and paternosters, her false hair veiled in white. She resorts to tears in order to wheedle permission for some of her own people to witness her death: she could not, after all, leave in the hands of Puritans responsibility for reporting the "religious melodrame" she contemplated. She sweeps into the execution chamber "as if coming to take a part in some solemn pageant," and drowns out the prayers of the Anglican dean with her own "powerful deep-chested tones," interspersing English with Latin so the audience might be sure in which faith she left the world.

Lest we miss the point, Froude punctures her piety with trenchant irony: "She prayed for the Church which she had been ready to betray, for her son, whom she had disinherited, for the Queen whom she had endeavoured to murder. She prayed God to avert his wrath from England, that England which she had sent a last message to Philip to beseech him to invade. She forgave her enemies, whom she had invited Philip not to forget" (H, 12:358). The black dress is removed to reveal a blood red costume that, he surmises, must have been carefully studied for the appalling "pictorial effect" it would create as she stood on the scaffold, surrounded by black figures. He turns the final action into a ghastly symbol of her own duplicity and of the degeneration of the Church she represents: "The coif fell off and the false plaits. The laboured illusion vanished. The lady who had knelt before the block was in the maturity of grace and loveliness. The executioner, when he raised the head . . . exposed the withered features of a grizzled, wrinkled old woman" (H, 12:361). Froude allows the brilliance of the acting but cuts short "the admiration and pity which cannot be refused her." He sternly reminds us that "she was leaving the world with a lie upon her lips. She was a bad woman, disguised in the livery of a martyr" (H, 12:362). Misplaced sympathy for her tragic end had obscured the fact that her execution, far from being the one blot on Elizabeth's reign, had been instrumental in paralyzing Catholic resistance and allowing the Queen to meet the Armada at the head of an undivided nation.

Arguments for political expedience notwithstanding, in this case Froude's eloquence backfired. Even readers with no illusions about Mary's innocence were repelled by the violence of his rhetoric and found his gloating triumph over her final humiliation in questionable taste.[27] Froude would perhaps not have strained so hard to blacken Mary had the contrasts between her and Elizabeth been sharper. His "mythic" view of the Reformation had dictated perspectives hard to maintain without some artificial heightening of the background. The heroine he needed to satisfy his melodrama formula dissolved in his hands, leaving only the crassest of pragmatists to embody the "good" cause. He originally conceived Elizabeth as a plain-dealing Tudor foil to Mary's caricature of Stuart fraud. She was to be a solitary heroine "braving and ruling the tempest" of Reformation politics (B, 172). She starts out as the perfect daughter to her manly and straightforward father: here was a queen who "rode, shot, jested, and drank beer; spat, and swore upon occasions; swore not like 'a comfitmaker's wife,' but round, mouth-filling oaths, which would have satisfied Hotspur" (H, 11:17-18). But he found Elizabeth's plain-dealing as hard to sustain as her heroism. As he delved deeper into archival evidence, Froude became more and more convinced that Elizabeth's greatness had actually been that of her advisors, and that she had been the champion of the Reformation in spite of herself.

At the outset he had refused to believe of Elizabeth what he so easily credited in Mary: that one exposed to great personal risk as leader of a country in crisis could be heavily influenced by personal motives. Further research revealed disquieting similarities between the two women, however. Having distinguished Mary from Elizabeth by the former's indulgence in her own licentious pleasures, he had with some embarrassment to account for Elizabeth's extended dalliance with Sir Robert Dudley, "technically honourable" though it might have been. He can rely only in part on our sympathy for the loneliness of the young queen with no one to guide her choice of friends, or for the isolation of the mature woman concealing the emotional emptiness of her life by idling with her human playthings. He tries shifting the blame to Anne Boleyn, arguing that Elizabeth's great and sovereign nature must have been "dashed with a taint which she inherited with her mother's blood" (H, 7:88). Nevertheless, one can trace his growing impatience as she trifled with half the crowns of Europe, too infatuated with Dudley to marry any, until it gathers to the final condemnation:

> Queens do not reign for their own pleasure, and the ignoble passion which had prevented her from making an honourable marriage when she was young, with a prospect of children, was no justification of her barren age which [in 1580] threatened the realm with convulsions. Individuals may trifle at their foolish will with character or fortune; sovereigns, on whom depends the weal of empires, contract duties from their high places, which their private humours cannot excuse them for neglecting. (H, 11:185)

His claim that Elizabeth's "unselfish interest in a great cause" allowed her to resist the personal temptations to which Mary succumbed also falters as evidence accumulates. He attempts at first to excuse a dishonesty and unscrupulousness equal to Mary's own by arguing that Elizabeth's "object in itself was excellent, and those who pursue high purposes through crooked ways, deserve better of mankind . . . than those who pick their way in blameless inanity" (H, 11:27-28). As he proceeds, however, he must more frequently acknowledge that her only object was to protect her throne and that she furthered the Reformation only insofar as it helped accomplish this end. Although wearied by repeated instances of her deceit, at the beginning of volume 12 he still defends her: dishonesty that would have irretrievably compromised a man's honor, deception that if pursued for a personal object would have been called "detestable treachery," might be "half pardoned for the general rectitude of her purpose," as well as for the inherent weakness of her sex (H, 12:25-26).

His final analysis affords only the most qualified praise, nonetheless. Vacillation must be expected from one who had no theological convictions. Elizabeth had realized (like the young Froude) that "the speculations of so-called divines were but as ropes of sand and sea-slime leading to the moon," but she had no larger or deeper convictions with which to replace them. If her insight were keen and her mind sharp, she lacked the "intellectual emotions which give the human character its consistency and power" (H, 12:583). Her personal bravery and economy hardly redeemed the grotesqueness of her vanity and affectation. In the end what was a powerful claim for Henry has faded to grudging acquiesence: "The greatest achievement in English history . . . was completed without bloodshed under

James Anthony Froude

Elizabeth's auspices, and Elizabeth may have the glory of the work" (H, 12:587). One cannot help feeling that it was really Froude's disillusionment with his badly tarnished heroine that convinced him to end his study at the Armada rather than follow her life out to its close as originally planned.[28]

This *History of England* is preponderantly a drama of palace intrigue. We get out of the court and stateroom periodically to the village, the battlefield, and the high seas, but we still miss that deep responsiveness to place that triggered the "imaginative archaeology" of Arnold and Carlyle and allowed even Macaulay to make cityscapes as real as his people. The battle of faith and its defenders carries for Froude much more weight than battles of men and ships. Granted, the materials for military history were disappointing. The vacillation and stinginess that were Elizabeth's trademarks told most heavily on her army and navy. The military chronicle of her reign offers an almost unremitting tale of ignominious defeats and ambiguous victories (e.g., H, 7:236, 529; 8:25). The heroism of English soldiers is repeatedly undercut by the pusillanimity of their commander-in-chief. Notwithstanding Froude's contempt for the Irish, their very barbarity informed their wars with an unqualified bravery and singlemindedness that inspires a lyric intensity he seldom could muster for the English (e.g., H, 8:429).

Luckily the Armada's defeat provided an unambiguous victory of surpassing historical importance. "It is all action," he wrote, "and I shall use my materials badly if I cannot make it as interesting as a novel." He closes his massive work in a "blaze of fireworks" (B, 310) that illuminated a moment of national triumph and solidarity. From the start Froude establishes his claim over the patriotic sympathies of his readers by presenting Spain's challenge as essentially political. By brushing aside theological issues, he treats England's response as a spontaneous outpouring of the national will—a rallying to the defense of age-old traditions of British freedom and independence that sets aside all differences of religious opinion. The spark of resistance flares first in the coastal towns, where news of the Spanish approach sets off saddling and arming and sends musters flocking to the ports. As it penetrates every corner of the country, the tidings set on fire "the patriotic heart of England" (H, 12:488). In the heat of this passion, chivalry is born anew and the commonplace is apotheosized into the heroic as all classes join in mutual support: "from Lyme, and Weymouth, and Poole, and the Isle of Wight, young lords and gentlemen came streaming out in every smack or sloop that they could lay hold of, to snatch their share of danger and glory at Howard's side"; if their strength was negligible, their presence proved to the crews that "the heart of England was with them" and thus "transformed every common seaman into a hero" (H, 12:489). Heroism and fortitude are needed all the more because of the government's inadequate support of its own troops. Froude's growing disgust with the Queen who "clung with the maddened grasp of passionate avarice" to the Burgundian diamonds while her navy starved, and niggled over every grain of powder while her admiral lay with empty magazines before an enemy twice his strength, is obvious. If it undercuts his portrait of national solidarity, this added disadvantage serves only to make the navy's final triumph over such great odds the more impressive.

Although himself an avid seaman, Froude viewed the action with the eye of the novelist rather than of the admiral. Precise, if largely imagined, details of weather and terrain place the reader on the scene: the early summer sun "shining softly on the white walls and vineyards of Coruña" as the majestic Armada drifted out on the purple waters, the "gibbous moon" that revealed to the Spanish the approach of the first English opposition, the "wild west wind" and "rolling breakers of the Atlantic" that wreck the remainder of the Armada on the Irish coast. We understand why the superstitious Spaniards view the English fireships, sent to force them away from Calais, as "some terrible engines of destruction," because Froude restores the scene as it would have appeared to them in all its shocking detail: "Certain dark objects which had been seen dimly drifting on the tide where the galleons lay thickest, shot suddenly into pyramids of light, flames leaping from ruddy sail to sail, flickering on the ropes and forecastles, foremasts and bowsprits a lurid blaze of conflagration" (H, 12:499). Major engagements are sketched in with sharp picturesque strokes: the Spanish ships moving like "Thames barges piled with hay" are never any match for the sharp low English ships, which shoot away "as if by magic in the eye of the wind" (H, 12:482). The decisive British attack pours "one continuous rain of shot" into the Spanish fleet, driving them into a confused and helpless mass; they are "hunted together as a shepherd hunts sheep upon a common" and herded onto the Flanders coast (H, 12:503). As the galleons heeled over, "their middle decks were turned into slaughter-houses, and in one ship blood was seen streaming from the lee scuppers" (H, 12:504).

James Anthony Froude

The taunts of the Spanish crews, daring the "Lutheran hens" to board, proved only "an idle bravado." The proud Castilian spirit was broken, and the remainder of the Armada chose to slink home via the Orkneys and Ireland. Froude drives home the ignominy of defeat by tracing out the grisly scenes of Spanish destruction as the survivors are savaged equally by the elements they had believed God controlled in the their favor and by the Irish whose religious camaraderie dissolves under the lure of plunder. Regardless of their position on the theological issues at stake, all readers could join in appreciating this brilliant celebration of English victory and proudly accord the *History* a place among the English classics.[29]

From the beginning Froude's work was better received by the general public than by the critics. And yet his brilliant style, unorthodox interpretations, and questionable accuracy would have made him no more controversial an historian than Carlyle or Macaulay had it not been for the much wider debate about the historian's function that crystallized around his career. His success crested at a time when the definition of "serious" history had begun to shift under the imposing pressures of a mass market and an emergent professionalism. Although his work supplied "scientific" scholars with ammunition against a popularization that they felt both challenged and undermined their standards, the general reader defended it as an eloquent testimony to the moral and imaginative power that the specialist would deny to history. Except among his staunchest supporters, Froude's revisions of sixteenth-century history converted few readers. But even many who disagreed with his interpretations paid tribute to the brilliance of his style and to the skill with which he brought to life actors in a thrilling historical pageant.[30]

Froude's accuracy found fewer defenders. The difficult work of deciphering and translating hundreds of manuscripts would have been a formidable challenge to any scholar. Froude proved an exceptionally careless copyist who compounded his errors by failing to make clear where he substituted paraphrases within quotations or excerpted without ellipsis marks. Goldwin Smith and E. A. Freeman were among the first to take him to task for factual errors in sixteenth-century history, and in later years T. Rice Holmes and W. S. Lilley found his *Caesar* and *Erasmus* similarly marred by misreadings, mistranslations, and mistakes.[31] Most reviewers recognized that his gravest errors concerned not accuracies of fact but accuracies of judgment—strong prejudice, not intellectual dishonesty, led him into so many misstatements and distorted emphases. But the same claims had been made against Macaulay, without branding him "essentially a rhetorician and not an historian," as A. V. Dicey said of Froude.[32]

When all is said and done, Froude's inaccuracy alone was not enough to disqualify him as a serious historian as defined by the standards of the 1870s and 1880s. It was certainly not enough to have turned "Froude's disease" into a byword for "constitutional inaccuracy" by the turn of the century had not more been at stake than errors alone.[33] As Freeman's attack makes clear, Froude served as a lightning rod for those who promulgated a new definition of the historian. Freeman's Anglican and Liberal sympathies were powerful sources of antipathy toward Froude, but professional jealousy was even stronger. Freeman resented the overwhelming popular success of a writer who ignored what he considered professional standards. The fact that Froude had undertaken far more primary research than Freeman did not absolve him of "original sin"; Freeman still claimed that he had tried to write about "a very difficult period of history without any proper apprenticeship to historical writing."[34] Froude's errors were "just the sort of things which superficial writers care nothing about, just the sort of things which superficial readers think it hypercritical to complain of; but . . . just the sort of things by which scholars judge whether a book is to be trusted or not."[35] Freeman and others attributed Froude's failings as much to the very nature of "literary" history as to the man himself. Goldwin Smith found it natural to find inaccuracy in a writer consumed by the desire for "pictorial effect."[36] He was joined by other commentators who worried about the way Froude's "historical romances" might warp the judgment of unsophisticated readers.[37]

Many reviewers blamed the readers themselves for encouraging unprofessional standards. As Henry Reeve put it, a "fiery spirit of partisanship" might be incompatible with justice and truth, but it "only renders the work more interesting and attractive to the reader."[38] William Donne unwittingly corroborated this charge by asserting that Froude's enthusiasm for the Protestant cause was a "better element in an historian's composition, than cold negation and apathy."[39] The tremendous vogue of historical writing of all sorts had, in the eyes of its critics, created an audience that was not just undiscriminating, but that actively preferred an entertaining style to solid scholarship, "pictorial effect" to accuracy. Frederic Harrison and Andrew Lang simply confirmed attitudes widely held at the turn of the century when they argued that it was impossible to combine the histrionic effect, sweeping judgments, and compelling narration essential to "literary" history with the cool objectivity, meticulous scholarship, and "infinite complexity of circumstance" demanded by scientific scholars.[40]

And yet, if some professionals believed they could uphold professional standards only by rejecting both the claims and methods of "literary" history, others were moved by the very violence of the attack against Froude to reaffirm the importance of imagination to full historical truth.[41] Nonprofessionals rallied in overwhelming numbers to support Froude, and by doing so to reaffirm the human and patriotic importance of history. Even Harrison admitted that the most meticulous scholarship was valueless if it never reached the public. Better that the general reader be beguiled into too lenient a view of the Tudors than that he "should feel no interest at all in them as men with purpose, brain, and courage."[42] T. Rice Holmes, like many readers, preferred the flawed diamond to the perfect crystal—the literary masterpiece that stirred the pulse and braced the patriotism of all who read to the scholarly omniscience that left them cold.[43] Even the *Saturday Review*, Froude's old nemesis, came to his defense in the nineties, affirming that minute accuracy was only "the small game of history," and that Froude's literary genius constituted adequate qualification for a Regius Professor.[44] If late Victorians acknowledged valid distinctions between a good historian and a good historical scholar, they still preferred the former as their public spokesman. Politics had much to do with Froude's appointment as Regius Professor, but so did the belief, still strong at the end of the century, that eloquence was at least as vital as scholarship—that it was as important to keep history alive in the imagination and in the heart as to satisfy the reason with cold hard facts and an austere objectivity.

Froude stands as one of the last great Victorian amateurs. Adopting the historian's vocation played a crucial role in his recoil from doubt into dogmatism. It gave him a way of legitimizing himself both professionally and ideologically. History was to him, as it was to Carlyle and Macaulay, a terrain reconstructed so as to make the present intelligible. He had found it necessary to free divine will and human purpose from their dependence on conflicting orthodoxies in order to protect the core of faith. In the long perspective of time, the doctrinal tides that had nearly shipwrecked him appeared as so many eddies on a stream whose course for the good was never turned aside. It is true that in order to vindicate this ultimate benevolence he felt he needed to find an historical refutation of specific doctrines. But his particular interpretations of the past were less important to his audience than his conviction that history taught morally and politically uplifting lessons and his genius at impressing these on the heart by way of the imagination.

In addition to endorsing Carlyle's political and social doctrines, Froude followed his example in the primary tenets of his historical faith as well: in his conviction that the elemental truths of the universe were manifested in the cyclical growth of beliefs and institutions, that man's nature was divine and its development consistent with moral law, that God's will was revealed in "the one great Bible which cannot lie": the history of the human race.[45] Like Carlyle he preserved historical truth from the corrosive effects of rationalism by locating it in the imagination, not the reason, and by declaring it accessible to poetic insight, not analytic proof. He too rejected "theories of history" as the tools by which ideologues manipulated this truth to legitimize their own world views, although he somewhat more forthrightly acknowledged the extent to which his own "myths" did the same. For both men history was a dramatic spectacle in which heroes and heroines were to enlarge our moral capacities by their example. Froude chose those heroes and heroines on the assumption that they would reinforce certain ideals, and like Carlyle with Frederick, he confronted difficult dramatic problems when he found them unequal to their task.

Despite this close affinity with Carlyle, in other respects Froude's artistic temperament had more common with Macaulay's. He lacked Carlyle's visionary power. His genius was narrative rather than metaphorical, better adapted to vivid outlines than to complex symbolism, and was never more brilliantly displayed than when engineering the melodramatic exposure of criminal queens and other traitors to the cause. His special pleading makes his characters seem more often paradoxical than complex. If he did not share Macaulay's cynicism and his insensitivity to the spiritual, he allowed his partisanship to determine which actions were consistent with "human nature" and which beliefs could be brushed aside as "mere" superstition. His

James Anthony Froude

casuistry, too, incurred charges that he was morally insensitive and/or intellectually dishonest, when in fact he was simply too convinced of the righteousness of his cause to recognize that what he saw as right and wrong others saw as a double standard. His investigation of manuscript sources, like Macaulay's immersion in popular literature, broke important ground in historical research, even while his mishandling of these materials discredited him as a serious scholar.

A family friend once described Froude as a man "apparently contradictory, almost inconsistent, because of his profound reverence for essential truth, and unsparing effort to arrive at it."[46] In his own intellectual journeying, Froude never seemed to find a secure resting place between Macaulay's sceptical reserve and Carlyle's leap of faith. For Macaulay truth was obvious because it was so limited. He never questioned whether his vision of reality was true—logic and common sense assured him it was. As for moral absolutes, it was enough to say that they were absurdly unfitted to guide practical behavior. For Carlyle truth was obvious because it dissolved all appearances. Moral absolutes were the only reliable reality. When Froude looked through facts he was overwhelmed by the fictionality of appearances but not by the reality of unified truth behind them. He posited the existence of such truth, but lacked the visionary power to sweep away all intellectual obstacles to reaching it. His strategy was one of compromise, not of transcendence. At times he placed truth beyond the reach of reason, but at others he appealed to reason to refute false truths. His scepticism was sometimes a weapon, sometimes a defense. If his struggle to arrive at truth led him into paradox, the journey was still necessary. Even readers who criticized him appreciated his willingness to undertake that journey for them.

The unprecedented amount of controversy over Froude's reputation does not indicate that he was below the standard of Victorian historiography so much as that he stood on the border line between conflicting definitions of what the historian should do and be. The very vigor of that controversy underlines the seriousness with which Victorians viewed the issues involved. Despite his scholarly failings, Froude became something of a patriotic fixture to a nation willing to overlook the eccentricities of his historical creed for his service in immortalizing great moments of the national past. To Frederic Harrison, the very fact that Froude was "attacked, admired, and condemned" by his readers was proof that at least his work would not be

History as Protestant Apologia

"put upon the shelf."[47] If he would always remain a talented amateur, a "popular writer of history" rather than a great historical scholar, still his narrative abilities served a vital purpose by nurturing the popular commitment to history's moral and imaginative functions at a time when the rise of professionalism was already beginning to fragment the audience for historical writing and to realign its priorities.

V

JOHN RICHARD GREEN
HISTORY AS NATIONAL BIOGRAPHY

Although forgotten by many now, John Richard Green was a bestselling historian in his day, one whose popularity rivaled Macaulay's. In the last quarter of the century, his *Short History of the English People*—the first serious work to give major emphasis to England's intellectual and social development—sold over 235,000 copies in England alone and enjoyed wide use as a school text.[1] He owed his success to many of the same sources as Macaulay: to his own highly engaging style and compelling historical imagination, as well as to a burgeoning middle class audience eager to improve themselves and particularly receptive to his cultural confirmation of whiggish progress. Green's divided allegiances made his position more anomalous than Macaulay's, however. If the success of the *Short History* placed him in the front rank of popularizers, his intellectual sympathies as well as his personal friendships have traditionally identified him as a member of the "Oxford School" of historians, along with E. A. Freeman and William Stubbs, other pioneering medievalists who brought a new rigor and thoroughness to the study of their period. The fact that Green felt the need to legitimize himself as a serious historian by following the *Short History* with two more original and minutely documented studies of early England suggests the conscious pressures of his position. Ultimately, years of invalidism took their toll on the quality of his scholarship, and his early death cut short the most promising late Victorian effort to bridge the gap between popular and professional expectations. Green's career has interest as much for his efforts to accommodate the popularizing impulse of Victorian history to the increasingly incompatible demands of the new scholarship, as for his success in providing the middle classes with a Whig history of their own social, intellectual, and economic evolution.

Green grew up steeped in the history of his native Oxford, where he was born in 1837.[2] He shook off the conservative influences of his childhood even sooner than Macaulay and Freeman, rebelling against his Tory, High Church family as early as 1850, when he was temporarily banished from his uncle's house for ridiculing the uproar over "Papal Aggression." The Whig sympathies of his prize essay condemning Charles I so alarmed his headmaster at the Magdalen College School that he recommended the boy be sent to a private tutor in 1852. Under his tutor's supervision Green prepared to win an open scholarship at Jesus College, where he matriculated in 1855. His reaction to the newly established School of Law and Modern History confirmed the criticisms made by its adversaries on the Oxford Reform Commission. He found the study of law dull and rebelled against the expectation that the student should confine himself to those selected fragments of books that would "pay" in the schools. Scorning the competition for prizes on these terms, he instead pursued an eclectic study of eighteenth-century writers and settled for a pass in physical science. He might have continued indefinitely his boycott of historical study had not he made the acquaintance of A. P. Stanley, then professor of ecclesiastical history. Stanley offered Green an example of a scholar for whom work was not simply a matter of classes and fellowships, and under his influence Green soon resumed his studies. These bore their first fruit in a series of twenty-two colorful narrative sketches of Oxford life in the eighteenth century, which appeared in the *Oxford Chronicle* during 1859 and 1860.[3] Although perhaps inspired by the contemporary popularity of Macaulay's *History*, these articles show how early Green developed his own distinctively picturesque and and anecdotal grasp of social history. They also illustrate his life-long conviction of the importance of municipal history in England's past, for they intentionally tell the story of Oxford's life as a town and not just as a university.

In "a fit of religious enthusiasm," Green took orders in 1861; inspired by Christian Socialism, he deliberately chose to work in the squalid parishes of London's East End for the next seven years. De-

John Richard Green

spite its demands on his time and already fragile health, Green always felt that his ministry among the poor had been vital to his understanding of history, convincing him that due attention should be given to the social condition of the masses in any account of the past. During this same period his sympathies with nationalism were also developing. With his friend Boyd Dawkins he founded a short-lived Jesus College magazine in 1862 to explore the College's roots in Welsh culture and history. Green's historical interests gravitated toward the early and middle ages, and although projected histories of Somersetshire, Ireland, the Archbishops of Canterbury, and the Angevin Kings were never completed, a paper on Dunstan he read before the Somersetshire Archaeological Society in 1862 won him the attention of E. A. Freeman. The acquaintance blossomed into a warm friendship and scholarly camaraderie despite their differences in temperament and historical approach. Through Freeman's intervention Green became a *Saturday* reviewer in the late sixties and early seventies, when the magazine was shaping educated opinion about "serious" history.

The strain of working late into the night turning out reviews and "middles" to defray mounting parish expenses eventually took its toll on Green's consumptive constitution. By the end of 1869 he had already been advised that his chances for life were precarious. The forced termination of all parish duties was fortuitous, for it enabled Green to avoid that break with the Church his growing scepticism would soon have necessitated. He had from early years acknowledged the authority of science, believing at first that it might be used to aggrandize the authority of religion by clearing away false interpretations from "True Revelation."[4] He hoped to find the "faith of the future" in the union of a nondoctrinal "Mysticism" with freedom of thought and inquiry (LG, 80). He stretched the limits of Broad Church liberalism to their utmost in an effort to accommodate the spirit of rational inquiry to sincere belief, but instead he wound up marooned between the separate spheres of "intellectual credence" and "religious faith" (LG, 164). In 1867 he noted with regret that he had lost Stubbs's confidence in "the old simple lesson that the world's history led up to God" and had found nothing to replace it (LG, 176). He avoided breaking openly with Christianity by settling for an assurance that "formularies" no longer literally credible might still be honored because they "have . . . an ideal truth, embody a great doctrine, continue the chain of Christian tradition" (LG, 164). Like

History as National Biography

Froude, Green exchanged the vocation of priest for that of historian, shifting his efforts from reconciling reason with dogma to the less controversial ground of historical interpretation. Green, however, sought no retreat from the perils of free thinking or from the antipathetic realities of the present. He not only approved the modern triumphs of liberalism but reconstructed history to justify them. As historian he transformed a gospel of Christian striving and conscience into a gospel of secular progress and social consciousness. If less explicitly providential than the interpretations of earlier historians, the national success story he told fulfilled the same romance patterns: the discovery and maturation of true identity, the struggle and triumph of the "good" cause.

The threat of death shadowed the remainder of Green's life. He began work on the *Short History* in 1869, hoping that if he lived it would serve as an introduction to future studies and that ten years of research would not be wasted should he die shortly after its completion. Forced to protect his health by spending his winters away from England and English libraries and receiving little support even from his friends for his then unorthodox approach to social history, he often found the *History* discouraging work. But his efforts were more than rewarded when it became an overnight best-seller after its release in December of 1874. Its success freed Green from his financial worries, and a temporary arrest of his disease allowed him to hope that time remained for more substantial achievements to answer the critics who would brand him merely a popularizer. He continued his historical labors through the decade, enlarging the *Short History* into the four-volume *History of the English People* (1877-80), editing a historical reader for the schools, supervising a series of historical and literary primers, and publishing with his wife *A Short Geography of the British Isles* (1879). He went on to expand his account of England's earliest days yet again in his most original work, *The Making of England* (1880). His desire to complete its sequel, *The Conquest of England*, kept him alive long after his doctors had given up hope, but he left the book to be finished and published posthumously by his wife after his death in 1883. To the end of his days Green remained an ardent liberal, deeply sympathetic with nationalistic movements in Europe and Ireland and driven by the desire to make real for his own people the evolution of their national identity and of the freedoms he believed were fundamental to it.

John Richard Green

In an early diary, Green accused himself of a dislike for "abstract thought" that tempted him to "subordinate general tendencies to particular events and principles to individuals" (LG, 104). He was perhaps too hard on himself, for what he later called his "impulse to try to connect things, to find the 'why' of things" (LG, 438) informed his "Herodotean" celebration of the particular with powerful explanatory continuities.[5] Underpinning these continuities was his conventional Whig belief in the "unity" of western history in general and English history in particular. In his earliest writings, cyclical recurrence unified past and present. Just as infancy more closely resembled senility than did robust manhood, he argued, so too in the history of mankind analogous cultural phenomena seemed to recur at varying intervals (OS, 27-28). The nineteenth century had more in common with the moral spirit of the Renaissance than with that of the worldly eighteenth century and shared a greater intellectual sympathy with the age of Pericles than with that of Dunstan (OS, 233; LG, 176). However, the dominant pattern of Green's thought lay not in the Carlylean alternation of epochs or in an Arnoldean comparison of cultures, and it was something more than a Whig celebration of political continuity. Green's ultimate aim was to depict "the organic life of a nation as a whole" (LG, 427), to reconstruct the evolution not of the English constitution but of the English people. He made literal the metaphor of national identity used by Carlyle and Arnold. His sense of continuity, like the tools he brought to the task, was that of the geologist or archaeologist. He set out to retrieve as many artifacts of his culture as possible, to demarcate the significant strata in which they were deposited and to extrapolate from external evidence the internal harmonies that defined each stage of evolution.

National identity was for Green the central reality of history. His conception of national life went far beyond even Arnold's moralized politics. "A State," Green believed, "is accidental; it can be made or unmade; but a nation is something real which can be neither made nor destroyed" (LG, 391). Political decrees could no more establish national consciousness than they could a mountain or a river: things that were not artifacts but organisms, the product of forces sometimes violent but always working from within to modify, not to create. To Green the conventional stuff of history constituted but "the outer forms" of a people's inner life, of that collective personality or state of mind that was central to his romantic sense of nationalism. He pointed to the French Revolution as proof that the "spiritual forces" sneered at by the *philosophes* were in fact "the deepest and strongest of realities" in political life, the mainspring from which the "outer phenomena" of change proceeded.[6] For Green two intertwined strands of national consciousness—the aspirations for brotherhood and for liberty—lay at the heart of these "spiritual forces." He condemned Disraeli's foreign policy for its insensitivity to the nationalistic sympathies reshaping nineteenth-century Europe and took care to make his own histories "spiritual" biographies of national life.

Because they recorded the history of states rather than peoples, political documents could supplement and correct history, but they could never *be* history in Green's eyes (LG, 150). To explain the great impulses that determined national identity, the historian needed to base political history on social history in its widest sense. Green could not rest satisfied with the limited attention given to sociocultural detail along "the old traditional lines of English historians"—Gibbon, Hume, Macaulay;[7] he became a crusader for nothing less than history that gave major weight to the moral, social, and intellectual development of the English people. Hence his manifesto in the introduction to the *Short History*:

> Whatever the worth of the present work may be, I have striven throughout that it should never sink into a "drum and trumpet history." It is the reproach of historians that they have too often turned history into a mere record of the butchery of men by their fellow-men. . . . If some of the conventional figures of military and political history occupy in my pages less than the space usually given them, it is because I have had to find a place for figures little heeded in common history—the figures of the missionary, the poet, the printer, the merchant, and the philosopher.[8]

Focusing on national identity became in effect Green's way of imposing the analytic insight of the "scientific" historian on the miscellaneousness of the antiquarian. Green shared with Freeman an early love of architectural history; nonetheless, he later ridiculed the pedantry of archaeological societies for setting aside "the real life of the people" for "fights over mouldings and endless discussions over conventual drains." He believed this same failure of "philosophic" insight prevented history's importance from being fully appreciated.[9] The *Short History* represented his attempt to "put facts on a philosophical basis" by showing political events to be "the outcome of

John Richard Green

social or religious currents of thought" (LG, 359). His scientific history was explicitly progressive: the historian escaped from "a mere bondage to details" by describing the moral, social, and intellectual "advance" of man.[10]

The beauty of Green's "philosophy" was that, like Carlyle's "science," it still guaranteed the primacy of the individual, the human, the suprarational. To Green, Freeman's exclusive attention to constitutional changes showed that he was not enough convinced of "the superiority of man in himself to all the outer circumstances that surround him."[11] Political documents were merely the manifestation of that "inner life" determined by thought, feeling, spirit. To comprehend this inner life, the historian had to sympathize with the age, to value the smallest datum for the genuine insight it offered into human experience. If he had periodically to step back from the crowd to get the "general effect" of where they were headed, he had also to move and feel with them. Thus Green's historian could still indulge the antiquarian's love of detail for its own sake and the romantic's yearning for empathy without forfeiting his claims to be "philosophical."

Philosophical insight guaranteed the traditional moral dimension in history as well. Green agreed with William of Malmesbury that history was the chief part of ethics and that "no historical teaching can be really sound or effective which shrinks from recognizing the power of human lives in the past over human conduct in the present."[12] He was as sceptical as Arnold of the value of strict impartiality or historicism, for either might subvert this didactic function. Criticizing Edith Thompson's *School History of England*, he argued that "there is no real impartiality in this avoidance of all expression of love for what is good and of hatred for what is evil in human conduct; and to avoid them, in fact, is to take the very soul out of history."[13] In Green's own judgments, morality unequivocally outweighed political expediency. The "moral grandeur" of Alfred's life lifted him to the level of the world's greatest men despite the narrowness of his impact on world history, but Godwin's complete lack of integrity made it a misuse of terms to call him "great" no matter how important his contributions to English unity. Like Arnold, Green believed the historian who posed as a mere chronicler similarly shirked his duty. Value-free narration was as impossible as it was undesirable. A principle of selection and judgment necessarily governed which facts were presented to readers, and to pretend, as Froude appeared to do, that readers were free to judge the facts for themselves was either disingenuous or simply irresponsible.[14]

Green proudly proclaimed his own point of view: he would go on "loving freedom" to the end (LG, 477). Focusing on national identity as the pulse of historical change was the logical fruition of his democratic sympathies. He opposed a "great man" theory of causation because he believed in the greater importance of "the people." Hero-worship, in addition to blinding the historian to the moral failings of the men he would deify (witness Froude's Henry or Freeman's Godwin) also ignored the weight of *Zeitgeist* in effecting change. Individuals still played a major role in Green's histories, but he treated them as he expected the subjects of a projected series of biographical primers to be treated, as types of their time, representative men (LG, 249-50). His point in arguing that the thoughts of even the most original thinkers were but "the expression of the great tide of feeling which is sweeping them, like the world around them, unconsciously on" was not to make the *Zeitgeist* all powerful as had Macaulay or Froude. Green stressed the power of these "tides of feeling" precisely because he considered them swelled by "great currents of popular sentiment." His anonymous millions did not need the efforts of a Carlylean hero to marshal them into order; they in effect created the real order of history. They shaped the spiritual progress of mankind far more than they were shaped by it.[15] The "spiritual forces" behind history were inherently more egalitarian for Green than for Carlyle, even if their purpose was the same: to make history morally meaningful by asserting the greater importance of mind and will over the material machinery of life.

Where Froude and Carlyle returned to the past to find principles for reordering the present and Macaulay to rejoice in disorder outgrown, Green affirmed constant principles of order unifying past and present. He sought to understand and to reconstruct the way the different layers of social, cultural, and political experience had formed that order. Notwithstanding their belief in underlying continuity, Carlyle and Macaulay both call attention to the disjunctures of history: to what had been lost, superseded, replaced, for better or worse. Green emphasizes the connectedness of past and present. He is always straining for the resemblances that reveal the kernel of identity in the transformation of the features over time. Reading history becomes for him

John Richard Green

a series of recognitions, of discerning the points at which the foreign becomes the familiar, the new the traditional.

The most obvious form this process took was in his extrapolation of the Whig view back before the thirteenth century. Along with Stubbs and Freeman, Green helped give scholarly credibility to the argument that representative democracy could claim the most ancient precedents, being implicit in the Teutonic institutions of the earliest "true" Englishmen.[16] Although able to criticize Freeman for a "Teutonic fanaticism," Green was no less convinced that the Teutonic invasions of the fifth century wiped out the whole organization of Roman government and society along with the people governed by it. The basis of Teutonic society was the free landholder, its guiding principle representation. At the heart of this society was the moot, where the kinfolk, later the wise men, met to dispense justice, frame their laws, and choose leaders who in peace time remained narrowly bounded by the customs and advice of their people. Green, like other Whig medievalists, traced a direct line between these village moots and modern parliament, and between representative democracy and Victorian success. No wonder that in his eyes

> it is with a reverence such as is stirred by the sight of the headwaters of some mighty river that one looks back to these village-moots of Friesland and Sleswick. It was here that England learned to be a "mother of Parliaments" . . . talk is persuasion, and persuasion is force, the one force which can sway freemen to deeds such as those which have made England what she is. The "talk" of the village moot, the strife and judgment of men giving freely their own rede and setting it as freely aside for what they learn to be the wiser rede of other men, is the groundwork of English history.

In the lineal descent of their institutions, Green's readers found proof that despite enormous change, they were "the same race still." It might be difficult to see the resemblance between the oak and the acorn, but the assurance of continuity between them guaranteed the stability and permanence of national identity.[18]

Green's account included the other fixtures of the Whig view as well. He emphasized more heavily the fact that the degradation of the freeman in a government becoming increasingly feudal and oligarchical was what allowed the successful Danish conquests of the eleventh century, although he also believed that neither these nor the Norman Conquest severed the social and political continuity of the

History as National Biography

English nation. He viewed the Great Charter as a reaffirmation rather than a manifesto of legal rights and dated modern political England from the reign of Edward I. He dispensed with York and Tudor challenges to parliamentary power in a more novel way, by labeling these reigns "The New Monarchy." The Tudor view of monarchical privilege "was the result, not of any gradual development, but of a simple revolution; and it was only by a revolution that the despotism of the New Monarchy was again done away" (SH, 303). The Long Parliament confirmed a historical truth as well as a legal one when it in effect returned English political development to the point where it had broken off, with the constitutional precedents of the Lancasters. Green's more democratic sympathies led him to assert that in England, "a reverence for the traditions of the past was made broad and living" by both "a deep conviction of abstract human right" and by "a practical sense of present necessities."[19] Despite this unwhiggish enthusiasm for "abstract" rights, he still agreed that reliance on precedent, not theory, accounted for the stability of English government and that by supporting the natural unfolding of progress, the English had attained a supremacy destined to grant them "the primacy of the world" in future ages.[20]

Green set his own stamp on the Whig view by tracing over this traditional Whig skeleton the more distinctive lineaments of "the people's" political advances. "In England, more than elsewhere," he reminded his readers, "constitutional progress has been the result of social development" (SH, iv). An early enthusiast for municipal history, he found the most significant role in this progress played by the urban middle classes. They emerge from his pages as the true custodians of English freedoms. Unlike their continental counterparts, English towns were coeval with the foundation of English society; the guild was an inevitable development of Teutonic life, the burgher the freeman within the walls.[21] English municipal freedom, like national freedom, was insured by the necessities of kings and by the slow growth of wealth and popular spirit, rather than by the violent revolts necessary to wrest liberty from continental seigneurs (OS, 21). Far from deploring the growth of commercial wealth as had Froude, Green asserted that it had allowed towns of the eleventh century to buy back those freedoms that had passed from the people at large into the hands of the feudal nobility, and from them into the hands of the Norman kings (SH, 94). The men of the borough-mote and merchant guilds had thus done more than knights and barons to make England

John Richard Green

what she is: "In the silent growth and elevation of the English people the boroughs led the way: unnoticed and despised by prelate and noble, they had alone preserved the full tradition of Teutonic liberty. The rights of self-government, of free speech in free meeting, of equal justice by one's equals, were brought safely across the ages of Norman tyranny by the traders and shop-keepers of the towns" (SH, 121).

Green was far from insensitive to the injustices provoked by class interest. Nonetheless, he found the urban middle classes defining the contours of virtually every significant stratum of English history. He documented far more fully than Macaulay the collective heroism of the middling orders. When he too sought a modern paradigm in Abbot Samson, he based it not on the Abbot's wise paternalism, but on his foresight in renewing the municipal liberties of Bury St. Edmond.[22] In his eyes Magna Charta claimed no liberties not already won by those plain burghers whom the barons despised. The decisive factor in Simon de Montfort's rise to power was the "new democratic spirit" at work in the towns, where "the purely industrial classes" were eventually successful in challenging the wealthy merchants for control of municipal administration (SH, 178). The union of the baronage with the commerical classes in the thirteenth-century Commons prevented Parliament from being paralyzed by the mutual jealousies of the four orders or from becoming the mere instrument of an aristocratic caste (SH, 248). The moral power of the middling orders was no less decisive a force in encouraging political development. Puritanism drew its greatest strength from their support. Its greatest attraction lay in its (distinctly un-Carlylean) promotion of greater social equality (SH, 458-59). The Puritans' seventeenth-century triumph marked the point at which "national opinion" had become what it remained ever since: "the supreme irresistible force in English politics" (HEP, 4:116). Green, needless to say, approved this force as heartily as Carlyle condemned it. Green also appreciated the way these classes kept alive the "old piety" through ages of ecclesiastical abuse and neglect and saw real value in the Methodist revival of moral and philanthropic zeal that sprang from their midst in the late eighteenth century (SH, 707). In his eyes more than crass self-interest had brought men of business into conflict with Whig monopoly at this same time: their earnestness was outraged by bribery and corruption, their patriotism by the politics of personal gain, their sense of efficiency by government mismanagement (HEP, 4:283). Green tacitly invited his readers to see in the Reform Bills of the nineteenth century the eventual triumph of this particular part of the English people; it was a moral as well as a political victory. Although no apologist for Philistinism, Green, like Macaulay, saw in the extension of the franchise a vindication of the inherent superiority of English political traditions. In the place of drums and trumpets he offered the Victorian middle classes a history of their own: a Whig view of the peaceful revolution which, through centuries of slow development, had finally brought them to power and seemed to identify their strengths and interests with the best qualities of the nation at large.

It would be misleading to suggest that this saga of political freedom constitutes all or even the most important part of national identity for Green. Freedom was for him what authority was for Froude and Carlyle: the central theme of his reading of history. The struggle of the English people to emerge as an independent nation and then to realize personal liberty in all its forms is the underlying pattern to which all else eventually relates. Green's inquiry into cultural evidence is no mere appendage to his political account, but the warp in his weave of national identity. "The Universities," "The English Towns" "The Friars," "The New Learning" demarcate essential features in England's progress toward its modern liberty of conscience, thought, and action. Green's eye for detail was omnivorous but not indiscriminate. He remains the "philosophical" historian who views every datum he includes in relation to this maturation of English liberties.

Green reads domestic detail for lessons more egalitarian than Macaulay's or Froude's. He notes the ingenuity and beauty of the Roman villa, but also reminds his readers of the squalid huts of serfs that once adjoined their frescoed walls, offering a silent indictment of the "union of material wealth with social degradation that lay like a dark shadow over the Roman world" (M, 45). The sumptuary laws that to Froude demonstrate the moral restraint of the upper classes reveal to Green their selfish anxiety about the laborer's and farmer's progress in comfort and wealth; he notes with satisfaction that such laws could do little to stop this progress as wages continued to rise after the Plague (SH, 295). In the display of commercial wealth that Froude reads as a sign of moral decay, Green finds the origins of the "peculiarly English" conception of domestic comfort. The rise of the commercial classes during Elizabeth's time improved the "mean appearance" of medieval towns with parapeted fronts, carved staircases, and quaint gables. The transition from medieval fortress to Elizabethan hall constituted an advance because it testified to the extinction of the feudal character of the noblesse; gilded turrets replaced battlements and Italian gardens replaced moats because comfort and refinement attained a greater priority than defense. Green's satisfaction with these signs stems not from Macaulay's relentlessly material standards of judgment, still less from his contempt for barbarity overcome. For one thing, to Green such architectural details are not relics of a world superseded; "we still gaze with pleasure" (SH, 400) on those gables and fretted fronts and in gazing possess them as something yet living. Even where he can no longer see the evidence of earlier stages of civilization, he affirms their contribution to present life and liberties. Once assimilated into English identity, earlier modes of life cannot be repudiated without denying identity itself.

From Green's consideration of literature, education, and religion emerges an analogous pattern of the gradual unifying and democratizing of English culture. Because progress in England's earliest days was aided by the development of a national literature, Green takes note of the "popular poetry" inspired by Ealdhelm (M, 337) and the expansion and consolidation of the Chronicle under Alfred, both of which helped unify national consciousness.[23] Layamon's English expansion of "Brut" demands attention despite its worthlessness as history because it shows that the language remained uncorrupted by one hundred and fifty years of Norman and Angevin rule. Green makes it symbolize the spirit of national resistance soon to triumph in Magna Charta (SH, 147). He most emphasizes those forms of literature that illuminate the spirit of the age and gauge its intellectual development. He finds in Cadmon "a type of the new grandeur, depth and fervor of tone which the German race was to give to the religion of the East" (SH, 64). Shakespeare represents the last flowering of the English Renaissance, Milton the "completest type of Puritanism," Dryden the reaction of the critical intellect against the Puritan temper.

Like his predecessors, Green placed great value on the ability of literature, especially popular literature, to "disentomb" the "common daily life of the past," and urged his fellow historians down the "bye-ways" of literature to learn how men had really lived (OS, 180). But he is really more interested in the sociology of literary development than in the lives these sources reflect. Literary evidence serves as a barometer of intellectual advance. If devoid of literary value, the homilies, grammars, and lesson books that poured out in the late tenth century testified to a "quickening of educational zeal among the people at large" (C, 298). Despite the "intellectual decay" of the fifteenth century, the popularity of compendia and abridgments showed that "literature was ceasing to be the possession of a purely intellectual class" (SH, 307). He attributes the impact of the Puritan Bible to the fact that at the time it was "the whole literature which was practically accessible to ordinary Englishmen"; it gave a loftiness to vulgar speech while it purified the temper of the whole nation.

Green traces the democratization of intellect even more directly in the history of university and Church. His analytical eye is trained on the social and political importance of religious institutions, not on the transcendent truths those symbols of spiritual health might have disclosed to Carlyle and Arnold. He finds the early Church significant because it poured a new spirit of manhood into a people crushed and degraded by Roman imperialism; it freed and invigorated man's moral and intellectual faculties and kept alive in its internal structure "the free democratic traditions of a world strangled by Caesarism."[24] Its administrative hierarchy later helped unify warring tribes into a single nation (M, 311-12), and its parish structure preserved the governing principles of the village moot (C, 16). In sharp distinction to Carlyle, Green characteristically gives greater emphasis to the Church's role in subverting outworn authority than in conserving tradition. Ostensibly purely ecclesiastical bodies, the universities played as significant a role in threatening feudalism with their democratic organization as they did in challenging the narrowness of medieval doctrine with their spirit of intellectual inquiry. Not surprisingly, Green's version of the Reformation differs significantly from Froude's. The new religion is for both an outgrowth of the new learning, but Green sees the Renaissance spirit struggling to triumph in spite of the narrowness and anti-intellectualism of reformers like Luther. In his eyes Henry championed the reformed Church not because of a conversion to its truer faith but as a further instrument of his tyranny over "old English liberties." Nonetheless, "the new spirit of inquiry, the new freedom of thought and discussion" awakened by Henry's imposition of a new religion eventually helped to break the spell of "the New Monarchy" over popular imagination in spite of him (SH, 366).

In short, for Green England's political development is only the most prominent feature in a landscape contoured by intellectual, social, and religious forces. Each stratum has contributed to the profile of the whole. For the English people, progress had meant the transi-

John Richard Green

tion from barbarism to civilization, from tribal jealousies to national unity, from oligarchy to democracy, from class privilege to class responsibility. It was made possible by the triumph of reason over superstition, self-determination over tyranny, public opinion over monarchical fiat. This victory of righteousness was no less inevitable and no less satisfying for being so thoroughly secularized. Green sought to demonstrate that the freedom of thought, the social justice, and the national identity he valued most highly in the present were the product of an organic development that affirmed these as deeply traditional and justified their continued advance in the future. He had gazed at the past with democratic eyes, and history had thrown back his own liberal image.

II

Green was more sensitive than earlier historians to the increasing strain between popular and professional historiography. Froude's wide popular success was a source of greater controversy to self-proclaimed professionals than to Froude himself. His assumptions, his talents, his conscious choices naturally aligned his priorities with those of the "literary" historians. Professional attacks bothered him, but not enough to make him question those priorities. To Green being a successful historian meant satisfying the expectations of both popular and professional audiences. His unconventional analyses of English history made this goal all the harder to achieve. It was a central concern of his career that his sociocultural syntheses would make history attractive to a wider audience and also gain legitimacy in the eyes of serious scholars. His situation was the opposite of Freeman's: Green's problem was to prove to professionals that popular history as he conceived it could be intellectually sound, Freeman's to overcome popular resistance to the ponderous detail of his scholarship.

The nature and scope of Green's research was determined by his sense of audience as much as by his increased emphasis on social and cultural history. Because the *Short History* and the *History of the English People* were aimed at "English readers of a general class" (SH, iv), Green eliminated footnotes in favor of chapter headnotes that briefly assessed the merits of the major secondary sources he had consulted. He also confined his research primarily to accounts in English. Although he hoped *The Making of England* and *The Conquest of England* would also appeal to a general audience, he intended these books to break new scholarly ground. *The Making of*

History as National Biography

England, for instance, demonstrates how archaeological and geological studies could be incorporated into the reconstruction of England's origins. The citations in both works give evidence that Green had read widely in specialized medieval scholarship. Nonetheless, these texts still draw almost exclusively from printed materials, even if some, like Bede, are used to furnish social evidence hitherto neglected. How Green might have extended his research had he lived is not clear; as things stand, however, there is little evidence in his work of the minute study of original sources that became a trademark of professionalism.

Green was a synthesizer by design. His desire to reach a large audience stemmed from his earnest belief in history's educational value, a value that could not be exploited fully so long as historical instruction remained so closely associated with dull primers and frivolous antiquarianism.[25] In writing the *Short History* and the *Short Geography*, he was inspired in large part by the plight of students for whom a study that should awaken the sympathies and train the mind too often amounted to little more than "a dry rattle of names and dates" (LG, 303). As a *Saturday* reviewer, Green was a stern critic of the *"bric-a-brac"* histories of superficial popularizers;[26] this made him all the more keenly aware of the needs of that growing middle class audience who "cry aloud for decent histories, and can't get 'em" (LG, 249), and all the more anxious to market his works at a price they could afford.[27] As a general editor, he valued Macmillan's projected series of short histories as a chance "to get right notions into the heads of the Many-Folk, of Herr Omnes" (LG, 445) and was even willing to admit a few drums and trumpets provided they won people's attention and interest to more "peaceful" subjects (LG, 475).

Finding the right voice for his ideal narrative cost him no little effort in the *Short History*. His pursuit of readability (*"the* thing I care about" LG, 384) had its perils. When Freeman and others criticized early drafts of the book for being too much in the *Saturday Review* style, Green repeatedly rewrote large sections already stereotyped. Freeman still thought that Green had sacrificed too much of the "real stuff" of history to his "power of brilliant *talkee-talkee.*"[28] In later years Green himself admitted that earlier portions of the *Short History* were marred by a fatal tendency to "essayism": to fall into a series of vignettes and slur over the uninteresting parts (LG, 445). On the other hand, he also had to satisfy critics like George Grove of Macmillan's, who judged an early draft of chapter one "too heavy"

John Richard Green

for " 'the upper forms in schools and for general readers' " (LG, 255). Green rewrote again to eliminate much of the detail he had packed so tightly. However, he stuck by his plan to replace the conventional political chronology with one based on social and cultural development—stuck by it despite criticism by Freeman and others that this made the narrative difficult to follow, especially for the beginning student.[29]

Although Green's concern with style stemmed largely from his desire to attract a large audience, he too shared the romantic assumption that the power of mind, spirit, and emotion in history demanded a creative method able to do justice to them. "There are times," Green wrote, "when poetic insight is the truest philosophy of history" (LG, 148), times when the historian's ability to feel with the subject yielded a more profound understanding than could analytical shrewdness. His advice to Kate Norgate suggests what his own creative method was like:

> When criticism has done its work comes the office of the imagination, and we dwell upon these names till they become real to us, real places, real battles, real men and women—and it is only when this reality has struck in upon us and we "see" that we can so describe, so represent that others see too . . . write when you feel they are real and life-like to you, do not be afraid of exaggeration or over-rhetoric (that is easily got rid of later on), but just strive after *realisation* and you will write history. (LG, 448-49)

Here are the familiar concerns with resuscitation and identification, with the constitutive power of the historian's vision.

Given the scantiness of legitimate historical sources for early history, like Arnold and Freeman Green turned to legends and traditions to serve the needs of insight and sympathy. Here too his advice to Norgate reveals his own approach. To "realize" the character of Fulc the Black, he wrote, "Help yourself by using the legends about him—telling them *as* legends, disproving their historical accuracy, if it be needful, but gathering from them the conception of character which after days formed of him, and using them as *colour* for your picture" (LG, 470). Green helps his reader to "see" Dunstan by coloring his own account with one such legendary detail. A brief digression into present tense restores to us one morning when, as Dunstan bends over his work, "his harp hung upon the wall sounds without mortal touch tones which the excited ears around frame into a joyous antiphon" (SH, 86-87). He similarly admits us into the Viking mind by contrasting the warrior's dauntlessness at sea with his superstitions about the land: "The boldest shrank from the dark holts and pools that broke the desolate moorland, from the huge stones that turned into giants in the mists of nightfall . . . and from the fell shapes into which their excited fancy framed the mists at eventide, shapes of giant 'moor-steppers,' of elves and trolls, of Odin with his wind-cloak wrapped round him as he hurried over the waste" (C, 56).

Nevertheless, Green leaves no doubt that "excited fancy" produced such impressions. For all his eagerness to hold the reader's interest, he was as concerned as Arnold and Freeman to make clear the line between fact and fiction—perhaps more so, since he felt his credibility more vulnerable. When James Bryce suggested that he use the Norse sagas to supplement the meager sources for early England, Green refused, saying that they were "unhistorical," and that he couldn't appear to trust them or to mix up authentic history with what was possibly fable.[30] Characteristically, he uses legendary evidence to establish the contemporary conception of historical figures or for sociological insights into the time. Alfred's traditional burning of the oat cakes, even "if nothing more than a tale, could never have been told of a man without humour," and is worth including for this insight (SH, 82). Carlyle would have used the miraculous return of Bishop Erkenwald's body to London to assess the age's capacity for hero-worship; Green recounts this story because it for the first time brings us face to face with the new burghers of the city, who struggled successfully against the religious houses for possession of the Bishop's remains (C, 455-56).

Green's most impressive examples of historical "seeing" involve his use of geological and archaeological detail to re-create a past. Like Arnold and Freeman, he was convinced that "History strikes its roots in Geography; for without a clear and vivid realization of the physical structure of a country the incidents of the life which men have lived in it can have no interest or meaning."[31] Like Macaulay and Carlyle, Green considered on-site visits essential, as much to verify details as to relive famous events in his imagination. But particularly in his account of England's earliest days, geographical evidence is far more than an aid to memory or imagination. In the absence of written evidence adequate to restore the past, Green taught his audience to read the story of England's origins in the physical record. As a *Times* reviewer put it, to Green a single geographical fact became like a single

John Richard Green

bone to Cuvier: it permitted the historical scientist to reconstruct the entire skeleton of a vanished organism.[32]

In the early pages of the *Making of England,* for instance, Green superimposes the terrain of ancient England over modern landmarks, noting how the distribution of wood and clearings controlled early settlement and determined the path of Saxon invasions (M, 8, 46). He gives a conventionally picturesque account of the "wild beauty" of Ebbsfleet, replete with landmarks that situate the modern reader on the scene. But he then goes on to use a detailed analysis of its terrain to confirm the tradition that this spot first felt the tread of English feet (M, 29-30). To Green, archaeological remains become so many clues to reading the mysteries of the past. The extension of Roman roads and towns tells how rapidly Britain was incorporated into the Empire; Camulodum's size and massive walls argue for its prominence in East Saxon society. From details of recent excavations, Green extrapolates the wretched decline of the Yorkshire cave-dwellers, refugees from the English invaders. The few enameled brooches and dainty sword hilts of ivory and bronze caught up by the fleeing provincials stand in pathetic contrast to the silent chronicle of their degeneration: "A few charred bones show how hunger drove them to slay their horses for food; reddened pebbles mark the hour when the new vessels they wrought were too weak to stand the fire, and their meal was cooked by dropping heated stones into the pot" (M, 68). In Green's hands even place names disclose the unfolding drama of civilization. Teutonic roots in village names corroborate the extermination of the Celt; the Comditch and Ayleswood that reflect the wild state of the land give way to the Knolton and Beaminster that record the spread of tunmoot and Church. Through an act of historical conjuration, "the birththroes of our national life" materialize from the dim territory formerly filled with "battles of kites and crows." Even more concretely than Arnold, Green merges the land itself into a living historical record.

Green's other triumph of historical vision lay in his realization of the daily reality of past worlds. His interest in domestic minutiae goes beyond Macaulay's and Froude's desire to particularize change with picturesque detail. His reverence for quotidian ritual goes beyond Carlyle's attraction to the costumes of Tradition. Green makes the life of the people the imaginative as well as the intellectual center of his historical explanation. In his hands the customary, the routine, the conventional emerge from the background to constitute the pattern of life itself; the focus closes in on "society" long enough to resolve its surface regularity into a myriad of concrete types. Green loves to enumerate the humble occupations that compose the common experience of the past. He lingers over the customary duties of the hayward, wood-ward, and bee-ward of Alfred's day (C, 330), over the spinster, ox-herd, cow-herd, and barn-man of the Saxon farm (M, 186-87). He notes with satisfaction the "characteristic figures" of mill and smith, hall and church, that prove Ecgbehrt's world already recognizably English (C,7). Green's social reality is literal and solid where Carlyle's is metaphorical and suggestive. Both value the anonymous routine of daily life, but where Carlyle prizes its silent obscurity as a sign of social health, Green wishes to feel "the quick pulse of popular life," to experience its robustness. There is something more distinctly Macaulayean in Green's proliferation of stereotypes in "Oxford During the Eighteenth Century." Employing a welter of detail from diaries, letters, newspapers, and incidental literature, Green raises up the crowded fabric of daily life: the coffee house lounger and the servitor, the "smart" and the freshman bumpkin, the belles who serve as the "toast" of the day; Oxford eating, drinking, sleeping and dressing, brawling in the streets and rhyming in the taverns. But if these types are exaggerated, they are never caricatured. Green senses too keenly the common humanity of the figures he creates to patronize them.

It is not always the familiarity of the past that Green stresses. The foreground of his eleventh-century Chester is recognizable enough: the "new commercial life" of the towns takes palpable shape in the sturdy burghers who tread their way among the piles of cheeses, bannock bread, and fish crates. But the motley crowd they confront is frankly exotic: the Dane who "strove in his northern tongue to draw buyers to his gang of slaves," the Welsh kerne wrapped in his blanket who "chattered as he might with the hardly less wild Cumbrian from the lands beyond the Ribble" (C, 443). Green's attraction to such scenes stems not from Macaulay's condescension to the barbaric but rather, as Burrow notes, from a real enthusiasm for frontier culture.[33] Green's purpose in superimposing the Oxford of the thirteenth century on that of the nineteenth is not to stress the superiority of the present. Indeed, to understand that older world we must "dismiss from our minds all recollections" of the new. From the venerable colleges and stately walks, "history plunges us into the mean and filthy lanes of a medieval town." Hundreds of boys, clustered around teachers as poor as themselves, take the place of the brightly colored train of doctors and Heads. The shock induced by this "stereoscopic" contrast leads us not to judge the past but to feel its reality more fully. Abandoning our modern preconceptions allows the thirteenth century to spring to life once more: "Now a mob of clerks plunges into the Jewry, and wipes off the memory of bills and bonds by sacking a Hebrew house or two. Now a tavern row between scholar and townsman widens into a general broil, and the academical bell of St. Mary's vies with the town bell of St. Martin's in clanging to arms" (SH, 159). For Green "the quick pulse of popular life" beats too exuberantly to allow condescension.

Works like the *Short History* and even the expanded *History of the English People* combined great fullness with great compression. Green had mastered the stylistic shorthand of the sketch—the firm outlines and few salient traits that projected the whole from a few parts. But what this style gained in vividness it often lost in subtlety and variety. To some readers the effect of reading the *Short History* was that of a "uniformity, sometimes almost a monotony, of picturesqueness; . . . we sometimes feel a fatigue like that which is experienced in turning over the pages of a picture-book."[34] The description is apt. Green's accounts often have the simplicity, assertiveness, and unmediated emotional appeal of the story book. Bede's death, for instance, is made intentionally hagiographical. In his final hours, completing the translation of John's Gospel parallels the waning of his own life. The symbolism is transparent, the incremental repetitions deliberately elegiac, the pathos overt:

> "There is still a chapter wanting," said the scribe, as the morning drew on, "and it is hard for thee to question thyself any longer." "It is easily done," said Baeda; "take thy pen and write quickly." Amid tears and farewells the day wore on to even-tide. "There is yet one sentence unwritten, dear master," said the boy. "Write it quickly," bade the dying man. "It is finished now," said the little scribe at last. "You speak truth," said the master; "all is finished now." (SH, 74)

Also typical is the way Green's elliptical brevity condenses Joan of Arc's martyrdom into prophetic melodrama: "Soon the flames reached her, the girl's head sank on her breast, there was one cry of 'Jesus!' 'We are lost' an English soldier muttered as the crowd broke up, 'we have burned a saint'" (SH, 293). Green's battle scenes possess the same compressed specificity and rapid pace. His brief account of Hastings drives forward with clipped, paralleled phrasing: "At three the hill seemed won, at six the fight still raged around the standard. . . . As the sun went down, a shaft pierced Harold's right eye." He looks aside from the main thrust of the action only for the most picturesque traditions. Taillefer tosses his sword and chants the Song of Roland, William rallies the Breton troops: " 'I live!,' shouted William, as he tore off his helmet, 'and by God's help will conquer yet!' " (SH, 108-9). In a single page, Green concentrates an account Freeman lingered over for fifty. There is no time for elaboration or qualification; in the brisk assertiveness of relentless action, he necessarily sacrifices shading for the sake of dramatic outlines.

The weaknesses of this method become most apparent when applied to major characters. Green has a good eye and ear for the telling gestures and turns of phrase that can fix individuals in a single stroke. A few sentences from his version of Cromwell taking the mace from the table restore the man in all his imperious rectitude and blunt audacity:

> "Come, come," replied Cromwell, "we have had enough of this;" and, striding into the midst of the chamber, he clapped his hat on his head, and exclaimed, "I will put an end to your prating!" In the din that followed his voice was heard in broken sentences—"It is not fit that you should sit here any longer! You should give place to better men! You are no Parliament." (SH, 564)

But this constant assertion of the typical leaves characters more vivid than complex. Green's penchant for enumeration enriches his characterizations quantitatively more than qualitatively. His usual pattern includes a list of salient physical and intellectual traits, illustrated by a few representative actions and interspersed with the revelatory observations of contemporaries: "The very spirit of the sea-robbers" from whom William of Normandy had sprung

> seemed embodied in his gigantic form, his enormous strength, his savage countenance, his desperate bravery, the fury of his wrath, the ruthlessness of his revenge. "No knight under Heaven," his enemies owned, "was William's peer." . . . No man could bend William's bow. His mace crashed its way through a ring of English warriors to the foot of the Standard. He rose to his greatest heights when other men despaired. His voice rang out as a trumpet when his soldiers fled before the English charge at Senlac, and his rally turned the flight into a means of victory. In his winter march on Chester he strode afoot at the head of his fainting troops and helped with his own hand to clear a road through the snowdrifts. (HEP, 1:125)

John Richard Green

The tight rhythms of the paralleled phrases reinforce the sheer weight of particulars being piled up here. Sir Thomas More is similarly itemized. Holbein's portrait captures "the inner soul of the man, his vivacity, his restless, all-devouring intellect, his keen and even reckless wit, the kindly, half-sad humour"; the New Learning seemed incarnate in "his gay talk, his winsomeness of manner, his reckless epigrams, his passionate love of music, his omnivorous reading, his paradoxical speculations, his jibes at monks, his schoolboy fervour of liberty" (SH, 326).

It is not that either man is caricatured. We see William's humanity as well as his savagery; we are shown More's stern inflexibility as well as his touching affection for his children's pets and games. But the shades of personality that put both darks and lights into perspective are usually missing. The endless stream of dazzling specifics overbears rather than convinces. The rapid parallels that underline Elizabeth's vanity and voluptousness are the tools of the Macaulayean essayist and entail their drawbacks:

> No adulation was too fulsome for her, no flattery of her beauty too gross. "To see her was heaven," Hattan told her; "the lack of her was hell." She would play with her rings, that her courtiers might note the delicacy of her hands; or dance a coranto, that the French ambassador, hidden dexterously behind a curtain, might report her sprightliness to his master. . . . Personal beauty in a man was a sure passport to her liking. She patted handsome young squires on the neck when they knelt to kiss her hand, and fondled her "sweet Robin," Lord Leicester, in the face of the court. (SH, 376)

The temptation is always to reap the dramatic benefits of sensational detail before or instead of taking judicious measurement. Although Green usually does not succumb to Macaulay's penchant for brittle paradox, characters for whom he lacks sympathy sometimes verge on caricature. He may admit that James I possessed much natural ability and learning, but it is "his big head, his slobbering tongue, his quilted clothes, his rickety legs, his goggle eyes . . . his gabble and rodomontade" (SH, 471) that stay in our memories. Once anatomized in this way, characters often struggle in vain to recover their integrity.

Green did strive for a deliberate balance in his characters. He objected to the hero-worship that lifted individuals "out of the sphere of human sympathies into a perfection that is simply uninteresting and unintelligible."[35] He was equally averse to the "herophobia" typical of the Philistines, "your 'right-and-wrong,' your 'truth and falsehood' people," who would sooner reduce a William of Normandy to a melodrama villain than allow his mixture of greatness and inhumanity to upset their simplistic categories (LG, 247). Itemization was a middle ground, but too often it left personalities inventoried rather than integrated. Green's characters are vivid and memorable, but they seldom seem more than the sum of their parts. Their characteristic turns of phrase and action do not resonate with a Carlylean suggestiveness of the intangible; these traits are not metaphors for a more complex whole. But then, Green had consciously chosen the style of information and instruction, not of prophecy and divination. He brought a much warmer humanity to this style than did Macaulay, but that did not entirely compensate for the kinds of oversimplification, the sacrifice of depth to breadth, that it encouraged.

The controversy over Green's reputation was less fierce than it had been over Froude's, but it was more complex, at least in part because Green was himself more self-conscious about the conflicts involved in trying to satisfy two different readerships. Its scope and tone marked the *Short History* as primarily a popular work; for reviewers it exemplified the strengths and weaknesses of the entire genre. Mrs. Oliphant applauded Green for clearing away the "scaffolding" of sources and footnotes; the *Short History*'s ability to trace the continuity of social life concealed within the "outer husk" of history made it for her "simply the ideal history we have been looking for."[36] Its accessibility to a wider public made it more valuable to *The Living Age* than "many books making higher claims to research and science."[37] The *Athenaeum* similarly complimented Green for his success in presenting "all the newest knowledge upon a very large section of history . . . in such a style that every one may read it with little effort."[38] *The Making of England* and *The Conquest of England* possessed similar virtues for F. A. Paley.[39]

On the other hand, the *Athenaeum* also complained that the *Short History* doled out ideas ready-made rather than encouraging independent thought and judgment.[40] John Brewer's Tory hysteria over Green's supposedly revolutionary sympathies was uncharacteristically extreme, but his general complaint—that works like *The Short History* placed dangerous views in "the hands of the young and incautious"—was one frequently lodged against popular history.[41] More typical was Brewer's suggestion that Green's desire for dramatic effect led him to invent unverifiable details.[42] Green's most formidable critic, James Rowley, made similar claims about the "exaggerations as culpable as misstatements that Mr. Green has been betrayed into by his unconscionable rhetoric." It was pure invention, Rowley argued, for Green's Jenny Geddes actually to fell the preacher with her stool and for his bishops to fall to their knees at the deathbed of Charles II.[43]

More damaging was Rowley's voluminous list of outright errors. Altough he implied that these resulted from Green's superficial preparation, most were minor mistakes that could have been corrected with an errata sheet. John Morley, who turned down Rowley's letters when first submitted to the *Fortnightly*, correctly perceived that his object was less to avenge truth than to avenge Froude. Although Green had himself deplored Freeman's attack on Froude, his close association with both the *Saturday* and with Freeman added to the glee with which critics pounced on the blunders of this more vulnerable member of "the Freeman school." Even Green's friends did not defend his reputation for accuracy in minute detail. His lack of verbal memory, the disruptive circumstances in which his books were composed, and the rapidity with which he revised them made many blunders inevitable. Green was aware of this and was grateful even to critics like Rowley for pointing out errors that could be removed in later editions. Although he was still not scrupulous enough with his corrections to satisfy S. R. Gardiner, Gardiner joined Stubbs and Henry Adams in confirming what Green himself believed of the *Short History*: that his mistakes did not undermine the cogency and soundness of his historical interpretations and that minute accuracy was impossible given the vast and comprehensive range of his books and the current state of specialized studies.[44]

Nonetheless, in many ways the scope of Green's work was the crux of the controversy. Freeman and James Bryce pointed to a more general problem than accuracy *per se* when they blamed Green for being too assertive about what could only be inferred or conjectured, especially in works like the *Short History* that afforded no space to discuss uncertainties. Stubbs was similarly dubious about how much success Green could achieve in synthesizing history for periods where the necessary specialized studies remained to be done.[45] Green's methodological choices were deliberate and made with full knowledge of how they challenged the prevailing assumptions of professional scholarship. He respected the efforts of men like Gardiner "to bring out the actual political facts and clear away loose talk." So much nonsense had passed under the name of "philosophies of history" that Green realized his own attempts to arrange facts on a philosophical basis might strike such men as "an attempt to bring the loose talk back again" (LG, 426). Despite his regret over the disapproval of the professionals, Green still intended his works to be an explicit protest against many of their assumptions about historical writing. He had long been averse to continental models for the new scholarship—to the tendency of French historians to limit themselves to the "étude" or specialized study, and to the exclusive concentration of German "pragmatic" historians on political documents. To Green the former approach smacked of "intellectual cowardice," the refusal to provide a comprehensive explanation of national life.[46] The "pragmatic" approach, on the other hand, did not look below the level of documents to the individual will or national spirit that produced them; it was too objective, too impersonal, to seize the real dynamic of change. What allies Green with the "literary" historians is less the picturesqueness of his style than this belief in the need for didactic judgments by the historian and his acknowledgement of the primacy of will and spirit in the historical process.

Green tried to bridge the gap between popular and professional expectations more directly when he became involved in the early planning for England's first "purely Historical Review." Plans for such a publication first surfaced in conversations between Green, W. Hunt, and James Bryce in early 1867, and later included A. W. Ward. From the beginning Ward and Bryce wanted what Germany and France possessed, "a purely scientific organ of historical criticism," one whose character was to be scientific and not popular, and in which "literary tone" was to be subordinate to critical rigor (LG, 433). Green, on the other hand, advocated a more popular format, both because he felt material of broader interest would be necessary to "float" the serious scholarship in the commercial market and because he had high hopes for the didactic potential of such historical writing. Although his journal would have maintained the strictly scholarly nature of original essays and reviews, it would also have demanded literary excellence of all submissions and included articles of greater topical interest to the general reader: background histories of current issues, "philosophical" biographies of eminent contemporaries, a quarterly summary of European events. He admitted, however, that such a scheme would likely fall between two stools: too scientific for the general reader and too popular to win the support of

John Richard Green

scientific scholars. The desire for commercial success would inevitably tend to make the review become more and more popular in tone and perhaps push it nearer to a distinct political line, moves sure to alienate serious writers still further. Green correctly perceived his own unsuitability as editor for such a review. Finally turning down Macmillan's offer of the post in 1876, he explained that he did not possess the confidence of historical scholars essential to such a position, and feared that he would be looked upon as a person imposed merely in the hope of securing a popular circulation. Moreover, he felt he would be able to pursue his particular approach to history more freely if not placed in official relation to writers so clearly unsympathetic to it (LG, 436).

It is no less true that Green felt keenly the criticism of those who refused to consider him a serious historian because of his popularizing and synthetic approach. He never expected the *Short History* to win him "historic fame" with the professionals, and in fact had continued his studies of the Angevin Kings while completing it in the hope of eventually winning their regard for his scholarly abilities in that way (LG, 258-59).[47] Disparagement of the *Short History* as a mere popularizing of other people's ideas spurred him to write *The Making of England*. Only with that book's success did he note "the cessation at last of that attempt, which has been so steadily carried on for the last ten years, to drum me out of the world of historical scholars and set me among the 'picturesque compilers' " (LG, 482).

His scholarly efforts notwithstanding, Green's sympathies remained with "literary" historians, and he achieved his greatest successes as a popularizer. His greater narrative genius enabled him to go farther than either Stubbs or Freeman in rescuing early England from the hands of the antiquarians and romancers and making it a living reality for his audience. "Philosophical enough for scholars, and popular enough for schoolboys,"[48] the *Short History* in particular was able to tap the widest possible segment of the later Victorian audience. According to Philip Gell, it survived the censure of the early professional school at Oxford, materially advancing the new popularity of historical study and widely influencing a whole generation of younger students: "It used to be said that when men leaving Oxford wished to improve their minds, if they were rich they traveled, and if they were poor they read Green's *Short History*."[49] At once compendious and accessible, the *Short History* enjoyed success as a school text and was no less attractive to nonacademic audiences, including the ever-increasing ranks of lower class readers newly educated at the Board schools and eager to gain useful knowledge.

Green's works struck many responsive chords in later Victorian thought. His drive for synthesis, if at odds with incipient specialization, nourished the still vital longing for a comprehensive "philosophical" ordering and control of facts.[50] His expanded history of culture harmonized well with the more complex conception of nationalism developing in Europe.[51] He offered convincing historical confirmation of the evolutionary concepts rapidly becoming commonplace in the mind of the time. If some found his liberalism a bit too enthusiastic, his version of the development of England's freedoms still enjoyed a wide appeal in the more egalitarian atmosphere of late Victorian society. Green moralized democracy even more thoroughly than Arnold. He had greater need to do so; deprived of its religious underpinnings in an increasingly sceptical age, ethical advance by itself was far too vulnerable a concept. Like Macaulay's, Green's story of temporal success served quasi-religious ends. He showed how evidence of political and social progress might satisfy his readers' longings to believe that the struggles of the race had made them better people, brought them to a more perfect world. Those many late Victorians troubled by orthodoxy and uneasy even with Carlyle's nondoctrinal mysticism could find in Green's secularized saga of continuous progress what the *Times* did: reassuring evidence that "in no chapter of the world's history is the truth of Hamlet's sentence more plainly proved than in that of England—'There's a divinity that shapes our ends, rough-hew them how we will.' "[52]

Green's role in late nineteenth-century scholarship remains a significant one. The idea of writing history as an integrated narrative of national civilization has become so commonplace that Green's achievement loses some of the impact it had at the time. In the competence and comprehensiveness of its account, the *Short History* broke new ground. Ironically, it was his very comprehensiveness and reorientation of historical priorities that distanced Green most significantly from the concerns of professional scholarship in his day. Specialization seemed increasingly necessary to achieve the minute accuracy of detail, the command of original sources, and the qualified judgments essential to professional standards. The breadth of Green's analyses demanded a level of generalization that made minute precision and qualification virtually impossible. To many serious scholars, his efforts to reach a popular audience with a readable narrative

John Richard Green

further compromised the objectivity and restraint they felt were essential to historical truth. Green's inaccuracy undoubtedly gave support to their fears, even though more of his errors were caused by his own disadvantages in time, health, and memory than by his desire for rhetorical effect or the need to generalize.

Green's shortcomings should not detract from the importance of his efforts to bridge the gap between general and specialized audiences. He had in effect to become a crusader for an audience earlier historians had taken for granted. There was no way he could escape being controversial; his position by definition challenged assumptions crucially important in the formative stages of professional identity. In the view of Frederic Harrison, himself poised between popular and professional positions, Green had usefully counterbalanced the weight of the new scholarship. Harrison lamented in 1898 that

> the historians of the present century, under the influence originally of Ranke in Germany, of Guizot in France, and Sir Henry Ellis and other editors of the Museum and Rolls records in England, have devoted themselves rather to original research than to eloquent narrative, to the study of special institutions and limited epochs, to the scientific probing of contemporary witnesses and punctilious precision of minute detail. The school of Freeman, Stubbs, Gardiner, and Bryce has quite displaced the taste of our grandfathers for artistic narrative and a glowing style. Where the older men thought of permanent literature, the new school is content with scientific research. Would that J. R. Green had lived out his life![53]

Few works of literary merit comparable to Green's succeeded in carving out a satisfactory middle ground between the rising tide of vulgarized history for the masses and the increasingly specialized literature of the professionals in the last quarter of the century. Few appealed so successfully to a large popular audience while building on such solid and extensive foundations. Few provided judgments of such genuine authority while avoiding the aridity and diffuseness that became the stereotype of much professional scholarship. Would that John Richard Green *had* lived out his life, if only to show whether it would have been possible to prevent the irreconcilability of popular and professional interests from becoming in many respects a self-fulfilling prophecy in the years to come.

VI

EDWARD AUGUSTUS FREEMAN
HISTORY AS PAST POLITICS

I have chosen to conclude with Freeman because of the extent to which he is at once traditional and transitional. He self-consciously placed himself in the tradition of Arnold's moralized historiography. An enthusiastic devotee of the late-Victorian cult of comparative method, he overlaid Oxford School medievalism with the "unity of history" and elaborated a full-scale "science" of historical cycles and racial continuity. He was a Whig who claimed Macaulay as a model, a romantic philhellene, an ardent (if somewhat abstract) democrat. He saw himself in the vanguard of modern historiography but was by temperament kindred to older, even ancient, traditions. Better than any contemporary, Freeman exemplified the ambiguities involved in defining a new status for the historian. Green was keenly sensitive to the conflicts between his own priorities and the requirements of "scientific" historiography; he made his choices. Freeman wanted popular acclaim, but on his own terms: he expected to succeed by making the general reader respect his professional authority. He intended much of his work to be popularizing in the most constructive sense—that is, devoted to correcting the general public's misconceptions about principles fundamental to western history. He was at once too condescending and too self-righteous a crusader to avoid alienating that audience. His violent attacks on Froude and other "amateurs" combined with his weighty erudition to make him the stereotype of a professionalism by definition hostile to the general public's needs and interests.

Edward Augustus Freeman

At the same time, if Freeman was a far more vocal publicist for professional history than William Stubbs or S. R. Gardiner, he was a considerably less successful practitioner thereof. His formidable display of laws and comparative method constituted the same wish-fulfilling imposition of order as earlier "unscientific" men of letters had indulged in. His "history for its own sake" was a moralized antiquarianism, his exacting scholarship a means of turning true facts into ultimate Truths. The Whig theorizing and Aryan mythmaking on which he based his claims for a scientific historiography were precisely what branded his work unscientific in the eyes of later scholars. His very contradictions make him more useful for my purposes, however, because they forecast wider issues in the evolution of professional identity, issues that I will return to at the close of my discussion.

Born in 1823 Freeman, like Green, began to break away from his conservative roots at an early age. The young boy's sympathy for Greek independence first undermined his relations' Tory influence and set the pattern for his later support for Aryan efforts to overthrow alien masters. At Oxford in the early forties, he was deeply impressed by Arnold's lectures but found much more compatible the religious principles of Newman. Yet Freeman was never tempted by conversion; indeed, unlike most historians I have discussed, he seems never to have experienced any serious challenge to his traditional High Church faith. The Oxford Movement's more important influence was indirect; it encouraged his interest in ecclesiastical architecture and medieval history. The latter bore early fruit in his 1845 essay, "The Effects of the Conquest of England by the Normans," which demonstrates how early he had formulated the central tenets of his interpretation of the Conquest. His contributions to *Poems Legendary and Historical* (1850) and *Original Ballads by Living Authors* (1850) show a different but no less characteristic side of his historical interests: his imaginative indulgence of a romanticized patriotism and a love of legendary heroism. These works were in effect his *Lays of Ancient Rome*. Another lifelong interest was evinced by his first significant publication, *A History of Architecture* (1849), predictably devoted to the glorification of Gothic. Freeman was active in delivering papers to local archeological societies throughout the fifties, and developed early that particular merger of architecture, archaeology, and municipal history that characterized his many later articles in the *Saturday* and other reviews. He played a role as a "conservative reformer" at Oxford in the early fifties, in favor of correcting abuses but hostile to those aspects of reform that he felt undercut a broadbased liberal education and encouraged superficial views of history. When he served as an examiner in the new School of Law and History during 1857, he had already begun to nurture ambitions to win one of its professorial chairs—ambitions that would have to wait thirty years for fulfillment.

He stood unsuccessfully for Parliament several times in the late fifties, styling himself a candidate in harmony with "the more advanced section of the existing Liberal party,"[1] and was a vociferous campaigner against the Bulgarian atrocities in the seventies. But his political interests were channeled more and more directly into the writing of history in his middle years. The first volume of a projected *History of Federal Government* (1863) outlined the "federal principle," one of those characteristic forms of Aryan political structure whose demonstration would occupy so much of Freeman's efforts in later years. Hoping to make himself a more attractive candidate for the Regius Professorship of Modern History at Oxford, he began his *History of the Norman Conquest* in 1865—a five-volume project not complete until 1876. This attempt to define the nature and origins of Aryan/Teutonic institutions spilled over into *The Growth of the English Constitution* (1872), *Comparative Politics* (1873), and the *Reign of William Rufus* (1882). During the same period he was engaged in several works of a more popular nature, among them *Old-English History for Children* (1869), *General Sketch of European History* (1872), and *History of Europe* (1875)—both part of Macmillan's series for the schools—and *The Historical Geography of Europe* (1881), not to mention a voluminous outpouring of articles for the *Saturday* and other reviews, many of which were later collected in his four volumes of *Historical Essays*. The prestige of his historical doctrines was confirmed in 1881, when in a lecture tour of the United States, he had the satisfaction of finding his favorite motto, "History is past politics, politics are present history," adopted as the epigraph for the new *Johns Hopkins University Studies in Historical and Political Science*. Freeman's contribution to the first volume (1882) characteristically treated American government as yet another realization of the Aryan impulse.

When Freeman finally attained the Regius Professorship of Modern History in 1884, he used the chair both to address theoretical questions (in lectures collected as *Methods of Historical Study*, 1886) and to continue his exploration of European medieval history. But his distaste (and lack of audience) for compulsory lectures and his failing health led him to put in increasingly less time and energy at Oxford as the decade waned. The final installments in his investigation of Aryan history comprised the *History of Sicily* (1891-92), and posthumous histories of *Western Europe in the Fifth Century* and *Western Europe in the Eighth Century and Onward* (1904). He died in Alicante, Spain, in 1892.

Despite the staggering output of Freeman's career—eight major historical studies and eight shorter popular ones, seven major essay collections, not to mention literally hundreds of review essays, lectures, and architectural studies—the major components of his theory of history are relatively few and static. Relying on the comparative method to establish the scientific legitimacy of his theories, Freeman expanded Arnold's belief in the unity of western history into a fullblown myth of Aryan dominance and superiority. In the process of reconstructing an Aryan family tree of representative democracies, he formulated what sounded like a classic Whig view of its most illustrious branch, the Teutonic. But beneath the familiar rhetoric of continuity through compromise and identity in progress operated a timeless kind of monism. Freeman was driven by a craving for order and unity deeper even than Arnold's. The dominant pattern that emerges from his elaborate blueprint of historical cycles is less one of progress than of eternal recurrence.[2] He paid lip service to the relativism and ambiguity necessary in historical judgments but could tolerate neither. His urge to classify, to subordinate to law, easily conflated scientific and ethical order. His overbearing display of objective investigation and scholarly authority protected moral absolutes that effectively prejudged all.

From his earliest inquiries into historical knowledge, Freeman sought to give his moral convictions the sanction of "scientific" order. As a young man, he withdrew from all dealings with the Royal Archaeological Institute because he felt that it was wrong to apply "to higher matters the merely antiquarian tone which belongs to inferior ones"; the Institute treated "consecrated things" like ecclesiastical art and architecture "merely as facts, curiosities, antiquities" (LF, 1:96). When he came to expand these charges against "archaeologians" as a group in the *History of Architecture*, he had already begun to link their impiety to their lack of "philosophical" perspective. In their enthusiasm for new artifacts, they recorded a "newly discovered

Anglo-Saxon charter . . . as a curiosity side by side with a newly discovered 'low-side window.' "[3] That is to say, not only did they consider an old barn no less important than a Christian minster, but they failed to recognize that their antiquarian pursuits should be means to a higher end: the study of man's political development. Their hostility to any attempt to mold theories or develop general principles from the details they amassed represented a failure of moral as well as philosophical insight. In Freeman's eyes such theories were "the vital principle" giving meaning to the "inert mass" of facts.[4] Only when the historian properly subordinated facts to the illustration of patterns and to the formulation of laws was he functioning in a "scientific" rather than in a merely antiquarian spirit. The study of coins, weapons, tools, and inscriptions became historical—and of moral value—only insofar as they contributed to the understanding of "man as a member of a political community."[5]

Declaring that "history is past politics" did not limit historical study so much as it might appear, for to Freeman political and moral action were in the highest sense one. Like Arnold, he believed that the study of history meant "the study of . . . man in his highest character"—that is, man acting "in his political capacity . . . as the member of an organized society, governed according to law."[6] In elaborating on the nature of "political science," he conveniently blurred the distinction between moral and methodological criteria. He had quite practical reasons for insisting that "right ruling" was a question of ethics, not expediency; arguing that "the same eternal laws of right and wrong" applied to present politics as to past was the basis of his opposition to Derby and Disraeli's pragmatic support of the Turks.[7] But he presented his position as being more valid because it was more philosophically sound. He argued that the "science of right ruling" meant something "higher" than following self- or party-interest precisely because it taught us "how to judge of causes and their effects . . . to judge of the character of acts, whether done yesterday or thousands of years ago." In the ability to recognize and apply valid analogies lay history's practical value: "The past is studied in vain, unless it gives us lessons for the present."[8]

In his own work, it is difficult to separate the moral from the political aspects of these lessons. With a self-conscious display of Whig practicality, Freeman, like Macaulay, professed to avoid the arbitrary dogmatism of "abstract" theory by deriving the laws of political behavior from the historical record and by allowing for contemporary values and circumstances when applying them. In practice the only laws he saw were the ones he looked for, and his own sympathies determined whether their validity was absolute or relative in a given instance. He ransacked history for "illustrative examples" that showed "what course, whether of true growth or of backsliding, the mind of man was taking" at any given time.[9] His preconceived standards of progress and decline blunted an historicist appreciation of past events and closed off inductive insights. Like Arnold and Macaulay, Freeman assumed that democratic governments were more moral, more characteristic of a politically "mature" society, than other political systems. While arguing that historical study "hindered the growth of any narrow political partizanship,"[10] he did not consider it partisan to assume that man appeared in his "highest form, as the citizen of a free commonwealth." In his eyes the record of despotic government hardly constituted "the history of a people at all."[11]

He acknowledged the dangers of substituting "abstract right" for an appreciation of the "circumstances, the habits, the beliefs, the prejudices, of each man's time" (HE, 1:119; see also HE, 1:109, 115) and even admitted that Arnold sometimes set too high a standard by failing to consider the weight of prevailing mores. But then, the values of others were always "abstract" in a way "the touchstone of morals" to which he brought all political questions (LF, 2:121) was not. Toleration, he argued, must not confound mere differences of opinion with "moral crimes"; tyranny was not just a political alternative for Freeman, but the "overthrow of all right" (HFG, xv). In opposing British aid to the Turks, he claimed the sanction of a "common morality"; his "scientific" study of history had taught him to view the Eastern Question as no less than a strife between Western civilization and Eastern barbarism, so that any aid to the "foul tyranny" of the Turks became simply "the work of the devil."[12]

His own attempts to correct modern censure by appealing to contemporary standards were often indistinguishable from special pleading for his Teutonic heroes. While relying on "universal" moral standards to condemn actions against his enemies, Freeman demanded of partisans of the right side nothing higher than the prevailing political morality of their age. He tried to mitigate the brutality of Frederick I of Italy, "a high and pleasing type of the pure Teutonic character," by comparing his actions with far greater atrocities in later history (HE, 1:280-84). To decide whether Godwin was guilty of treachery in the death of the Atheling Alfred, he resorted to precisely the kind of arguments that outraged him when Froude made them. He assumed that "an English patriot" of Godwin's stature simply could not be guilty of any wrong more heinous than acting like "a wary and hard-headed statesman" instead of a "sentimental and impulsive hero."[13] Like Froude's, Freeman's relativism was employed to protect higher absolutes—to vouch for the righteousness of all in his Teutonic pantheon. If his pretensions to scientific method were greater than those of fellow historians, so too was his dogmatism. He might at times treat laws as if they denoted only practical rules of thumb,[14] but in practice only a set of axioms could brace the rigid polarities of his world view.

In arguing for history's scientific nature, Freeman was caught between conflicting positions. He could not assume the essential unity of moral and physical truth as had Arnold; he could not dismiss out of hand history's claims to be scientific as had Froude. Although he wished to claim for the historian a professional status commensurate with the scientist's, for moral and intellectual reasons he needed to free historical study from the determinism of both Positivism and physical science. He actually shared a great many of the moral biases of his nemeses, Froude and Kingsley. He considered history a form of the "protest of mind against matter in a material age" and held up the study of man as inherently nobler than the study of rocks and tides (LF, 1:118-19). He distrusted a positivistic science of history in large part because he suspected that "it has very little to do with the grand personal drama" of human life,[15] since it treated men as "mere walking automata" (HE, 1:51), enslaved to inflexible law. Like Froude, Freeman argued that the existence of free will made it impossible to reduce historical actions to any "grand scientific law" such as that favored by "the school of Mr. Buckle" (HE, 1:50).

If Freeman wanted to prevent history's annexation by pseudoscience, he was just as concerned to claim for his studies a place among legitimate sciences. He objected to "the strange way in which the name of *science* is often confined to certain branches of knowledge" in order to assume "some special merit and dignity" for them (M, 118). In reaction to this "unfair monopoly of a name," Freeman purposefully returned to the older sense of *scientia* and was thus able to treat history's claims to be a science as "a question of words and nothing else" (M, 152). While appearing to acknowledge the authority of the scientific, Freeman actually diluted the scientist's truths until they offered no significant challenge to the historian's. Like the physical sciences, he argued, history assigned outward facts or phenomena to the working of certain laws or principles. But in both cases these laws were "only generalizations from instances, a high class of probabilities" (LF, 1:118). The physical scientist could not claim a "mathematical certainty" for his laws either, Freeman opined, so that his "deductions from experience" differed only in degree from those of the historian (M, 150).

In fact, Freeman charged, the natural philosopher could only describe how effects followed causes—he could not explain why they did so. When pushed back to a first cause, he had nothing more palpable than "Force" to refer to—an explanation that Freeman dismissed as no more philosophical than a reliance on personal will or an omnipotent being (M, 147).[16] In this regard the historian might have more difficulty establishing facts, but once they were established he was in a better position to assess "the real causes of the facts," for "surely," Freeman asserted with bland confidence, "We know more about the human will than we know about Force" (M, 152). He was content to assume that in the study of human affairs, "We can reach that high degree of likelihood which we call moral certainty"—the same certainty on which men were content to base their daily actions (M, 151). "Moral certainty" was of course for Freeman's purposes far more useful than "mathematical certainty." It was quite compatible with the free will necessary to release history from determinism, but it also permitted valid generalizations about human nature. A science of history possessing "moral certainty" combined the best of both worlds: freedom and order.

In theory Freeman distinguished between narrative histories and the "political science" that abstracted lessons from them. The first was the obvious arena for the "grand personal drama" of human life. Although heroes, especially Aryan ones, towered over Freeman's own narratives, he stopped short of a Carlylean hero-worship, asserting that "the course of history is not a mere game played by a few great men."[17] Rather, Freeman professed the "old-fashioned belief" that God had created a world in which "every man, however obscure he may deem himself, has laid upon him . . . a historical responsibility, a share in guiding the course of the world for good or for evil."[18] The exercise of each man's will helped determine the common will, his unconscious acts the spirit of the age. The actions of the great differed only in degree from those of the lesser. In Freeman's "practical" way of looking at heroes, the great man was able to lead his nation only to the extent that he was thoroughly identified with its virtues and limitations.[19]

In practice the "grand personal drama" of history interested him only insofar as it reenacted the larger patterns discovered by "political science." Harold and William provide imaginative foci to the *Norman Conquest*, but they function less as autonomous individuals than as vehicles of racial destiny. Freeman's deepest engagement lay not with the individual fact, but with the system of historical meaning to which it belonged. He controlled the multitudinousness of experience by subordinating each datum to a master plan. The next best thing to the permanence he longed for was the constant duplication of the same patterns. This duplication accounted for the fact of change without having to surrender the security of the eternal.

Nowhere are his strategies clearer than in the grandiose theory of racial continuity he based on the comparative method. The philosophical prestige of comparative studies at the time made them the natural choice of a mind that wished to endow its craving for analogical system with scientific status. This approach seemed already to have revealed the geneaology of Indo-European language and myth in the same way that evolutionary theory had explained the development of physical life. In an early essay Freeman compared the methodology of comparative philology to that of geology and noted with approval its gradual triumph over obscurantists who had originally tried to deny linguistic evidence, just as others had tried to deny the paleontological evidence against special creation (HE, 2:244-45).

Despite Freeman's pretensions to a similar scientific objectivity and disinterestedness, he had clearly chosen this method because it so convincingly validated his foregone conclusions. He pronounced the comparative method "the greatest intellectual achievement of our time" because it had brought "a line of argument which reaches moral certainty into a region which before was given over to random guess-work."[20] "Moral certainty" was vital for two reasons. First, the comparative method enabled the historian to extrapolate with confidence a meaningful pattern into what might otherwise be an uncharted void or a jumble of disparate evidence. He could use analogies revealed by comparative study to provide internal "proof" of the organic continuity of Aryan development—a continuity for which no external evidence could be found. Secondly, the comparative method justified the historian in basing cultural identity on factors subject to free will—always the realm of "moral certainty"—rather than limiting him to traits subject to the determinism implicit in "mathematical certainty."

Freeman wanted to define race philologically so that he could treat "national character" and "spirit of the age" as "undoubted facts" without also having to equate these with "unchanging physical forces, over which personal agency has no control."[21] He intended this definition to be a scientific advance over popular theorizing about race, but he was also concerned to disassociate racial theory from the materialist ethnology of scientists like T. H. Huxley. As early as 1865 Huxley had exposed the fallacies in trying to treat community of language as proof of racial unity in the physical sense and opted instead for a zoological definition based on skull shape and related traits. In later years he more specifically refuted arguments for Teutonic and Aryan purity similar to those held by Freeman.[22] Freeman's own "Race and Language" (1877) acknowledged these counterarguments but continued to defend his "historical" definition of race. No nation could claim purity of blood from a physiological point of view, Freeman argued; nevertheless, for all "practical" purposes, political or historical (HE, 3:226), such communities could be defined by a common stock of cultural traditions, chief among them language. The real issue of course was that Freeman considered ethnology a purely physical science, based on traits over which man had no control. Language, on the other hand, depended upon behavior perhaps "unconscious" but still "unconstrained." Thus, he could assume that philology concerned itelf with "the aggregation of endless acts of the human will" (M, 61). Freeman went on to argue that although community of language was no certain proof of community of blood, it provided the same degree of "moral proof" available in other areas of human history and thus provided a valid working definition of race.

Practicality, scientific order, moral certainty—what higher recommendations did Freeman's theory of Aryan continuity need to claim intellectual prestige in the late nineteenth century? Here was the "vital principle" that vindicated the lesson he had first learned from Arnold: that the political life of the western world constituted "one living whole" (M, 7). Here was the organic unity that allowed history to be read "not as a mere chronicle of events . . . but as the living science of causes and effects" (HE, 2:234). A cyclical pattern further reinforced this unity. Like Arnold, Freeman rejected as artificial the distinctions between ancient and modern history, arguing that "the later days of a people, amidst countless differences of detail, may have more real likenesses, more identity of principle, with its very early days, than with intermediate times from which . . . they are separated by much slighter differences" (HE, 4:250). The laws of political cause and effect remained valid because the same political forms reconstituted themselves from age to age of Aryan development. Freeman devoted a major part of his work to tracing the common descent of Aryan constitutions from Greece, through Rome, and by way of the Teutons to the most recent British parliament and American congress. So compelling was the genetic metaphor that he believed he could "describe either an Homeric [assembly] or an English micklegemot all the better for having seen a [Swiss] Landesgemeinde" (LF, 1:417). He naturally saw ontogeny recapitulating philogeny in the American colonies as well: colonial governments had reproduced Teutonic institutions prevalent in the fifth and sixth centuries, thus giving new life to traditions that "in their older home had well nigh died out."[23] Everywhere the "germ" of Aryan government was planted, it generated the same species of constitution.

Although Freeman's philhellenic enthusiasms produced conflicts of interest,[24] he was a self-proclaimed panegyrist for the Teutonic branch of the Aryan family tree. In an early pamphlet concerning the new school of modern history at Oxford, he lamented the exclusive concentration on ancient history and called on his countrymen to recognize "that the soil of Teutonic Christendom has brought forth as glorious works of art and genius, as mighty deeds of national and individual greatness, as aught that southern heathendom can boast" (LF, 1:120). Freeman's *History of the Norman Conquest* and related works aimed not merely at correcting this neglect, but at demonstrating that the political traditions unique to the despised "barbarian" Teutons were in fact directly responsible for the stability and greatness of modern England.

In pursuit of this end he joined forces with Green and Stubbs to build for the Whig view an historical foundation in the Middle Ages. Not content with ruling out all taint of Roman absolutism in English institutions, he went on to argue that England became "in the days of its earliest independence, a more purely Teutonic country than even Germany itself" (HE, 1:51). Among all the nations of modern Europe, England could still claim for "its political institutions the most unbroken descent from the primitive Teutonic stock" (CP, 45). Freeman's peculiar emphasis in the Whig debate fell on his insistence that the Conquest had made "no formal change whatever" in the constitution. It was a turning point, not a beginning. William had "claimed the Crown by legal right," and "he professed to rule . . . according to the laws of his predecessor and kinsman King Eadward."[25] Even William's tyranny was conducted under legal forms that tacitly legitimized the very freedoms he sought to stifle. Freeman assigned something like the status of a "fortunate fall" to the Conquest. "Had there never been a time of foreign tyranny," he claimed, "our liberties might have crumbled away without our knowing it" (HNC, 5:459). As it was, the Conquest did not "crush or extinguish the Old-English spirit" but rather invigorated it. The Normans, once "washed clean from the traces of their sojourn in Roman lands" (HNC, 3:405), returned to the Teutonic fold as worthy proselytes (HE, 1:52).

Although more explicit about the dangers of false analogies between parliaments of the ninth and nineteenth centuries, like other Whig medievalists Freeman held that in principle "there is absolutely no gap between the meeting of the Witan of Wessex which confirmed the laws of Aelfred . . . and the meeting of the Great Council of the Nation" in 1873 (CP, 47). True, as Burrow points out, Freeman at times resorted to an implicitly discontinuous series of revivals or restorations in order to preserve this continuity. The English reformed by "falling back on a more ancient state of things," by "calling to life again the institutions of earlier and ruder times," by casting aside "the slavish subleties of Norman lawyers" and "the innovations of Tudor tyranny and Stewart usurpation" (GEC, 21). Still, restorations did not negate the principle of continuity; if anything, they made more explicit the mythic dimensions of this loss and recovery of national identity.[26] And of course they also created classic examples of modern periods that shared more "identity of principle" with the distant than with the nearer past.

For Freeman as for other Whigs, there were greater modern advantages to reading English history not as a series of purifications but rather as a palimpsest in which all emendations could still be read, or to figuring the constitution as a building that had often been repaired but never razed and rebuilt (GEC, 55-56). The paths of precedent had always been for the English the paths of progress because they had early learned how to reform without destroying, unlike the "clever constitution makers" of France (CP, 234). Altogether "guiltless of political theories," England's "stout knights and citizens" had pre-

History as Past Politics

served the fabric by mending it before it tore. Because political change in England had always been "conservative because progressive, progressive because conservative," Freeman could claim ancient English history as the true possession of the "Liberal, who, as being ever ready to reform, is the true Conservative, not of the self-styled Conservative who, by refusing to reform, does all he can to bring on destruction" (GEC, 55, viii). By also portraying the English constitution as an organism growing "almost in obedience to a natural law" (GEC, 66), Freeman turned change into a fulfillment of genetic destiny, the maturation of the "germ" into the fully realized organism.

More importantly, he made this genetic destiny part of a larger, implicitly providential pattern. With a chauvinism typical of his age, Freeman taught that only the Aryans possessed a *"history* in the highest sense."[27] Western culture was synonymous with the successive achievements of Greek, Roman, and Teuton. Each had championed the progressive side in the eternal struggle for light against darkness, freedom against bondage, civilization against barbarism.[28] Like Arnold, Freeman imposed on Aryan legatees the responsibility for sustaining the upward spiral of progress on behalf of the whole world. In widening the franchise or opposing the Turks, the Victorians were reenacting that eternal struggle. Their achievements and their duties became charged with a cosmic significance.

Dignifying the temporal with the eternal is, in more or less explicit form, the standard means by which the Victorian historian reconciled progress to permanence. In Freeman's case that juxtaposition of temporal and eternal conceals conflicts that ultimately belie the whiggish present-mindedness and relish for progress he seems otherwise to exemplify. Burrow skillfully illuminates the contradictory nature of Freeman's devotion to the past, a devotion "so intense as to amount to a reluctance to recognise it as irrevocably past."[29] His elaboration of Aryan cycles simply enacts on the largest scale an obsession with parallels pervasive enough to constitute something close to typological or figural thinking. For such a mind it is always a short step from analogy to identity, to the collapsing together of types that makes the past eternally available. This is also the appeal of his two models for change, restoration and continuity. Both were "forms of triumph over time . . . because they offered alternative images of eternity: the tying of the ends of history into its eternal circles and the architectural palimpsest as the symbol of the co-existence of all ages."[30] Freeman did not, like Macaulay, value the past because it had made possible the present success. Rather, he defined success in terms of its accurate recapitulation of tradition. In this respect his reverence for the past had more in common with Carlyle's. But where Carlyle allowed—indeed, required—the building to be razed so that the traditional could be re-created in new forms, Freeman could be secure only with palpable permanence: either the old building with all its repairs, or a return to the purity of the *ur*-form. If he was guilty of anachronism, it was not because he applied his contemporary political beliefs to the past, but because "apart from history he had no contemporary politics at all."[31]

Freeman resists easy classification. Among the most enthusiastic champions of modern methodology, he was in a more profound sense the least reconciled to modernity of the six authors here discussed. A vocal public proponent of greater rigor and objectivity, he was driven by a private mythology that imposed its own evaluative criteria on all judgments. If the contradictions run deep, they are only the most extreme examples of ambiguities that in fact pervaded the transition to professionalization. It was his longing for a unitary standard of truth, some key that would make all phenomena morally intelligible, that made Freeman the sage and Freeman the scientist one and the same. Like Arnold, he wished to co-opt scientific methodology so that it served, not threatened, the moral function of history. So convinced was he of the truth of his reading of western history that it never occurred to him that he had put the cart before the horse—chosen the methodology to justify, not to verify, the teleological pattern of history, and thus compromised the objectivity of the historian in the very process of trying to vindicate it.

II

If we consider in more detail Freeman's strategies as a practicing historian, we find his affinities to the "literary" tradition even stronger. The apparent contradictions in Freeman's position arise less from what he actually did as an historian than from his self-consciously polemical role in the late Victorian debate over old and new models of historiography. It was in his public personae as the Regius Professor, the Froude-Slayer, the scholarly heavy that he gained the reputation as chief antagonist to the "literary" cause. His unfortunate penchant for rhetorical overkill obscured what was in fact the main thrust of his efforts as a publicist: to aggrandize, not to belittle, the traditional aims of historical study.

History as Past Politics

Consider, for example, his position on the reform of historical education at Oxford: it was weighted much more to older conventions of liberal education and didactic historiography than to specialized professionalism. He objected to the founding of a school of modern history in the early fifties not just because it would distort the underlying unity of history and deal with periods still too controversial for balanced judgment, but also because the specialism it encouraged would subvert the ideals of liberal education. He believed that the main purpose of undergraduate study in history should be to train students' minds in the principles of historical philosophy, and felt that this could be achieved simply by approaching the curriculum of the old school of *Literae Humaniores* in a more scientific (that is, comparative) spirit. The passing of the Oxford Act and the Examination Statute over the objections of Freeman and others meant that when he returned as Regius Professor in the eighties, he found an educational system conducive to neither sound tutoring nor a research professoriate. Examinations had degraded teaching into a trade, he charged, and were driving students from the generalist college tutor to the specialized "combined lecturer," affiliated with no college and therefore dispensing education in a moral and social vacuum.[32] These lectures also usurped the role of the professors, who, because they had little control over examinations and their lectures "did not pay in the schools," often found themselves, as did Freeman, speaking to almost empty benches. The heavy lecturing duties attached to the Professorship further undermined its effectiveness and authority. To require of a professor forty-two lectures a year was to make research not less but more difficult—indeed, downright "penal."[33]

Freeman declared that the professor's duty was not to prepare students for examinations but to be a representative of learning, to guide those interested in knowledge for its own sake to the study of "original authorities" (M, 16). He actually valued the close reading of primary texts not as a source of original research but as an heuristic model closest to that of the old school of *Literae Humaniores*: the "old-fashioned study of 'books'" represented an antidote to the "delusive" pursuit of "subjects" and "periods" (M, 36). Far from styling himself a professor in the German mode who was "bound to utter something new every time he officially opens his mouth" (HE, 4:201), he felt it entirely appropriate to use the Regius Chair to outline "the great periods of history" (M, 38) or to summarize the historical background of topical issues. He considered an understanding of basic principles more important to accuracy than the exhaustive research "the last German book" could boast of (M, 289). His quite traditional priorities were summed up at the end of his Inaugural lecture, where he declared that enabling his listeners better to play their part in the present by providing clearer knowledge of "those earlier forms of public life out of which our own has grown" was an object higher than the "search after truth for its own sake" (M, 40).

Freeman drew the battle lines between the old and new historiography much more broadly when addressing the position of history outside the academy. But his very willingness to play so active a role in the wider public debate was a sign of a commitment to an ideal broader than professionalism alone. Endowing the historian with professional status was a way of cementing his traditional authority, not of defining its replacement. Freeman took on the crusader's role with relish. From his earliest essays for the *Saturday Review*, he never tired of insisting that the serious historian should, like any other professional, be expected to master the methodology of his science before beginning his work and to meet scholarly standards in executing it. His harrying of Froude was only the most notorious instance of his broader assault on dilettantes who had taken up history because they had nothing better to do and whose works belonged in the drawing room, not on the historical shelf.[34] As we have seen, the physical scientist provided a ready model for the kind of authority Freeman desired. He regretted that the wide popularity of historical writing made it much harder to convince readers of the importance of "scientific" levels of expertise. The public assumed that the scientist's position was backed by an expertise that admitted of no challenge from mere laymen. But history possessed nothing like science's technical terminology to "frighten away fools" (LF, 2:202); England had no equivalent to the German *Gelehrten* to expose imposters and render authoritative judgments (LF, 2:185). When the historian ventured (as Freeman so often did) to correct misconceptions, he was charged with pedantry; the public assumed that in historical controversies, every side had "an equal 'right to their own opinion' " (M, 86). As a result, although crackpot scientific views had been rooted out of sources "laying any claim to a scientific character," the historical equivalent of "flat earth" theories still flourished in "publications of considerable pretensions" (M, 90).

Freeman linked the issue of authority to the broader one of audience expectation and discrimination. He lamented that readability was more important than accuracy to the general reader and that the historian who wished to reach an audience that read for pleasure and amusement was thus tempted to sacrifice fact for effect (M, 99). Freeman was particularly zealous in lauding the virtues of men like Stubbs and Finlay, who sacrificed popularity to the painstaking, meticulous work of "real" scholarship.[35] He was particularly resentful of an audience whose taste for pretty pictures and lively paradox made Froude a best seller, while it condemned the scrupulous Gardiner to obscurity (M, 100-102), and he was particularly hard on men like Charles Kingsley, who discredited the Regius Professorship by bringing history "down to the lowest level of the sensational novelist" in *The Roman and the Teuton*.[36] In part Freeman's animus against popular writers may be attributed to repeated criticisms of his own dullness and pedantry,[37] heaped on top of his disappointment at being so long passed over himself for a professorship. But we should also remember how easily his attempt to raise the standards of historical writing would have appeared to him as no less than a defense of truth against falsehood, of good against evil (M, 102-3, 112).

The crucial point about Freeman's role in this debate is that precisely because the promulgation of truth was so important to him, he could not accept J. R. Seeley's remedy to the professional's identity crisis: "To make sure of being judged by competent judges only, we ought to make history so dull and unattractive that the general public will not wish to meddle with it."[38] He might applaud the efforts of the Rolls Series to provide reliable texts for serious students of history,[39] but he was not willing that scholars should abandon the general reader to the rising tide of popularized history that flooded the mass market in the second half of the century. The circulating libraries and the middle class thirst for self-help were creating a lucrative business for the practitioners of "the art of history made easy"—topical and often sensationalized farragoes of romance and history, detail and digressions—all the more pernicious because their uncritical audience took their statements on trust.[40] It was not history's popularization that Freeman objected to, but its vulgarization in this way. Accepting the expectation of the general public that some kind of history be "served up to it," Freeman proclaimed it the duty of the serious historians "to improve its taste, to guide its voice, and to teach it to speak the right way."[41]

In attempting to practice what he preached, Freeman displayed a broader range of styles than his defense of professionalism might suggest. In the seventies he contracted to write a series of short histories for Macmillan's Historical Course for the Schools, hoping thereby to supplant "the many wretched compilations and epitomes which misled and bewildered the minds of young readers by their blunders, and disgusted them by their dullness" (LF, 2:31). *Old-English History for Children* he designed as an experiment to prove that "clear, accurate, and scientific views of history . . . may be easily given to children from the very first"—specifically, that they could be taught "to distinguish true history alike from legend and from willful invention."[42] This did not mean excluding those legends that had so often usurped the place of true history, but presenting them as did Arnold, in the antiquated style of the King James *Old Testament*.

Freeman was particularly concerned to promulgate his theory of Aryan continuity in a form accessible to the general reader. He aimed to make his *History of Federal Government* "instructive and interesting to any thoughtful reader, whether especially learned or not," by avoiding "technicalities" in the text and relegating discussion of detailed points to notes that he hoped would satisfy "the requirements of the most exacting scholar" (HFG, xv). He left the *Growth of the English Constitution* in the form of its original "popular lectures," hoping that its "more highly wrought shape" would catch the attention of readers and lead them to the "proper sources of more minute knowledge" (GEC, vi). The *History of the Norman Conquest* itself was to be a major scholarly work, but one he also hoped would attract that "strangest of beings, the general reader" (LF, 1:336). His goal was to clothe "with flesh and blood the dry bones" of his old English heroes, whose "living personal interest" had up until then been obscured by "fantastic legends" or "summaries of the most repulsive dryness" (NC, 1:xvi-xvii). Even Stubbs's recent constitutional history would need to be "translate[d] . . . into thunder and lightning" (LF, 2:88) in order to impress the true greatness of English continuity on the public mind.

Far from ruling out imagination in historical research, Freeman agreed with contemporaries that—under proper restraint—it was essential to perceiving history's patterns (M, 282). Far from believing excellence of style to be incompatible with excellence of matter, he felt that combining both was the best way of winning over the serious reader to the cause of truth.[43] He objected to the spasmodic excesses of historical sensationalism precisely because they reduced great moments to tawdry bombast (HE, 1:326-27). But to acknowledged masters of historical narrative like Arnold and Macaulay, he accorded higher honors than to their more scholarly German brethren. Though concerned to improve the historian's image in the public eye, Freeman's goal was not professionalism for its own sake. Although he recognized the legitimacy of a separate genre for fellow specialists, he devoted his major efforts to upgrading popular historical writing—to mediating, not widening, the gap between popular and professional audiences. In styling the historian a professional, he was trying to combine, not to replace, the Victorian sage with the historical scientist.

Freeman's own research techniques, for example, were essentially conventional rather than innovative. He might have lauded facts "drawn from the fountain-head" as the appropriate corrective to crude theories promulgated by "the philosophical school or the picturesque school,"[44] and have styled himself merely an illustrator or harmonizer of original texts: "I wish no one to read me instead of my authorities" (M, 270). But the voluminous *History of the Norman Conquest* was more a synthesis of existing accounts than a compilation of original research. His command of the narrative sources of Anglo-Saxon history was unrivaled at the time, but his repugnance to working in libraries kept him from consulting any "original authorities" not available in print. He would often hold up the painstaking drudgery of the plodding dryasdust as the virtue that separated the scholarly sheep from the dilettante goats. Yet he felt the German insistence on mastering every scrap of the whole historical *Literatur* for every issue to be an unreasonable one,[45] and excused his own less than exhaustive analysis of Domesday, for example, by saying that only an editor would sit down to read it through, word for word (NC, 1:xi).

He believed that he provided evidence voluminous enough to allow readers to double-check him and draw different conclusions if they wished. But he seldom realized how much he distorted that evidence by trying to force syntheses from contradictory accounts or the extent to which his own assumptions biased his choice of data.[46] His forerunners on the Norman Conquest, Thierry and Palgrave, he found guilty of failing to distinguish the relative value of different authorities in their eagerness to support their own theories (NC, 1:xv). Freeman dutifully cautioned his readers against the panegyric excesses of English sources, but too often his own critical method amounted to little more than examining the English account of some fact and then comparing the "Norman perversion of it" (NC, 2:4 n.).

English encomium was usually allowed to presuppose some legitimate basis for praise, Norman invective to result from "interested invention" (e.g., NC, 2:21, 1:472). He never tired of holding up Froude as the classic case of the gullible amateur, a "confiding innocent" who took Henry's royal proclamations and acts of parliament at face value. No experienced historian could be so naive, Freeman scoffed. Yet he used documents in a similar way to prove "parlimentary subserviency" in an age of Tudor *"unlaw."*[47] The methodology of those who disagreed with him always struck him as less professional than his own.

Freeman's treatment of myth and legend offers the most illuminating parallels to earlier historians. On the one hand, myth was fundamental to his reconstruction of Aryan nationalism; on the other, it would appear a primary obstacle to a scientific reading of history. As early as 1866, Freeman had pinpointed the tendency to prefer romance to fact as the bane of popular historical writing and attempted to lay down guidelines for distinguishing between the two (HE, 1:1-39). At times this involved verifying details by known facts or analyzing their internal consistency. More often, it meant using comparative methods to expose similar accounts as imitations of a genre. Freeman noted with a kind of grim satisfaction that the result of textual criticism was "to tear away all shreds of likelihood, all shreds of possibility, from the choicest, the most beautiful, the most cherished, legends"; still, he resented the fact that "this often makes our studies unpopular; people quarrel with us because we rob them of their beloved fables, and they . . . say that they will believe the fables in spite of us and our evidence" (M, 139-40). The serious historian might permit readers their artistic pleasure in pretty stories, but he had to insist that belief was a matter of fact, not taste.

For all the self-righteous severity Freeman mustered in the persona of the embattled professional, it is important to see that here too his motives were the same as Arnold's and Carlyle's: to try to establish a groundwork of fact upon which a legitimate hero-worship might be raised. His real objection to sacrificing history to "silly stories" was that as a result, "the real actions of very remarkable men are utterly forgotten" (HE, 1:8). For England in particular, substituting history for legend "almost always tends to exalt instead of to depreciate the ancient heroes of our land." For "truths like these it is worth while to surrender a few pleasant fables," Freeman argued; "but on the other hand, we must beware lest sound criticism degenerate into indiscriminate scepticism" (HE, 1:39). Their precise historical accuracy might remain in question, but mythic accounts should still be allowed some germ of truth that testified to Aryan ideals. Freeman thus parted ways with Grote, who censured all attempts to pin down historical truth in Trojan legends. He likewise drew the line at theories (like Max Müller's and G. W. Cox's) that reduced all Aryan myths to expressions of natural phenomena, fearing that "if Achilleus and Odysseus are ruled to be the sun, later heroes of mythology and romance, Arthur and Hengist and Cerdic and the Great Karl himself, may some day be found out to be the sun also" (HE, 1:2). If this naive literalism was largely a pose, it did not rule out a quite serious concern that too thoroughgoing a scepticism about early history might erode respect for genuine tradition as a legitimate historical source. Like Arnold, Freeman used scientific methods not to discredit myth and legend, but rather to give authority to the "right" ones. It was all the more gratifying to praise famous men when imagination and fact were thus joined.

Myth, superstition, and folklore also played an important role in Freeman's re-creation of the mind or spirit of the age. "The history of opinions about facts is really no small part of the history of those facts" (M, 267), he reminded his readers. Hagiography, outdated histories, and popular literature also helped reconstruct that opinion. Even traditional documents like Domesday had a double value, providing the legal record but also letting the reader behind the scenes: "Every human relation, every position of life . . . the wail of the dispossessed, the overbearing greed of the intruder, the domestic details of courtship, marriage, dowry, inheritance, bequest, and burial, all are there" (NC, 5:44). Most often, the mind of the time served Freeman as it did Froude and Macaulay. He was too obviously the judicious lawyer highlighting detail that supported his case, leaving in shadow what did not. References to daily life in Domesday are muted except where they demonstrate the injustice of Norman rule (e.g., 5:44-45); legendary accounts are brought to the fore mainly when they argue for his good opinion of Teutonic heroes (e.g., NC, 3:361). Freeman might (in appendixes) insert disclaimers about the reliability of superstition and folklore, but in the text he takes full advantage of the rhetorical weight they lent to his own interpretations. He manipulates "the feelings of those times" about oaths in such a way as to condemn William for making Harold swear fealty, rather than faulting Harold for breaking the oath (NC, 3:252). To heighten the portentousness of William's last year of life, he lets "our ancient tongue . . . set forth the full horrors of such a time" (NC, 4:695). Quoting the words of the chronicler and going on to cite other catastrophes that popular belief anachronistically placed in the same year allows Freeman to reinforce, without actually having to credit, the sense that some ritual revenge was being wrought upon the usurper.

Despite the vast detail of Freeman's major work, there is little of the texture of daily life, few of the individual faces of custom, that captured Macaulay's and Green's imaginations. Lack of data was a factor, although Green overcame the same liability with significant success. We might also argue that "history as past politics" necessarily meant that only lead actors deserved center stage. The more persuasive explanation lies in the demands of Freeman's mythology. His focus is always on the archetype, not on the individual, on the public spectacle, not on its private contexts. The universalizing pull of his cycles flattens into insignificance the quotidian and the personal. It is the infrastructure rather than the "pulse of life" that attracts him most. When he makes significant detours from the main course of the political narrative, it is to linger in places where the historical record has in effect solidified; in the streets of cities, in the surrounding terrain.

Freeman's contributions to "comparative urban history and historical travelogue" were substantial.[48] He credited Green with first teaching him that towns too had personal lives with relevance to the principles "animating" their architecture. The *Norman Conquest* is studded with capsule histories of towns along the way (e.g., IV, 87, 196, 202), and his frequent travels abroad yielded dozens of travelogue "middles" for the *Saturday Review*. For Freeman, capturing the "local character" of a town seldom meant resuscitating its teeming street life as it had for Green. He is more interested in establishing "its position in the history of the world"—its role in the wider drama of Aryan history (HE, 4:v). He cherishes the physical structure of cities as a literal palimpsest that preserves in miniature all strata of cultural evolution. Nothing fascinated him more than finding spots where he could see the whole history of the world "stamped for ever on the stones of a single building" (M, 316). Like Carlyle's inventory of Cromwell-land, his capsule histories become catalogues of the famous men and deeds associated with place. Yet the effect of Carlyle's stereoscopic imposition of perspectives is to draw the past into the immediacy of the present. Freeman valued place less for the dynamic immediacy of its history than for the monumental fixity that constituted permanent presence. The effect of his miniature travelogues in the *Norman Conquest* is not to make us feel time's evanescence, but to stabilize—even immobilize—us in the density of the historical record. The cross threads of universal history actually wind up muting local color. When Freeman conducts us on a walking tour of Falaise, where legend joined William's parents for the first time, like Carlyle he positions us as "the traveller [who] gradually ascends to the gate of the castle, renowned alike in the wars of the twelfth, the fifteenth, and the sixteenth centuries" (NC, 2:177). But associations that for Freeman enrich the scene—Talbot's tower leads on to his role in Aquitaine, the castle's keep to Henry's siege—diffuse the focus of the reader who could not glimpse the private patterns that ordered this relentless cross-referencing. Freeman's allusive density enriched an otherwise sketchy period in the *Norman Conquest,* but the tendency to turn coincidence into connection became to some an exasperating mannerism.[49]

Where the land itself was concerned, it was also for Freeman less a case of seeing how the organic shaped human history than of learning to read the marks of "deathless history . . . written for ever on the everlasting page of the soil, the hills, the sea" (M, 319). Again he credited Green with helping him appreciate the importance of terrain to military history; Green or their mutual friend, the geologist Boyd Dawkins, often accompanied Freeman in on-site visits, by then *de rigeur* for "the finished historian" (M, 314). But Freeman valued geography mainly for its reinforcement of political distinctions. He never tired of correcting popular misunderstanding of geographical—and hence political—divisions and devoted his entire *Historical Geography of Europe* to tracing the major contours of political geography from the days of early Greece to the present. Not surprisingly, the *Geography* became a tedious chore long before its final appearance in 1881. Freeman lacked the attachment to landscape that for Arnold galvanized streams and rivers into the veins and arteries of a living being. To climb a mountain for any reason other than a better view of historical sites seemed pointless to him. The effect of geographical detail in the *Norman Conquest* is static rather than dynamic. Such evidence simply fixes a site with more precision (e.g., Harold's landing place at Porlock, NC, 2:322) or thickens the density of allusion. The *felsen* or steep rocks from which Falaise took its name acquire value not from their sublimity but because there "the good old Teutonic speech still lingers in local nomenclature" (NC, 2:178). Freeman's nature, like his cities, is no more than the fixed repository of a fossil record.

In his early reviews of the *Norman Conquest*, Green had taken Freeman to task for neglecting the "moral, social, and intellectual advance of man." Freeman protested in private that such was not his "mission,"[50] but he responded in the final volume with a survey of the Conquest's "local," "social," and "ecclesiastical effects," and of its impact on culture. If this section (or the appendixes touching points of social and cultural history along the way) does little to restore the organic relationship between social and political life that pervades Green's work, Freeman's analysis is far more substantial than the survey either Froude or Macaulay provides at the outset. If the needs of Freeman's political argument dominate this discussion, so too did theirs. But by putting this section last, Freeman does underline its subordination to his political interests. Although he acknowledges the interaction of custom and innovation, we sense this data less as part of a living environment than as so many more analogical layers of artifacts, deposits of the same political glacier. Social and ecclesiastical change he treated so as to document the working of that same "general law" of continuity (NC, 5:505) that we see everywhere; the Conquest simply furthered changes already under way. His discussion of its impact on language, literature, and art (which he equates with architecture) duplicates familiar paradigms as well. Noting that he will treat philology "only as it illustrates the political history" of the time (NC, 5:vi-vii), he dutifully uses the predominance of Teutonic vocabulary and syntax to buttress his claim that Norman influence represented only an infusion into a dominant stock (NC, 5:538). Here, however, the fossil record showed evidence of catastrophic destruction that uniformitarian arguments could not rationalize away. Freeman could not help feeling that these infusions "marred for ever the purity of our ancient tongue" (NC, 5:651). His penchant for choosing germanic over latinate words, which became an obsession in later life, represented his personal attempt at reparation. The same sense of corruption and loss hangs over his discussion of literature. The tameness of the *Roman de Rou* is contrasted with the old heroic songs of the English folk (NC, 5:586-88); the translator of Wace is condemned for unleashing a flood of "wretched fables" to drive out "the true history and worthier legends of our fathers" (NC, 5:590). Burrow quite rightly detects "an un-Whiggish sense of irrevocable disinheritance" behind all this mourning.[51]

Freeman is luckily able to find more consoling evidence of both purity and continuity in architecture. The argument permits full indulgence of his earliest and deepest love. He rummages through the architectural record of all western Europe, comparing, classifying, ranking, until each specimen has been securely placed in one vastly branching family tree. In the process he is able to defend the "primitive Romanesque" of pre-Conquest England as not a corruption, but a more perfect carrying out of the true Roman form (NC, 5:603-4). The Norman Romanesque that replaced it still kept English architecture in the family, and insofar as that replacement had begun with good King Edward, Freeman could still argue that the Conquest had merely given a fresh impulse to causes already at work; once again, it was a turning point, not a beginning.

In turning to consider Freeman's stylistic strategies, we must to an extent distinguish between the different audiences he served. His most avowedly popularizing works—the outlines and school texts—were by their very nature largely devoted to summary and synthesis. Freeman could make few concessions to good stories for their own sake in such works. *Old-English History*, which he originally wrote for his own children, is an important exception. It tells at length selected legends like the story of King Edwin "because it is such a famous and beautiful tale," but it brackets such stories apart from the rest of the text and consciously antiquates the style to distinguish them from "true history" ("Then Aethelfrith sent unto Raedwald, saying, 'Slay me Edwin mine enemy, and I will give thee much gold and silver.' But Raedwald would not hearken").[52] In Freeman's own narrative voice there is much of the confiding dogmatism of the earnest schoolmaster. He coaxes the naive reader along in a story-telling singsong, prompting the correct judgments ("You will perhaps say that our forefathers were cruel and wicked men . . . but you must remember . . . that it is not fair to judge our fathers by the same rules as if they had been either Christians or civilized men") and gently but firmly inculcating the lessons of the Aryan catechism ("We should always think with reverence of our own fathers and kinsfolk, and think what great nations have grown out of the people who were then looked down upon as *Barbarians*").[53]

Freeman's grand style is more dignified but no lighter in its touch.

Edward Augustus Freeman

He was a great admirer of Macaulay's "English undefiled" (M, 105) and claimed that it had taught him the need for clarity, simplicity and judicious repetition.[54] The results of Freeman's imitation would scarcely have flattered Macaulay. Freeman's attempts at lucidity translated into a doggedly insistent prose that hammered home the same ideas in the same simplistic cadences and virtually unvaried phrasing. His conviction that what every schoolboy knew was a jumble of anachronisms and misnomers turned Macaulay's breezy allusiveness into labored antiquarianism, his easy authority into an overbearing dogmatism. Freeman strove for dignity and grandeur but achieved at best what Green called "a sort of undertaker-solemnity," all anthems and no timbrels (LG, 302, 222). Freeman's limitations were in part temperamental. Subtlety of any kind irritated him. He could trust the black and white garishness of Macaulay's prose, but instantly suspected Froude's elegant nuances. Not surprisingly, his taste for fiction was highly limited. His essential dogmatism admitted no toleration for alternative realities. He was also the least novelistic of my six historians. The aesthetics of sympathy brought one a bit too close to familiarity. Freeman was jealous for the reputations of his Aryan pantheon and required a conventionally histrionic heroism to keep them larger than life.

The History of the Norman Conquest in England was first and foremost a patriotic epic, the latest in a long chain of Aryan sagas: for Freeman, part of both a literary and an historical tradition. He had begun his career as a composer of ballads celebrating Aryan heroes; when it came time to tell the story of his own nation in prose, he naturally adopted the same mode. However often he might acknowledge the weight of relative standards of behavior, he measures the stature of any individual with pretensions to greatness against centuries-old ideals of military valor and honor. Whenever he wishes to deepen the resonance of important moments, he automatically borrows analogies from that tradition: the battle of Maldon naturally struck him as having a "thoroughly Homeric character," its record in verse as breathing "the true fire of the warlike minstrelsy common to Greek and Teuton" (NC, 1:273-74). Such conscious parallels helped not only to make good his claim that the achievements of Teutonic Christendom rivaled those of the ancient world, but also to aggrandize England's special providential role in Aryan history.

Casting English history in terms of this epic tradition necessarily meant stressing the importance of individuals, in refutation of Positivist claims against individual freedom. Despite his disclaimers about hero-worship, Freeman was instinctively attracted to "great man" explanations: to situations where the "spirit of a gallant army" could be "foully damped by the malice of a single traitor" one year, and rallied to victory in the next by "the efforts of a single hero, boldly struggling against every difficulty" (NC, 1:322). On the other hand, if individuals hold the center stage in the *History*, judgments always reach beyond the individual. Freeman's handling of men and events encourages us to gauge their stature as silhouetted within ever widening frames of perspective: to judge their significance first to English, then to Aryan, and finally to Universal history. William and Harold play the leads in the "great drama" of the Conquest, but it is their role in the "great struggle of nations and tongues and principles" that gives them interest, not vice versa (NC, 1:532). Freeman begins, rather than ends, with a summation of Harold's and William's vices, virtues, and political significance. There is little or no sense of a character evolving in either man. The moral and political estimates of each are fixed at the outset, the rest of their characterization tailored to vindicate these. As a result they do not come home to us as personalities in the way that Carlyle's Cromwell or even Froude's Henry does. This effect derives partly from the amount of verifiable detail Freeman had at his disposal, but is more a question of his own narrative choices and abilities. Lengthening the field of focus necessarily subordinated individual personalities to the larger pattern. The principles he represents, not the man himself, emerge as the real source of dramatic interest.

Harold's place in the ranks of English heroes is assured from the beginning. Freeman casts him not as the usurping Godwinson but as "the hero and the martyr of our native freedom" (NC, 2:37), a consummate military commander and an even more accomplished statesman whose goal was ever to keep England free from foreign domination. He was in all things Teutonic: even those foreigners he promoted were "natives of . . . kindred Teutonic lands" (NC, 2:41). Freeman takes great pains to keep his motives as pure as his lineage. He devotes a substantial portion of the narrative in volume 3 to the most controversial point of Harold's reign, whether or not he had sworn an oath to place William on the throne after Edward's death. He continues his special pleading in lengthy appendixes, content only when he can turn the final blame against William.

Edward Augustus Freeman

Freeman's usual strategy for aggrandizing Harold's position consisted not of directly refuting "Norman calumny" but of magnifying the terms of comparison. He begins by comparing Harold, the "champion of England against the Southern invader," (NC, 2:44) to Constantine Palailoges, who fell, sword in hand, defending his native Greece against invading Turks. Freeman consciously heightens the drama surrounding Harold's election and reign, enlarging their scope until he seems a political leader of international proportions. Referring to the Bayeux tapestry, Freeman lingers for five pages over the hesitant expression on Harold's face when he is formally offered Edward's crown. He attributes to him a conception of its political significance clearly more Freeman's than Harold's. By noting that Harold was not of noble blood, Freeman isolates him in world history; by measuring him against a rogue's gallery of tyrants, he easily inflates Harold's distinction:

> For him, no son of a kingly father, no scion of legendary heroes and of Gods of the elder faith, to see with his own eyes the diadem of Ecgbehrt and Cerdic ready for his grasp, was of itself a strange and wondrous feeling, such as few men but him in the world's history can have felt. He was not like others before and since, who by fraud or violence have risen to royalty or more than royalty. Harold was not a Dionysios, a Caesar, a Cromwell, or a Buonaparte, whose throne was reared upon the ruins of the freedom of his country. He was not an Eastern Basileus, climbing to the seat from which a fortunate battle or a successful conspiracy had hurled a murdered or blinded predecessor. (NC, 3:22)

Having suitably intensified the awe with which Harold must have viewed the English crown, "freely offered in all its glory and greatness," (NC, 3:23), Freeman then turns to other reasons for Harold's hesitation: to his consciousness of assured challenges by Tostig, his brother, and by William, to his memory of the ignominious oath he had sworn to the latter and would now have to break: "No wonder then if, as the picture sets before us, he looked at the Crown at once wistfully and anxiously, and half drew back the hand which was stretched forth to grasp the glittering gift. And yet the risk had to be run. A path of danger opened before him, and yet duty no less than ambition bade him to enter upon the thorny road" (NC, 3:24). By arguing on Harold's behalf that William would challenge the throne regardless of who held it, and that only Harold was an adversary mighty enough to protect it, Freeman casts his decision in the light of self-sacrifice rather than self-interest: "The danger then had to be faced. The call of patriotism distinctly bade Harold not to shrink at the last moment from the post to which he had so long looked forward, and which had at last become his own. The first man in England, first in every gift of war and peace, first in the love of his countrymen, first in renown in other lands, was bound to be first alike in honour and danger" (NC, 3:25). Arnold himself could not have conjured up a more noble set of motives for a silent hero.

Freeman maintains the note of quavering sanctity through Harold's coronation, the highlight of which was the voiced consent of the people to his election: a classic Whig anachronism, here intensified into a moral victory: "Never was there a more lawful ruler in this world than Harold, King of the English and Lord of the Isle of Britain—King, not by the mouldering titles of a worn-out dynasty, not by the gold of the trafficker or the steel of the invader, but by the noblest title by which one man can claim to rule over his fellows, the free choice of a free people" (NC, 3:47). Harold's endorsement by the most hallowed traditions of English political life is made more poignant by their imminent disruption. To drive home Harold's position in the saga of English liberties, Freeman pauses in the account of his final laying to rest at Waltham for one of those parallels that were his trademark. He looks forward two hundred forty years to the day when the body of Edward I lay temporarily at Harold's side. In Freeman's hands comparison becomes typological, and coincidence reveals the major contours of English liberty:

> With Harold, our native Kingship ends; the Crown, the laws, the liberties, the very tongue of Englishmen, seem all fallen never to rise again. In Edward the line of English Kings begins once more. After two hundred years of foreign rule, we have again a King bearing an English name and an English heart—the first to give us back our ancient laws under new shapes. . . . In the whole course of English history we hardly come across a scene which speaks more deeply to the heart, than when the first founder of our later greatness was laid by the side of the last kingly champion of our earliest freedom. (NC, 3:521)

If a man be judged by the company he keeps, Harold's good reputation would be assured by the way Freeman frames his portrait. Held fast in the interlocking circles of English history, Harold becomes by implication larger than life, a martyr to causes most sacred to the Whig view.

Notwithstanding Harold's symbolic importance, it is William who is the more personally realized—and not just as the villain of the piece. This is true in part simply because Freeman had more materials to work with: one of the perquisites of success was more and better press. William's characterization draws more fully upon the conventional materials of the Victorian historian: we see his portrait in the later years of his reign (NC, 4:622), hear his voice in direct quotations (NC, 4:707), are treated to the detailed deathbed scene (NC, 4:708-9), and mythic alternatives to the standard biography. Although Freeman wants us to remain at an awestruck distance, his efforts to make William larger than life work at cross-purposes with his political sympathies. Only the highest superlatives quite satisfy him: "No man that ever trod this earth was ever endowed with greater natural gifts; to no man was it ever granted to accomplish greater things" (NC, 2:164-65). But knowing that this sheer force of character helped crush old English freedoms necessarily qualifies Freeman's admiration. He casts his qualifications in ethical rather than political terms, however. Only when William's actions are looked at "without regard to their moral character" may he "fairly claim his place in the first rank of the world's greatest men." William's preeminence, like Harold's, earns him the right to be judged by international standards. But William is hardly a match for the much more punishing competition of the world's "pure patriots." Harold easily looked good in the exclusive company of tyrants; William, if not damned, is at least compromised, by much fainter praise:

> If we cannot give him a niche among pure patriots and heroes, he is quite as little entitled to a place among mere tyrants and destroyers. William of Normandy has no claim to share in the pure glory of Timoleôn, Aelfred, and Washington; he cannot even claim the more mingled fame of Alexander, Charles, and Cnut; but he has still less in common with the mere enemies of their species, with the Nabuchodonosors, the Swegens, and the Buonapartes, whom God has sent from time to time as simple scourges of a guilty world.   (NC, 2:165-66)

Although admitting that considering his upbringing and the mores of his time, William was to be commended for not being worse, Freeman never lets relativism devalue the moral and patriotic hierarchies that structure history. Finally, of course, these hierarchies are one and the same: it was because William "stretched forth his hand to grasp the diadem which was another's" that he was not "one of the best, as well as one of the greatest, rulers of his time" (NC, 2:171).

Another strategy Freeman uses to universalize the moral judgments against William is to let the eye of contemporaries see the hand of God in policies Freeman wished to condemn as immoral. Freeman's own well-publicized campaign against fox hunting undoubtedly encouraged him to find William's laying waste of populated lands to create the New Forest especially blameworthy. He allows contemporaries to draw conclusions from the fact that William's son was to be treacherously murdered there: "Our age shrinks, and it is often wise in shrinking, from seeing the visible hand of God in the punishments which seem, even on earth, to overtake the sinner. The age of William was less scrupulous: the men of his own day . . . saw in the life of William a mighty tragedy, with the avenging Atê brooding over the sinner and his house" (NC, 4:610). Freeman goes on to elaborate the classical analogy. At "the highest pinnacle of earthly greatness . . . the pride of greatness and victory overcame him. They led him on to those deeds of greater wrong by which the avenger, as in the tales of old Hellas, was wont to punish earlier deeds of lesser wrong." In the view of the eleventh century, the disgraces of William's later years were "so many strokes of the sword of the avenger," (NC, 4:610-11) punishing William for harrying Northumberland, allowing the death of Waltheof, and desolating Hampshire for his own pleasure. "To speculations beyond his range the historian can say neither Yea nor Nay," Freeman sagely cautions. This would-be disclaimer hardly obscures the fact that Freeman willingly chooses to see a "poetic justice" (NC, 4:701), if not an outright act of divine vengeance, in the tragic downfall of a once mighty ruler whose base actions had lowered him to the level of meaner men. The condemnation gains more authority by being modeled on a paradigm of western culture. In condemnation, as in celebration, the terms of comparison assume maximum breadth of judgment.

The Battle of Hastings (or of "Senlac," as Freeman rechristened it), the thematic as well as literal center of his major work, provides us with the set piece that most effectively demonstrates Freeman's handling of events. Apart from the conventional devices of Victorian military history—speculations on the thoughts of soldiers, citation of battle cries and dialogue, notes on the modern appearance of the field—we are struck most forcefully by the Homeric echoes that sound throughout the account. This was the crux of the "great struggle of tongues and nations and principles"; its importance in world history demanded a suitably grand style of presentation, one that gave great warriors and great nations their due. The handling of details, focus, and action is calculated to convince us that this epic of Norman and Teuton equals in gravity and splendor any in the Aryan canon.

Like Carlyle at the battle of Dunbar, Freeman begins by allowing us behind the lines on the night before the fighting. The Normans, "under the influence of that strange spiritual excitement which had persuaded men that an unprovoked aggression on an unoffending nation was in truth a war of religion" (NC, 3:454), occupied themselves with prayer and devotion. What the French source slightingly refers to as "singing and drinking" in the English camp, Freeman converts into the symbolic moment when "spirit-stirring strains of old Teutonic minstrelsy" were heard for the last time "in the air of a free and pure Teutonic England." To underline this point, he speculates that "they sang, we well may deem, the song of Brunanburh and the Song of Maldon; they sang how Aethelstan conquered and how Brihtnoth fell." He thus converts a Norman slight into a solemnly patriotic preparation for battle, as fitting as all the "pious oratory" on the other side. Paralleled accounts of the morning's preparations follow: the generals' speeches to their men, a survey of the troops, a closeup shot of each side as battle positions were taken up. Freeman closely follows the *Roman de Rou* in its account of the nobles who rode with William, but he characteristically pauses to allude to each man's past or future significance in the saga, to weigh up his vices and virtues, before passing on. We glimpse Robert Montgomery, who would found a mighty house in the conquered isle, Roger of Norfolk—"a man false alike to his native country and its foreign King"—and Eustace of Boulogne, who had murdered unarmed Englishmen on their hearthstones and would soon bear the ignominy of being the only man to show craven fear (NC, 3:460-61). The effect is not so much to personalize the account as to make it resonate with historical associations: in this moment lay the intersection of many strands of personal and national history. The surveying eye moves on, noting the regional identities and characteristic weapons of the common soldiers as they approached the field of combat. It reserves the closeup for William and Odo, leaving them dramatically spotlighted at "the innermost center of the advancing host": "There, in the midst of all, the guiding star of the whole army, floated the consecrated banner, the gift of Rome and of Hildebrand, the ensign by whose presence wrong was to be hallowed into right. And close beneath its folds rode the two master-spirits of the whole enterprise, kindred alike in blood, in valour, and in crime" (NC, 3:463). After a description of each leader, the perspective widens back out again, to close with a roll call of "the chivalry of Normandy, the future nobility of England": the men who gained a foothold by wrong but whose children would win the rights of the Great Charter (NC, 3:466).

In turning to the English side, Freeman had no such record as Domesday to aid him: "The heroes who fought against [the French] for hearth and home are nameless" (NC, 3:467). After giving a paraphrase of Harold's exhortation to his troops, he fills in by taking time to refute Norman aspersions cast on English conduct. He then follows with a parallel survey of the weaponry and battle positions of the English, and similarly closes in, first on the ensign bearing the Dragon of Wessex—"the sign which had led Englishmen to victory at Ethandun and at Brunanbuhr, at Penselwood and at Brentford"— and then to the leaders beneath it. Freeman gradually constricts our focus, slowing the action with self-conscious repetition and paralleled phrasing, to apply maximum concentration on the hero at the center of this scene, as he is at the center of the *History* itself:

> There, as the inner circle of the host, were ranged the fated warriors of the house of Godwine. Three generations of that great line were gathered beneath the Standard of its chief. There stood the aged Aelfwig, with his monk's cowl beneath his helmet. There stood young Hakon the son of Swegen, atoning for his father's crimes. And, closer still than all, the innermost centre of that glorious ring, stood the kingly three, brothers in life and death. There, in their stainless truth, stood Gyrth the counsellor and Leofwine the fellow-exile. And there, with his foot firm on his native earth, sharing the toils and dangers of his meanest soldier, with the kingly helm on his brow and the two-handed axe upon his shoulder, stood Harold, King of the English. (NC, 3:474-75)

The stage is now set for the fighting to begin. Freeman admits the traditional account of Taillefer's throwing his sword in the air and striking the first blow, but decidedly deflates its picturesque appeal with a no-nonsense observation: "A bravado of this kind might serve as an omen, it might stir up the spirits of the men on either side; but it could in no other way affect the fate of the battle" (NC, 3:477). He skims through the first Norman assault, ending with balanced parallels that underscore the literal and symbolic opposition in the scene: "Javelin and arrow had been tried in vain; every Normal missile had found an English missile to answer it. The lifted lances had been found wanting; the broad-sword had clashed in vain against the two-handed axe; the maces of the Duke and of the Bishop had done their best. But . . . the old Teutonic tactics . . . proved too strong for the arts and the valour of Gaul and Roman" (NC, 3:479-80). As one would expect, hereafter the battle focuses on individual combat. Freeman relates the story that William, seeing the Breton troops in retreat, personally rallied them by baring his head to show that he still lived and exhorting them to return to the fray. He chooses the version that has William kill Gyrth with his own mace for similar reasons: these hand-to-hand struggles were the stuff of epic heroism and made overt the symbolic significance of the battle. The epic parallels become explicit in Harold's reaction to his brother's fall: "The deed of Metaurus had been, as it were, wrought beneath the eyes of Hannibal; Achilleus had looked on and seen the doom of his Patroklos and his Antilochos. The fate of England now rested on the single heart and the single arm of her King" (NC, 3:485). So important to Freeman was "the great personal struggle which was going on beneath the Standard" of the English that he attributed a similar preoccupation to the English troops: this explained why the French were able to penetrate the barricade for the first time. He completes the account of how Norman "craft," in the form of a false retreat, allowed French troops finally to break through the shield wall with another sampling of the "more remarkable" instances of hand-to-hand combat from Wace (NC, 3:492).

Despite the fact that his audience was well aware of the battle's outcome, Freeman tries to maintain suspense to the end. With the Breton retreat, "for the moment the day seemed lost" (NC, 3:481); even after the French breakthrough "the fight was still far from being over. It was by no means clear that some new chance of warfare might not again turn the balance in favour of England" (NC, 3:491-92). Not until that one arrow "more charged with destiny than its fellows" pierced Harold's eye is the cause conceded as lost (NC, 3:497). All that is left to do is to "call up before our eyes the valiant deaths of those few [English] warriors of Senlac whose names we know" (NC, 3:500). Compared with one of Carlyle's battle pieces, Freeman's seems peculiarly static, almost ritualized. We are clearly watching a pageant, not participating in one. Freeman's intention is not so much to duplicate the experiential reality of the fighting as to sing his song of arms and the man in terms befitting its importance: to convince his audience that "never was a battle more stoutly contested between able generals supported by more valiant soldiers" (NC, 3:505). His main tactic is not to strive for imaginative originality, but to sound echoes of time-honored conventions of epic heroism; not so much to personalize the battle as to universalize it.

When the *History of the Norman Conquest* began first to appear, periodicals like the *Athenaeum* and the *Pall Mall Gazette* hailed Freeman for delivering England's early history from the hands of trivializing romancers and dryasdust chroniclers alike. They praised the life and spirit of his prose and appreciated his success in raising the tone of historical writing.[55] But Freeman ended by pleasing neither general nor professional audiences. The same journals soon began to weary of his prolixity and repetitiveness.[56] Despite Freeman's obsession with the laws of political science and his dislike of excessive specialization, he became in public eyes a classic example of the new scholar who rejected all synthesis until every fact had been catalogued.[57] Although he recognized the importance of style to history, the violence of his attacks on Froude and Froude's readers stereotyped Freeman as hostile to any literary concessions. Frederic Harrison's "The History Schools (An Oxford Dialogue)" caricatured Freeman's supposed positions in the manuscript-sifting pedant, Aethelbald Wessex.[58] Harrison also pointed out the ways Freeman's almost exclusive attention to the Aryans and to history before 1300 undercut the very "unity of history" he touted.[59] Instead of being converted by the Aryan gospel, reviewers resented Freeman's assuming "the tone of a prophet of a new revelation."[60] The *Athenaeum* pronounced his argument for Aryan continuity self-defeating.[61] The intemperance of his Francophobia discredited his analyses for some, the fulsomeness of his praise for liberty and its Teutonic defenders strained his hero-worship for others.[62] Freeman's tendency to "treat modern politics like an archaeologist" demonstrated how very *un*practical a politician he was.[63] With so few converts to his credit, Freeman had good reasons for feeling a baffled messianism.[64]

If the general audience found his antipathies and enthusiasms too intense for sound views, one can imagine how fellow professionals reacted. C. H. Pearson matched him source for source in questioning Freeman's idealization of Harold, and ended by paying him the dubious compliment of finding him a more vivid portraitist precisely because he was such a prejudiced special pleader.[65] J. H. Round's ferocious pedantry and professional jealousies quite outdid anything Freeman had inflicted on Froude. After criticizing Freeman's battle of "Senlac" in excruciating detail, Round dismissed Freeman's work in terms echoing Freeman's own criticisms: blinded by democratic zeal and carried away by his "homeric" dramatization of heroes, Freeman had drawn more upon the "resources of his imagination" than on the judicious analysis of sources.[66] Others agreed that the epic poet in Freeman was incompatible with the "calm and unprejudiced observer" the historian should be and wrote him off as merely the last of those who wrote history as romance.[67] For the new school of Maitland and Tout, it was Freeman's anachronistic attempts to justify present politics by past precedent that discredited his scholarship.[68] While maintaining an attitude of respect, the *English Historical Review* treated him more as a synthesizer than an original researcher.[69]

Freeman was in a sense a casualty of changes in audience expectations, but much more so of his own inherent strengths and weaknesses. His popular success was limited not because he cared too little for general readers, but because he had too much invested in his message to them. His immersion in private myths blinded him to measure and proportion in his public elaboration of them. What were to him analogies that demonstrated the master plan struck his audience as irrelevant pedantry; the lengthy analyses of sources intended to salvage truth more often convinced them of its elusiveness and made Freeman out a casuist. Having converted his own beliefs into moral absolutes, he self-righteously attacked the disagreement of others as defiance of a common morality. His avenging zeal more than once carried him beyond the limits of good taste and good judgment. To be sure, Freeman did serve his audience well in more general ways. Although the continuity of English history had by then become a commonplace, it was still reassuring to have it made "scientific" by such an authority. The public could and did take comfort in the thumping assurance of his patriotism and appreciated his giving the Conquest the full-dress treatment it had long deserved. And surely for every one reviewer who deplored Freeman's simplistic partisanship, there were a dozen readers secretly comforted by his reduction of all western history to one vast psychomachia: to a clearcut struggle between good and evil in which England—provided she forsook the Turk—could place herself complacently on the side of faith, civilization, and progress.[70]

Freeman revealed the central imperatives of Victorian historical writing all the more openly because he thought that he had justified his positions by scientific scholarship alone. Just as much as Arnold and Carlyle, he was concerned to rescue the past from obscurity and determinism, to endow historical study with the "moral certainty" that made human action possible and meaningful. He needed to argue for the unity of history in order to vindicate the universality of his own assumptions about political behavior. He advocated the most exacting methods of source criticism in order to set his hero-worship on a firmer basis. His scholarship was more scientific—in the sense of being more thorough and more self-conscious—than that of his men-of-letters predecessors, but the important point was that he adopted the guise of the new German professionalism in order to aggrandize, not to undercut, the emotional authority of the Victorian sage. Like those predecessors he signalled his request for a belief that went beyond mere credence by adopting a self-consciously "literary" approach—an epic style that justified the awe and reverence his vision deserved.

By pointing up how easily traditional Victorian assumptions about history's cultural value could be assimilated to the new academic professionalism, Freeman's career forecasts a pattern distinctive to England. At the ancient universities, the power of historical thinking would continue to outweigh the command of specialized skills in the study of history. History's main purpose would remain the teaching of useful lessons. The historical scientist's research would have to be "applied," not "pure," if he were to fulfill his highest duties. To an extent unprecedented elsewhere, English historians remained responsive to the wider society's demand for practical and uplifting history. Freeman demonstrates the resulting contradictions between public and professional priorities in their most flagrant form: the further ramifications of those contradictions will be the subject of my epilogue.

CONCLUSION
DESIRED PRESENTS AND RE-ORDERED PASTS

If the nineteenth century was the age of history, histories themselves were a genre that most efficiently reconciled the contradictory needs of Victorian consciousness. Victorian histories asserted the authority of the real but provided the satisfactions of romance. They emplotted the actual so as to demonstrate the triumph of good over evil, recovery over loss, identity over disinheritance. As art that could both entertain and educate, histories escaped the evangelical disapproval and Utilitarian scorn that "mere" literature aroused. Macaulay's penchant for conjuring up historical romances while at the same time insisting on the clear distinction between fact and fantasy provides the classic example of the tension between imagination and reason, escapism and pragmatism. Historical study satisfied even so rationalistic a mind as Macaulay's by uniting "the clear discernment of truth and the exquisite enjoyment of fiction." It satisfied the exacting consciences of Arnold and Carlyle for similar reasons: they could counter fears of self-indulgent escapism by turning their histories into "tracts for the times."

Even more important was history's ability to reconcile faith with reason. In the hands of these writers, history brought the facts of the past to bear on the truths of belief. It confirmed with law the order posited by faith. In an increasingly secular age, history took the place of dogma as the mainstay of meaningfulness. Without knowledge of his past, man became for Carlyle an "aimless exile" from the spiritual community, deprived of a soul because he was deprived of a history. The very process of studying history satisfied quasi-religious needs by reestablishing this spiritual community and paying tribute to its ideals. Arnold defined the "power of connecting ourselves with the past" as "one of the very divinest parts of our nature." Studying history became an act of reverence toward all things "noble and just, and wise and holy" in human achievement. For Carlyle and Froude this meant hero-worship. The Whig might revere institutions more than individuals, but his alternative faith had similar purposes: to locate a teleological order in the past and to create a tradition that demanded and inspired emulation in the present. What was true for Macaulay, the most rationalistic of the six, was to an extent true of them all: the scenes of major historical events replaced religious shrines as the holy ground of a modern faith. History provided the sacred text and a secularized communion of saints for a religion in which "Admiration, Hope, and Love" bolstered the orthodox creed.

As Arnold's Christian teacher, Carlyle's poet-seer, or even Freeman's professional, the historian became the high priest for this religion, an interpreter who was supposed to provide consolation, direction, and inspiration for his flock. Arnold viewed his historical work in the same light as his clerical responsibilities: both were ways of wrestling actively with the doubt and scepticism of the secular world. For Arnold the priest and the historian were one because all knowledge was one. Victims of Truth's fragmentation, Froude and Green chose the latter vocation after failing at the first. Carlyle struggled with increasing difficulty to make historical study affirm the prophet's voice. Freeman succeeded by refusing to acknowledge a distinction between his moral and scientific messages. By devoting himself to historical writing, Macaulay retreated from his public duties and private griefs into a world of controllable experience. Like the others, he sought there a realm of more stable ideals and more conscious order than he found in the present.

For all six, public mission as well as private needs made objectivity and impartiality suspect if not irresponsible. Where ethical issues were concerned (and for the Victorians, where were they not?) impartiality became "unworthy indifference." Like Green, all six historians considered moral judgment "the very soul of history." Not just understanding but belief itself was at stake in historical investigation: the penalty for failing to make the past intelligible was scepticism.

Conclusion

Carlyle evinced the most anxiety about the difficulties of discerning landmarks in history's dark void, but even Freeman feared that being too critical in analyzing sources threatened to make us despair of finding any reliable record of human achievement. There was in this sense no such thing as a search for truth "for its own sake."

For twentieth-century thinkers, one's way of knowing determines what one can know. For the Victorians what one believed determined one's way of knowing. Spiritual facts were revealed to the eye of imagination. There was a certain practical motive in supplying history with rousing narratives and purple patches: history had to have "the interest of romance" in order to retain its hold on "imaginative and moral feelings"; it needed art to "brand" lasting instruction on the mind. Here Arnold and Macaulay were in essential agreement. Choosing to downplay their scholarly apparatus in order to preserve readability appeared natural to them. This choice had become more polemical for Freeman and Green. Still, both were willing to make concessions in professional standards in the hope of holding the attention of the general public. However, far more significant in determining the literary shape of historical narrative was the conviction that imagination was necessary to understanding, that "poetic insight" was often "the truest philosophy of history." Given the complexity of great personalities, only poetry was adequate to re-create them. Given the fragmentary nature of the historical record, only an act of imagination could reconstitute the "scattered bones" into an organism, transform the "shot rubbish" into a reflection of the cosmic whole. To bridge the gap between past and present consciousness, the historian had often to project what he could not confirm. Carlyle was not the only one who felt that some invention could produce a truer, because more fully realized, picture. Verisimilitude often had greater persuasive power than "hard facts" because meaning in history was the domain of the suprarational—of inspiration, of sympathy, of will. The literary coherence of the Victorian history was an invitation to belief: a pact between the writer, the reader, and the past.

The different registers of Victorian history correspond to the different levels at which the reader could enter and experience. If engaging what Arnold called "poetical feelings" in itself enlarged one's mind, merely witnessing the pageant of great individuals engaged in great deeds was inspiring to the reader—all the more when he could believe such romantic scenes had "really" happened. Purple prose and the grand style were intended to overawe the worshipper in the same way as did ecclesiastical pomp. But recognition of the familiar compelled a more powerful belief than did pageantry. In a secularized faith, sympathy did the work of conversion, and sympathy rested on the acknowledgement of a shared humanity. Glimpses of the private man or woman—More showing off his children's rabbit hutches, Cromwell troubled by hypochondria—did more than merely highlight or round out their portraits. They asserted the authenticity of common experience, the basis of claims that these characters were "friends and brethren." The fabric of common experience extended far beyond individuals to domesticate an alien world. The landmarks of daily life were as important as those of city and battlefield to force the reader from observation into participation. Through the minute documentation of the "life-method" of ordinary people, the historian proved that by-gone ages "were actually filled with living men." Believing that these ages would be unintelligible without some understanding of the shared consciousness that characterized them, he gladly stooped to materials formerly beneath "the dignity of history." The proliferation of quotidian detail authenticated this consciousness as it made the past habitable by imagination. In its "faithful representing of commonplace things," the Victorian narrative history aimed at asserting the authority of the ordinary in the same way as did many novels of the period. The crowded canvasses of both genres also testify to the multi-dimensionality and complexity of the historical process, the novel through its minutely detailed backgrounds, panoramic scale, and interwoven plots, the history through its layering of the private and public, the political and the social, the individual and the mass.

Belief in history's imaginative truths led to art; belief in its philosophical truths led to *Wissenschaft*. Order finally made claims more urgent than individuality. Imaginative realization of the historical datum was a means to an end, for history's meaningfulness rested on patterns accessible by law. Unlike the thinkers of the eighteenth century, the Victorians sought laws that subordinated detail without denying its particularity. They viewed society not as a machine but as an organism. It was not man himself but the process of social evolution that was the same. Recognizing resemblances in the development of different societies confirmed history's "continuity," its interrelatedness. It introduced system into the historian's work, making it scientific rather than merely antiquarian. The attraction of modeling historical change on nature lay partly in its reconciliation of identity

Conclusion

with growth, permanence with variation. If change were in effect seasonal, even the most violent contrasts corresponded to a deeper regularity. If present were related to past as the man to the boy, the tree to the sapling, history could claim unity without uniformity. Manifestations of early stages of development were not scorned as backwards but appreciated as appropriate to their context and essential to growth. The historian could acknowledge the validity of relative standards of conduct without abandoning himself to them. More importantly, "natural" change conveniently secularized teleology. The dynamic behind the historian's version of evolution was not random mutation but the fulfillment of genetic programming. The growth of the germ into the organism became a realization of lineage, the perfecting of something innate. In some (usually) unarticulated sense, this development was predetermined, subject to higher, ultimately benevolent, laws. The distinction between process and progress was more useful for being ambiguous. The historian could manipulate the determinism and regularity of the system to serve his own ends.

Notwithstanding his willingness to borrow the authority of the natural, each historian imposed a system of absolutes on the freedom and relativism of the organic. Nature was not self-sufficient; nurture made the man intellectually superior to the boy, the tree more fruitful than the sapling. Cycles were not self-validating. History spiraled toward some goal. For each historian that goal was defined differently, but once defined, it ordered history according to its own priorities. Ultimate truth might be served by submission to authority or growth into self-determination, by the triumph of silent faith or of rational talk. In either case the definition of truth rationalized blindspots and made some ages more "immediate to God" than others, based on the extent to which they furthered a desired conception of progress.

Such a conception of change gave the historian an argument for reshaping society in his own image. He interpreted the political and social structure he desired for his own society as the issue of a progress that conflated the fulfillment of God's will with the maturation of the organism. This interpretation exploited the coercive power of both the providential and the natural. God's will would ultimately triumph, but man still had to decide whether or not to help further His scheme. Nature would take its course, but growth could lead to disease or deformation if maturation were obstructed. So long as people cooperated with the natural course of change, the evolution toward the good society was guaranteed. Defy that process, however—resist the Reform Bill or shirk the responsibilities of a true aristocracy—and social chaos would come again.

Implicit in such explanations is a tension between a benevolent determinism and a responsible free will that structures the treatment of causation in all six historians. Only Macaulay went so far as to insist that the spirit of the age acted independently of even the greatest individuals—that "without Copernicus we should have been Copernicans." But the others managed to escape this conclusion only by fusing the hero with the spirit of his time or people. Human progress advanced unconsciously in a tide that the hero might guide or the genius epitomize, but that neither originated nor really controlled. Even Carlyle's heroes were modelers, revealers, guides, not creators. By making the spirit of the age a manifestation of the divine plan and the choice of whether to cooperate with it a meaningful one, these historians robbed the "force of circumstances" of its tyrannical influence. If the great man were merely the most prominent specimen of this spirit, his actions still gained significance from their contribution to progress. Victorians feeling lost in the rapid tide of change in their own day could take comfort in history's assurance that the direction of change was ultimately toward the good. Meanwhile, the possibility of retribution or temporary breakdown prevented a fatalistic abandonment to circumstance and kept up the pressure for continued individual struggle.

It was not so much their deficiencies as researchers as the controlling power of their desired patterns that made Victorian historians seem amateur by later standards. Although it is true that most of them relied heavily on standard secondary sources for their data, Macaulay and Carlyle made significant use of original documents, and Froude undertook extensive archival research. They all helped to expand historical understanding by widening the scope of investigation to include geographical, artistic, intellectual, economic, and religious forces. Their treatment of historical sites, mythic and popular literature, religion, and race bespeaks a conception of historical explanation beyond the reach of the Enlightenment. And yet despite the greater complexity of their analyses, various factors prevented them from realizing the full importance of such sociocultural factors and from fully integrating them into historical explanation. This was inevitable given the breadth of their syntheses and the fragmentary state of research materials at the time. The real problems were more polemi-

Conclusion

cal than practical, however. Sociocultural evidence possessed no real autonomy in historical explanation because it became simply another means of vindicating the historian's preconceived sense of order. No inductive revelations were likely given the strength of the patterns already in the historian's mind. Each selected data to condone or condemn the mind of the time; each ransacked culture for analogues to a schema already imposed by his own political and moral precepts.

The Victorian need to demonstrate order and purpose in history made it difficult for the historian to appreciate any fact for its own sake, to understand any event entirely in terms of its context. Finally, only what still "reached to the surface" of the present was worthy of preservation; nineteenth-century needs and interests controlled the historian's perception of what survived. Froude and Carlyle took a "Whig view" of history as much as did Macaulay, Green, or Freeman in this respect: all of them judged and ordered events according to the priorities of the present. They overlooked the specific historical context of events in order to fashion them into anticipations or prototypes of issues decisive for their own society. Preaching the virtues of objectivity and impartiality as so many of them did was no guarantee of either. All were aware of and attempted to practice the scientific analysis prescribed by Ranke. But their foregone conclusions about the righteousness of certain causes made them truly critical of only what contradicted these conclusions. The coherence of history depended upon the timelessness of the values by which they judged it. Seldom could they accept opposing judgments as a matter of intellectual disagreement rather than sinful indifference to Truth. Their need to impose value-laden schema on the past finally made their capacity for romantic empathy highly selective and discredited their claims to what later ages would mean by "scientific" accuracy.

This is precisely why they served their audience so well. Each historian projected his ideal version of modern order back onto the past: each concentrated on materials most easily shaped to mirror that order. The historian devised a genealogy to make recognizable the traits of modern society. The Victorian history promised the general public that insofar as they could endorse and emulate the values of a designated tradition, its history could become their own; they became part of the fulfillment of Teutonic, Protestant, and middle-class destiny. Works so conceived put history's own seal of approval on selected aspects of Victorian success and offered a rationale for continued progress in the same direction. The historian's highest duty

Desired Presents and Re-ordered Pasts

was to make sense of the past in order to make sense of the present. In reality he reversed this process, first asserting a desired present and then assembling a past to justify it. If his powerful impulse toward order undercut historical objectivity and distance, it provided something of much greater use for society at large: a place and purpose in the flux of time.

The Victorian historian's desire to be both sage and scientist was the ideal of an age whose central task was reconciliation, the reconciliation of its different ways of knowing and of its different intellectual and social constituencies. Like other Victorian thinkers, the historian was engaged in defining some communality of vision for a society whose traditional unities were breaking down. When Matthew Arnold placed the authority of a universal culture over the anarchy of individual judgment, when John Henry Newman reaffirmed the existence of timeless truths overriding perennial change and falsehood, when George Eliot tried to replace truth of doctrine with truth of feeling, each was asserting the integrative power of some "idea of the world" over the "multitudinousness" of existence, the power of some common Reality over the increasing number of individual realities. The historian was similarly a mediator: his address to a wide audience was the counterpart of his belief in a shared order; his integration of the rational, the moral, and the imaginative made possible his refusal to surrender truth to relativism. The compartmentalization of intellectual life in the next century was the most prominent sign of the erosion of shared certainties. As a teacher the historian sustained the cultural ideals of an earlier age. His continuing belief in the humanizing power of history—a Victorian legacy—preserved to him an integrity of vision fewer and fewer professionals could claim (or wish to claim) in the multinormative world of the twentieth century.

EPILOGUE
AMATEUR IDEALS AND PROFESSIONAL IDENTITIES

The last fifty years have witnessed great changes in the management of Clio's temple. Her inspired prophets and bards have passed away and been succeeded by the priests of an established church; the vulgar have been excluded from the Court of the Gentiles; doctrine has been defined; heretics have been excommunicated; and the tombs of the aforesaid prophets have been duly blackened by the new hierarchy. While these changes were in process the statue of the Muse was seen to wink an eye. Was it in approval, or in derision?

In his anxiety to defend "Clio, A Muse,"[1] G. M. Trevelyan was too hasty in proclaiming the *Götterdämmerung* of "literary" history. John Osborne uses Trevelyan's own success to convince us of the continued vigor of the belletristic tradition in the twentieth century.[2] Perception is often more important than reality in shaping public debate, however. Trevelyan's metaphors suggest how much was thought to be at stake in the new revelation, and why the public antagonism between the rival faiths had reached such a high pitch by the turn of the century. The most important issue in defining professional identity was not the historian's methodology or expertise *per se* but his relationship to his audience. The professional's public image was formed less by the actual traits of his work than by his claims about that work. Pluralism undermined the status professionals were trying to claim for themselves; in order to safeguard their new authority, many felt they had to repudiate the old one. Public expectations about writing and evaluating history had to be rejected lest they compromise that new authority. My purpose here is to examine both the rhetoric and the reality of the debate that surrounded the professional's struggle to define his position. I will argue that in England the continuities between the amateur and professional traditions were more significant than the apparent conflicts. The ideals of the old faith were decisive in forming the responsibilities of the new. Particularly at Oxford and Cambridge, historical study developed in ways that necessarily qualify generalizations about the professional's growing alienation from the needs and interests of a more general public.[3] Many mourned the death of the amateur tradition too soon.

On the face of it, the professional's credo did challenge the assumptions of the "literary" tradition in explicit ways. For the historian as man of letters, a network of values connected the separate facts of history and gave them meaning. Insight and imaginative identification enabled the historian to see the truth more clearly than analysis and criticism. His authority rested on his effectiveness as a moral teacher; his first priority was to shape history to attract and instruct a wide general public. Professional status rested on different assumptions. For the professional the new research ideal of advancing knowledge outweighed the liberal ideal of training mind and character as the goal of learning.[4] To support professional standards, history had to be viewed as a body of objective and systematic knowledge, attained by technical training whose standards fellow experts determined. Although the certification of this training came more and more to mean university study leading to an academic career, the exact course of training and employment was less important than the expertise such experience guaranteed. This expertise would provide a basis for attempts to convince the public that only the professional was qualified to make and evaluate historical judgments and to determine the priorities that should direct historical study.[5]

The clearest of those priorities was epitomized in the cult of origi-

Epilogue

nal research. Freeman paid lip service to this ideal; William Stubbs was a more important convert since he actually practiced what Freeman only preached. In his Inaugural Lecture as Regius Professor at Oxford in 1866, he looked forward to founding an historical school that would join "with the other workers of Europe in a common task" and build "not upon Hallam and Palgrave and Kemble and Froude and Macaulay" but on newly collected records and manuscript materials.[6] The opening of archives and the outpouring of published texts and documents in the second half of the century provided the new researcher with plenty to do. So great became the volume of available manuscript materials that by 1895 Lord Acton feared "a lifetime spent in the largest collection of printed books would not suffice to train a real master of modern history" in his own day. Nevertheless, he stood by his claim that "history, to be above evasion or dispute, must stand on documents, not opinions."[7]

The cult of original research had important implications for the shape of historical writing. The exigencies of the research ideal militated against the broad-scale syntheses beloved by the "literary" school. Stubbs, like S. R. Gardiner and Frederic Maitland, two other early professionals, was prominent as an editor. The more synthetic works of such men concentrated on specialized subjects like legal history that lent themselves to minute documentation. Early examples include Stubbs's *Constitutional History of England* (1873-78), Maitland's *History of the English Law before the Time of Edward I.* (with Frederick Pollock, 1895), and *Domesday Book and Beyond* (1897). When a professional undertook a more comprehensive political narrative like S. R. Gardiner's *History of England from the Accession of James I. to the Outbreak of the Civil War* (1863-87), he carefully distinguished his approach from the conventions of "literary" history. Resisting the conjectures of a Macaulay or a Hume, Gardiner preferred simply to present the evidence in as much detail as possible, leaving final judgments to the persevering reader. To avoid the distortions of the Whig view, he steadfastly refused to foreshadow results; to prevent his knowledge of the outcome from influencing his reconstruction of events, he sent his drafts off to the publisher before continuing the narrative. He considered picturesque detail untrustworthy and, even if true, trivial. Rather than trying to make the reader feel like an eyewitness, Gardiner instead asked his audience "to supply a chorus of doubt, and to keep in mind that they read, not an account of that which certainly happened, but of that which appears to me to have happened after such inquiry as I have been able to make."[8]

Histories of Gardiner's scope were becoming the exception rather than the rule in the professional camp, however. More typical in some respects was the *Cambridge Modern History*, organized according to a "judicious division of labour" among specialists who were enjoined by Acton to be strictly impartial: "This is essential not only on the ground that impartiality is the character of legitimate history, but because the work is carried on by men acting together for no other object than the increase of accurate knowledge."[9] In its most extreme form, the research ideal militated against any kind of conclusive exposition at all. The assumption that having to produce written results for the public took time away from research was a central argument of those supporting the reallocation of college funds to endow research at the universities in the late nineteenth century.[10] Mandell Creighton claimed that Stubbs resented all distractions from editing manuscripts, and "wrote his *Constitutional History* more because something was expected of him than because he enjoyed doing it."[11] J. H. Round, who had proclaimed in 1895 that in history as in science " 'the minute sifting' of facts and figures is the only sure method by which we can extend knowledge," grew increasingly resistant to summarizing any results. He turned down Acton's invitation to contribute to the *Cambridge Modern History* on the grounds that preparing even such a specialized synthesis would be "alien" to his commitment to research.[12] And Acton himself despite (or perhaps because of) his prodigious erudition left only brilliant fragments behind him.

Whatever practical constraints new standards for research imposed on the historian's work were finally less influential than assumptions about audience in molding professional identity. The rising chorus of criticism directed at "literary" historians from the seventies on reflected less a debate over style than over professional authority. Professionalism required that history be shaped not by the demands of the marketplace but by the criteria of what J. R. Seeley called a "sufficient *corps* of specialists . . . to whose judgment historians might appeal with confidence."[13] H. A. L. Fisher viewed the problem in the same light: "So long as history is allowed to be concerned with truth, the true historian will prefer to be judged, not by the public, who enjoy his style, but by the one or two specialists who can test his facts."[14] But as Freeman's case makes clear, too much was at stake for early professionals to rest content with a separate but equal audience

Epilogue

for their work. Professional authority depended upon convincing the public that serious history was an undertaking only trained scholars could conduct and whose merits only they could judge. The great influence exercised by "literary" historians like Froude constituted a rival authority, one that would-be professionals like Freeman felt compelled to discredit in order to distinguish their own postion. Rhetorical exaggeration on both sides of the ensuing debate rapidly moved the alleged incompatibility of popular and professional standards toward a self-fulfilling prophecy.

Part of this exaggeration was inspired by changes in the late Victorian reading public, changes that increased professional anxiety about defining and maintaining standards. The rise of mass culture and the rise of specialization were not only contemporaneous but in important ways mutually reinforcing. In the same period that historical study was being professionalized, a rapidly expanding lower-middle class, educated in the Board schools and newly enfranchised, was becoming affluent enough to create a market for an accessible literature that could both entertain and further educate them.[15] The concerns of professional historians about the type of writing that attracted such audiences were typical of more general fears. Many commentators believed that the dramatic growth of popular literature in the second half of the century had drastically reduced its overall quality.[16] In the same vein, Stubbs blamed the stream of "trashy books" and superficial journalism on publishers trying to exploit the taste of the "half-educated" for "sensational and picturesque" historical writing.[17] Professionals came to feel that they had to counteract not only the influence of Froude, Carlyle, and Macaulay, but also that of the inferior popularizers whom their success had encouraged. Freeman's defense of Macaulay and Gardiner's of Green notwithstanding, most "literary" historians were held guilty by association with vulgarized history. If Macaulay simply mirrored the most Philistine prejudices and Green provided ideas "ready-made," how much more superficial must the latest Mudie's favorite be? If writers of Froude's and Carlyle's genius misled readers with "dangerous" views, if the "striving for pictorial effect" warped the judgment of even the best minds, what damage might really unscrupulous popularizers do?

Fine distinctions were soon lost in the assault on all writing enjoyed by an audience whose frivolous taste and short attention span seemed to pose grave threats to the quality of all serious literature.

Criticisms of specific "literary" historians tended to harden into the categorical position that artistic imagination and compelling narration were completely incompatible with objective scholarship. The artist, Fisher argued, was too easily carried beyond the boundaries of his evidence: he might be tempted "to add a touch here and a touch there, ignore the inconvenient little facts, and traduce the inconvenient little persons, until his canvas ceases to represent the original, although it may be full of power and beauty and psychological insight."[18] Picturesque history was labeled superficial by definition, producing what Mandell Creighton called "a purely external view of the course of affairs."[19] J. R. Seeley stated the professional complaint in its baldest form: "History only becomes interesting to the general public by being corrupted, by being adulterated with sweet, unwholesome stuff to please the popular palate."[20]

With battle positions like these being drawn, it is no wonder that the self-proclaimed dullness and aridity of works like Creighton's *History of the Papacy* or Stubbs's *Constitutional History* were held up as tokens of their professionalism, or that the *English Historical Review* felt compelled to proclaim in its first issue that "no allurements of style will secure insertion for a popular *réchaufée* of facts already known or ideas already suggested."[21] There was continued anxiety that the *Review* might be "too popular," but Mandell Creighton, its first editor, discounted that possibility: "My fear is lest it die of dullness; but oh how the dullards croak with dread lest the atmosphere in which they live should by any chance be rarefied."[22] Although early issues still included some materials of interest to "an educated man, not specially conversant with history,"[23] true to Green's prophecy Creighton decided that the *Review* could not be popularized "without entirely changing its character and making it useless to students."[24]

And yet, the exaggerated rhetoric of this debate implied more dramatic distinctions between popular and professional styles than actually existed. We have seen that beneath Freeman's crusty professionalism lurked the epic poet *manqué*. J. B. Bury's pronouncement that "history is a science, no less and no more," did not preclude a significant role for literary art and imagination.[25] Maitland was acclaimed as a stylist even by those who did not read him; modern appreciations of Stubbs reveal far more artistry than his own disclaimers allowed for.[26] The length and detail of professional histories limited their audience, but the professionals' well-publicized disparagement

Epilogue

of popular taste did far more than the quality of their prose style to alienate the general reader. While the boundaries of professionalism were still being drawn, many of the new historians adopted a harder public line about the literary dimensions of history than their own work justified in order to stake out new ground for themselves.

In the process, of course, they made the public all the more protective of its own turf. The resentful reactions of readers whose taste and judgment were so widely impugned joined with professional fears of appearing "too popular" to accentuate further the differences between the two positions. The public's treatment of Gardiner and Stubbs, for example, makes clear that despite the rebuffs of the professionals, they were slow to accept their dismissal as qualified judges of what constituted "good" history. The *Saturday Review* and the *English Historical Review* might approve of Gardiner's leaving out the "tawdry trappings" and "tinsel embroidery" that vulgarized popular works; for them and for the *Academy* Gardiner's admitted deficiencies as a writer in no way detracted from his qualifications as historian.[27] But more middle-brow periodicals resented Gardiner's failure to fulfill their expectations about historical writing. Finding "the actors depicted in a small weak way," the *Athenaeum* for instance disputed Gardiner's protest that the period in question was "wanting in dramatic interest"; even had that been true, the reviewer went on to note, "the writer should have concealed the fact with the utmost art." Gardiner apparently took to heart other criticism of his disproportionate detail and somewhat improved the readability of later volumes of his *History*. But readers continued to plead in vain to know "his thoughts" and the moral of his story. If some reviewers finally acknowledged Gardiner's stature as a scholar, they continued to believe that his lack of proportion, conclusiveness, and vivid characterization prevented him from being an historian in the full sense of the word.[28] Stubbs found himself in a similar position: the "casual critics" of history whom he attacked in his Oxford lectures "had their revenge in deciding that my writings were not literature."[29] The *Saturday Review* and the *English Historical Review* might be predictably complimentary of his achievements, but more popular journals labeled him rather an editor and lexicographer than an historian.[30]

Defenders of "literary" history went on the offensive as well. We have seen how popular audiences made their preference for Macaulay and Froude a challenge to scholarly detractors of their favorites. Among the high popularizers of the nineties, men like Augustine Birrell, Andrew Lang, and Hugh Crothers attacked professional works for leaving the reader "adrift, without human companionship, on a bottomless sea of erudition" and called for more readable narratives in which the audience could be uplifted and emotionally involved.[31] Lang was far from defending the rhetorical excess preferred by the "vile herd," considering it as injurious to good art as to good science. But he warned that "from Mr. Froude the public will never be won, till some scientific historian writes about his topic as agreeably, with less bias and more accuracy."[32]

It was not just history's literary value that was at stake here: the cult of objective research seemed to threaten the very intelligibility of the past. At the turn of the century, even fellow professionals worried because "many of the ablest and most learned historians restrict their efforts to the determination of the facts by scientific process and deem it futile to attempt more."[33] It was this position that Frederic Harrison parodied in Aethelbald Wessex, the tutor of the Freeman school who insisted that no synthesis could take place until every fact had been catalogued; he went so far as to wish that "histories were not published at all in the current English of literature, but were plain and disconnected propositions of fact." Satire aside, Harrison was concerned that the "paleo-photographic" method of research might be able to accumulate vast amounts of data but made it impossible to master or use them.[34] John Morley, just as aware of the shortcomings of "literary" history, concurred with Harrison's reservations about "history for its own sake." Like so many Victorian readers, Morley did not "in the least want to know what happened in the past, except as it enables me to see my way more clearly through what is happening today." From his point of view, scientific history was simply becoming "narrow, pedantic and trivial. It threatens to degenerate from a broad survey of great periods and movements of human societies into vast and countless accumulations of insignificant facts, sterile knowledge, and frivolous antiquarianism."[35] The hostility and mistrust of the general public inspired the stereotype of the scholar who was incapable of decisive judgments and feared that practical applications sullied his pure intellectuality.[36] They were also at the root of suspicions that researchers sought merely sinecures, so that "the endowment of research may degenerate into the research of endowment."[37]

In addition to being interpreted as a renunciation of the historian's responsibility to the general public, pronouncing "literary" history

Epilogue

and scientific scholarship to be incompatible actually worsened the very situation the early professionals had wanted to correct. As Lang put it, "Men of real information are demoralised by writing for the public, while the non-specialist (the abandoned 'populariser') is a person of contemptible character."[38] The quality of popularized work tended to sink rather than improve as the market expanded. The merchandizing of history unleashed a deluge of what Trevelyan described as "publishers' books" of the type "generically known as 'Criminal Queens of History,' spicy memoirs of dead courts and pseudobiographical chatter about Napoleon and his family. . . . The public understands that this kind of prurient journalism is history lightly served up for the general appetite, whereas serious history is a sacred thing pinnacled afar on frozen heights of science, not to be approached save after a long novitiate."[39] Trying to strike a happy medium between popular and "scientific" history became considerably more of a challenge once "literary" history had been tarred by the same brush as this kind of vulgarization. This situation left those readers who had in earlier years formed the audience for the great reviews and Victorian histories with far less literature of comparable excellence, and further emphasized the fragmentation of the norm for serious history, once identical with the literary masterpieces of Macaulay, Carlyle, and Froude.

This fragmentation placed the early professionals in an anomalous position. They were struggling to win public acknowledgment of their authority, but found their definition of that authority contradicting the public's. The amateur ideal had taught the public to measure the historian's authority by the moral uplift and practical guidance he provided. Professional authority was based on specialized expertise, applied to advance knowledge for its own sake. The susceptibility of the amateur ideal to vulgarization only reinforced the professionals' inclination to limited research rather than broad synthesis, to address fellow professionals rather than cater to the public. The general audience might be willing to acknowledge the authority of professional expertise, but insofar as they saw it as by choice exercising no relevant power over their lives, they withheld the cultural authority of the historian from men who were to them "merely" scholars. The winning of professional authority at the expense of this cultural authority was an outcome few early professionals were willing to accept. Freeman's example confirms a wider pattern. Attacks on "literary" amateurs were a publicistic way of aggrandizing the historian's position; calls for more professional levels of training were a way of increasing his authority. But for many of those who waged such attacks, what gave the historian his stature in the first place was still conventional Victorian assumptions about history's function and value. I have shown how the exigencies of public debate exaggerated differences between "literary" and professional historians where style and audience were concerned. If we turn to consider the professional in his native habitat, the History School, we find a similar situation. The triumph of the research ideal was in many ways more apparent than real; especially at the ancient universities, the enduring vitality of liberal education provided a medium in which traditional assumptions about history's practical and moral importance continued to thrive. Historical study within the academy provided a way of salvaging the most important goals of "literary" history without the problematic literary form, but it also complicated the question of professional identity. Their continuing allegiance to history's preeminent importance as a moral and political guide in the service of a wider society prevented many Oxbridge historians from becoming alienated from the needs and interests of a more general public in the sense that many American and European scholars did. On the other hand, this allegiance left them implicitly at odds with professionalism's call for an audience of experts and the pursuit of knowledge for its own sake. In either case I would argue that the transition from "literary" to professional history in England was less a break than a continuum in which, by and large, the demands of professionalism accommodated themselves to the assumptions underlying "literary" history rather than vice versa.

The university was the natural home of the new professional historian, and virtually all of the early professionals held academic positions from the eighties on. From the beginning, however, historical study at Oxford and Cambridge was divided between the liberal ideal and the research ideal in ways that paralleled the rivalry between "literary" and professional historiography outside the academy. The first step toward professionalization had been to gain recognition of history as a distinct academic discipline, apart from moral science or humane letters. The first set of university reforms established an examination school in modern history at Oxford in the 1850s; a separate Historical Tripos was established at Cambridge in 1873. Attempts by the first Oxford Reform Commission to empower a German-style

Epilogue

professoriate met with vigorous and ultimately successful opposition from the tutors, however. The key issue was whether history was "to provide useful citizens of the State, or furtherers of historical research."[40] To the tutors, who defended the liberal ideal of education as character formation, men whose major purpose was the advancement of knowledge and the training of fellow professionals were "unsuitable and even dangerous instruments" for the moral education of the young.[41] Their position weighed most heavily in the Oxford University Bill of 1854. New schools and chairs were created, but the tutors were able effectively to exclude the professors from having any significant impact on college governance or the examination process, especially after mandatory lecture attendance was dropped in 1861. Their continued strength foiled efforts to enhance the power and status of the professoriate in 1872, preventing professors from becoming *ex officio* chairmen of the new Boards of Faculties and influencing the colleges to reduce the funds reallocated to the professoriate.[42] Here was a case where the tutors' status as professional teachers conflicted with the professoriate's desire for institutional power commensurate with their own status as professional scholars. It is true that part of the tutors' increasing professionalism involved some specialization on their part—e.g., many of them became the "combined lecturers" who prepared students for exams in the new schools.[43] But this specialization remained compatible with and subordinate to the college-based ideal of liberal education. The professors might have gained the apex of the pyramid of academic prestige, but the Oxbridge tutors continued to exercise effective control over the educational process. Thus from the beginning ambiguity existed about who controlled historical knowledge and for what ends.

In the case of history, this control placed significant limits on professional training. When Charles Firth became Regius Professor at Oxford in 1905, he renewed the call for professional training on a par with that of the continent. His suggestion that the History School require a thesis based on original sources—something he viewed as a necessary preliminary for postgraduate work—met with concerted resistance from tutors and lecturers, who charged that it was incompatible with the chief purpose of the Honors School: "a liberal education through history."[44] Even Firth's claims that the School could accommodate both forms of education failed to mollify them, and his proposals met with little success in his lifetime. He and Paul Vinogradoff did conduct two postgraduate seminars at Oxford, but Vinogradoff complained that his students did not take to this continental style of education.[45]

At Cambridge the professors met with more success in accommodating the Tripos to specialized research, but some of the same conflicts arose.[46] From the late nineteenth century, two views opposed one another. One group valued history for its practical uses in preparing citizens and statesmen for their duties in society. Its proponents—men like J. R. Seeley and Oscar Browning—felt that study should be organized around subjects about which a student could formulate and test theories, theories that would in turn form the basis of a "political science." A. W. Ward represented the "pure" historians, who believed that history should be studied for its own sake, an aim best served by specifying periods whose facts had to be determined and mastered. The political scientists controlled the shape of the 1873 Tripos. Attempts to accommodate both approaches in the reforms of 1897 were mutually unsatisfactory, resulting in what to Maitland resembled "rather the programme of a Variety Show than the sober programme of an Historical School."[47] Although emphasis on outlines increased under Acton and on research techniques under Bury, not until the 1929 reforms was the domination of political science conclusively broken. And even then, the sections on economic and constitutional history tended to remain issue-oriented and encouraged practical rather than professional aims.

With these constraints on graduate study, postgraduate schools grew only slowly at the ancient universities. It was rather the civic and provincial universities, from the beginning dominated by the professoriate and more heavily influenced by the occupational professionalism of scientific and technical fields, that provided the first significant support for post-graduate work. During the first quarter of the century, the History School shaped by T. F. Tout at Manchester became "a Mecca for serious-minded young scholars from the older universities."[48] Albert Pollard's hopes of founding a research center in London were realized in 1921 when the Institute for Historical Research first opened its doors. Although dismissed at first as a mere "Ph.D. factory," the Institute gradually gained support and recognition as a center for advanced work.

The slow progress of a more professional training at the ancient universities was in significant ways reinforced by many of the professors. For Freeman, as we recall, the discovery of practical political

Epilogue

lessons was more important than "the search for truth for its own sake." His proselytizing for "original authorities" notwithstanding, as a teacher he much preferred the old-fashioned mastery of great books. At Cambridge J. R. Seeley shared as much in Freeman's practical view of historical education as he did his peevish irritation at dilettantes. Seeley's belief that history was first and foremost "the school of statesmanship" (a school whose "laws" similarly endowed his own prejudices with "scientific" status) worked against specialized scholarship and an appreciation of the contemporary context of events in the same ways as had "literary" history. Sheldon Rothblatt makes clear that Seeley advocated more rigorous intellectual standards as a means of producing better leaders, not better historians; he was himself a better example of the professional teacher, rather than the professional scholar.[49]

Even men with more compelling professional credentials continued to let the practical priorities of the larger society dictate the ends of historical study. Stubbs shared Freeman's belief that scientific scholarship was only a means to an end. In the same Inaugural lecture where he called for the founding of a research school on the continental model, he also stated that his aim was "to train not merely students but citizens . . . to be fitted not for criticism or for authority in matters of memory, but for action" in the greater community. He viewed history as "next to Theology itself . . . the most thoroughly religious training that the mind can receive."[50] Acton echoed Stubbs's views thirty years later when he became Regius Professor at Cambridge. He thought modern history had a particular value for "men in general" because it was filled with "inestimable lessons" still relevant to the present. He rated its gift of "historical thinking" higher than that of "historical learning" because better adapted to the "formation of character and the training of talent." Notwithstanding his call for strict impartiality, he enjoined his students "to try others by the final maxim that governs your own lives, and to suffer no man and no cause to escape the undying penalty which history has the power to inflict on wrong."[51] At the turn of the century, Firth at Oxford and George Prothero at Edinburgh were other advocates of original research who also acknowledged history's importance as a moral and political guide. H. W. C. Davis was making the same claim as Regius Professor at Oxford in the twenties, and his successor, Maurice Powicke, publicly encouraged amateur writing.[52]

The attitude prevalent in Seeley's time—that Regius Professors had

227

a message to convey to the world at large—never really died out, despite a gradual upgrading of the scholarly credentials of appointees. Maitland turned down the chance to succeed Acton in 1901 for this very reason: "The Regius Professor of Modern History is expected to speak to the world at large," he argued, "and even if I had anything to say to the W. at L., I don't think I should like the full houses and the limelight. So I shall go back to the Year Books."[53] Gardiner likewise had rejected the chance to succeed Froude because he could not face the lecturing requirements.[54] Given the public mission associated with many professorial chairs, it was quite appropriate that Charles Oman and G. M. Trevelyan should win them after distinguishing themselves as popular historians. Up to the present, men of such stature as George Kitson Clark and R. W. Southern (who became Chichele Professor at Oxford in 1961) continue to defend general education as the primary end of historical study at their universities and to lament the loss of direction earlier furnished by the belief in history's practical importance.[55]

The belief in this importance by no means ruled out more professional standards of scholarship. But it did operate in British historiography to compromise objectivity and critical perspective, in large part because it was so inextricably intertwined with the kind of anachronisms implicit in the Whig view. Stressing the preservative nature of historical innovations and reconstructing a series of precedents linking past logically and directly to present gave the subject a ready-made continuity, itself taken as proof that history was a "scientific" discipline, not a random collection of facts. In the work of Stubbs and Freeman, the specifics of the Whig view had won the early professional seal of approval. Bury and Acton were less partisan, but their reading of western history as the progress of political and intellectual freedom offered less provincial and less immanent versions of the same assumptions.[56] If there was gradual recognition of the Whig view's particular anachronisms and fallacies of intentionality among early twentieth-century professionals like Pollard and Tout, the belief in history's political relevance was kept alive by the continued emphasis on constitutional development and political science in the History Schools. The increased prestige of bureaucratic efficiency in government at the turn of the century simply encouraged new anachronisms as administrative historians rehabilitated absolutism in an attempt to reconstruct the origins of the modern state and civil service.[57] In other words the details of the interpretation

Epilogue

changed, but the impulse underlying the Whig view—to use evidence of precedent and tradition to explain and thus legitimize a present or desired political order—remained unquestioned.

In some respects early professional research methods actually encouraged rather than eliminated present-mindedness. By isolating historical phenomena from other relevant aspects of their context, narrow specialization made heteronomous interpretations more rather than less likely.[58] The continued reliance on facts speaking for themselves made unconscious value judgments all the harder to detect.[59] The compatibility of political apologetics with professional scholarship had been demonstrated by Ranke himself. Georg Iggers points out the ways Ranke's "hermeneutical" emphasis on political documents and on the self-justifying "individuality" of the state constructed from them served inherently conservative ends by excluding as irrelevant to historical understanding factors such as the economic or social analyses offered by socialism. It is noteworthy that this "classical" model of historical study remained firmly entrenched in both England and Germany well into the twentieth century, despite challenges raised elsewhere by a variety of more sociologically-informed approaches to history.[60]

Persisting belief in its practicality helps explain why history became the "queen of the liberal arts" at least temporarily in the early twentieth century. In the first quarter of the century, nearly one third of the undergraduates at Oxford were reading for the History School; as many as two hundred took the History Tripos each year in the late twenties and early thirties.[61] As Kitson Clark points out, however, few of these viewed themselves as future historians: history had become a haven for students who "were not clear what else they wanted to do." Many of these were destined to fill posts in domestic and imperial administration at a time when the British government was assuming new functions at home and abroad. History seemed suited in a number of ways to serve their needs. In addition to providing a genealogy for the new bureaucratic elite, it also afforded a more general frame of reference from which to view and to understand the problems they would encounter. G. N. Clark argues that it was in part a shortage of modern studies capable of supplying such background that motivated the *Cambridge Modern History*, a work aimed, in Acton's words, "to bring home to every man . . . the ripest conclusions of international research." It was precisely because of his conception of its audience that Acton intended it not as a chronicle of facts for their own sake, but a compendium whose proportions were shaped by what he judged to be their relative philosophical importance to world history. The *History* represented not so much a scholarly advance as a codification of nineteenth-century assumptions about what constituted "universal" history.[62]

Remarks by R. W. Southern suggest a more important class dimension to history's early twentieth-century popularity. In his eyes the tutors' success in keeping historical education general and unsystematic worked to "enlarge the minds of men who would meet just such conditions in the world they were to rule." Historical study "met a large variety of intellectual and practical needs in the last days of British supremacy in the world."[63] It provided not only an ideologically stabilizing view of the national past, but the kind of mental training and character development that certified the new ruling elite. As Phillip Elliott has pointed out, opening the competition for the Home and India Civil Service in the late nineteenth century wound up giving the universities a new purpose at a time when they seemed to have lost their sense of direction.[64] The ideal candidate for higher level administration was not the specialist but the generalist, the man whose liberal university education had cultivated in him the mental properties that would enable him to handle any situation. This model of leadership drew far more from the older ideal of the gentlemanly professional than from the occupational professionalism of the expert or specialist. It tended not to open the governing elite to the business and commercial classes, but to institutionalize the connection between the new professional classes and the older social elite.[65] History had from the earliest days been one of the subjects for the Civil Service examinations. The method its study entailed was even more significant than its content. It had the advantage of providing practical information while offering the kind of intellectual discipline and character formation that distinguished liberal education from utilitarian training. The Oxbridge history schools were all the more effective in continuing to train the gentleman professionals of the future precisely because they failed to make themselves more professional from the historian's point of view. The increased rigor of historical studies benefitted these men not as future historians but as the future custodians of an increasingly diverse society, a society where control depended upon a more complex but not necessarily a more technical or specialized understanding of problems and issues. Such attitudes also suggest reasons for the more rapid development of

Epilogue

specialized and technical training in history at the provincial and civic universites, since these were patronized by the classes largely shut out of the ancient universities and less influenced by the stigma attached to utilitarian training.[66]

In the culturally dominant ancient universities, professionalization of historians meant first and foremost professionalization of liberal educators in history. The Historical Association, founded in 1906, reflected this bias: its original purpose was to improve historical teaching, especially in the secondary schools, although professionals like Pollard, Firth, and Tout succeeded in moving it toward more scholarly concerns in later years.[67] The control and upgrading of secondary education was a priority of early professionals in Germany and America as well, but the extent to which the ends of liberal education continued to exert their control over the way history was taught in England is distinctive. At the ancient universities, specialization and rationalization accommodated themselves to liberal education, not vice versa. In history as in other disciplines, a professional hierarchy developed with the more research-oriented professoriate at the top. But this hierarchical principle was implicitly challenged by the egalitarianism of the tutorial ideal, in which equality was based not so much on specialized expertise as on an equality of "voice and status among qualified practitioners."[68] Research achievements were never the sole or even most important criterion for rewards within this system. These factors help account for the continued high priority placed on teaching over research at these universities. A. H. Halsey and M. H. Trow's generalizations about British academics today hold true with particular force for historians: "They reinforce and reflect a set of attitudes which may be distinguished from professional careerism through specialised research and which encourage a way of academic life emphasizing teaching and, in the best sense, amateurism."[69]

In another respect, of course, their commitment to teaching made historians like other academics members of "the key profession," to borrow H. J. Perkin's term. In the early twentieth century, they began to control the process by which other professionals were selected and educated. But in the case of history they controlled it by supplying mental discipline more than a body of expertise. Rather than reinforcing the theoretical underpinnings of professional knowledge, the "historical power" of judgment provided by undergraduate education prolonged pragmatic and anachronistic assumptions implicitly at odds with history's claims to be scientific. This suggests that late Victorian fears about history and the historian were somewhat misaimed. Rejecting "literary" style as inappropriate did not entail loss of faith in history's moral and political utility. Many historians did turn away from the needs and interests of the general public, but not to the needs and interests of fellow professionals exclusively. They aided the process—implicit in professionalization—whereby knowledge became the domain of an elite, but not by establishing a monopoly of expertise over knowledge in precisely the way other professionals did. Making historical study more rigorous enhanced its prestige more than its autonomy; that prestige attracted more members of a social elite seeking credentials of general intellectual ability than it did future historians. The "literary" historians had assumed that history's purpose was to make the world morally and intellectually intelligible to a wide audience; for the Oxbridge historians, historical study became a primary means by which a liberally educated ruling class could command society.[70] The withdrawal of historians into the academy did not signify so much a break with the wider society as a different way of influencing it. It is no coincidence that history's popularity as a field of study began to decline after 1930. With the final dissolution of the constitutional bias of historical study and of the credibility of the Whig view, history could no longer offer the same comprehensive explanation of the past. At the same time, the new research methods introduced by scholars like Namier only underscored the growing intractability of professionals where such explanation was concerned.[71]

Other factors distinguished the early development of professionalism in England from that in Europe and America. Joseph Ben-David notes that the dominance of the ancient British universities ruled out the kind of competition that spurred advances in research and technical training in Germany.[72] Felix Gilbert cites the importance of government support and control in stimulating historical study and shaping the educational and archival bureaucracies on the continent. He also notes that the acceptance of critical methods and scholarly standards in England was imitative and incomplete because it "did not arise from a need to adjust the universities to the requirements of a changed political structure" in the sense that this was true in Europe.[73] Doris Goldstein argues that the relative lack of support from government and universities made all the more important the role of voluntary organizations like the Royal Historical Society and the

Epilogue

British Academy in developing a sense of community among British professionals.[74] In the United States, the hopes of Herbert B. Adams that the American Historical Association would provide a "channel through which the aristocracy of culture might, in historical matters, exert a vigorous, uplifting influence on national policies" never materialized. Without such an alliance between the patrician intellectuals and the academicians as existed in England, the professionals turned inward to their own concerns and the men of letters stopped writing of their own accord.[75] The prestige of the German research model had been higher from the start in the United States, and graduate study developed much more rapidly.[76] By 1910 sixteen American universities were training doctoral candidates in history, and had already produced approximately two hundred fifty Ph.D.s in history.[77] The more egalitarian nature of the American university kept teaching an important function, but did not give it the prestige it enjoyed in Britain.

The assimilation of history to the liberal ideal helps explain why the status contradictions between teaching and research, endemic in academic professionalism, never became so acute in the case of English historians. It also testifies to the lasting influence of the amateur tradition in endowing the British historian with continuing cultural authority—the kind of authority that many disciplines forfeited as the price of professionalization. The animating ideals of the amateur, the sage, the man of letters, the "literary" historian, lived on in their twentieth-century successors who continued to measure historical knowledge not in terms of expertise alone—who by believing in history's humanizing power helped to make that power a continuing reality.

NOTES

INTRODUCTION

1. Wilfred Ward, "The Time-spirit of the Nineteenth Century," *Edinburgh Review* 194 (July 1901):92-131.

2. Henry Sidgwick, "The Historical Method," *Mind* 11 (April 1886):203.

3. George Eliot, *The Writings of George Eliot—Essays and Leaves from a Note-Book* (Boston: Houghton-Mifflin, 1908), p. 198.

4. J. W. Burrow, *A Liberal Descent* (Cambridge: Cambridge University Press, 1980), p. 194.

5. George Levine, *The Boundaries of Fiction* (Princeton: Princeton University Press, 1968), p. 116. I have also benefitted from Levine's discussion of nineteenth-century novelists in *The Realistic Imagination* (Chicago: University of Chicago Press, 1981), pp. 14-20 in particular.

6. Duncan Forbes, *The Liberal-Anglican Idea of History* (Cambridge: Cambridge University Press, 1952).

7. R. N. Stromberg, "History in the Eighteenth Century," *Journal of the History of Ideas* 12 (April 1951):299.

8. David Hume, *The Letters of David Hume*, ed. J. Y. T. Greig (Oxford: Clarendon, 1932), 1:170.

9. William Robertson, *The History of America* (New York: Samuel Campbell, 1798), 1:xii.

10. Edward Gibbon, "Preface to the Fourth Volume of the Quarto Edition," *The Decline and Fall of the Roman Empire*, ed. J. B. Bury (London: Methuen, 1896), 1:xii.

11. *The Miscellaneous Works of Edward Gibbon*, ed. John, Lord Sheffield, 2d ed. (London: Murray, 1814), 5:487.

12. Ibid., 4:63 (my translation).

Notes

13. Ernst Cassirer, *The Philosophy of the Enlightenment*, trans. C. A. Koelln and James Pettegrove (Princeton: Princeton University Press, 1951), pp. 199, 220; David Norton, "History and Philosophy in Hume's Thought," in *David Hume: Philosophical Historian*, ed. David Norton and Richard Popkin (Indianapolis: Bobbs-Merrill, 1965), pp. xxxvii-viii.

14. David Hume, *The History of England* (London: Caddell, 1792), 2:143.

15. David Hume, *Essays and Treatises on Several Subjects*, new ed. (London: Millar, 1758), p. 294.

16. Henry St. John, Viscount Bolingbroke, *The Works of Lord Bolingbroke* (Philadelphia: Carey and Hart, 1841), 2:226, and Gibbon, *Miscellaneous Works*, 4:65.

17. Gibbon, *Miscellaneous Works*, 4:631.

18. Hume, *History of England*, 3:297.

19. For this interpretation of the *philosophes'* search for "man in general," see Carl Becker, *The Heavenly City of the Eighteenth Century Philosophers* (New Haven: Yale University Press, 1932), p. 98 *et passim*.

20. David Hume, "An Enquiry Concerning Human Understanding," in *David Hume: Philosophical Historian*, p. 52.

21. For examples, see Ernest C. Mossner, "An Apology for David Hume, Historian," *PMLA* 56 (1941):667-69.

22. Gibbon, *Decline and Fall*, 3:71. Leo Braudy explores the ambiguities and complexities in Gibbon's explanation of cause in *Narrative Form in History and Fiction: Hume, Fielding, and Gibbon* (Princeton: Princeton University Press, 1970).

23. Friedrich Meinecke, *Historism: The Rise of a New Historical Outlook*, trans. J. E. Anderson (London: Routledge, 1972), p. lv.

24. Samuel Taylor Coleridge, *The Friend*, 3d ed. (London: Pickering, 1837), 1:276.

25. Samuel Johnson, *Rasselas* (Oxford: Clarendon, 1927), p. 50; William Blake, "Marginalia to Sir Joshua Reynolds' *Discourses*," in *The Poetry and Prose of William Blake*, ed. Geoffrey Keynes (London: Nonesuch, 1927), p. 977.

26. Isaiah Berlin, "Foreword," in Meinecke, *Historism*, p. ix.

27. Ibid.

28. Quoted by Emery Neff, *The Poetry of History* (New York: Columbia University Press, 1947), p. 23, who cites this as the first use of *einfühlen* with this connotation.

29. Peter Gay, "The History of History," *Horizon* 11, no. 4 (1969):117.

30. Susan F. Cannon, *Science in Culture* (New York: Science History Publications, 1978), p. 20.

Notes

31. Philip Harwood, "The Modern Art and Science of History," *Westminster Review* 38 (October 1842):370, 353.

32. Ibid., p. 363.

33. Hayden White, *Metahistory* (Baltimore: Johns Hopkins University Press, 1973).

34. "Preface," *History of the Latin and Germanic Nations from 1494-1514*, quoted in Fritz Stern, ed., *The Varieties of History from Voltaire to the Present* (New York: World, 1956), p. 57.

35. Quoted by George Gooch, *History and Historians in the Nineteenth Century* (Boston: Beacon, 1959), p. 74.

36. Georg Iggers, "The Image of Ranke in American and German Historical Thought," *History and Theory* 2 (1962):17-40, analyzes discrepancies between Ranke's practice and his reputation.

37. One hundred forty thousand sets of Macaulay's *History of England* were sold within a generation of its first publication, as noted by Alexander Milne, "The Victorian Historian," *Colorado Quarterly* 15 (1967):304-5. Green's *Short History* sold thirty-five thousand copies in its first year, according to Richard Altick, *The English Common Reader: A Social History of the Mass Reading Public 1800-1900* (Chicago: University of Chicago Press, 1957), p. 388.

CHAPTER I: THOMAS ARNOLD

1. Arthur Penrhyn Stanley, *The Life and Correspondence of Thomas Arnold, D.D.*, 7th ed. (London: B. Fellowes, 1852), pp. 15-16. Hereafter cited parenthetically as LC.

2. Thomas Arnold, *The Miscellaneous Works of Thomas Arnold, D.D.* (London: B. Fellowes, 1845), pp. 483-84. Hereafter cited parenthetically as MW.

3. Thomas Arnold, "The Oxford Malignants and Dr. Hampden," *Edinburgh Review* 63 (April 1836):238-39. The title of the essay was not Arnold's but his editor's. For other criticisms of the Tractarian position, see Arnold's appendix to his Inaugural Lecture as Regius Professor.

4. Susan F. Cannon, *Science in Culture*, chap. 2. See also Charles Richard Sanders, *Coleridge and the Broad Church Movement* (Durham: Duke University Press, 1942), pp. 6-11.

5. Thomas Arnold, *History of the Later Roman Commonwealth*, 2d ed. (London: B. Fellowes, 1849), 2:454-55. Hereafter cited parenthetically as LRC.

6. See Susan F. Cannon, *Science in Culture*, chap. 1, for the use of scientific models of proof as an authority in other intellectual fields in the early nineteenth century.

Notes

7. Thomas Arnold, *Introductory Lectures on Modern History*, 4th ed. (London: B. Fellowes, 1849), p. 21. Hereafter cited parenthetically as L.

8. Thomas Arnold, "The Historians of Rome," in *History of Roman Literature*, ed. Henry Thompson, 2d ed. (London: John Joseph Griffin and Co., 1852), p. 333.

9. Thomas Arnold, "Early Roman History," *Quarterly Review* 32 (June 1825):77-78.

10. "Oxford Malignants," p. 234.

11. Thomas Arnold, *History of Rome*, 4th ed. (London: B. Fellowes, 1845), 1:xi. Hereafter cited parenthetically as R.

12. Duncan Forbes, *The Liberal Anglican Idea of History* (Cambridge: Cambridge University Press, 1952), p. 124.

13. For Arnold's own approach, see in particular his "Two Sermons on the Interpretation of Prophecy," in *Sermons*, vol. 1, 5th ed. (London: B. Fellowes, 1845), and "On the Right Interpretation and Understanding of the Scriptures," in *Sermons*, vol. 2, 4th ed. (London: B. Fellowes, 1845).

14. *Sermons*, 1:370-71.

15. Thucydides, *History of the Peloponnesian War*, trans. Thomas Arnold, 3d ed. (London: Whittaker and Co., 1847), 1:503.

16. Ibid., 1:503; 3:xvi.

17. *Sermons*, 2:391.

18. Thucydides, *History*, 1:521.

19. Ibid., 1:519.

20. Ibid., 1:509.

21. See, e.g., "Early Roman History," p. 85 and *Lectures*, p. 277.

22. Thucydides, *History*, 3:xv-xvi.

23. Thomas Arnold, "Introductory Dissertation: On the Credibility of Early Roman History," in *History of the Roman Republic*, ed. E. Pococke, 2d ed. (London: Joseph Griffen and Co., 1852), p. 2.

24. "Historians of Rome," p. 339; R, 3:479.

25. "Historians of Rome," p. 347.

26. See, e.g., the Inaugural Lectures of Kingsley, Stubbs, Froude, Freeman, or Goldwin Smith.

CHAPTER II: THOMAS CARLYLE

1. For a discussion of Carlyle's early intellectual development see in particular Carlisle Moore, "Thomas Carlyle and Fiction: 1822-34" (Ph.D. diss., Princeton University, 1940); Hill Shine, "Carlyle's Early Writings and Herder's *Ideen*," in *Booker Memorial Studies*, ed. Hill Shine (New York: Russell, 1969) and *Carlyle's Fusion of Poetry, History, and Religion by 1834*

Notes

(Chapel Hill: University of North Carolina Press, 1938). Other aspects of Carlyle's thought about history are addressed in Peter Allan Dale, *The Victorian Critic and the Idea of History* (Cambridge: Harvard University Press, 1977), C. F. Harrold, *Carlyle and German Thought* (1934; rpt. London: Anchor, 1963), Hill Shine, *Carlyle and the Saint Simonians* (Baltimore: Johns Hopkins University Press, 1941), René Wellek, "Carlyle and the Philosophy of History," *Philological Quarterly* 23 (October 1944):55-76, and Louise Young, *Thomas Carlyle and the Art of History* (Philadelphia: University of Pennsylvania Press, 1939).

2. Shine, *Fusion*, p. 55.

3. Thomas Carlyle, *Two Note Books*, ed. C. E. Norton (New York: Grolier Club, 1898), p. 151.

4. Thomas Carlyle, *Critical and Miscellaneous Essays*, in *The Works of Thomas Carlyle*, ed. H. D. Traill, centenary ed. (New York: Scribner's 1896-1901), 3:54. Hereafter cited parenthetically as E. All further citations are to this edition of Carlyle's *Works*.

5. Carlyle, *Sartor Resartus*, p. 202.

6. Carlyle, *Two Note Books*, pp. 187-88.

7. James Anthony Froude, *Thomas Carlyle: A History of His Life in London 1834-1881* (London: Longmans, 1884), 2:259. For a complete discussion of Carlyle's attitude toward the scientific, see Carlisle Moore, "Carlyle: Mathematics and 'Mathesis,' " in *Carlyle Past and Present*, ed. K. J. Fielding and Rodger Tarr (New York: Vision, 1976), pp. 61-95.

8. Carlyle, *Past and Present*, p. 241. Hereafter cited parenthetically as PP.

9. Thomas Carlyle, *Letters of Thomas Carlyle to John Stuart Mill, John Sterling, and Robert Browning*, ed. Alexander Carlyle (London: Fisher, Unwin, 1923), pp. 82-83.

10. Thomas Carlyle, *History of Friedrich II. of Prussia, Called Frederick the Great*, 1:18. Hereafter cited parenthetically as FG.

11. Thomas Carlyle, *Historical Sketches*, p. 297. Hereafter cited parenthetically as HS.

12. Thomas Carlyle, *Oliver Cromwell's Letters and Speeches*, 1:7. Hereafter cited parenthetically as OC.

13. Froude, *Life in London*, 1:333.

14. George Levine, *The Boundaries of Fiction*, p. 72.

15. Wellek, "Carlyle and the Philosophy of History," p. 70.

16. Thomas Carlyle, *The Correspondence of Thomas Carlyle and Ralph Waldo Emerson 1834-1872* (Boston: Houghton Mifflin, 1884), 2:6-7.

17. *Two Note Books*, p. 132.

18. Thomas Carlyle, *The French Revolution*, 2:2. Hereafter cited parenthetically as FR.

Notes

19. Wellek, "Carlyle and the Philosophy of History," p. 57.

20. Here I concur with Wellek's refutation of Shine's position in *Carlyle and the Saint Simonians.*

21. Thomas Carlyle, *Lectures on the History of Literature,* ed. J. Reay Greene (New York: Scribner's, 1892), p. 104.

22. Thomas Carlyle, *On Heroes, Hero-Worship, and the Heroic in History,* p. 1.

23. George Macaulay Trevelyan, "Carlyle as an Historian," *The Living Age* 5 (November 1899):367-68.

24. Thomas Carlyle, *New Letters of Thomas Carlyle,* ed. Alexander Carlyle (London: John Lane, 1904), 2:11.

25. Thomas Carlyle, "The Guises," *Victorian Studies* 25 (Autumn 1981): 32. For parenthetical notes, see, e.g., pp. 19, 57, 58.

26. Hedva Ben-Israel, *English Historians on the French Revolution* (Cambridge: Cambridge University Press, 1968), p. 138. See also C. F. Harrold, "The Method and Sources of Carlyle's *French Revolution,*" *PMLA* 43 (1928):1150-69, who points out that Carlyle's method of citing sources was at times fragmentary and misleading.

27. Thomas Arnold, *Introductory Lectures on Modern History,* pp. 294-97.

28. See W. Aldis Wright, "The Squire Papers," *English Historical Review* 1 (1886):311-48 for a full examination of the issue. Carlyle did, it should be noted, present the Squire Papers as being of doubtful authenticity in the third edition of *Cromwell,* 2:342-43.

29. Reginald Palgrave, "Carlyle, the 'Pious Editor' of Cromwell's Speeches," *National Review* 8 (1886-87):588-604.

30. See, e.g., *Letters to Mill, Sterling, and Browning,* pp. 76-7.

31. Carlyle, *New Letters,* 1:268-69; Froude, *Life in London,* 1:325-26.

32. Richard A. E. Brooks, *Thomas Carlyle: Journey to Germany Autumn 1858* (New Haven: Yale University Press, 1940).

33. Carlyle, *New Letters,* 1:217.

34. Carlyle, *Two Note Books,* p. 171.

35. Ben-Israel, *English Historians,* p. 130.

36. Carlyle, *New Letters,* 1:254-55.

37. C. F. Harrold, "The Method and Sources of Carlyle's *French Revolution,*" (Ph.D. diss., Yale University, 1925), 1:191-204.

38. H. M. Leicester, "The Dialectic of Romantic Historiography: Prospect and Retrospect in *The French Revolution,*" *Victorian Studies* 15 (1971):6-7.

39. Ibid., p. 8.

Notes

40. Thomas Carlyle, *Life of Schiller*, pp. 95-96.

41. Carlyle, *New Letters*, 1:33.

42. Froude, *Life in London*, 1:75.

43. John Clive, "Introduction," in *The History of Friedrich II. of Prussia Called Frederick the Great*, by Thomas Carlyle (Chicago: University of Chicago Press, 1969), pp. xxviii-xxix.

44. Morse Peckham, *"Frederick the Great,"* in *Carlyle Past and Present*, p. 203.

45. Leicester, "Prospect and Retrospect," p. 11.

46. John Holloway, *The Victorian Sage* (London: Archon, 1962), pp. 73-74.

47. Carlyle, *Emerson Correspondence*, 1:130.

48. Edward Hamley, "Carlyle: Mirage Philosophy and the History of Frederick," *Blackwood's Magazine* 85 (February 1859): 150.

49. J. F. Stephen, "Mr. Carlyle," *Saturday Review*, 19 June 1858, pp. 638-40.

50. Robert Vaughan, "Oliver Cromwell's Letters and Speeches," *British Quarterly Review* 3 (February 1846):53.

51. "Carlyle's Frederick the Great," *British Quarterly Review* 29 (January 1859):262; see also Hamley, "Mirage Philosophy," p. 151; William Stigand, "Carlyle's Frederick the Great," *Edinburgh Review* 110 (October 1859):376; W. Frederick Pollock, "Carlyle's Frederick the Great," *Quarterly Review* 105 (April 1859):276-77.

52. See, e.g., H. H. Lancaster, "History of Frederick the Great," *North British Review* 43 (September 1865):41, and G. H. Lewes and Frederick Greenwood, "Our Survey of Literature, Science, and Art," *Cornhill Magazine* 6 (July 1862):107.

53. J. R. Seeley, "Political Somnambulism," *Macmillan's Magazine* 43 (November 1880):42, 35.

54. Oscar Browning, "The Flight of Louis XVI. to Varennes. A Criticism of Carlyle," *Transactions of the Royal Historical Society* 3 (1886): 319-41.

55. Frederic Harrison, *The Choice of Books and Other Literary Pieces* (London: Macmillan, 1886), p. 410. Harrison, of course, considered Carlyle "unscientific" because he was not a Positivist. See similar criticisms in Lewis James, "Carlyle's Philosophy of History," *Westminster Review* 132 (1889): 427.

56. James Russell Lowell, *My Study Windows* (Boston: Osgood, 1872), p. 134.

57. James Mozley, "Thomas Carlyle," *Quarterly Review* 132 (April 1872):192.

Notes

CHAPTER III: THOMAS BABINGTON MACAULAY

1. Leslie Stephen, "Macaulay," *Cornhill Magazine* 33 (May 1876):570.

2. James Anthony Froude, *Thomas Carlyle: A History of the First Forty Years of His Life 1795-1835* (London: Longmans, 1882), 2:231. "Charlatan," quoted by R. C. Beatty, "Carlyle and Macaulay," *Philological Quarterly* 18 (1939):32.

3. John Clive, *Macaulay: The Shaping of the Historian* (New York: Knopf, 1973); see also Jane Millgate, *Macaulay* (London: Routledge, 1973) and Joseph Hamburger, *Macaulay and the Whig Tradition* (Chicago: University of Chicago Press, 1976).

4. Thomas Babington Macaulay, *Napoleon and the Restoration of the Bourbons*, ed. Joseph Hamburger (New York: Columbia University Press, 1977).

5. George Otto Trevelyan, *The Life and Letters of Lord Macaulay* (Oxford: Oxford University Press, 1978), 1:171. Hereafter cited parenthetically as LM.

6. Margaret Macaulay, *Recollections of a Sister of T. B. Macaulay* (London: privately printed, 1864), pp. 85-86.

7. Thomas Babington Macaulay, *The Works of Lord Macaulay*, ed. Hannah Trevelyan (London: Longmans, 1866), 8:446. Hereafter cited parenthetically as W.

8. William Madden, "Macaulay's Style," in *The Art of Victorian Prose*, ed. George Levine and William Madden (New York: Oxford, 1968), p. 129.

9. *Macaulay*, p. 149.

10. George Levine, *The Boundaries of Fiction*; my reading of Macaulay owes a great deal to this work, as well as to Madden's and Millgate's interpretations.

11. *The Letters of Thomas Babington Macaulay*, ed. Thomas Pinney (New York: Cambridge University Press, 1977), 3:115.

12. Levine, *Boundaries of Fiction*, p. 106.

13. For examples, see Hamburger, p. 216, notes 48 and 49.

14. Hamburger, p. ix *et passim*.

15. John Clive, "Introduction," *Selected Writings*, by Thomas Babington Macaulay, ed. John Clive and Thomas Pinney (Chicago: University of Chicago Press, 1972), pp. xi-xii; Clive, *Macaulay*, p. 184.

16. Clive, *Macaulay*, pp. 105-7; J. W. Burrow, *A Liberal Descent*, pp. 41-42.

17. Herbert Butterfield, *The Whig Interpretation of History* (New York: Norton, 1965).

18. Burrow, *A Liberal Descent*, pp. 33-35.

Notes

19. Clive, *Macaulay*, p. 95.

20. Burrow, *A Liberal Descent*, p. 102.

21. James Spedding, *Evenings with a Reviewer, or Macaulay and Bacon* (Boston: Houghton Mifflin, 1882), 1:xiii-xiv. For similar criticism see also John Paget, "Lord Macaulay and Dundee," *Blackwood's Magazine* 88 (August 1860):158-59 and Cotter Morison, *Macaulay* (London: Macmillan, 1882), pp. 157-61.

22. John Paget, "Macaulay and the Highlands of Scotland," *Blackwood's Magazine* 86 (August 1859):163-64 and "Macaulay and Marlborough," *Blackwood's Magazine* 85 (June 1859):661, 670-76. Paget's four reviews of Macaulay's *History* were later collected as *The New Examen*.

23. Sir Charles Firth, *A Commentary on Macaulay's History of England* (London: Macmillan, 1938), pp. 65-66. For Macaulay's misuse of source materials, see also George Kitson Clark, *The Critical Historian* (New York: Basic Books, 1967), pp. 99-111.

24. *Letters*, 4:27-28; LM, 2:58, 183.

25. *Works*, 6:382; *Letters*, 1:280.

26. See Madden for a discussion of Macaulay's various styles.

27. G. S. Fraser, "Macaulay's Style as Essayist," *Review of English Literature* 1 (October 1960):9-10.

28. Madden, p. 130; see also Levine, *Boundaries of Fiction*, p. 84.

29. Clive discusses the propulsive aspects of Macaulay's style in "Macaulay's Historical Imagination," *Review of English Literature* 1 (October 1960):25. For further discussion of the static quality of Macaulay's narrative, see also Levine, *Boundaries of Fiction*, pp. 150-51 and Millgate, pp. 127-29.

30. Madden, pp. 143-44.

31. Burrow, p. 86.

32. Ibid., p. 67.

33. Levine, *Boundaries of Fiction*, pp. 130-31.

34. Millgate, p. 165.

35. Quoted in David Alec Wilson, *Carlyle to Three Score and Ten* (London: Routledge, 1929), p. 15. See Millgate for a discussion of Macaulay's failure to provide a complex appreciation of William's character, chap. 9.

36. Stephen, "Macaulay," p. 575.

37. Burrow, pp. 64, 84, 73. See also Robin Gilmour, *The Idea of the Gentleman in the Victorian Novel* (London: Allen and Unwin, 1981), for links between "manliness" and middle class ideals.

38. Millgate offers insightful analyses of these and other narrative devices in chap. 7.

39. Macaulay told Ellis that witnessing a division over the Reform Bill was like "seeing Caesar stabbed in the Senate House, or seeing Oliver taking the mace from the table" (LM, 1:187).

40. Millgate points out that such detail was also intended to touch the consciences of readers still faced with the problem of just treatment of the Irish, p. 151.

41. Millgate treats such details as examples of Macaulay's attempt to make memory concrete, see pp. 149-50.

42. Margaret Oliphant, "Macaulay," *Blackwood's Magazine* 80 (August 1856):128-29.

43. William Greg, "Macaulay's History of England," *North British Review* 25 (May 1856):79, 109. See also Walter Bagehot, "Mr. Macaulay," *Literary Studies*, ed. R. H. Hutton (London: Longmans, 1898), 2:1; William Thackeray, "Mr. Macaulay's Essays," *Stray Papers* (London: Hutchinson, 1901), pp. 202-4; and James Moncrieff, "Macaulay's History of England," *Edinburgh Review* 105 (January 1857):142-81.

44. Archibald Alison, "Macaulay's History of England," *Blackwood's Magazine* 65 (April 1849):402. See also Oliphant, "Macaulay," *Blackwood's Magazine* 80 (September 1856):365, 378.

45. Moncrieff, pp. 143-44, 181; David Brewster, "Macaulay's History of England," *North British Review* 10 (February 1849):199; Oliphant (August 1856), 141; John Croker, "Macaulay's History of England," *Quarterly Review* 84 (1849):554.

46. Henry Reeve, "Lord Macaulay," *Edinburgh Review* 111 (January 1860):275; see also James Moncreiff, "Macaulay's History of England—Fifth Volume," *Edinburgh Review* 114 (October 1861):284-85; J. F. Stephen, "Lord Macaulay," *Saturday Review*, 7 January 1860, p. 9.

47. J. A. Froude, "Lord Macaulay," *Fraser's Magazine*, n.s. 13 (July 1876):681; John Morley, "Macaulay," *Critical Miscellanies* (London: Macmillan, 1886), 1:265, 270; Leslie Stephen, pp. 569-70, 581.

48. Morley, p. 290; Margaret Oliphant, "Macaulay," *Blackwood's Magazine* 119 (May 1876):635; Morison, p. 53; Leslie Stephen, p. 579.

49. "Lord Macaulay and His Writings," *Eclectic Magazine* 50 (July 1860):299; Margaret Oliphant, *The Victorian Age of English Literature* (New York: Tait, 1892), 1:175-76.

50. Frederic Harrison, "Lord Macaulay," *Studies in Early Victorian Literature* (London: Edward Arnold, 1906), pp. 71-72. See also A. V. Dicey, "Morison's Macaulay—I," *Nation*, 22 February 1883, p. 175; E. C. Foxcroft, "The Limitations of Lord Macaulay," *Fortnightly Review*, n.s. 72 (1902):822.

51. A. V. Dicey, "Macaulay—I," *Nation*, 22 May 1876, p. 338; Herbert Paul, "Macaulay and His Critics," in *Men and Letters* (London: John Lane,

Notes

1901), pp. 290, 302. See also E. C. Whitehurst, "Lord Macaulay as an Historian," *Westminster Review* 107 (April 1877):204-23.

52. J. Wells, "Macaulay as a Man of Letters," *Fortnightly Review*, n.s. 124 (1928):453; see also G. M. Trevelyan, *Clio, A Muse and Other Essays* (London: Longmans, 1931), p. 46.

53. Bagehot, 2:5.

54. William Gladstone, "Macaulay," in *Gleanings of Past Years, 1844-78* (New York: Scribner's, n.d.), 2:287-88.

55. Henry Lancaster, "Lord Macaulay's Place in English Literature," *North British Review* 33 (November 1860):455; John Skelton, "A 'Last Word' on Macaulay," *Fraser's Magazine* 62 (October 1860):441.

56. Leslie Stephen, p. 574.

57. Pieter Geyl, *Debates with Historians* (Glasgow: Collins, 1955), p. 35.

58. Madden, p. 129.

CHAPTER IV: JAMES ANTHONY FROUDE

1. Hilaire Belloc, ed., "Preface," *Essays in Literature and History*, by James Anthony Froude (London: Everyman, 1906), p. xiv.

2. For the details of Froude's early life, see Waldo Hilary Dunn, *James Anthony Froude: A Biography*, 2 vols. (Oxford: Clarendon, 1961-63); hereafter cited parenthetically as B. Froude's early life is also interpreted by Basil Willey in *More Nineteenth-Century Studies* (1956; rpt. New York: Harper and Row, 1966) and by Burrow, *A Liberal Descent*.

3. James Anthony Froude, *Short Studies on Great Subjects*, 4 vols. (London: Longmans, 1867-83), 4:227. Hereafter volumes under this title will be cited parenthetically as SS.

4. Quoted in Herbert Paul, *The Life of Froude* (New York: Scribner's 1906), p. 66.

5. Burrow, *A Liberal Descent*, pp. 268-69.

6. James Anthony Froude, *The History of England from the Fall of Wolsey to the Defeat of the Spanish Armada*, 12 vols. (New York: Scribner's, 1871), 12:580. Hereafter cited parenthetically as H. This title was adopted in vols. 11-12, replacing the original *The History of England from the Fall of Wolsey to the Death of Elizabeth*.

7. SS, 4:227-28; Raymond M. Bennett, "Letters of James Anthony Froude," *Journal of the Rutgers University Library* 11 (December 1947):12. Burrow notes the pervasively anti-doctrinal bias of Froude's thought and connects his interpretation of sixteenth-century Protestantism with his view of nineteenth-century doubt, *A Liberal Descent*, p. 272.

8. James Anthony Froude, "A Legend of St. Neot," in *Lives of the English*

Notes

Saints, ed. John Henry Newman, 4 vols. (London: James Toovey, 1844), 2:74-75.

9. James Anthony Froude, "Inaugural Lecture," *Longman's Magazine* 21 (December 1892):153. Hereafter cited parenthetically as "Inaugural."

10. George Eliot, *Adam Bede*, ed. John Paterson (Boston: Houghton Mifflin, 1968), p. 150.

11. James Anthony Froude, "Kircaldy of Grange," *Fraser's Magazine* 47 (May 1853):536.

12. James Anthony Froude, "Suggestions on the Best Means of Teaching English History," in *Oxford Essays 1855* (London: Parker, 1855), pp. 78-79. Hereafter cited parenthetically as "Teaching History."

13. James Anthony Froude, *The Life and Letters of Erasmus* (London: Longmans, 1894), p. 212.

14. James Anthony Froude, *The English in Ireland in the Eighteenth Century*, 3 vols. (London: Longmans, 1872-74), 1:5.

15. James Anthony Froude, *Caesar: A Sketch* (London: Longmans, 1879), p. 7.

16. James Anthony Froude, *The Divorce of Catherine of Aragon* (London: Longmans, 1891), p. 18.

17. Burrow, *A Liberal Descent*, p. 250.

18. James Anthony Froude, "The Morals of Queen Elizabeth," *Fraser's Magazine* 48 (October 1853):373.

19. James Anthony Froude, "Preface," *The History of England from the Fall of Wolsey to the Defeat of the Spanish Armada*, 12 vols. (London: Longmans, Green and Co., n.d.), 1:iv.

20. *The Divorce of Catherine of Aragon*, p. 18.

21. "The Morals of Queen Elizabeth," p. 372.

22. James Anthony Froude, "The Edinburgh Review and Mr. Froude's History of England," *Fraser's Magazine* 58 (September 1858):360.

23. *The Divorce of Catherine of Aragon*, p. 13; "Preface," *The History of England* (Longmans), 1:ii. Burrow discusses a number of other more particular resemblances between Froude's interpretation and the Whig view, *A Liberal Descent*, pp. 242, 270-73, 276-77.

24. Burrow detects a distinct nostalgia on Froude's part for the Catholicism left behind, *A Liberal Descent*, pp. 263-65.

25. *Caesar: A Sketch*, p. 5.

26. See Burrow's discussion of Henry's whiggish traits, *A Liberal Descent*, pp. 259, 278.

27. See, e.g., Margaret Oliphant, "Mr. Froude and Queen Mary," *Blackwood's Magazine* 107 (January 1870):110.

Notes

28. Burrow notes that Froude's dislike of constitutional history was another reason for neglecting the end of Elizabeth's reign, when disputes over the constitution loomed large, *A Liberal Descent*, p. 237.

29. F. D. Maurice, "Froude's History of England, Vols. V and VI," *Macmillan's Magazine* 2 (August 1860):276.

30. T. E. May, "Froude's Reign of Elizabeth," *Edinburgh Review* 124 (October 1866):511; Henry Reeve, "Mr. Froude's History of Queen Elizabeth," *Edinburgh Review* 131 (January 1870):2.

31. Goldwin Smith reviewed the *History* in the *Edinburgh*: "Froude's King Henry VIII.," 108 (July 1858):206-52; "Froude's History of England, Vols. V-VIII," 119 (January 1864):243-79. Smith's "Froude's Reply to the Edinburgh Review," 108 (October 1858):586-94 was a reply to Froude's "The Edinburgh Review and Mr. Froude's *History of England*."

Freeman's reviews of the *History* began in the *Saturday Review* for 1864: "Froude's Reign of Elizabeth [First Notice]," 16 January 1864, pp. 80-82; "Froude's Reign of Elizabeth [Concluding Notice]," 30 January 1864, pp. 142-44; "Froude's Reign of Elizabeth—Vol. III," 27 October 1866, pp. 519-20; "Froude's Reign of Elizabeth—Vol. III [Second Notice]," 3 November 1866, pp. 550-51; "Froude's Reign of Elizabeth—Vol. IV," 24 November 1866, pp. 642-44; "Froude's Reign of Elizabeth—Vol. IV [Second Notice]," 1 December 1866, pp. 677-78. Freeman also reviewed the first volume of "Froude's Short Studies," 11 May 1867, pp. 601-2. His articles entitled "Mr. Froude's Life and Times of Thomas Becket" appeared in the *Contemporary Review* in four installments: 31 (March 1878):821-42; 32 (April 1878):116-39; 32 (June 1878):474-500; and 33 (September 1878):213-41. Freeman summed up in "Last Words on Mr. Froude," *Contemporary Review* 35 (May 1879):214-36, and Froude replied in "A Few Words on Mr. Freeman," *Nineteenth Century* 5 (May 1879):618-37.

See also W. S. Lilley, "The New Spirit in History," *Nineteenth Century* 38 (October 1895):629, and T. Rice Holmes, "Mr. Froude and His Critics," *Westminster Review* 138 (July 1892):179 82.

32. A. V. Dicey, *Nation*, 14 December 1871, p. 388.

33. Freeman first used the term "constitutional inaccuracy." "Froude's disease" was coined by Charles Langlois and Charles Seignobos, *Introduction to the Study of History*, trans. G. G. Berry (London: Duckworth, 1898), p. 125.

34. Freeman, "Froude's Reign of Elizabeth—Vol. III," p. 519 and "Froude's Reign of Elizabeth [First Notice]," p. 81.

35. Freeman, "Froude's Reign of Elizabeth [Concluding Notice]," p. 143.

36. Smith, "Froude's History of England—Vols. V-VIII," p. 247-48.

37. See, e.g., Lilley, "The New Spirit in History," p. 629 and Montague

Notes

Burrows, "Mr. Froude's Queen Elizabeth," *Quarterly Review* 128 (April 1870):544.

38. Henry Reeve, "Mr. Froude's History of Queen Elizabeth," p. 21.

39. William Donne, "Froude's History of England," *Fraser's Magazine* 54 (July 1856):33.

40. Frederic Harrison, "The Historical Method of Froude," in *Tennyson, Ruskin, Mill and Other Literary Estimates* (London: Macmillan, 1899), p. 233; Andrew Lang, "Freeman vs. Froude," *Cornhill Magazine* 93 (February 1906):251.

41. Langlois and Seignobos offer the best examples of the rejection of "literary" history, while A. B. Hart defends the importance of imagination in his presidential address to the American Historical Association, "Imagination in History," *AHR* 15 (January 1910): e.g., 237-38, 250-51.

42. Harrison, "The Historical Method of Froude," p. 230.

43. Holmes, "Mr. Froude and His Critics," p. 187.

44. "Mr. Froude's Appointment," *Saturday Review*, 9 April 1892, p. 411.

45. James Anthony Froude, "Preface," *The Nemesis of Faith*, 2d ed. (London: Chapman, 1849), p. xii.

46. Quoted in Dunn, *Biography*, 1:ix. The speaker is Mrs. William Harrison, Kingsley's daughter.

47. Harrison, "The Historical Method of Froude," p. 224.

CHAPTER V: JOHN RICHARD GREEN

1. The publication data for the *Short History*, cited by York Powell and Charles Firth, "Two Oxford Historians," *Quarterly Review* 195 (1902):542n., does not include the authorized and unauthorized American editions of the book, or the substantial circulation of the *History of the English People*, which gave essentially the same account of history but with greater expansion in the eighteenth-century sections.

2. The standard biography is Leslie Stephen's *Letters of John Richard Green* (London: Macmillan, 1901). Additional information can be found in R. B. McDowell, *Alice Stopford Green: A Passionate Historian* (Dublin: Allen Figgis, 1967). The *Letters* will hereafter be cited parenthetically as LG.

3. These essays, along with two more from the *Saturday Review* and *Macmillan's* written later in his career, were reprinted in J. R. Green and George Roberson, *Studies in Oxford History* (Oxford: Clarendon, 1901). Hereafter *Studies in Oxford History* will be cited parenthetically as OS. Green was instrumental in the founding of the Oxford Historical Society, which sponsored the book's publication after his death.

4. Jesus College MS. 198, Green to Boyd Dawkins, 28 April 1861.

Notes

5. James Bryce, "John Richard Green," in *Studies in Contemporary Biography* (1903; rpt. New York: Macmillan, 1927), pp. 150-51. Bryce notes that Green himself considered Herodotus "more precious" than Thucydides, for "his view was so much wider."

6. J. R. Green, "Freeman's Norman Conquest," *Saturday Review*, 13 April 1867, p. 470.

7. Alice Stopford Green, "Introduction," *A Short History of the English People*, 2d ed. (New York: American Book Co., 1911), p. xiii. See also LG, 427.

8. John Richard Green, *A Short History of the English People* (New York: Harpers, 1875), pp. iii-iv. This edition will hereafter be cited parenthetically as SH.

9. John Richard Green, "St. Edmondsbury and the Archaeological Institute," *Saturday Review*, 31 July 1869, p. 147.

10. John Richard Green, "Freeman's Norman Conquest," *Saturday Review*, 13 April 1867, p. 470.

11. Ibid., p. 471.

12. John Richard Green, "A School History of England," *Saturday Review*, 1 November 1873, p. 573.

13. Ibid., p. 574.

14. John Richard Green, "Guizot's Life of Barante," *Saturday Review*, 16 November 1867, p. 636.

15. John Richard Green, "Foulkes' Christendom's Divisions," *Saturday Review*, 23 November 1867, p. 667.

16. See in this regard Burrow's discussion of the idea of Teutonic freedoms in *A Liberal Descent*, especially chapter 5.

17. John Richard Green, *The Making of England* (London: Macmillan, 1882), pp. 193-94. Hereafter cited parenthetically as M.

18. "Two New Books on English History," *Times*, 4 February 1882, p. 4.

19. John Richard Green, "Freeman's Growth of the English Constitution," *Saturday Review*, 4 May 1872, p. 574.

20. John Richard Green, *History of the English People*, 4 vols. (New York: Harpers, 1879), 4:271. Hereafter cited parenthetically as HEP.

21. John Richard Green, "English Town Gilds," *Saturday Review*, 25 June 1870, p. 838.

22. John Richard Green, *Stray Studies from England and Italy* (London: Macmillan, 1876), pp. 214-16.

23. John Richard Green, *The Conquest of England* (London: Macmillan, 1883), p. 167. Hereafter cited parenthetically as C.

24. John Richard Green, "Stubbs's Inaugural Lecture," *Saturday Review*, 2 March 1867, p. 280.

Notes

25. John Richard Green, "St. Edmondsbury and the Archaeological Institute," p. 147; "School History of England," p. 573.

26. See, e.g., "Cobbe's Norman Kings," *Saturday Review*, 18 December 1869, pp. 800-801, or "Hughes' Alfred the Great," *Saturday Review*, 30 April 1870, pp. 582-84.

27. H. R. Haweis, "John Richard Green: In Memoriam," *Contemporary Review* 43 (May 1883):733.

28. Jesus College MS. 201, Freeman to Green, 21 September 1873.

29. Freeman consistently argued that the unconventional organization of the *Short History* kept it from being useful to students who didn't already know the traditional outlines of British history. He told Green that A. W. Ward had agreed that the book would not be suitable as a beginning text, even for Ward's students at Owens College, Manchester; Jesus College MS. 201, Freeman to Green, 16 May 1875. Nonetheless, G. P. Gooch notes that the book became widely used as a manual for schools and as a companion for advanced students, *History and Historians in the Nineteenth Century*, p. 331. R. L. Schuyler similarly claims that Green fulfilled his aim of replacing the abridged Hume as a standard reference work, "Green and His Short History," *Political Science Quarterly* 64 (1949):333.

30. Bryce, "John Richard Green," p. 163.

31. John Richard Green and Alice Stopford Green, *A Short Geography of the British Isles* (London: Macmillan, 1880), p. xi.

32. "Two New Books on English History," *Times*, 4 February 1882, p. 4.

33. J. W. Burrow, *A Liberal Descent*, p. 203.

34. "John Richard Green," *Living Age*, 5 July 1902, p. 10.

35. John Richard Green, "Freeman's Norman Conquest—Vol. II," *Saturday Review*, 22 August 1868, p. 267.

36. Margaret Oliphant, "New Books," *Blackwood's Magazine* 118 (July 1875):90.

37. "John Richard Green," *Living Age*, 5 July 1902, p. 19.

38. "Green's Short History of the English People," *Athenaeum*, 6 March 1875, p. 322.

39. F. A. Paley, "The Origins of English History," *Edinburgh Review* 155 (April 1882):407; "Green's Conquest of England," *Edinburgh Review* 159 (April 1884):410.

40. "Green's Short History of the English People," *Athenaeum*, p. 323.

41. John S. Brewer, "Green's History of the English People," *Quarterly Review* 141 (April 1876):323.

42. Ibid., pp. 285-86.

Notes

43. James Rowley, "Mr. Green's Short History of the English People; Is it Trustworthy?" *Fraser's Magazine* 92 (September 1875):408-9.

44. Samuel R. Gardiner defended Green in "Mr. Green and Mr. Rowley," *Academy*, 11 December 1875, pp. 604-5, although in a later review of vol. 4 of the *History of the English People* he took Green to task for not having improved his accuracy, *Academy*, 10 July 1880, p. 19. See also Henry Adams, "Green's Short History of the English People," *North American Review* 121 (July 1875):216, 222, and *The Letters of William Stubbs*, ed. W. H. Hutton (London: Archibald Constable, 1902), p. 154.

45. Bryce, "John Richard Green," pp. 158-59; Jesus College MS. 202, Freeman to Green, 14 March 1876 and 26 March 1876; *The Letters of William Stubbs*, p. 154. The *Athenaeum* was even hasher, denouncing Green's "childish omniscience" about so wide an array of historical questions as "charlatanry"—"English History for Public Schools," *Athenaeum*, 1 January 1876, p. 18.

46. John Richard Green, "Historic Study in France," *Saturday Review*, 17 October 1868, p. 526.

47. Green's notes for his projected study of the Angevin kings show that he had no intention of abandoning his method of writing history as sociocultural synthesis, even in this more scholarly work. See British Museum Add. MSS. 40,170 and 40,172.

48. Bryce, "John Richard Green," p. 139.

49. Philip Gell, "John Richard Green," *Fortnightly Review*, n.s. 33 (May 1883):738.

50. Certain aspects of this longing fed the ideal of "universal knowledge"; see Sheldon Rothblatt's discussion in *Tradition and Change in English Liberal Education* (London: Faber, 1976).

51. See Burrow's discussion of the relationship between German investigations of ancient law as the basis of national identity and the interpretations of late Victorian medievalists like Green, Stubbs, and Freeman, *A Liberal Descent*, pp. 119-25.

52. "Green's Short History of the English People," *Times*, 30 December 1874, p. 3.

53. Frederic Harrison, "The Historical Method of Froude," *Nineteenth Century* 44 (September 1898):373.

CHAPTER VI: EDWARD AUGUSTUS FREEMAN

1. W. R. W. Stephens, *The Life and Letters of Edward A. Freeman*, 2 vols. (London: Macmillan, 1895), 1:209. Hereafter cited parenthetically as LF.

2. J. W. Burrow, *A Liberal Descent*, p. 225.

Notes

3. E. A. Freeman, *A History of Architecture* (London: Masters, 1849), p. xv.

4. Ibid., p. 4.

5. E. A. Freeman, *Lectures to American Audiences* (Philadelphia: Porter and Coates, 1882), p. 209.

6. Ibid., p. 208.

7. E. A. Freeman, *The Ottoman Power in Europe* (London: Macmillan, 1877), p. viii.

8. Ibid., pp. viii-ix. Freeman made much the same connection between moral and scientific positions in his "Sentimental and Practical Politics," *Princeton Review*, 55th Year (March 1879):311-44.

9. E. A. Freeman, *The Methods of Historical Study: Eight Lectures* (London: Macmillan, 1886), p. 119. Hereafter cited parenthetically as M.

10. E. A. Freeman, *The History of Federal Government in Greece and Italy* (1863; rpt. London: Macmillan, 1893), p. xv. Hereafter cited parenthetically as HFG.

11. E. A. Freeman, *Historical Essays, Third Series* (London: Macmillan, 1879), p. 237. Hereafter all volumes of the *Historical Essays* will be cited parenthetically as HE with volume number. The first series was published in 1860, second series 1873, fourth series 1892. Citations from the first series are to the 4th ed., 1886.

12. E. A. Freeman, "National Morality," *Princeton Review*, 54th Year (November 1878):655, 657.

13. E. A. Freeman, *The History of the Norman Conquest in England*, 3d ed., rev. (Oxford: Clarendon, 1877), 1:500-1. Hereafter cited parenthetically as NC.

14. E. A. Freeman, "On the Study of History," *Fortnightly Review* 35 (1881):330.

15. E. A. Freeman, "Pearson's Early and Middle Ages of England," *Fortnightly Review* 9 (April 1868):398.

16. Robert M. Young points out that the resort to "Force" as an explanation was an attempt on the part of scientists to bridge the mind/body, will/mechanism gap; see his "The Role of Psychology in the Nineteenth-Century Evolutionary Debate," in *Historical Conceptions of Psychology*, ed. Mary Henle, et. al. (New York: Spring, 1973), p. 198.

17. "On the Study of History," p. 331.

18. *Lectures to American Audiences*, p. 224.

19. Ibid., p. 220.

20. E. A. Freeman, *Comparative Politics* (New York: Macmillan, 1874), p. 1. Hereafter cited parenthetically as CP.

21. *Lectures to American Audiences*, p. 216.

Notes

22. See in particular Huxley's "On the Methods and Results of Ethnology" and "On Some Fixed Points in British Ethnology" in *Selected Works of Thomas Henry Huxley* (New York: Appleton, n.d.), vol. 7.

23. E. A. Freeman, "Introduction to American Institutional History," *Johns Hopkins University Studies* 1 (1882):15.

24. Burrow, *A Liberal Descent*, p. 182, discusses such conflicts.

25. E. A. Freeman, *The Growth of the English Constitution from the Earliest Times* (London: Macmillan, 1872), pp. 69-70. Hereafter cited parenthetically as GEC.

26. For Burrow's discussion of continuity, see in particular *A Liberal Descent*, chap. 8, and "Editor's Introduction," *The History of the Norman Conquest of England* (Chicago: University of Chicago Press, 1974), pp. xiv-xviii.

27. E. A. Freeman, *General Sketch of European History* (London: Macmillan, 1872), p. 2.

28. E. A. Freeman, "A Review of my Opinions," *Forum* 13 (April 1892):155.

29. Burrow, *A Liberal Descent*, p. 226.

30. Ibid., pp. 224-25.

31. Ibid., p. 164.

32. E. A. Freeman, "Oxford After Forty Years," *Contemporary Review* 51 (1887):618-20.

33. Ibid., p. 611.

34. See, e.g., E. A. Freeman, "The Art of History Making," *Saturday Review*, 17 November 1855, pp. 52-54 and "Creasy's History of the Ottoman Turks [I]," *Saturday Review*, 17 May 1856, pp. 61-62.

35. See, e.g., E. A. Freeman, "The Use of Historical Documents," *Fortnightly Review* 16 (September 1871):335.

36. E. A. Freeman, "Mr. Kingsley's Roman and Teuton," *Saturday Review*, 9 April 1864, p. 446. See also "Kingsley's Hereward," *Saturday Review*, 19 May 1866, pp. 594-95.

37. See, e.g., Frederic Harrison's "A Pedantic Nuisance," *Nineteenth Century* 19 (January 1886):87-105, attacking Freeman's idiosyncratic use of names and spelling.

38. "On the Study of History," p. 326.

39. See, e.g., E. A. Freeman, "Stubbs' Registrum Sacrum Anglicanum," *Saturday Review*, 24 July 1858, pp. 86-87 or "Medieval London," *Saturday Review*, 4 June 1859, pp. 689-97.

40. E. A. Freeman, "Dr. Doran Again," *Saturday Review*, 10 January 1857, pp. 37-38; see also "The Art of History Making."

Notes

41. "On the Study of History," p. 329.

42. E. A. Freeman, *Old-English History [for Children]*, new ed. (London: Macmillan, 1878), p. vii.

43. "On the Study of History," p. 327; see also *Methods*, p. 106.

44. E. A. Freeman, "Stubbs' Registrum Sacrum Anglicanum," p. 86.

45. E. A. Freeman, *The History of Sicily from the Earliest Times* (Oxford: Clarendon, 1891), 1:xi.

46. M. E. Bratchel, *E. A. Freeman and the Victorian Interpretation of the Norman Conquest* (Ilfracombe: Arthur Stockwell, 1969), gives examples of Freeman's distorting syntheses, p. 27.

47. "The Use of Historical Documents," pp. 323-24.

48. Burrow, *A Liberal Descent*, p. 183.

49. G. W. Prothero, "Review of *Historical Essays, Fourth Series*," *English Historical Review* 8 (April 1893):385.

50. Jesus College MS. 200, Freeman to Green, 11 February 1872 and 1 November 1872. Freeman's concern was at least in part that Green's criticism would make the public think he was deficient by the standards of fellow professionals.

51. Burrow, *A Liberal Descent*, p. 211.

52. E. A. Freeman, *Old-English History*, pp. 59, 51.

53. Ibid., pp. 23, 28-29.

54. E. A. Freeman, "Lord Macaulay," *International Review* 3 (September 1876):690.

55. Review of *The History of the Norman Conquest*, vol. 1; *Athenaeum*, 16 March 1867, p. 345; "Mr. Freeman's Historical Essays," *Pall Mall Gazette*, 23 November 1871, p. 1811; review of *The Growth of the English Constitution* and *The Unity of History*, *North British Quarterly* 56 (1872):520. Freeman reviewed for both the *Athenaeum* and the *Pall Mall Gazette*.

56. Review of *The History of the Norman Conquest*, vol. 2, *Athenaeum*, 25 July 1868, pp. 104-5; "Mr. Freeman's Norman Conquest—Vol. IV," *Pall Mall Gazette*, 2 March 1872, p. 851.

57. See, e.g., "Mr. Freeman's Historical Essays," *Pall Mall Gazette*, p. 1811, or C. F. Adams, "The Sifted Grain and the Grain Sifters," AHR 6 (1900-1901):217.

58. Frederic Harrison, *The Meaning of History and Other Historical Pieces* (New York: Macmillan, 1900), p. 118.

59. Frederic Harrison, *Tennyson, Ruskin, Mill, and Other Literary Estimates*, p. 243.

60. Review of *Historical Essays, Second Series*, *Athenaeum*, 22 February 1873, p. 245.

Notes

61. "The Politics of the Aryan Race," *Athenaeum*, 24 January 1874, pp. 123-24.

62. See, e.g., review of *Historical Essays, Second Series, Athenaeum*, 22 February 1873, p. 245, and "Mr. Freeman on the English Constitution," *Pall Mall Gazette*, 26 April 1872, p. 1575.

63. Review of *Historical Essays, First Series, Athenaeum*, 14 October 1871, p. 493.

64. Burrow, *A Liberal Descent*, p. 213.

65. C. H. Pearson, "Earl Godwin and Earl Harold," *North British Review*, o.s. 52 (April 1870):28-68.

66. John Horace Round, *Feudal England* (London: Swan Sonnenschein, 1895), pp. 389, 393.

67. H. A. L. Fisher, "Modern Historians and their Methods," *Fortnightly Review*, o.s. 62 (December 1894):805.

68. P. B. M. Blaas, *Continuity and Anachronism* (The Hague: Martinus Nijhoff, 1978), p. 266; see also Charles Langlois and Charles Seignobos, *Introduction to the Study of History*, p. 320.

69. See reviews of *The Methods of Historical Study* by A. W. Ward, *English Historical Review* 2 (1887):358-60 and of *Historical Essays, Fourth Series*, by G. W. Prothero, *English Historical Review* 8 (April 1893):384-89.

70. This is precisely the kind of public reaction that observers like James Fitzjames Stephen felt the Bulgarian Atrocities campaign stirred up; see R. T. Shannon, *Gladstone and the Bulgarian Agitation 1876* (London: Thomas Nelson, 1963), pp. 47-48.

EPILOGUE

1. G. M. Trevelyan, *Clio, A Muse and Other Essays*, p. 140.

2. John W. Osborne, "The Endurance of 'Literary' History in Great Britain: Charles Oman, G. M. Trevelyan, and the Genteel Tradition," *Clio* 2 (1972):7-17.

3. For such generalizations see, e.g., Richard A. E. Brooks, "The Development of the Historical Mind," in *The Reinterpretation of Victorian Literature*, ed. Joseph E. Baker (Princeton: Princeton University Press, 1950), p. 137, or J. R. Hale, *The Evolution of British Historiography* (London: Macmillan, 1967), p. 56. Although T. W. Heyck's concern is not professionalization *per se*, he uses historians as one example of the withdrawal of intellectuals from the needs and interests of the general public in his *The Transformation of Intellectual Life in Victorian England* (New York: St. Martin's, 1983).

4. For a discussion of the research ideal, see Sheldon Rothblatt, *Tradition and Change in English Liberal Education*, pp. 157ff.

Notes

5. This definition is offered as a consensus that avoids some of the knottier problems of how to define professionalization. It draws from such accounts as William Goode, "Community within a Community: The Professions," *American Sociological Review* 22 (1957):194-200; Bernard Barber, "Some Problems in the Sociology of the Professions," *Daedalus* 92 (1963):669-88; Everett C. Hughes, "Professions," *Daedalus* 92 (1963):655-68; and Phillip Elliott, *The Sociology of the Professions* (New York: Herder, 1972), p. 5. Opposing definitions of professionalization with particular relevance to Victorian and Edwardian England are surveyed by Elliott, pp. 55-56, and by Susan F. Cannon, *Science in Culture: The Early Victorian Period*, pp. 147-63. Andrew Abbott's analysis of differences between public and professional perceptions of professional status suggests that in some respects the case of the British historian is a variation of conflicts inherent in professionalization: "Status and Strain in the Professions," *American Journal of Sociology* 86 (1981):819-35. Doris Goldstein stresses the importance of a sense of community to the professionalization of history in "The Organizational Development of the British Historical Profession, 1884-1921," *Bulletin of the Institute of Historical Research* 55 (1982):180-93.

See also Doris Goldstein, "The Professionalization of History in Britain in the Late Nineteenth and Early Twentieth Centuries," *History of Historiography* 3 (1983):3-26, and John Kenyon, *The History Men* (London: Weidenfeld and Nicolson, 1983) for other treatments of professionalization that I was unable to incorporate into my own analysis.

6. William Stubbs, *Seventeen Lectures on the Study of Medieval and Modern History*, 3d ed. (Oxford: Clarendon, 1900), p. 14; see also p. 110.

7. Lord Acton, *Essays in the Liberal Interpretation of History*, ed. William McNeill (Chicago: University of Chicago Press, 1967), pp. 329, 332.

8. Frederick York Powell and Charles Firth, "Two Oxford Historians," *Quarterly Review* 195 (1902):560.

9. Acton, *Essays in the Liberal Interpretation of History*, pp. 397-98.

10. See, e.g., C. E. Appleton, "Economic Aspects of the Endowment of Research," *Fortnightly Review*, o.s. 22 (October 1874):521-22. See also essays by Mark Pattison and A. H. Sayce in *Essays on the Endowment of Research* (London: King, 1876).

11. *Selections from the Correspondence of the First Lord Acton*, ed. J. N. Figgis and R. V. Laurence (London: Longmans, 1917), 1:309.

12. J. H. Round, *Feudal England*, p. x. "Minute sifting" is an allusion to Lord Kelvin's presidential address to the Royal Society in 1871. The comment about research is quoted in P. B. M. Blaas, *Continuity and Anachronism*, p. 56.

13. J. R. Seeley, "Political Somnambulism," *Macmillan's Magazine* 43 (November 1880):43.

Notes

14. Herbert A. L. Fisher, "Modern Historians and Their Methods," *Fortnightly Review*, o.s. 62 (December 1894):811.

15. Richard Altick, *The English Common Reader: A Social History of the Mass Reading Public 1800-1900*, chaps. 13 and 15.

16. See, e.g., Margaret Oliphant, "The Byways of Literature," *Blackwood's Magazine* 84 (August 1858):200-216; Thomas Wright, "On a Possible Popular Culture," *Contemporary Review* 40 (July 1881):25-44; B. G. Johns, "The Literature of the Streets," *Edinburgh Review* 165 (January 1887):40-65; and Edward Dowden, "Hopes and Fears for Literature," *Fortnightly Review*, o.s. 51 (February 1889):166-83.

17. Stubbs, *Seventeen Lectures*, pp. 58-59, 114; see also 61-62.

18. H. A. L. Fisher, "Modern Historians and Their Methods," p. 812.

19. Mandell Creighton, "Picturesqueness in History," *Cornhill Magazine*, o.s. 75 (March 1897):305.

20. J. R. Seeley, "History and Politics—Part IV," *Macmillan's Magazine* 41 (November 1879):32.

21. "Prefatory Note," *English Historical Review* 1 (January 1886):5. Doris Goldstein identifies James Bryce as the author of the prefatory note, "The Organizational Development of the British Historical Profession," p. 182.

22. Louise Creighton, *Life and Letters of Mandell Creighton* (London: Longmans, 1904), 1:337.

23. "Prefatory Note," *English Historical Review*, p. 5.

24. Louise Creighton, *Life and Letters of Mandell Creighton*, 1:343.

25. J. B. Bury, *Selected Essays*, ed. Harold Temperley (Cambridge: Cambridge University Press, 1930), p. 3. See Doris Goldstein's analysis of tensions and ambiguities in Bury's position, "J. B. Bury's Philosophy of History: A Reappraisal," *AHR* 82 (1977):896-919.

26. On Maitland see Andrew Lang's comments in "History as she ought to be wrote," *Blackwood's Magazine* 166 (August 1899):266. On Stubbs see Burrow, *A Liberal Descent*, pp. 137, 145-46, and Robert Brentano, "The Sound of Stubbs," *Journal of British Studies* 6 (1966-67):1-14.

27. "Gardiner's Personal Government of Charles I.," *Saturday Review*, 22 December 1877, p. 774; J. K. Laughton, "Gardiner's History of the Commonwealth and Protectorate 1649-60, Vol. III," *English Historical Review* 13 (1898):167; J. R. Seeley, "History of the Great Civil War," *Academy*, 21 May 1887, pp. 353-54; see also F. York Powell, "S. R. Gardiner," *English Historical Review* 17 (1902):275-79.

28. "Gardiner's History of England," *Athenaeum*, 21 March 1863, p. 392; "Prince Charles and the Spanish Marriage," *Athenaeum*, 8 May 1869, pp. 629-30; see also A. V. Dicey, "Gardiner's History," *Nation*, 11 April 1895, p. 280; F. W. Warre-Cornish, "Gardiner's Protectorate," *Quarterly Review*

Notes

187 (April 1898):446-70; G. L. Beer, "Gardiner: An Appreciation," *Critic* 38 (1901):546-47.

29. William Stubbs, *Seventeen Lectures,* p. vii. He also complained that his work was better appreciated in Germany than in England, p. 32.

30. F. W. Maitland, "William Stubbs," *English Historical Review* 16 (1901):421, claims Stubbs as a fellow professional while admitting his defects for the general audience. H. Adams criticizes Stubbs for the same traits, "Stubbs' Constitutional History of England," *North American Review* 119 (1874):235.

31. Samuel Crothers, "That History Should be Readable," in *The Gentle Reader* (Boston: Houghton Mifflin, 1903), pp. 167-200; Augustine Birrell, "The Muse of History," in *Obiter Dicta* (New York: Scribner's, 1887), 1:196-223; Andrew Lang, "History as she ought to be wrote," pp. 266-74.

32. Lang, "History as she ought to be wrote," pp. 268, 272.

33. Charles Colby, "Historical Synthesis," in *Congress of Arts and Sciences,* ed. Howard Rogers (Boston: Houghton Mifflin, 1906), 2:48. This is part of the proceedings from the session on Historical Sciences, held as part of the 1904 St. Louis Exposition.

34. Reprinted in Frederic Harrison, *The Meaning of History*; see pp. 105, 135, 137.

35. John Morley, *Critical Miscellanies,* 3:9; *Diderot and the Encyclopedists* (London: Macmillan, 1886), 2:212.

36. John Hobson, "The Academic Spirit in Education," *Contemporary Review* 63 (February 1893):240.

37. James Bryce, "The Future of English Universities," *Fortnightly Review,* o.s. 39 (March 1883):387.

38. Lang, "History as she ought to be wrote," p. 268.

39. G. M. Trevelyan, *Clio, A Muse,* pp. 174-75.

40. Sir Charles Oman, *On the Writing of History* (New York: Dutton, 1939), p. 230.

41. E. G. W. Bill, *University Reform in Nineteenth-Century Oxford* (Oxford: Clarendon, 1973), p. 97.

42. Arthur Engel, "Emerging Concepts of the Academic Profession at Oxford 1800-1854," in *The University in Society,* ed. Laurence Stone (Princeton: Princeton University Press, 1974), 1:349.

43. Ibid., pp. 347-48. Engel also points out that while the number of professorial chairs increased to 47 in 1892 from 25 in 1850, there were still not enough for these to be viewed as the normal promotion for college dons; see p. 351. The interdependence of specialization and academic professionalism discussed by Rothblatt, *Tradition and Change,* pp. 185-86 was, in the period I discuss, not yet decisive in determining professional advancement for tutors.

Notes

44. A. T. Milne, "History at the Universities: Then and Now," *History* 59 (1974):40.

45. R. W. Southern, *The Shape and Substance of Academic History* (Oxford: Clarendon, 1961), p. 18.

46. The following account is drawn from Jean O. McLachlan, "The Origin and Early Development of the Cambridge Historical Tripos," *Cambridge Historical Journal* 9 (1947-49):78-105, and George Kitson Clark, "A Hundred Years of the Teaching of History at Cambridge, 1873-1973," *Historical Journal* 16 (1973):535-53.

47. Quoted by McLachlan, p. 95.

48. Milne, "History at the Universities," p. 39.

49. Sheldon Rothblatt, *The Revolution of the Dons* (London: Faber, 1968), p. 179. Seeley was Regius Professor of Modern History at Cambridge from 1869 to 1895.

50. William Stubbs, *Seventeen Lectures*, pp. 21, 10.

51. Lord Acton, *Essays in the Liberal Interpretation of History*, pp. 331-12, 351.

52. McLachlan, "Cambridge Historical Tripos," p. 87; E. S. de Beer, "Sir Charles Firth 1857-1936," *History* 21 (1936-37):4; Oman, *On the Writing of History*, p. 253; Gareth Stedman Jones, "The Pathology of English History," *New Left Review* 46 (1967):32.

53. C. H. A. Fifoot, ed., *The Letters of Frederic William Maitland* (Cambridge: Cambridge University Press, 1965), p. 349.

54. Milne, "History at the Universities," p. 37.

55. Kitson Clark, "A Hundred Years of the Teaching of History," p. 552; Southern, *The Shape and Substance of Academic History*, p. 18.

56. Doris Goldstein stresses Bury's departures from nineteenth-century assumptions about history, "J. B. Bury's Philosophy of History: A Reappraisal." My reading of her evidence suggests that despite his epistemological innovations, he retained more conventional attitudes toward such things as the practical value of historical study: see p. 914, e.g.

57. I disagree with P. B. M. Blaas's Kuhnian view that the early professional school had overthrown the Whig paradigm by the early twentieth century. Some of his own evidence suggests to me that the change was far from so conclusive and not complete so early. See, e.g., his remarks on administrative history, *Continuity and Anachronism*, pp. 293-95, 364, 373.

58. Ibid., p. 367.

59. Gareth Stedman Jones, "The Pathology of English History," pp. 41-42.

60. Georg Iggers, *New Directions in European Historiography* (Middletown, Conn.: Wesleyan University Press, 1975), pp. 21, 30-31. Gareth Stedman Jones offers a rather more polemical account of the connections between

Notes

political apologetics and historiographical conservatism in England in "The Pathology of English History."

61. Jones, p. 31; Kitson Clark, p. 538.

62. G. N. Clark, "The Origin of the Cambridge Modern History," *Cambridge Historical Journal* 8 (1945):57-64; Felix Gilbert, "European and American Historiography," in *History*, by John Higham with Leonard Kreiger and Felix Gilbert (Englewood Cliffs, N. J.: Prentice-Hall, 1965), p. 345.

63. R. W. Southern, *The Shape and Substance of Academic History*, pp. 5, 17.

64. Elliot, *The Sociology of the Professions*, p. 47; see also Christopher Kent, *Brains and Numbers* (Toronto: University of Toronto Press, 1978), pp. 17-18.

65. Elliott, pp. 49, 54-55. See also Joseph Ben-David and Z. Zloczower, "Universities and Academic Systems in Modern Societies," *European Journal of Sociology* 3 (1962):45-84.

66. Ben-David and Zloczower, pp. 63-64. See also A. L. Halsey and M. A. Trow, *The British Academics* (London: Faber, 1971), p. 40.

67. Goldstein, "The Organizational Development of the British Historical Profession," p. 189. See also Milne, "History at the Universities," p. 43. A typical result of efforts to professionalize teaching is *Essays on the Teaching of History*, ed. William Archbold (Cambridge: Cambridge University Press, 1901).

68. H. J. Perkin, *Key Profession: A History of the Association of University Teachers* (New York: Augustus Kelley, 1969), p. 5. See also Ben-David and Zloczower, pp. 69-70.

69. Halsey and Trow, pp. 239-40; see also their survey of attitudes toward teaching and research, pp. 280 ff.

70. Ben Knights, *The Idea of the Clerisy in the Nineteenth Century* (Cambridge: Cambridge University Press, 1978), pp. 211-12 makes this argument for university education in general.

71. See, e.g., Blaas's account of the lack of cooperation Colonel Wedgewood met with from Namier and J. E. Neale for his proposed biographical history of Parliament, pp. 332-34.

72. Ben-David and Zloczower, "Universities and Academic Systems," p. 66.

73. Felix Gilbert," European and American Historiography," p. 336.

74. Goldstein, "The Organizational Development of the British Historical Profession," p. 181. Goldstein also notes conflicts between amateur and professional ideals in the early stages of the Historical Society and the British Academy, pp. 184, 187.

75. Higham, Kreiger, and Gilbert, *History*, p. 14.

Notes

76. Laurence Veysey, *The Emergence of the American University* (Chicago: University of Chicago Press, 1965) and Burton Bledstein, *The Culture of Professionalism and the Development of Higher Education in America* (New York: Norton, 1976) examine academic professionalism in America.

77. Higham, Kreiger, and Gilbert, *History*, p. 19.

INDEX

Acton, John Emerich Dalberg, Lord, 217, 218, 228
   at Cambridge, 226, 227, 228, 229-30
Adams, Henry, 165
Adams, Herbert B., 233
Addison, Joseph, xvi
Alison, Archibald, 99
Arnold, Matthew, 2, 76, 214
Arnold, Thomas
   and Carlyle, compared, 6, 11, 12, 16, 33-34, 35, 37, 38, 39, 40, 48, 58, 59, 62
   and Freeman, compared, 16, 173, 174, 175, 176, 179-80, 182, 183, 187, 189, 190, 192, 198, 205
   and Froude, compared, 12, 111, 119, 120, 133
   and Green, compared, 16, 145, 147, 154, 157, 158, 159, 168
   and Macaulay, compared, 12, 19, 66, 67, 69, 71, 72, 73-74, 75, 76, 77, 78, 81, 82, 85, 92, 101, 102
   biographical survey, 1-4
   characterization in, 21-24
   concern with audience in, 18-19, 209
   creative method of, 17-18
   influence on Freeman, 171
   laws of history in, 5, 7-9
   model of change in, xxi, 9-11, 39, 40
   model of science, 4-5
   moral function of history in, xv, xxvii, 5-6, 207, 208
   on Carlyle, 21, 27
   progress in, xiv, 11-14, 30, 39
   scholarly methods of, 14-17
   style of, 19-21, 209
   summary, 29-32
   treatment of class or social groups, 24-25
   treatment of events by, 25-28
   treatment of geography by, 17, 28-29
   works
      Englishman's Register, 3
      History of Rome, xxiv, 3, 6, 15-16, 18, 20, 24-25, 28-29
      History of the Later Roman Commonwealth, 2
      "Introductory Dissertation on the Credibility of Early Roman History," 15
      Introductory Lectures on Modern History, 3
Aryan race
   advance of civilization by, 182
   history of 171, 178, 179, 180, 182, 187, 195, 196, 204
   political institutions of, 172, 173, 180
   traits of, 177, 179, 189, 190, 194, 195
Audience, concern with, xiii, xiv, xv-xvi
   by Arnold, 18-19
   by Freeman, 186-88

Index

by Green, 155-57
by Macaulay, 85-86
by professional historians, 216, 218-19
Bagehot, Walter, 99, 101
Barante, M. de, 7
Belloc, Hilaire, 105
Ben-David, Joseph, 232
Ben-Israel, Hedva, 50
Birrell, Augustin, 221-22
Blaas, P. B. M., 259n.57
Blake, William, xx
Brewer, John, 164
Brewster, David, 99
British Academy, 233
Brooks, Richard, 49
Browning, Oscar, 61, 226
Bryce, James, 158, 165, 166, 249n.5, 257n.21
Buckland, William, 4, 16
Bunsen, Chevalier, 6, 11
Buckle, Henry T., xxvi, 176
  History of Civilization in England, 110
Burrow, J. W.
  on Freeman, 181, 182-83, 194
  on Froude, 108, 116-17, 129, 245n.7, 246nn.23, 24, 247n.28
  on Green, 160
  on Macaulay, 79, 81, 87, 90, 93
Bury, John B., 220, 226, 228, 259n.56
Butterfield, Herbert, 78

Cambridge Modern History, 218, 229-30
Cambridge University
  Regius Professors of Modern History at, 225-26, 227-28
    Acton as, 227, 228
    Kingsley as, 186
    Kitson Clark as, 228
    Seeley as, 259n.49
    Trevelyan as, 228
  study of history at, xxvi, 216, 224, 225, 226, 227, 228, 229-32
Cannon, Susan F., xxii, 4
Carlyle, Thomas
  and Arnold, compared, 6, 11, 12, 16, 33-34, 35, 37, 38, 39, 40, 48, 58, 59, 62
  and Freeman, compared, 177, 183, 189, 191-92, 196, 201, 203, 205
  and Froude, compared, 106, 108, 109, 111, 113, 114, 115, 117, 118, 119, 120, 121, 123, 124, 125, 126, 127, 128-29, 133, 135, 137, 138, 139
  and Green, compared, 145, 147, 148, 151, 152, 154, 158, 159, 160, 164, 168
  and Macaulay, compared, 39, 48, 66, 67, 69, 71, 72, 73, 74, 75, 76, 77, 81, 82, 83, 85, 87, 89, 90, 92, 94-95, 98, 101, 102, 103
  biographical survey, 33-34
  characterization in, 54-58
  critical reaction to, 61-62
  hero-worship in, 41-43, 112, 208, 212
  influence on Froude, 105, 107
  model of change in, xxi, 38-41, 42-43
  model of science in, 35-36
  moral function of history in, xxvii, 34-35, 207, 208, 209
  on Macaulay, 66, 91
  responsibilities of historian in, 36-38
  scholarly methods of, 45-49, 212, 240n.26
  social history in, 43-45
  style of, 49-54
  summary, 62-65
  treatment of events, 58-61
  uses of history in, xi
  works
    "Biography," 41
    "Diderot," 42
    "Early German Literature," 39
    The French Revolution, 33, 38, 44, 49-50, 51, 52, 53-54, 58-59, 61-62, 63
    "The Guises," 46
    History of Friedrich II. of Prussia, called Frederick the Great, 33, 41, 49, 54, 56-57, 60-61
    Oliver Cromwell's Letters and Speeches, 33, 44, 47-48, 57-58, 59-60, 61, 63
    Past and Present, 33, 53, 54-55
    Sartor Resartus, 38
    "Signs of the Times," 41
Celtic race, 116
Change, model of, 210-12
  in Arnold, 9-11, 39, 40

Index

in Carlyle, 38-41, 42-43
in Froude, 113-15
in Green, 145-46, 148-49
in Macaulay, 76-78
in romantic history, xxi
in Whig history, 39, 40
Characterization, treatment of
  by Arnold, 21-24
  by Carlyle, 54-58
  by Freeman, 195-200
  by Froude, 127-33
  by Green, 162-64
  by Macaulay, 91-94, 243n.35
Clark, G. N., 229
Class of social group, role of, xv
  in Arnold, 24-25
  in Carlyle, 44
  in Green, 151-52
  in Macaulay, 93-94
  in romantic history, xx-xxi
Clive, John, 54, 67, 74, 79
Coleridge, J. T., 18, 20
Coleridge, Samuel Taylor, xx, xxii
Cox, G. W., 190
Creighton, Mandell, 218, 220
  History of the Papacy, 220
Croker, John, 99
Crothers, Hugh, 222
Cuvier, Georges, 159

Davis, H. W. C., 227
Dawkins, Boyd, 143, 192
Derby, Edward Stanley, Earl of, 174
Dicey, A. V., 136
Disraeli, Benjamin, 174
Donne, William, 136

Eliot, George, xii, 88, 92, 94, 110, 124, 214
Elliott, Phillip, 230
Emerson, Ralph Waldo, 58, 59, 107
Engel, Arthur, 258n.43
Enlightenment, treatment of history by, xvi-xix, xxvii
  influence on Arnold, 6-7, 30
  influence on Macaulay, xxvii, 76, 81, 102
  influence on Ranke, xxiv
  reaction against, by Carlyle, 36

Events, treatment of
  by Arnold, 25-28
  by Carlyle, 58-61
  by Freeman, 200-204
  by Froude, 133-35
  by Green, 161-62
  by Macaulay, 94-99, 244n.39, 40, 41
Evidence. *See* Scholarly Methods

Finlay, George, 186
Firth, Sir Charles, 225-26, 227, 231
  Commentary on Macaulay's History of England, 84
Fisher, H. A. L., 218, 220
Forbes, Duncan, 8
Freeman, Edward Augustus
  and Arnold, compared, 16, 173, 174, 175, 176, 179-80, 182, 183, 187, 189, 190, 192, 198, 205
  and Carlyle, compared, 177, 183, 189, 191-92, 196, 201, 203, 205
  and Froude, compared, 119, 120, 176, 189, 190, 193, 195, 196
  and Green, 141, 143, 156-57, 165
  and Green, compared, 142, 146, 147, 148, 149, 155, 157, 158, 162, 167, 170, 171, 180, 191, 192, 193, 195
  and Macaulay, compared, 174, 175, 182-83, 190, 191, 195
  attacks on Froude, 109, 135, 136, 170, 183, 185, 186, 204
  biographical survey, 170-73
  characterization in, 195-200
  comparative method in, 178-80
  concern with audience in, 186-88
  conflicts with professionalization in, xv, 183-85, 188, 209, 218-19, 223, 226-27
  critical reaction to, 204-5
  defense of professionalization by, 185-86, 223-24
  hero-worship in, 175-76, 177-78, 189-90
  model of science in, 176-77
  moral function of history in, 173-76, 208, 209
  on Arnold, 170, 175, 188
  on Green, 165, 250n.29
  on Macaulay, 170, 188, 195

Index

scholarly methods of, 188-89, 217
social history in, 190-91, 193-94
style of, 194-95
summary, 205-6
treatment of events by, 200-204
treatment of geography by, 191-93
treatment of myth by, 189, 190-91
Whig history in, 170, 171, 173, 180-83, 198, 213, 228
works
  Comparative Politics, 172
  "The Effects of the Conquest of England by the Normans," 171
  General Sketch of European History, 172
  The Growth of the English Constitution, 172, 187
  Historical Essays, 172
  Historical Geography of Europe, 172, 192
  History of Architecture, 171, 173
  History of Europe, 172
  History of Federal Government, 172, 187
  History of the Norman Conquest in England, 172, 178, 180, 187, 188, 191-92, 195, 196, 202, 204-5
  History of Sicily, 173
  Methods of Historical Study, 172
  Old-English History for Children, 172, 187, 194
  "Race and Language," 179
  Reign of William Rufus, 172
  Western Europe in the Eighth Century and Onward, 173
  Western Europe in the Fifth Century, 173
Froude, Hurrell, 106, 108
Froude, James Anthony
  and Arnold, compared, 12, 111, 119, 120, 133
  and Carlyle, compared, 106, 108, 109, 111, 113, 114, 115, 117, 118, 119, 120, 121, 123, 124, 125, 126, 127, 128-29, 133, 135, 137, 138, 139
  and Freeman, compared, 119, 120, 176, 189, 190, 193, 195, 196
  and Green, compared, 118, 144, 148, 150, 152, 154, 155, 159
  and Macaulay, compared, 101, 106, 113-14, 115, 118, 121-22, 123, 124, 125, 126, 133, 135, 137, 138-39
  biographical survey, 105-9
  characterization in, 127-33
  critical reaction to, 135-37
  hero-worship in, 112-13, 208
  model of change in, 113-15
  moral function of history in, 111-12
  on Macaulay, 100
  progress in, 145-19
  role of imagination in, 109-10
  scholarly methods of, xxvii, 119-24, 212, 217
  social history in, 117-18, 120, 121
  style of, 124-27
  summary, 137-40
  treatment of events by, 133-35
  works
    John Bunyan, 108
    The Council of Trent, 109
    The Divorce of Catherine of Aragon, 109, 120
    The English in Ireland in the Eighteenth Century, 108, 115
    English Seamen in the Sixteenth Century, 109
    History of England from the Fall of Wolsey to the Defeat of the Spanish Armada, 105, 107, 108, 109, 116, 120, 122, 129, 133, 135
    Julius Caesar, 108, 115, 135
    "A Legend of St. Neot," 107, 109-10
    Life and Letters of Erasmus, 109, 135
    Life and Times of Thomas Becket, 108, 109
    Life of Carlyle, 105
    The Nemesis of Faith, 105, 107
    "The Science of History," 110

Gardiner, Samuel R., 217-18, 221, 228
  and Freeman, compared, 171
  as professional historian, xv, 165, 186
  History of England from the Accession of James I. to the Outbreak of the Civil War, 217, 221
  on Green, 165, 219, 251n.44

Index

Gay, Peter, xxii
Gell, Philip, 167
Geography, treatment of
  by Arnold, 17, 28-29
  by Carlyle, 48-49
  by Freeman, 191-93
  by Green, 158-59
  by Macaulay, 83, 88-90
  by romantic historians, xxi
Gibbon, Edward, xvii-xviii, xix, xx, 106, 146
  Decline and Fall of the Roman Empire, xvii
Gilbert, Felix, 232
Gilmour, Robin, 243n.37
Gladstone, William, 102
Goldstein, Doris, 232, 257nn.21, 25, 259n.56, 260n.74
Gooch, George Peabody, 250n.29
Greeks, racial traits of, 24, 182, 195
Green, John Richard
  and Arnold, compared, 16, 145, 147, 154, 157, 158, 159, 168
  and Carlyle, compared, 145, 147, 148, 151, 152, 154, 158, 159, 160, 164, 168
  and Freeman, compared, 142, 146, 147, 148, 149, 155, 157, 158, 162, 167, 170, 171, 180, 191, 192, 193, 195
  and Froude, compared, 118, 144, 148, 150, 152, 154, 155, 159
  and Macaulay, compared, 141, 142, 146, 148, 151, 152, 153, 158, 159, 160, 163, 164, 168
  biographical survey, 141-44
  characterization in, 162-64
  concern with audience in, 156-57
  conflicts with professionalization in, xv, 165-67, 209
  creative method, 157-58
  critical reaction to, 164-65
  hero-worship in, 148, 163-64
  model of change in, 145-46, 148-49
  model of science in, 146-47
  moral function of history in, 147-48
  on Freeman, 165, 193, 195, 254n.50
  scholarly methods of, 155-56
  social history in, 142, 145-46, 152-55, 159-61, 251n.47
  summary, 167-69
  treatment of events by, 161-62
  treatment of geography by, 158-59
  Whig history in, xv, 141, 142, 145, 149-52, 213
  works
    The Conquest of England, 144, 155, 164
    The History of the English People, 144, 155, 161, 248n.1, 251n.44
    The Making of England, 144, 155-56, 59, 164, 167
    A Short Geography of the British Isles (with Alice Stopford Green), 144, 156
    A Short History of the English People, 141, 144, 146-47, 155, 156, 161, 164, 165, 167, 168, 250n.29
    Studies in Oxford History, 142, 160, 248n.3
Greg, William, 99
Grote, George, xxvi, 190
Grove, George, 156

Hallam, Henry, xv, 70, 217
Halsey, A. H., 321
Hamburger, Joseph, 73
Hare, J. C., 18, 29
Harrison, Frederic
  "The History Schools (An Oxford Dialogue)," 204
  on Carlyle, 61-62, 241n.55
  on Freeman, 204, 222
  on Froude, 137, 139-40
  on Green, 169
Harrold, C. F., 51, 240n.26
Hart, A. B., 248n.41
Harwood, Philip
  "The Modern Art and Science of History," xxii-xxiii
Herder, Johann, xxi
Herodotus, xviii, 21, 145, 249n.5
Hero-worship, xiii, xv, 208, 212
  in Arnold, 21-24, 26
  in Carlyle, 41-43, 112, 208, 212
  in Freeman, 175-76, 177-78, 189-90
  in Froude, 112-13, 208
  in Green, 148, 163-64

267

Index

Heyck, T. W., 255n.3
Higher Criticism of the Bible, 2, 8-9
Historical Association, 231
Historicism, xix-xx, xxii, xxvii
   reaction against, by Arnold, 6, 7
   reaction against, by Carlyle, 38
   reaction against, by Froude, 120-21, 122, 123-24
   reaction against, by Green, 147-48
History
   dignity of, xxi, 36, 49, 81, 210
   laws of, xii-xiii, xv, xxvii, 210
   in Arnold, 5, 7-9
   in Enlightenment, xvii
   in Froude, 110-11
   in Macaulay, 71, 73-74
   social, xxvi, 210, 212-13
   in Arnold, 24-25
   in Carlyle, 43-45
   in Freeman, 190-91, 193-94
   in Froude, 117-18, 120, 121
   in Green, 142, 145-46, 152-55, 159-61, 251n.47
   in Macaulay, 81-83, 90-91
   unity of, xv, 9-10, 145, 170, 173, 204
Holloway, John, 55
Holmes, T. Rice, 135, 137
Hume, David, xvi, xvii, xviii-xix, xix-xx, xxii, 146, 217
   History of England, xvi, xix, 250n.29
   Treatise on Human Nature, xix
Hunt, W., 166
Huxley, Thomas Henry, 179

Iggers, Georg, 229
Imagination, role of
   in conveying moral significance of history, xiii, xiv, xxii-xxiii, 209
   in reconstructing historical facts, xiii, xxi-xxiii, xxvi
   in Arnold, 17-18
   in Carlyle, 36-38, 50, 56-58
   in Freeman, 187-88, 189-90
   in Froude, 109-10, 126-27
   in Green, 157-58
   in Macaulay, 68-72
Institute for Historical Research, 226

Johnson, Samuel, xx

Keble, John, 2
Kemble, John, 217
Kingsley, Charles, xxvi, 107, 176, 238n.26
   The Roman and the Teuton, 186
Kitson Clark, 228, 229

Lang, Andrew, 137, 222, 223
Langlois, Charles, 247n.33, 248n.41
Leicester, H. M., 51, 52, 55
Levine, George, 38, 69, 71, 90, 243n.29
Liberal-Anglican School, xv, 8, 12
Lilley, W. S., 135
"Literary" history
   equated with dilettantism, xv, xxv, 136-37, 164-65, 185-86, 218-20
   moral function of, xxvi, xxvii, xxviii, 166, 207-9, 216
   traits of, xiii
Literature, as historical evidence
   in Arnold, 16
   in Carlyle, 53
   in Freeman, 193-94
   in Green, 153-54
   in Macaulay, 82-83
Livy, xviii, 21, 26
Lloyd Henry
   History of the Late War, 56
London, University of, 5, 119
Lowell, James Russell, 63

Macaulay, Margaret, 68, 69
Macaulay, Thomas Babington
   and Arnold, compared, 12, 19, 66, 67, 69, 71, 72, 73-74, 75, 76, 77, 78, 81, 82, 85, 92, 101, 102
   and Carlyle, compared, 39, 48, 66, 67, 69, 71, 72, 73, 74, 75, 76, 77, 81, 82, 83, 85, 87, 89, 90, 92, 94-95, 98, 101, 102, 103
   and Freeman, compared, 174, 175, 182-83, 190, 191, 193, 195
   and Froude, compared, 101, 106, 113-14, 115, 118, 121-22, 123, 124, 125, 126, 133, 135, 138-39

268

Index

and Green, compared, 141, 142, 146, 148, 151, 152, 153, 158, 159, 160, 163, 164, 168
biographical survey, 66-68
characterization in, 91-94, 243n.35
concern with audience in, 85-86, 209
critical reaction to, 99-101
laws of history in, 71, 73-74
model of change in, 76-78
model of science, 72-73
progress in, 74-76
role of imagination in, 68-72
scholarly methods of, xxvii, 83-85, 212, 217
social history in, 81-83, 90-91
style of, 86-88
summary, 101-4
treatment of events by, 94-99, 244n.39, 40, 41
treatment of geography by, 83, 88-90
Whig history in, xv, 67, 78-81, 103, 213
works
  Essays, 68, 93-94
  "Hallam's Constitutional History," 70
  "History," 70
  History of England, 68, 69, 75, 78, 81, 82, 84, 85-87, 93-94, 97-98, 99, 100, 101
  History of France, 67
  Lays of Ancient Rome, 19, 68, 69, 171
  "Milton," 70, 75
Mackintosh, 16
Madden, William, 87
Maitland, Frederic, 205, 220, 226, 228, 258n.30
  Domesday Book and Beyond, 217
  History of the English Law before the Time of Edward I. (with Frederic Pollock), 217
Manchester University, 226, 250n.29
Maurice, F. D., 107
Meinecke, Friedrich, xx
Mill, James, 78, 85
Mill, John Stuart, 48
Millgate, Jane, 69, 91, 243nn.35, 38, 244nn.40, 41

Moncrieff, James, 99
Montesquieu, Charles de Secondat, Baron de, xix
Morison, Cotter, 101
Morley, John, 100, 101, 164, 222
Müller, Max, 190
Myth, treatment of, xxvi
  by Arnold, xxiv, 15-16, 19-21, 69
  by Cox, 190
  by Freeman, 189, 190-91
  by Froude, 109-10
  by Green, 157-58
  by Grote, 190
  by Macaulay, 69
  by Müller, 190
  by Niebuhr, xxiv, 15-16
  by romantic historians, xxi

Namier, Sir Lewis, 232, 260n.71
Narrative, imposition of order by, xiii-xiv, xviii, xxiii, 51-54
Neale, J. E., 260n.71
Newman, John Henry, 105, 106, 107, 108, 171, 214
  Lives of the Saints, 107
Niebuhr, Barthold, 18, 19, 29, 85
  as romantic historian, xxiii
  influence on Arnold, xxiv, 2, 14-15, 16, 19
  scholarly methods of, xxiii-xxiv, 14-15
Norgate, Kate, 157

Oliphant, Margaret, 99, 101, 164
Oman, Sir Charles, 228
Organic
  change conceived as, xxi, xxvii, 210-12
  by Arnold, 9-12
  by Carlyle, 39-41
  by Froude, 113-15
  by Macaulay, 75-76
Osborne, John, 215
Oxford Movement, 3, 106-8, 109, 171, 237n.3
Oxford University
  Regius Professors of Modern History at, 31, 225-26, 227-28
  Arnold as, 3-4

269

Index

Firth as, 225-26
Freeman as, 109, 172-73, 183, 184-85
Froude as, 108, 109, 112, 137, 228
Stubbs as, 217
study of history at, xxvi, 216, 224-26, 227, 228, 229-32, 258n.43
Freeman on, 171-72, 184-85
Froude on, 119
Green on, 142

Paget, John, 84
Paley, F. A., 164
Palgrave, Sir Francis, 188, 217
Palgrave, Reginald, 47-48
Pearson, Charles, 204
Peckham, Morse, 54
Perkin, H. J. 231
"Philosophical," treatment of history as, xii, xiii, xvii, xxvi
by Arnold, 1, 4-5
by Carlyle, 35-36
by Enlightenment, xx
by Freeman, 173-74
by Green, 146-47, 168
by Macaulay, 71, 73
Pollard, Albert, 226, 228, 231
Pollock, Frederic
History of the English Law Before the Time of Edward I. (with Frederic Maitland), 217
Polybius, 17, 27, 28
Positivism, xiii, xv, xxv, xxvii, 241n.55
reaction against, by Carlyle, 39
reaction against, by Freeman, 176, 195-96
reaction against, by Froude, 110, 115
Powicke, Maurice, 227
Price, Bonamee, 8-9
Professionalization
conflicts with "literary" history, xii, xv-xvi, xxv-xxvi, xxvii-xxviii, 61-62, 215-16, 218-24
for Freeman, 170-71, 183-86, 188, 205-6
for Froude, 135-37
for Green, 141-42, 155, 165-67, 168-69
priorities of, xxv-xxvi, 216-17, 218-19, 256n.5

Progress, xv, xxvii, 211-12
in Arnold, xiv, 11-14, 30, 39
in Enlightenment, xviii-xix
in Froude, 115-17, 118-19
in Green, 152-55
in Macaulay, 74-76
in Whig history, 39
Prothero, George, 227

Ranke, Leopold von, xx, xxiv-v
and Macaulay, compared, 73, 84
scholarly methods of, xxiii-xxv, 213, 229
Realism, influence of, xiii, xiv, xxvi, 210
Reeve, Henry, 136
Research. *See* Scholarly methods
Robertson, William, xvii
History of Scotland, 42
Romance, as pattern for history, xiii-xiv, 111, 207
Romans, racial traits of, 13, 24, 154, 182
Romanticism
influence of
on Arnold, 16
on Carlyle, xv, 34, 62
on Froude, 120
on Green, 145, 147, 157
on Macaulay, 81-82, 102-3
reaction against
by Arnold, 6
by Macaulay, 68-69
Romantics, treatment of history by, xx-xxiii, xxvi
Rothblatt, Sheldon, 227, 251n.50, 258n.43
Royal Historical Society, 232, 260n.74
Round, John Horace, 204-5, 218
Rowley, James, 165
Rugby School, 2, 3, 10

Schiller, Friedrich, 41
History of the Revolt of the United Netherlands, 53
Scholarly methods, xv, xxvi-xxvii, 212-13
in Arnold, 14-17
in Carlyle, 45-49, 212, 240n.26
in Enlightenment, xvi-xvii
in Freeman, 188-89, 217

270

Index

in Froude, xxvii, 119-24, 212, 217
in Green, 155-56
in Macaulay, xxvii, 83-85, 212, 217
in Niebuhr, xxiii-xiv, 14-15
in professional history, xxv, 216-18, 229
in Ranke, xxiv-xxv, 213, 229
in romantic historians, xxi, xxiii-xxiv
Schuyler, R. L., 250n.29
Science, model of
　in Arnold, 4-5
　in Carlyle, 35-36
　in Enlightenment, xvii-xviii, xxii
　in Freeman, 176-77
　in Green, 146-47
　in Macaulay, 72-73
　in romantic historians, xxii-xxiii
"Scientific," treatment of history as, xii-xiii, xxiii, xxv, xxvii, 210, 213
　in Arnold, 7-10
　in Carlyle, 35-36
　in Freeman, 174-75, 176-77, 179-80
　in Green, 146-47
　in Macaulay, 71, 72
　in professional history, 222-23, 228
　in romantic historians, xxii-xxiii
Scott, Sir Walter, xxiv, 41-42, 70
　Quentin Durward, xxiv
Seeley, J. R., 186, 218, 220, 226, 227, 259n.49
Seignobos, Charles, 247n.33, 248n.41
Shakespeare, William, 36, 57
Shine, Hill, 240n.20
Sidgwick, Henry, xii
Smith, Goldwin, 135, 136, 238n.26
Southern, R. W., 228, 230
Spedding, James, 84
Spirit of the age. *See Zeitgeist*
Stanley, Arthur P., 3, 6, 7, 9, 29, 142
Stephen, J. F., 61, 99-100, 255n.70
Stephen, Lesley, 66, 92, 100, 102
Sterling, John, 50
Strauss, David Friedrich, 8
St. Simonians, 39
Stubbs, William
　and Freeman, compared, 171, 180, 187
　and Green, compared, 141, 143, 149, 167
　as professional historian, xv, 165, 186,
219, 258n.30
Constitutional History of England, 187, 217, 218, 220
　scholarly methods of, 217, 218
　style of, 220, 221
　Whig history in, 228
Style, xiii, 209-10
　of Arnold, 19-21, 209
　of Carlyle, 49-54
　of Freeman, 194-95
　of Froude, 124-27
　of Green, 156-62
　of Macaulay, 86-88
　of professional history, 220-21
　See also Audience, concern with; Characterization, treatment of; Events, treatment of; Geography, treatment of

Tacitus, xviii
Teutonic race
　advance of civilization by, 13, 173, 180, 181, 182, 195
　language of, 159, 193
　political institutions of, 149, 150, 151, 180, 249n.16
　traits of, 24, 114, 116, 153, 175-76, 190, 195, 196, 201, 203, 204, 213
Thackeray, William M., 99
Thierry, Augustin, 188
Thompson, Edith
　School History of England, 147
Thucydides, xviii, 2, 9, 249n.5
Tout, T. F., 205, 226, 228, 231
Tractarians. *See* Oxford Movement
Trevelyan, George Macaulay, 45, 223, 228
　"Clio, a Muse," 215
Trevelyan, George Otto, 83, 86
　Life and Letters of Lord Macaulay, 100
Trevelyan, Lady Hannah, 69
Trollope, Anthony, 92, 94
Trow, M. H., 231
Turner, Sharon, xv, 106

Utilitarianism, xiii, xv, xxvii, 1, 73, 76, 110, 115, 207

Vaughan, Robert, 61

271

Index

Voltaire, xix
Vico, Giambattista, 9
Vinogradoff, Paul, 225-26

Ward, Adolphus W., 166, 226, 250n.29
Wellek, Rene, 38, 47, 240n.20
Whig history, xiv, xxvii, 208, 213, 232
  and Carlyle, compared, 39, 40
  and Froude, 105, 114, 118, 122, 246nn.23, 26
  and Gardiner, 217
  in Acton, 228
  in Bury, 228
  in Freeman, 170, 171, 173, 180-83, 198, 213, 228
  in Green, xv, 141, 142, 145, 149-52, 213
  in Macaulay, xv, 67, 78-81, 103, 213
  in professional history, 228-29, 259n.57
  in Stubbs, 228
White, Hayden, xxiii
Wissenschaft, as model for history, xiv, xxiii, 4, 210
Wordsworth, William, xxii, 17, 18, 20, 50
  Lyrical Ballads, 18

Young, Robert M., 252n.16

Zeitgeist, 212
  in Freeman, 179
  in Froude, 106, 113-14
  in Green, 148
  in Macaulay, 77, 93